THE
ENVOY

FROM KABUL TO THE WHITE HOUSE,
MY JOURNEY THROUGH A TURBULENT WORLD

ZALMAY
KHALILZAD

St. Martin's Press

New York

www.stmartins.com

Design by Letra Libre, Inc.

Library of Congress Cataloging-in-Publication Data

Names: Khalilzad, Zalmay, author

Title: The envoy : from Kabul to the White House, my journey through a turbulent world / Zalmay Khalilzad.

Description: First edition. | New York : St. Martin's Press, 2016. | Includes bibliographical references and index.

Identifiers: LCCN 2015043831| ISBN 9781250083005 (hardcover) | ISBN 9781250083012 (e-book)

Subjects: LCSH: Khalilzad, Zalmay. | Ambassadors—United States—Biography. | United Nations—Officials and employees—Biography. | United States—Foreign relations—2001-2009. | United States—Foreign relations—Iraq. | Iraq—Foreign relations—United States. | United States—Foreign relations—Afghanistan. | Afghanistan—Foreign relations—United States.

Classification: LCC E901.1.K48 A3 2016 | DDC 327.2092—dc23

LC record available at http://lccn.loc.gov/2015043831

First Edition: March 2016

10   9   8   7   6   5   4   3   2   1

CONTENTS

Preface From Kabul to Baghdad   1
         Kabul, June 20, 2005

≺ PART I ≻
EARLY LIFE

1   Poppy Fields and Tree-Lined Boulevards   9
    Afghanistan, 1951–1965
2   Journey to the Other Side of the World   26
    The United States, 1966–1967
3   Into the Cauldron of Politics   35
    Kabul and Beirut, 1968–1974
4   Aspiring Strategist   45
    Chicago and New York City, 1974–1980
5   The Mujahedeen and the Halls of Power   57
    New York and Washington, D.C., 1980–1989
6   Containing Saddam   67
    Washington, D.C., 1988–1992
7   Crafting Grand Strategy for a Unipolar World   76
    Washington, D.C., 1991–1992
8   One Nation's Disintegration, One Man's Destiny   83
    Washington, D.C., 1993–2001

≺ PART II ≻
BUSH ADMINISTRATION

9   The Calm before the Storm   93
    Washington, D.C., January–September 2001
10 America under Attack   105
    Washington, D.C., September 2001

11   A Quest for Leaders in Tyranny's Shadow   114
Washington, D.C., and Bonn, Germany, September–
December 2001

12   Return to Kabul   128
Kabul and Washington, D.C., January–June 2002

13   *Loya Jirga*   141
Kabul, June–July 2002

14   Eyes Elsewhere   151
Washington, D.C., December 2002–February 2003

15   Planning Postwar Iraq inside Iraq   161
Ankara, Turkey, and Salahuddin, Iraq, February 2002

16   Iraq: From Liberation to Occupation   168
Washington, D.C., and Baghdad, March–May 2003

17   Accelerating Success in Afghanistan   176
Washington, D.C., May–November 2003

18   Ambassador   189
Kabul, November 2003–January 2004

19   Builders versus Spoilers   198
Afghanistan, 2003–2005

20   Fruits of Democracy   212
Kabul, 2004–2005

21   Preparing for Iraq   225
Washington, D.C., November 2004–July 2005

22   Repairing Iraq   237
Baghdad, July–December 2005

23   Forging a National Unity Government   254
Baghdad, December 2005–May 2006

24   Struggling to Break the Cycle of Sectarian Violence   266
Baghdad, 2006–2007

25   Permanent Representative to the United Nations   284
New York, 2007–2009

═══ PART III ═══

AMERICA IN THE WORLD

26   A More Dangerous World   307
2016 and Beyond
Afterword   322

Acknowledgments   324
Index   326

FROM KABUL TO BAGHDAD

KABUL, JUNE 20, 2005

ASCENDING THE GRAY, METAL STAIRCASE TOWARD THE COCKPIT, I WAS INVITED TO take a spot in the second row of seats, just behind the captain. Behind me, the cargo hold loomed, completely empty, cavernous, big enough to carry an M1 Abrams tank.

Previously when I hitched rides on C-17s, I traveled in the company of gigantic earthmoving equipment or combat vehicles on their way to Afghanistan's Bagram Airbase or Kandahar. It was my last day as a special presidential envoy and ambassador to Afghanistan, and this plane had been sent to transport me to my new post as ambassador in Baghdad. Its flight, in fact, was probably the first one ever between the two war-ravaged capitals. It was an especially emotional departure for me since the place I was leaving behind was the nation of my birth. After the Soviet invasion of Afghanistan in 1979, I wondered if I would ever return. Then I had come back as a senior diplomat after the attacks of 9/11. Now I was leaving again, with business very much unfinished.

Was I letting Afghanistan down? Certainly, the U.S. ambassador does not determine the fate of a nation. But I had spent the past three years helping Afghan leaders construct and strengthen a fragile government after a quarter century of revolution, occupation, and civil war. I had mediated disputes among warlords and induced them to cooperate with the national government. I had helped Afghan leaders put down the foundation of national institutions, such as the Afghan National Army. I had confronted the challenges posed by plotting neighbor states. Afghanistan, as well as the United States and other friendly powers, was struggling with a reemerging Taliban insurgency. We had made progress—more than many thought possible—but we certainly weren't finished.

I had been asked by President George W. Bush to move on to Iraq, a country falling into sectarian conflict. I was needed there, my superiors had said, right away.

The giant plane taxied down the runway. Before us were the peaks of the Hindu Kush, some still covered with snow even in late June. As we climbed, I looked down on a country that over the centuries had been the seat of great empires, occupied by armies of conquerors such as Alexander the Great, and afflicted by tyrants and turmoil. It also was the birthplace of the Persian Sufi mystic and writer Rumi and the home of poets, the world's earliest glassmakers and miners, and agile merchants on a bustling way station of the Silk Road.

I reflected on the historical drama that had brought me back to Afghanistan. Even as a young person, I had perceived the rise of what I called the "crisis of Islamic civilization"—a crisis grounded in the collapse of the civilization's dominant position in the world in the fifteenth century and the failure of all subsequent empires and national governments to deliver for their peoples. As a young visitor and an immigrant to the United States, I saw that other countries had found a better path. In my early career, I had warned that this crisis was producing a wave of violent Islamist extremism. It ultimately resulted in the attacks of 9/11.

I could not sit still or get the sleep I needed. Instead, I paced the hollow belly of the C-17, and let my thoughts wander to my youth.

I recalled my first glimpse of the presidential palace—more recently the site of my negotiations and meetings with Afghan politicians—when I was still a young boy recently arrived in Kabul from my birthplace in Mazar-i-Sharif. It was then still the royal palace of King Zahir Shah. It had been only a short stroll from Independence Square, with green spaces adorned with sculpted shrubbery and flowerbeds.

I had been dazzled by the palace's huge walls, the honor guards posted outside, and the historic black cannons that stood as monuments of the Afghan victory over the British in the nineteenth century—a testament to the fact that my people had fought for independence and defeated the greatest empire on the planet. An enormous Afghan national flag flying from the central tower above the main gate had given the structure an added sense of grandeur. The architects had achieved their intended effect: I had felt awed by their physical embodiment of the Afghan state. It seemed as enduring and formidable as Afghanistan's mountains.

In the 1950s, there were no serious security issues, no bombs exploding, and no insurgents. Ordinary citizens could walk right up to the palace gates. Those were, in the familiar American expression, "the good old days." But, as seemed to be my homeland's fate throughout the centuries, they were not to last.

The Soviet Union's bitter, decade-long occupation, coupled with American disengagement and neglect after the Soviet withdrawal, left the country to the tender mercies of fractious leaders of armed internal factions and acquisitive regional powers such as Pakistan, Iran, and Russia. Instability in Afghanistan produced toxic results: proxy warfare among regional powers, an explosive escalation in the opium trade, massive refugee populations in neighboring countries, energized militant Islamist ideologies, the rise of transnational terrorist groups such as al Qaeda, and the victory of the Taliban. The Taliban regime imposed a cruel tyranny and an unending civil war against the anti-Taliban groups in the north and entered into an alliance with Osama bin Laden, who plotted the 9/11 attacks while living in Afghan territory.

My last three years, shuttling back and forth between Washington and Afghanistan, had been an exhausting, difficult process of helping to make Afghanistan a "normal country."

My last meeting with President Hamid Karzai had occurred just an hour or so earlier in his office. Though we joked with each other as we had done in hundreds of previous meetings we both felt mixed emotions. On the one hand, Afghanistan was now on a better trajectory. The Afghan people as a whole were optimistic about the future and supportive of their government and the U.S. presence. The economy was growing, and progress was occurring in a wide variety of areas. After the presidential elections in October 2004, insurgent violence almost entirely dissipated. We had reports that senior Taliban leaders viewed the high turnout in the national election as a strategic defeat. Some leaders took the view that the insurgency was no longer viable and that reconciliation with the Afghan government was the right course of action. On the other hand, we were uncertain about whether this hopeful state of affairs was permanent or just a pause in the fray.

I was leaving Afghanistan because of a call between President Bush and Iraq's president Jabal Talabani. Iraq was approaching a deadline for the drafting of its constitution. Progress was slow. Near the end of the conversation, Bush had asked whether he could do anything else for the Iraqi leader. Talabani had replied, "Yes, send Zal."

Talabani was a fascinating leader. His easy-going manner belied his reputation as a tough, lifelong Peshmerga fighter and shrewd political operator.

His request was flattering. And I could understand that he wanted a partner, someone with whom he could work out the difficult issues over countless cups of tea. He wanted an American ambassador whom he trusted and who he knew could get things done, in both Baghdad and Washington.

The last time I had seen Talabani was two years earlier, in April 2003, in Baghdad, shortly after the toppling of Saddam Hussein's regime. I had been tasked with convening conferences across Iraq to identify leaders who would be able to work with exile groups to form an interim government. Sovereignty was to be transferred to this new administration as soon as possible. But the process had been suddenly abandoned when President Bush announced that Paul Bremer would be going to Baghdad instead, to head the Coalition Provisional Authority, which would serve as the U.S. occupation government in post-Saddam Iraq.

A few hours after the announcement, Bush had called me. He hoped I wouldn't take this 180-degree turn personally. In his typical laid-back style, he said, "We all love you, Zal. We think the world of you."

I appreciated the compliment, but I responded that I did not understand why we were shifting from a plan to devolve power as quickly as possible to the Iraqis themselves to a plan that would amount to us being an occupying force like the one that had ruled defeated Japan after World War II.

The president explained it all in narrow personal and administrative terms. The problem was that if both Bremer and I went to Baghdad, Bremer would be reporting through the Department of Defense to Donald Rumsfeld and I would be reporting through National Security Council Advisor Condoleezza Rice. Rumsfeld and Rice were not working well together. You couldn't have two senior officials in the field responding to principals in Washington who were at odds with each other. The president needed the Department of Defense to be in the lead, and that meant Bremer.

There seemed to be little understanding of just how consequential it would be to shift from self-government to occupation. I raised my concerns with Rice and her deputy, Stephen Hadley, but they told me that it was too late.

To make matters much worse, the Iraqi national army was dissolved soon after the occupation decision. Also, the purging of the old regime— de-Baathification—was taken too far, affecting many Iraqis who were not complicit in Saddam's crimes. Hundreds of thousands of Iraqis, experienced at warfare and governance, were now jobless, displaced, resentful, and without a future. They filled the ranks of the insurgency. We had scored, as my sons might have said, an own-goal.

Looking back, my greatest regret is that I was unable to reverse the decision. It was inevitable that an American-led occupation, however benign its intentions, would lead to armed opposition. Arab nationalism, bitter memories of European imperialism, ethnic and sectarian enmities, and the vast weaponry and materiel from Saddam's armories were a precarious combination. And it was not long before the country was ablaze.

Interrupting my pacing in the C-17, I reached into my pocket and unfolded a note I had received from my family. The paper was an elegant piece of stationery with perforated edges, left over from the birth announcement of our older son. It had a four-leafed clover pasted on the page along with messages of support and love from my children and my wife, wishing me luck in Iraq. The lucky clover was one we had found on our last carefree family outing to a swimming pool.

Near the clover my wife, Cheryl, inscribed a message. Referring to an idyllic park set on the banks of one of the tributaries to the Danube River near the apartment where we had once lived in Vienna in our first years of marriage, she wrote, "Let this remind you of the *Gaensehaeufl* and cool sunny days and good ice cream and those who love you just for you. And let it bring you luck and God bless you and we are here for you."

We were about to land. I was handed an armored vest—something I had never worn in Kabul—and reflected that I would need all the luck a four-leafed Austrian clover could convey.

PART I

EARLY LIFE

ONE

POPPY FIELDS AND TREE-LINED BOULEVARDS

AFGHANISTAN, 1951–1965

I WAS BORN IN THE NORTHERN AFGHAN CITY OF MAZAR-I-SHARIF ON THE FIRST DAY of spring. Called Nowruz, the day marks the start of the New Year on the solar calendar. My hometown derived its name—"blessed tomb"—from the majestic blue shrine located in the center of the city. The shrine is the reputed burial place of Imam Ali, the son-in-law and cousin of the Prophet Mohammed.

As is the custom, my extended family gathered for a ceremony a few days after my birth. Amid heaping servings of rice, chicken, lamb, and pastries, members of the family debated various possibilities for my name. In the end, it was the family matriarch, my paternal grandmother, Hawa, who made the decision. I would be named Zalmay, an Afghan name from the Pashtun part of the country meaning "youthful."

I remember the vivid colors of spring in Mazar-i-Sharif. The city was radiant with the red of hundreds of thousands of poppies growing wild. The poppy blooms were everywhere, in the fields, along the streets, almost anywhere soil, water, and sun came together. In those days, houses were built with a mixture of mud and straw, which, when dried, was sufficiently durable to withstand the elements—much like the adobe used in the American Southwest. They had flat roofs crowned with domes, all made of mud. In the spring, poppies would take root, imparting a hue of red to the entire city. Even the ancient fort of Quala-i-Jangi was crowned with the poppies—the wild flowering an expression of the optimism of spring.

My father, Khalilullah, had come to Mazar in the 1930s from the eastern province of Laghman. He used to tell us the story of how he traversed the central range of the Hindu Kush to reach the north. There were no cars in Afghanistan at the time. Traveling on horseback and by foot, he was in search of opportunity. In those days, it was no small matter for a young man to set off into the unknown. On the day of his departure, his family held a symbolic funeral, never expecting to see him again. It took him several months to reach Mazar, but he quickly grasped the potential of its wide-open spaces and smaller population. Upon his return to Laghman, he was able to persuade his mother, one brother, and one sister to join him in Mazar. Together they settled in a neighborhood near the Blue Mosque.

He also brought a wife back with him. Typically, a woman received a house or parcel of land as dowry. This is why marriages among relatives were preferred—that way, property stayed in the family. The groom and the bride usually did not see each other until the wedding and had little to say about the decision. In this, my father had an advantage. My mother lived next door, and he had caught glimpses of her. He liked what he saw, which set talks between the families in motion.

In traditional Afghan society, people did not keep accurate track of their ages or celebrate their birthdays, but my mother estimated that she was between nine and twelve years old at the time of her marriage. She gave birth to her first child around age fifteen.

My father was, according to family estimates, twenty-two years old at the time of his marriage. While not from a privileged social background, he was educated by local standards. He had completed elementary school, so he became a civil servant in the finance ministry. Eventually he became a director in the provincial finance department in Mazar. He was known for his integrity, foresight, and exceptional work ethic. He supported his new wife comfortably on his monthly salary of a few dollars.

My mother, Bibi Zahra, or Shah-Koko, as she was more generally called, was a slight, pale little woman, filled with unremitting drive and immense willpower. She seemed always in a race against time to complete her household tasks according to self-imposed deadlines. I called my mother Ayah, a common term of endearment for "mom."

Families in those days were large, but many children failed to survive their first years. Women gave birth often, in many cases starting when they were too young to sustain pregnancies safely. Clean water was not always available, and medical care was rudimentary. In the 1950s, the infant mortality rate in Afghanistan hovered around 250 per 1,000 live births. My family's experience was worse than the average. Over the course of her lifetime, my mother would give birth thirteen times, but only seven of her children would survive—three boys and four girls. Two of the other six died before reaching their first birthday.

My birth as a healthy boy was cause for celebration. Of my five older siblings, only one survived, and to everyone's distress, that one was a mere girl, my sister Aziza. My mother knew the realities facing women in Afghanistan, and, in a sense, felt culpable for bringing girls into a world where they would become victims of social injustice.

When I finally arrived in 1951, the all-important and longed-for son, all stops were pulled out to protect me. My ear was pierced with a gold earring to declare me the slave of Ali, who, it was hoped, would then look after me. Many years later, when I was at the University of Chicago, my colleagues calculated the odds of my surviving to the age of twenty and declared me to be a miracle.

Being the only son and, later, when two more boys joined the family, the oldest son, I was spoiled. Additional sisters followed—Latifa, Malika, and Bassima. There were also children who didn't survive. One of the most searing memories of my childhood was the night when my sister Hafiza passed away. She cried desperately for days, particularly at night. I remember the moment when those cries stopped. I knew I had lost my sister.

I remember that a pharmacist came to see her and gave her some medicine. But no doctor came by, and she was never taken to a hospital. I believe she had appendicitis.

My parents were sad but fatalistic. I was despondent and furious. When I kept asking why Hafiza had died, they repeated that it was the "will of God." Even at that young age, I suspected that more could have been done—an intuition confirmed to me as I learned more about poverty and underdevelopment.

During my childhood, my father would leave for work early in the morning. When he returned in the evening, he would bring groceries from the market, often including something special for us children—roasted chickpeas and raisins, pine nuts, or candy. We often waited in great anticipation to see what he would bring us. Generally, men did the shopping during those years.

My mother would also rise early and, after her prayers, prepare breakfast. I would wake up to the scent of a hot pot of "sheer chai"—sweet tea with milk—a great incentive to get up. She was a good cook. Her quince and sour cherry marmalades were famous in the neighborhood. One of my favorite dishes was *qabuli palaw*, in which lamb and chicken are buried in mounds of rice mixed with almonds, pistachios, strips of orange peel, shredded carrots, and raisins. Another was *burani-banjan*, in which pan-seared eggplant and tomatoes seasoned with coriander and hot peppers were mixed with *chaka*, a type of cottage cheese made by draining the liquid from yogurt.

We children received our first education at home. Etiquette was important, and children were expected to be well behaved. During any gathering, the seating order was strictly determined by age and rank. Positions were reshuffled every time a new person entered the room. Children were at the bottom of the hierarchy, but they received a great deal of affection from adults—sometimes too much, when a series of visitors energetically pinched their cheeks.

⤛　⤜

FOR MANY AMERICANS, Afghanistan evokes images of endless armed conflict, bombed-out buildings, and severe poverty. They see it as an ungoverned and backward land.

For much of the twentieth century, however, Afghans enjoyed more peace and stability than did many developing countries. Few Afghans questioned the legitimacy of the Durrani dynasty. King Zahir Shah, who ruled from 1933 until 1973, was largely seen as a benevolent monarch who was gradually introducing social and economic progress. A fatherly figure, Zahir Shah was a Pashtun from a tribe in the south and spoke only Dari, a dialect of Persian and the language of the north. Because of his softhearted nature, he was incapable of signing death warrants. Famously, when pressed to do so, he would leave the country and a less squeamish deputy would sign.

The king's cousin, Daoud Khan, the prime minister who eventually deposed him, was a forceful modernizer. The Afghan government in Mazar provided basic services, including schools, civil administration, police, postal delivery, records of property rights, and roads. Local courts resolved disputes and enforced the law. While poor, Afghanistan had functioning institutions and a reasonable level of stability. It was also a very stratified society, in which rank, privilege, and connections played an enormous role. You could buy a ticket to a sporting event or a concert, but its value mattered little if someone more important wanted your seat.

The country's recent history hardly compares to the glories of the past. Afghans are the descendants of a line of great empires. In the area of northern Afghanistan where I grew up, we occupied the remains of the great civilization that was centered in the city of Balkh, situated seventy kilometers south of the Amu-Darya River, which now separates Afghanistan and Uzbekistan. The ancient Greeks wrote of Central Asia as "a land of 1,000 cities," and some of those cities date back nearly 5,000 years. Balkh was so prosperous that the Arabs later described it as the "Mother of Cities."

Historian Frederick Starr has described Balkh as one of the greatest cities of late antiquity. Its outer walls, more than one hundred kilometers in length, enclosed a suburban region and gardens. The inner area, called Bala Hisar, housed a palace and government buildings and was ten times the size of ancient Troy. A center of culture and intellectual innovation, Balkh was the city in which Zoroaster, who founded a religion that profoundly influenced Judaism, Christianity, and Islam, began his teaching. Alexander placed the capital of his Kingdom of Bactria in the city, and it became a center of Hellenic culture. Later it was a major center of Buddhism in the pre-Islamic era. The great Sufi poet Maulana Jalaluddin Rumi was from a Balkh family.

Mazar also has a significant role in the schism between Sunni and Shia—the central fault line in the Islamic world from the early days of the religion until today. The divide dates back to the struggle over the succession of the Prophet Mohammed. Some—whose latter-day adherents are the Shia—contended that leadership should stay within the house of the Prophet and believed that Mohammed had personally specified Ali as his successor. Others, who came to be known as Sunnis, argued instead that Mohammed's closest disciples should select the successor from among themselves. The Sunnis won this power struggle, and Abu Bakr became the first caliph. Shia Muslims rejected him and his immediate successors as usurpers. After the death of the third caliph, Uthman, Ali ascended to the role of leader and, in Shia parlance, became the first Imam. This period was one of sectarian strife, and Ali was soon assassinated by those in rival factions.

Afghans believe Ali's body was brought from the Iraqi city of Najaf to Mazar. The legend has it that he was to be buried wherever the camel carrying his body stopped to rest. With impressive energy and endurance, the camel proceeded all the way to Mazar before sitting down. Most other Muslims, particularly Shias in the Arab and Persian world, contend that Ali was buried in Najaf, where a huge shrine attracts thousands of religious pilgrims every year. This is no deterrent to the Afghans, who stick firmly to their story, though a popular poem offers a conciliatory slant: "People say Ali is buried in Najaf, Come and see in Mazar the blessed shrine . . . The sun is one but its rays are everywhere."

WE LIVED CLOSE to the center of the city on Sia-Gerdak Street, near the Blue Mosque. Our home was a suburban-style, one-story house surrounded by tall walls. The houses in residential neighborhoods across the city were built in a similar fashion. On most blocks, residents knew each other by name, and usually the heads of households were similar in terms of social status and professional occupation.

The perimeter wall of our home enclosed a courtyard. On the left stood a big, beautiful tree, with a fragrant smell in the spring. A few steps up, there was a room for receiving guests and then a wall with another, smaller door that led to the family's private living area. Inside, there were several rooms to the right, and across, on the left, was a raised stage-like platform where we kept rope beds. We moved the beds onto the roof to sleep outdoors in the summertime, where we could enjoy the evening breeze, look at the stars, and smell the fragrance of the courtyard's flowers.

Our street had a small mosque with an ornamental pool. Its standing water, which we drank, had a greenish hue and was the source of many stomach ailments, as children swam in the pool and people cleansed themselves there before prayer.

In the 1950s, Mazar was a humble town. It did not have a university, though it did boast two high schools, Lycee Sultana Razia for girls and Lycee Bakhtar for boys. Mazar had no radio station. In fact, the only accessible signal was that of the national radio station in Kabul, which had been built by German engineers in 1937. The town had one movie theater, which exclusively played Iranian and Indian films. There was no public transportation, public water supply, sewer system, or library. Health care was primitive at best.

Like virtually all Afghans, my father and mother were observant Muslims. Both prayed regularly. When I turned eight, I began to accompany my father to the mosque for prayers. I was always serious about this duty; I wanted to be a pious person. Along with the other children in the neighborhood, I attended Koran classes held by a cleric in the nearby mosque. He was, let us just say, not a gifted pedagogue, and we did not look forward to his instruction. We mostly learned to repeat verses of the Koran in Arabic, with little to no effort expended on discussing or understanding their meaning.

Still, the religion I grew up with helped me learn right from wrong and gave meaning to everyday life. At twelve I started fasting during the month of Ramadan. The bad news was that I would be famished by the time we could eat after nightfall. The good news was that we got to wake up at three in the morning—well before sunrise—and enjoy a meal of tea and sweets made especially for the holiday. This early morning meal had to sustain us until dusk, so we made the most of it.

During the Nowruz holiday season, storytellers would regale crowds gathered in the street with battle tales from the early days of Islam. The more senior storyteller would declaim his narrative in a booming voice. His junior assistant would repeat the account in softer tones. I was mesmerized by these storytellers and joined their audiences as often as I could after school. They told of the great exploits of Ali, who prevailed over powerful enemies against extraordinary odds through his skill as a swordsman. He was a gifted commander, often finding ways to outsmart his opponents. He had the additional benefit of divine or magical powers, which could enhance the size of his sword or multiply the number of its blades during critical moments in battle. The storytellers would also recite poems about his sons, Hassan and Hussein. The narrative reached its climax when Hussein was killed in the Battle of Karbala.

At this point, the senior storyteller would break down sobbing as though Hussein's death had happened only days, not centuries, ago. The anguish was genuine, reflecting the grief that Shia Muslims still feel about their failure to support Hussein at this crucial battle. But even those of us in the audience who were not Shia would be overcome with emotion as we learned Hussein's fate. Great weeping would ensue. Many years later, this experience helped me to understand the culture of guilt, grief, and perserverance in the face of oppression that permeates the Shia leaderships in Iraq and Iran.

I have reflected a great deal on how extreme versions of Islam overwhelmed the more benign understanding of my childhood. Islam arrived in Afghanistan in the seventh century and quickly came to permeate every aspect of Afghan society. About 99 percent of Afghans are Muslim. Some 80 percent are Sunni, and 19 percent are Shia. Religion helped to overcome other fissures in society, particularly ethnic differences and social inequalities. It served as a rallying cry during wars against foreign powers, and it was a powerful source of political legitimacy to national, tribal, and religious leaders.

Looking back, I can now see that the power of Islam created a competitive dynamic between civil, tribal, and religious power. Islam provided authority and legitimacy to religious leaders. In my lifetime, the central government's power ebbed and flowed depending on the reforms it was pursuing and the level of strife in the country. During King Zahir Shah's reign, religious leaders were kept at arm's length and prevented from exerting much power. During periods of crisis, when political stability was threatened or the state collapsed, civil authorities used religion to achieve social unity. Religious leaders rose to political prominence as Islam became the sole common denominator in Afghanistan's diverse society. After the Soviet invasion, in 1979, religious leaders and their foreign patrons played a central role in mobilizing the country's diverse ethnic groups, tribes, and resistance factions in the fight against occupying forces. Tragically, this environment facilitated the rise of religious radicals and jihadists.

◄ ►

IN 1959, when I was eight years old, we moved to the northern district of Char Bulak, where my father was appointed the head of the finance department.

Char Bulak was in the middle of expansive plains near the Soviet border. Our house was an hour's ride on horseback from the government buildings where my father worked.

I went to elementary school on horseback. My horse, Wazir ("minister" in Dari), was calm and well behaved, and one of our two servants would ride alongside me. Classes at my all-boys school went from morning to early afternoon. When the teacher entered the room, the students would stand up to show respect. Our subjects included religion, through which we learned to recite the Koran. Then we came home for a late lunch—the main meal of the day.

On the way home from school, my friends and I would sometimes engage in impromptu races on horseback. I remember one such race vividly. *"Bidao, Wazir,"* I commanded in Dari as I urged my horse to a faster pace. "I know a shortcut!" I boasted to my friends. As Wazir and I veered off the trodden dirt paths and crossed untended gardens, his galloping hooves burst melons growing wild on the ground, creating a rhythmic thundering as we went.

Home at last, I couldn't wait to boast of my victory to my biggest fan.

"Ayah!" I called, yelling for my mother as I burst through the front door. "We raced home and I won!"

"That's wonderful," she responded dryly. "Now do your homework."

My mother was a strict disciplinarian, particularly in matters of education. She insisted that the entire family—including our four sisters—receive the best education available. She herself had never been allowed to go to school. In 1920s Afghanistan, it simply wasn't an option. I sensed that, to some degree, she was trying to achieve her own aspirations through her children.

My mother knew that education not only had pecuniary benefits; it would allow me to serve the country as well.

With regard to my sisters, my mother emphasized that educated girls were less likely to be abused by their husbands. It did not take a great leap of faith for us to see her point. When I was growing up in Mazar, my uncle Osman was infamous for his temper. Neighborhood children, including me, would vanish from the streets like ghosts whenever we saw him, not knowing what might trigger his wrath. My father would often run down the street to Osman's house when he heard that his brother was unleashing his anger on his helpless wife.

On matters of education, my parents were fully in agreement. My father tended to be liberal in his views, and I suspect that my mother hardened his conviction that education was important for both boys and girls. When Mazar opened a grade school for girls, my father made sure that Aziza, then six years old, was the first name on the list of those who would attend.

So heeding my parents' command, I took my schoolbooks to the room I shared with my two brothers. It was stiflingly hot and we had no electricity, but we had time-tested technology to cool us off: a rope attached to a suspended cloth on which we could pull to create some movement in the stifling air.

Every night, my mother asked about our homework, and she often demanded to inspect it. Since she could not read, I wondered, but never asked, what she was looking for.

As I was finishing up my homework, my father would come through the front door in a dust-covered suit. There was a great deal I admired about him. But he was also impatient and short-tempered.

"There is nothing wrong with them!" I remember him saying angrily one day, as I walked into the kitchen. "They were the best tomatoes in the market!"

"They're not firm," my mother judged, poking at them disapprovingly.

"You're never satisfied!" my father shouted, his face flushing red with anger.

"They even smell rotten," my mother added, lifting one disdainfully to her nose.

My father easily became enraged by criticism, though, unlike his brothers, he was rarely violent. Still, my mother's behavior puzzled me. Why did she keep criticizing my father's purchases knowing he would storm out of the house to cool off? Though she might be right, her approach was not helping matters. Why repeat a pattern if it only gets the same undesired result?

I had long since concluded that it was better to manage my father than confront him. The tactics I learned early on to avoid conflicts with my father represented some of the tools for working with friendly leaders in challenging circumstances, though not necessarily with adversaries.

—＜　＞—

WE MOVED BACK to Mazar before I started fourth grade. I attended an all-boys school that stood in the shadows of the Quala-i-Jangi fortress.

Focus and discipline were sometimes challenges for me in my elementary school years, when my interest in academics flagged for a time. Cinemas had come to Mazar, and Indian action movies were very popular. One day I decided that going to the movies sounded better than going to school. A day of playing hooky stretched into a second day, then a week. At first it was a lark, but as the days passed, the potential consequences began to dawn on me. The problem was that I was too scared to go back to class. In those days, corporal punishment was the norm. If you misbehaved, the teacher would take out a long stick and strike you repeatedly on the hands. I finally decided to confide in a much older cousin. I hoped that he would invent some sort of cover story, or at least facilitate an amnesty. However, my cousin turned me in. As punishment I was hit with a stick on the face of my hands more than a dozen times—both at school and at home.

By age ten, I was obsessed with kite fighting, an Afghan pastime depicted in Khaled Hosseini's best-selling novel *The Kite Runner*. At that time, other sports such as soccer or cricket had not gained much of a following, partly due to a lack of facilities. But kite fighting was enormously popular in Mazar. Only much later did I learn that elsewhere in the world, kite flying was a peaceful and aesthetic pastime during which one took pleasure just in the beauty of a colorful kite catching the wind. This was not the case for us. We viewed kites as vehicles of combat.

Before launching your kite, you carefully soaked the string in a mixture of mushy boiled rice and pulverized glass, turning it into a flying razor. Then you took aim against the strings of your adversaries. The right angle and speed would ensure that you sliced their kites right out of the sky and sent them crashing to the ground. The object of the game was to have the last kite still flying.

Any money gifts I received I immediately invested in my armory of kites and string. One of my cousins, nicknamed Landye ("Shorty"), was a master at holding his *charkha* ("steel string"). When he prevailed, he would offer the losing party his signature sweet smile. He generously shared his tricks with me. You needed to release additional string just when your kite was at the optimal angle vis-à-vis the opponent's. Therefore, it was best to approach an adversary's kite when he had released all of his string but you still had some in reserve. You needed to come up under his string from the downwind side. This allowed you to pull past and across his line, creating the fatal friction that cut down your adversary's kite.

Sometimes, you would down the other kite in short order, giving you the chance to reel back your string quickly and prepare for another engagement. Other times, your string would not cut through completely. This was risky. An inconclusive engagement could fatally entangle your kite with the enemy's. At best, it created a period of vulnerability to other kite fighters.

My mother was not keen on my kite-fighting exploits. She thought that it took away from my time on studies, and also feared that my competitive intensity would end in disaster. She was not just being overprotective, as I learned with great sadness. My friend Hazrat lived a few houses down the road from us. One day, when he was running across the roof and navigating his kite, he fell off the roof, hitting his head on the ground. He died on impact. All of the children in the neighborhood were in shock and mourning for weeks.

This tragedy rekindled my mother's fear that she could lose yet another child, and she ordered me to focus on my studies instead. As she suspected, I found it impossible to abide by her orders. On one occasion, she put on her burqa and went out in search of her young *bazi-gosh* son—the one "who didn't listen." She spotted me from afar, but, preoccupied by the excitement of battle, I didn't see her coming.

As she got closer, she gripped a stick that she had concealed and then suddenly charged at me. "Didn't I tell you not to fly kites!" she screamed as she struck me. I ran from the scene, embarrassed and humiliated. But my mother was not done. She rushed home, grabbed my kites, which I had hung like beautiful paintings, and tore them apart one by one, before smashing the reels against the floor and throwing the wreckage of my passion into the blazing oven in the backyard. It took me several weeks to reconstitute my kite collection and reach an agreement with my mother. I would fly kites only once a week, after I had done my homework. I had to promise to exercise extreme care when on rooftops.

MY FIRST IMPRESSIONS of the wider world came through the radio. By providing news from a national Afghan perspective, and offering cultural programming, such as poetry reading, music, and dramas, the radio contributed to a sense of national unity.

My parents would listen to the news. I remember reports of tensions with Pakistan over disputed borders and trade restrictions. Our family followed the conflicts between India and Pakistan. We rooted for New Delhi, not so much because we loved India but because Pakistan was our principal adversary.

We heard about state visits from senior Soviet officials. I was broadly aware of the Cold War but, as a kid, never imagined that the conflict would affect Afghanistan. I sometimes saw foreigners in the markets. Based on their fair complexion, I assumed they were part of Soviet teams. By the late 1950s, the Soviets were building roads, highways, and the airport at Mazar-i-Sharif. At the time, I didn't understand the strategic design behind their efforts. The Soviet Union would use this infrastructure for their invasion in 1979.

My father, despite serving in government, hardly ever offered political views. I do not remember him commenting on government affairs or expressing opinions about particular officials. He was a classic civil servant, carrying out duties efficiently as directed. My mother was more interested in politics, consuming as much news as possible and weighing in freely on whether leaders were making the right decisions for Afghanistan.

I remember when the king visited Mazar. As he rode down the main street in an open car, other children and I trotted alongside the motorcade. The king wore leather gloves, and people ran up to the vehicle to kiss his gloved hands in adulation. I wondered why everyone greeted him so enthusiastically in light of the country's obvious problems.

I was already aware that, after a glorious history, Afghanistan had become isolated and underdeveloped. The British had squeezed us from the south, the Russians from the north. Afghanistan had once been a big player, controlling vast territories, but now it had been pushed to the margins. Parts of our former lands had been incorporated by Pakistan after the British withdrew from India. The territory of Panjdeh to the north and west was taken from Afghanistan by Russia as part of a long-since-expired agreement; it then belonged to the Soviet Union and present-day Turkmenistan.

These reminders of loss did not engender hopelessness but, rather, fed the idea that Afghanistan could again expand and rise to power. Every year, this optimism was underscored in the public mind with a military parade that sought to demonstrate the country's might in a rather exaggerated way.

—◄   ►—

WHEN I WAS in eighth grade, my father announced to us that we were moving to Kabul. He had been appointed to a position in the Ministry of Public Works to oversee its work in the northern province of Konduz.

When it was time to leave Mazar, we loaded our possessions onto a bus for the perilous, two-day trip. The route took us along a narrow, unpaved road that snaked through the mountains. Often, it seemed to be barely carved out of the mountainside, with a sheer rock wall on one side of the bus and a cliff looking down on a river far below on the other.

On the second afternoon of our trip, I noticed a big limousine trying to get around a Chevy truck ahead of it. With no shoulders on the road, it was difficult for cars to pass each other. The truck either wouldn't or couldn't let the limo pass. When the narrow road briefly widened, the fancy car seized the opportunity and flew past the truck, only to slam on its brakes and come to a halt. The truck was forced to stop, as was our bus.

"What's going on?" I asked my father. "Quiet!" he snapped.

I moved forward in the bus to see for myself. The driver of the limo was opening the car's back door. Out stepped a well-dressed, bald, clean-shaven man. His bearing radiated arrogance and power. "Daoud Khan," my father whispered. "He's the king's cousin. Husband of the king's sister. Former prime minister. He ruled the country when the king was young."

Daoud's face was full of rage. My jaw dropped as I watched him and his chauffeur drag the truck's driver out of his vehicle, throw him to the ground, and beat and kick him senseless.

"We should do something!" I pleaded. My mother agreed, but my father refused, as did others on the bus. "Are you crazy?" he said. "Do you know who that guy is? He could kill us!"

Daoud then moved toward the truck driver and bit off his left ear. Blood ran down his cheek and neck. The ear, bloodied and covered in spittle and dust, lay on the side of the road.

I felt sick to my stomach. I was shocked by the injustice and brutality of a powerful figure abusing others with such impunity.

I thought back many times to what I had seen. What did the incident say about the country I loved?

KABUL WAS MUCH more sophisticated than Mazar. The capital city had a population of some 500,000, about ten times that of Mazar. It was a clean, pleasant city, quite green, with main boulevards—particularly the road to Darulaman Palace—lined with grand old trees. Its trolleys, airport, and multistory buildings were hallmarks of modernity. The houses in Kabul were often constructed from brick or concrete instead of mud. Some were small villas, with beautiful, elaborate gardens. Many homes and public places had Western furniture, including couches and dining tables.

On holidays, crowds larger than any I had ever seen would gather for festivities, attend concerts and cultural events, and stay out late. I recall the sound of Afghan music and the scent of kebabs and corn cooking on open grills. Social interactions were much more open in Kabul, with men and women sitting together—a change I liked.

Kabul at the time was a relatively cosmopolitan city. Indians would come to shop for goods unavailable in their socialist economy. U.N. Secretary General Ban Ki-moon later told me that, as a diplomat in Delhi during this period, he would notify his friends and colleagues before his trips to Kabul. They in turn would provide him with lists of goods to bring home that were unavailable in Delhi—blue jeans were a popular item.

It was not uncommon to see Pakistanis, who came to escape the oppressive summer heat in the Indus River plain, enjoy Kabul's nightclubs and entertainment and indulge in the guilty pleasure of Indian movies, which were banned in their own country.

Backpackers from the United States and Western Europe filled Kabul's hotels, favorite stops on the so-called Hippie Trail. Citroën, the French automobile company, organized a Paris-to-Kabul-to-Paris automobile rally that attracted 1,300 participants in 1970.

My family initially lived in downtown Kabul and later moved to a cottage before settling in a larger house in Karte Char. Located to the west of the central city along Darulaman Road, beyond the city's zoo and behind the national parliament building, Karte Char was one of Kabul's better suburbs.

I now had a room to myself. It was square, with cream white walls and a light hanging from the ceiling. The window had teal curtains, and the floor was covered with a handmade red carpet. My bed was a typical Afghan futon, called a *toshaak*, and had white sheets, pillow shams, and a dark purple blanket. My books were usually scattered around the bed for easy access. I had a radio that I had bought with my savings.

I enrolled in Ghazi High School, an all-boys school with a British-influenced curriculum. Among my schoolmates in Kabul, I was initially viewed as a country bumpkin from up north. I used to wear a karakul hat in order to tamp down my unruly curls—a cause of endless teasing from my new peers. It did not help that there was a girls' high school called Rabia Balkhi nearby. The boys of Ghazi and girls of Rabia Balkhi would talk, joke, and make plans to get together—an openness with which I was unfamiliar. I was initially teased for being so shy, but soon found my bearing.

By the time I made it to Kabul, I had become a good student. I often got up early in the morning to study in my room, wrapped in a blanket to ward off the chill. I had a mirror, which I would use on most afternoons to practice my English presentations.

In seventh and eighth grades, I received the top marks in my class. This meant that I had the dubious distinction of being "captain." When the teacher walked into the room, it was my duty to call out to all the students, "Stand up!" I also had to keep track of attendance. When the teacher left the classroom, I was expected to keep order. Naturally, I was accused of being a teacher's pet and found myself on the wrong side of the class bullies.

Literature and history were among my favorite subjects. I was fascinated by the *Shahnameh*, an epic poem relating the story of Persian dynasties. We also read more modern Afghan poets, such as Pazhwak, whose work dwelled on patriotic themes and appealed to Afghan nationalists yearning to reunite with their brethren on the Pakistani side of the Durand Line.

I grew to appreciate how Afghanistan as a country had emerged from the cauldron of competing empires. For centuries, countries as we understand them today did not exist. Instead, empires led and named for dynastic families rose and fell. I was struck by the violent history of Afghanistan. Rulers led military campaigns against neighboring lands, sometimes to spread development and progress, sometimes to bring back treasures and cultural influences, and at times to conquer and destroy. The same set of factors seemed to doom once-great empires: domestic infighting, poor leadership, and an inability to adapt to innovations in technology, weapons, or economic trends.

Afghan history reinforced to me that the country had the potential to do great things. There was nothing inevitable about its current state. I was particularly interested in two of Afghanistan's recent leaders. One was Abdur

Rahman Khan, the so-called Iron Amir, who forged a modern state from 1880 through 1901. Through force of will and arms, he created a centralized, top-down state in which he appointed all the provincial governors and extended Kabul's administrative reach to the most distant villages. While I recognized that a strong hand was needed to establish order, I thought the Iron Amir was too quick to resort to brutal methods instead of taking on the more painstaking tasks of power-sharing and consensus-building.

The story of Afghanistan's failed modernizer king, Amanullah Khan, who ruled from 1919 to 1928, made an impact on me as well. Like the leaders of Turkey and Iran at the time, he had embarked on an ambitious experiment in modernization, seeking not only to build state institutions but also to liberalize Afghanistan's conservative social norms. He was the first Afghan head of state to travel to Europe, stopping in Turkey and Iran on the way. Unfortunately, Amanullah lacked the political skills to enforce his program. His modernization program generated a severe backlash from traditional and religious forces in Afghan society.

Amanullah Khan compounded his problems by taking on the British in India, calling for an end to colonialism and encouraging unrest among Pashtun tribes in areas subordinated to British rule. The British encouraged Afghan tribal leaders, who were already antagonistic to the modernization program, to rebel against Kabul. Amanullah Khan abdicated in 1929 and went into exile in Italy.

While Amanullah's reforms were discredited in their time, Afghans of my generation admired him as a progressive nationalist. When I was leaving Afghanistan as ambassador in 2005, I was honored that President Karzai bestowed on me Afghanistan's highest medal, named after King Amanullah.

The issues of state-building and reform were salient at the time. In the 1960s, Zahir Shah came into his own as a ruler. The king was taking important steps to modernize Afghanistan. He crafted a new constitution in 1964, which led to the election of a national parliament the following year. The power and influence of government institutions, the business community, and the intellectual class grew relative to landowners and tribes. Local religious leaders were weakened by their growing financial dependence on the state and private sector. With foreign assistance, the government was able to complete important national infrastructure projects—notably the "ring road" connecting Afghanistan's principal cities and major hydroelectric dams on the Kabul River.

Still, cautious by nature, Zahir Shah was careful not to antagonize the traditional religious and tribal establishment—which was particularly regressive on women's issues.

At a time when I was beginning to see the injustices around me through a more political lens, I was dissatisfied with the pace of the king's reforms. I was already aware of the sexism that abounded in Afghanistan. But it was only in Kabul that I came to appreciate the country's deep ethnic divide. While Afghanistan had four major ethnic groups and several minor ones, the Pashtuns and the Tajiks were dominant.

The Hazaras were always given the hard, lowly jobs. In the national army, Hazara conscripts would be assigned as servants in the homes of state officials. There were Hazaras in my school, and I saw that there were limits to how high they could rise.

This was true, albeit to a lesser degree, for Uzbeks, Turkomen, and other ethnic minorities as well. In the plains of the north, the Uzbeks and Turkomen might have land or considerable wealth. However, in Kabul, they were regarded as simpletons. In institutions such as the military and the diplomatic service, the highest ranks were reserved exclusively for Pashtuns or Tajiks.

I never became desensitized to the plight of the Hazaras. I remember one time I saw a small group of Hazaras struggling to pull a heavy carriage up a hill. I approached them and offered to give them a hand. I was surprised when they refused my help. They were afraid that I would get hurt.

In the tenth grade, I received a poignant reminder of the advantage that I enjoyed as a male. Class rank determined one's eligibility to compete for a place in the coveted American Field Service (AFS) exchange program to the United States. Just like today, each AFS student would live for a year with an American family and attend a local high school. I was well positioned, having finished ninth grade at the top of my class, and was allowed to take the written and oral examinations to join the program. I had known several students who had been in the AFS program in previous years and was eager to go abroad.

My year was supposed to be the first in which girls were allowed to compete for slots. Just after we were seated for the exam, however, the girls were asked to leave. A government minister vetoed the girls' participation at the last minute, arguing that it was inappropriate for girls of that age to travel to America without family members.

I was struck by how unfair it was to deny smart Afghan girls the opportunity to compete and succeed. But I also felt a degree of ambivalence about the decision, knowing that my chances of being accepted into the program were now much higher.

After passing the written test in Dari, I was interviewed in English to assess how well I could manage with an American family. After a nerve-wracking wait, I was informed that I would be spending my junior year in the United States.

An orientation program followed. I started to get a better feel for American ways but, like most Afghans students, did not fully grasp the immense distance separating Afghanistan and the United States or the profound differences between our societies and cultures. I knew that America was a modern and powerful country. From the news and movies, I had images of great American cities with tall buildings. But I thought they were not much different from those in India. As we prepared for the trip, I learned about the intriguing nature of America—a country of immigrants that played an important role in the world.

In the days before my departure, it hit me that I was leaving my family and setting out for the other side of the world. Waking before dawn the morning I was flying out, I felt a sense of both excitement and unease. Unlike my father's family, who held a symbolic funeral for him when he left Laghman for Mazar, my family followed a more recent Afghan tradition. They held up a copy of the Koran, under which I walked three times. As I was leaving the house, my sisters sprinkled water on the floor behind me to ensure that I would come back.

TWO

JOURNEY TO THE
OTHER SIDE OF
THE WORLD

THE UNITED STATES, 1966–1967

AS OUR PLANE APPROACHED NEW YORK'S JOHN F. KENNEDY AIRPORT IN AUGUST 1966, a yellowish glow grew brighter outside the window. It had been just forty-eight hours since I left Kabul aboard an Ariana Airlines flight. We had hopped from Kabul to Tehran to Brussels and were now approaching our final destination.

I had never seen so many lights in my life. At first, this dazzling display was a puzzle to us twenty-four Afghan exchange students. In Afghanistan, only for major celebrations would strings of lights be hung in parade or concert areas. We naturally concluded there must be some huge event under way in New York.

My knowledge of the United States was sketchy and idiosyncratic. From radio news and various films, Afghans understood that America was an enemy of the neighboring Soviet Union (for which I had never had much affinity), that it was involved in a difficult conflict in Vietnam, and that it was a rich and powerful nation. As a boy, I envisioned America as a glamorous and fashionable place. There were markets back home where one could purchase secondhand garments from America. The idea that someone would discard perfectly good clothes to be sold elsewhere made a deep impression on me. Americans must be so wealthy that they could wear their clothes just once or twice and then give them away. The glittering skyline confirmed this impression; people here were so wealthy they could turn night into day.

There were massive crowds at the airport gates, at the immigration checkpoint, at the baggage carousel, and at the customs counter—more people than I'd ever seen in one place and all of them in a hurry. And that was just the airport.

Our group boarded buses to go to our hotel in Manhattan. We looked out at the city in amazement. Every once in a while I caught a quick look from one of my Afghan peers: What have we gotten ourselves into? There were billboards everywhere. I could not understand what most said. Even though I had studied English in school, in reality I could barely read or string together anything beyond the simplest phrases.

I knew a little bit about the family with whom I would live—the Perras of Ceres, California. The father, Medrick, was a designer and precision tool-and-die maker for a local manufacturing company. His wife, Ruth, was a schoolteacher and helped run the family walnut orchard. Their daughter, Lorraine, had married and left home already. One son, Mark, was studying science at a nearby junior college. The other son, David, was a high school student a couple of years younger than me. From the letter I had received from them, they seemed like a warm and nice family. Still, I was more than a little uneasy.

The culture shocks came in quick succession. From our hotel, where AFS students would stay for a few days of orientation, the city seemed massive, with skyscrapers stretching as far as I could see down the long avenues. The buildings looked like mountains. How did people get up so high?

When I arrived at the hotel, I discovered the answer. I cocked my head skeptically at the first elevator I had ever seen, a metal box with doors that seemed to open menacingly to swallow you up.

"After you," I told the others.

The hotel room presented new puzzles. It was a very hot and humid August night. Neither my roommate, Najib Shikiba, nor I grasped the fact that there was an air conditioner. We did not know what that box in the window was, much less how to turn it on. Soon we were suffocating from the heat. To escape the stifling room, we decided to explore the city. It was even hotter there. The heat seemed to rise from the street like steam. Our hotel was on one of the big avenues, and I marveled at the traffic lights lined up one after another into the distance as far as I could see. I had never before seen the red, green, and yellow lights signaling to cars. Traffic police enforced order at the major intersections in Kabul. It did not take long before we concluded that setting out on our own was a bad idea.

In the morning, it took me some time just to figure out the concept of a shower. In Afghanistan you cleaned yourself by taking warm water from the stove, carrying it to the bathroom in a bucket, and then using a small cup to throw water on yourself. My roommate and I finally managed to turn on the water before learning the hard way that you needed to regulate the temperature.

On the first day in New York, the AFS officers explained that the American host families were volunteers. It was my first encounter with the powerful way Americans self-organize to achieve civic good. Americans take this for granted. For a young Afghan, it was a revelation.

We had time to sightsee too. Americans looked extraordinarily big and tall. I felt very small, though maybe I was just feeling out of place. The diversity of the people was strange to me, as well. People of European, Asian, and African descent all mingled in the swirl of the city sidewalks. I had never seen someone of African descent before. Afghanistan had some ethnic diversity, but this was much more striking. The crowds overwhelmed me.

I was starting to feel sick from the oppressive heat and humidity. As the orientation drew to a close, I approached the AFS administrator.

"I want to go back to Afghanistan," I told him. "It's too hot and humid here. I can't breathe."

The administrator looked up my name on a list and assured me that I'd be okay. "This is New York," he said. "You're going to California."

"Is it different there?" I asked.

With a hint of a smile, he simply said, "You'll find out."

The next day, I bid a sad goodbye to my friends, among them Ashraf Ghani, and headed west. Because of an airline strike, we had to travel by bus. There were young people from all over Europe, Latin America, and the Middle East, but I was the only Afghan. I could communicate to a limited extent with a couple of Iranians because of the similarities between Dari and Farsi, but it was difficult to connect enough words in my limited English vocabulary to convey more than the simplest idea to anyone else.

As we headed west, the prosperity of America started to sink in. Afghans in rural areas were only slightly above subsistence farmers. Here, the farms were like villas, and I saw giant machines that worked enormous fields in near-perfect geometric patterns. The huge bridges, spanning immense rivers, were incredible to me. I compared the American highways with the road that linked Mazar to Kabul, which was mostly unpaved and often rutted by erosion. Here, the paved roads were so smooth you could drive at high speeds. If you miscalculated, there were even guardrails to catch you.

Our first scheduled stop was in Colorado, but we took brief respites along the way. The people at these stops were well dressed, and there were restaurants everywhere. The number of cars was overwhelming. All the towns and even isolated houses had electricity. When we stopped in Chicago, I was impressed not just by the size and architectural design of the Wrigley Building but also by the sheer scale and extent of everything else that had been built. America was a young country compared with Afghanistan. How had the Americans had enough time to build all these structures?

We drove day and night to make better time. In the Midwest, we saw miles of corn and more corn and then miles of wheat and more wheat. The rough-hewn edges of the beautiful Rocky Mountains reminded me of Afghanistan.

When we reached our first overnight stop in Colorado, we had driven three days and two nights, so we were grateful for the chance to shower and rest. The AFS program had arranged for us to spend a night with local families. I remember thinking how Americans did everything in such a well-organized way. I was assigned to a welcoming family in a nice house. They showed me to my room. Knowing how long we had been on the road, one of the parents kindly offered, "Why don't you take a bath?" I had mastered the shower but had not yet encountered a bathtub. I stared at the tub, flummoxed. Americans were unfailingly kind, but it was difficult for them to appreciate how little I knew about modern things and how different the circumstances of daily life were in less developed countries.

Once I was spruced up, it was off to a potluck dinner. This was my first experience with the concept of bringing food to a dinner at someone else's house. In Afghanistan, where the role of an Afghan host is to serve food in abundance, it would be mortifying to ask your guests to bring their own food.

Two days later, when our bus finally arrived in San Francisco, the Perra family was at the terminal to pick me up. They were a picture-book family: Dad and Mom and the kids. They drove an American-made family sedan with round back taillights. The parents both wore the heavy-framed glasses that were stylish in those days. On that day, the boys wore the checkered, light dress shirts that were cool enough for a summer day but sufficiently formal for greeting a new houseguest.

The Perras later told me that they had asked for an exchange student from somewhere other than Europe. Since I arrived with a prayer rug and Afghan cookbook, I probably fit the bill.

I was directed into the backseat with the kids. David seemed a little shy, while Mark, the older son, was more forward. When we stopped in a restaurant to eat, it was a challenge to figure out what to order. American food was a mystery to me, and I did not recognize most of the dishes, even in the colorful pictures on the laminated menu. I settled on something involving chicken, though I may have ordered "kitchen" when I spoke to the waitress. The Perras were very friendly and solicitous, and I remember the relief I felt as I became comfortable with them. We drove on, eighty or ninety miles east down an interstate and then on Highway 99 into the Central Valley. After passing through Modesto, we arrived in Ceres, a rural town with a population of a little more than 5,000. It had one main street with a general store, restaurants, a post office, and a gas station. Along one section of the main street, houses were built on large plots of land, and then farmland extended into the distance.

The Perras had about nine acres, with an orchard of walnut and almond trees that the family harvested every year. They also grew vegetables and corn, as everyone seemed to do in this community. Medrick, the father, liked to work on old cars and had a 1930s classic that he would spend time on after work. He also had a tractor and a pickup truck as a second car. Their house was a modest but comfortable one-story ranch. It had a family room with a dining area and a kitchen at one end of the house. The couches and chairs in the family room were arranged for watching the television.

In Afghanistan I vaguely knew about televisions but had never actually seen one. There were other novel devices: the refrigerator, the electric range, and the telephone. At the other end of the house were the bedrooms and bathrooms. There was a master bedroom, and the two smaller bedrooms, one for David and the other for me. When Mark came over from the junior college, he stayed with David. The Perras had a nice backyard, where they sometimes played croquet.

I woke up that first morning in California and found only Ruth at home. The others had gone to work. She asked me what I wanted for breakfast. She could see I was struggling for the right English words, so she asked whether I wanted eggs. Asked how I wanted them prepared, I confidently requested "fired" eggs. She smiled and asked what else I would like. My intention was to ask for toast but instead I requested "cookies." My language skills were a work in progress.

I had arrived in August, a couple of weeks before the beginning of the school year. The time flew by amid a whirlwind of meetings with neighbors. Yet, even in those early days, I was beginning to discern bit by bit some of the reasons for America's success.

Americans had an appealing openness about them. I saw this as the Perras took me to meet friends around town, as well as the teachers I would have in school. I was a young boy from a country they had never heard about. Yet I was never treated as an outsider. Everyone was unfailingly warm, and their hospitality instantly put me at ease. The people of Ceres seemed genuinely interested in Afghanistan, though they knew almost nothing about the country, not even where it was on a map. Despite this limitation, I came to see that something in the culture enabled Americans to create immediate connections with others.

David was working that summer doing small jobs for various people around town in order to make some money for the school year. I wanted to do the same, and the Perras helped me get a series of jobs. One involved vaccinating chickens. It was terrible. I had to put droplets into the eyes of the chickens—thousands of them. The chicken coops reeked, and the stench stayed with me when I came back to the house at the end of the day. I also spent long hours harvesting almonds and grapes, which I found difficult because of the hours in the strong sun. In Afghanistan this work would have been considered lower class and looked down upon. Here, any and all work was seen as a valuable social contribution and as evidence of maturity.

When I calculated how much I was being paid and its equivalent in Afghan currency, it seemed like a lot, though it must have been minimum wage. I was vaguely insulted, though, when I picked almonds for the Perras and they offered to pay me. When I worked for my family in Afghanistan, I did so without compensation. I refused to take the money at first but, over time, learned that the American practice was for children to accept allowances from their parents. Maybe, I thought, this was how Americans taught their children the value of work.

This work ethic, as well as the American spirit of entrepreneurialism, was infectious. Despite the days spent vaccinating chickens, I enjoyed all the chicken dishes Ruth prepared for the family. Chicken was much more plentiful and affordable in America than it was in Afghanistan. I began to think that when I went back home, I should start a chicken farm. Afghans loved chicken, and I was convinced that I could get rich in this business.

The Americans around me seemed to practice a tolerant and practical kind of religious faith. The Perras, who were Presbyterians, attended church every Sunday but were not intensely religious. It was eye-opening to see men and women attend services together. There was some singing, but mostly you sat and listened to a sermon that related faith to your personal life and challenges.

Religion was important to people, and some demonstrably sought to express their faith through their daily actions. Yet, upon learning that I was a Muslim, there was not a hint of a negative judgment. Most of all, people were curious and interested in learning the differences between Christianity and Islam. Sometimes the discussions focused on whether or not Islam was a true religion. I explained that, according to Islamic beliefs, God said that Judaism and Christianity were true religions and that Islam was the final prophecy to mankind. Americans, with a myriad of faiths and denominations, seemed able to explore these ideas at an intellectual level without descending into rancorous disputes about which faith was the valid one.

The social equality of 1960s America was also striking to me. Both the husband and wife worked in the home. The wife usually did more of the cooking, but the husband had his share of yard work and chores. Unlike those in Afghanistan, where the husband was the dominant figure, American couples seemed to treat each other as equals and as friends. Everyone had a voice in dinner table conversations.

This took time for me to accept. Once, I was trying to back up the family tractor to unload some wood. Having never learned to drive in Afghanistan, I was struggling with the chore. Seeing my frustration, Ruth took my place behind the wheel and backed the tractor up with precision in seconds. I remember thinking that my father would have been cross with me for not being able to do something that a woman could do with such ease.

In an interview many years later, Ruth recalled that when I was getting ready to leave America, she asked me what American customs I would like to see adopted in Afghanistan. I answered, "The way a man treats his wife."

Social equality also existed in the wider community. There were no leading families or feudal landowners as far as I could tell. Everyone could buy land and own a business. I noticed that Americans, even school-aged children, reflexively resolved disputes by putting issues to a vote. No one ever questioned the legitimacy of the decision of the majority.

As the school year began and I started grade twelve, my English was quickly improving, but keeping up with note-taking in class was a struggle. I learned to swim and play basketball. Having always been in all-boys schools, I found the presence of girls distracting—and fascinating. It took me even more time to adjust to the American dating scene.

I was deeply impressed by the American talent for organization. Coming from the more anarchic environment of Afghanistan, I had the impression that everything in America functioned as if it were being carried out by a military organization. During field trips, the bus rolled up on time, and the kids were lined up and ready to go. The people at our destination were prepared and expecting us. Arrangements for lunch and drinks had been made and went off without a hitch. Guides completed their tours with precision. The bus got us all back to school just as our families were arriving to pick us up. It was a marvel to watch. This kind of thing could never happen in Afghanistan.

During the school year, I spoke about Afghanistan at meetings of organizations like the Rotary or Lions Clubs. These talks were part of my responsibilities as an AFSer. I was supposed to introduce Americans to my country and the wider region. Again, I was gratified to see that the leaders of the community were eager to know about Afghanistan. I was struck by the fact that adults would sit and respectfully listen to a young person like me.

As my year as a student went on, I became more comfortable and easy-going. When I talked about Afghanistan, I started to work in a few jokes, both to make people laugh and to test whether they could tell that I was joking. In Afghanistan, I would say, we went on dates on camels, and on very special dates we went on double-hump camels.

I learned about the vital role that volunteer civil society groups played in America. They raised money for good works, such as refurbishing play-grounds or offering scholarships. In Afghanistan, most people would expect the government to do these things.

As the year progressed, I started to focus beyond Ceres on broader aspects of the American system. I was impressed by the fact that each state had its own legislature, each county its own board of commissioners, and each town its own mayor and council.

However, the private sector made an even more powerful impression. Af-ghanistan was a market economy, but not like this. In America, if you were a leading businessman, you were consequential and respected as a leader of the community. Afghans believed that those who made money in business were schemers who had won ill-gotten gains.

As a non-American visiting for the first time, I was amazed at the ease of assimilation into American society. I met an Afghan immigrant who managed a restaurant. He seemed to have become a genuine American without losing a sense of his identity.

⤙   ⤚

AT THE END of our American year, the AFSers reconvened in New York City before flying home. We had all been profoundly changed by our experiences. Certainly we all spoke better English. However, the bigger change was that we were all Americanized, both in subtle and not-so-subtle ways. Everyone looked healthier and more relaxed. Most of us wore faded blue jeans and T-shirts. A year earlier we were wearing suits when we arrived in New York. Now, we were more self-assured. We were also much more fun.

I had not thought a great deal about political philosophy or world politics before my year abroad. The contrasts between Afghanistan and America, and the countless conversations about Afghanistan and world events, had changed that for good. I now knew there was a better way to organize society, even if I did not know how to apply those ideas in Afghanistan. As I thought about college, I was still focused on practical pursuits such as engineering, but politi-cal questions were more and more on my mind.

On a personal level, I was profoundly touched by the love and kindness my American hosts had shown me. They had imbued me with a deep affection for America. I remained in close touch with the Perras over the years, and in the 1980s they hosted my brother, Tory, while he pursued a degree at Modesto Junior College.

Even my exposure to America's challenges left me with a positive impression of the country. I became aware of the growing social turmoil in the U.S. In 1966 the civil rights movement was well under way, opposition to the Vietnam War was building, and the women's liberation movement was growing. Even as the tumultuous decade of the 1960s tested American unity and social cohesion, I saw that American society had reasonable ways to address profound disagreements.

I wondered how Afghanistan could navigate the process of change on a similar scale. Even as a young person, I sensed that modernizing Afghan society would be difficult, and I doubted whether it could be accomplished in my lifetime.

Not for a moment did I anticipate that I would represent the United States in an effort to help Afghans modernize their country. But from the time I left California, I came to see myself as a person with two homes and two affiliations. And in an odd, rather unusual twist of history, I would become an advocate for each to the other.

THREE

INTO THE CAULDRON OF POLITICS

KABUL AND BEIRUT, 1968–1974

I RETURNED TO KABUL A CHANGED PERSON. MY CLASSMATES HAD ONCE TEASED ME for being a country bumpkin. Now they now gave me a hard time for having become so "Americanized." I sported American-style shorts, which no local would dream of wearing, and often mixed English words or phrases into my speech. It took time to readjust to Afghan food, which was heavier and oilier than what I had become accustomed to in California.

My time in America had sharpened my eye when it came to conditions in Afghanistan. I struggled with the fact that my country was so poor and underdeveloped compared with the United States.

Plus, I had to make some choices about my future. With equal parts encouragement and pressure from my family, I entered medical school at Kabul University.

Almost immediately, I came to doubt that medicine was right for me. The odor of formaldehyde and the sight of blood made me feel faint. Still, I stuck with it. I knew how important it was to my family.

I maintained my connection to the United States through the American community in Kabul. I attended events sponsored by the U.S. embassy and helped the AFS program expand into other parts of Afghanistan. I also supported American AFS students who came to Afghanistan for the summer and needed some cross-cultural mediation. A frequent complaint of the American students was the lack of privacy—their adopted families did not allow them to spend even a few minutes alone. To the Afghan mind, if someone withdrew to his or her room, this meant that he or she was depressed or unhappy. Why else would they not immerse themselves in boisterous, welcoming togetherness? When they sought some time alone, someone would immediately be dispatched to see what was troubling the American. Of course, the students just wanted some relief from all the noisy socializing of an Afghan extended family.

Another thing that made the Americans uncomfortable was the constant insistence from their Afghan "mothers" that they eat more. In Afghan culture, pressing food upon your guests is an imperative, since they in turn are obliged to decline the offer initially even if they would like to have more. I was called upon to "translate" the conflicting courtesies.

One day, while strolling across the Kabul University campus with some friends, I saw an announcement for a USAID scholarship to the American University of Beirut (AUB). It listed the fields of study that were available, and the fact that medicine was not among them piqued my interest. On a whim, I decided to take the application exam. I was surprised when, a couple of weeks later, I was told that I had earned a spot in the program. My English-language skills were strong enough that I would only need a few weeks of additional instruction before enrolling at AUB in the fall.

But I eventually declined the scholarship. U.S. ambassador Robert Neumann* cornered me when he saw me at a Fourth of July celebration at the U.S. residence. Neumann, along with the Afghan minister of education, urged me to try AUB during the summer session. I could always come back and resume my medical studies in the fall if I did not like it.

My father, who probably would have supported my going to AUB, was away on an extended assignment in Kunduz Province. So the decision was up to my mother. She hesitated, but concluded that a few weeks at AUB would not be the end of the world.

THE MOMENT I got off the plane in Beirut, I fell in love with the city. While I worked hard on academics, I did my share of lounging on the Mediterranean

---

*Neumann's son Ronald, in the then-unimaginable future, would succeed me as U.S. ambassador to Afghanistan.

beaches and enjoying the Beirut nightlife. I also played a good deal of pinball with my fellow Afghan, Qadir Ahad. Pinball facilities were popular hangouts for young men. We didn't just tamely pull the levers, but would grab the entire machine and attempt to jolt our way to victory. The indulgent proprietor, worried for his machines, would deliver rebukes in a resigned tone of voice. I can still hear him: "*Ya shabab!*" (Oh, you young people!)

I was intrigued by Lebanon and its cosmopolitan, flourishing capital. Lebanon was incomparably more prosperous, sophisticated, and advanced than Afghanistan. Members of leading Saudi and Gulf families liked to visit Beirut and enjoy its worldly pleasures before returning to their own austere and stern societies. I was impressed by how many languages even the average shopkeeper commanded. To be fluent in Arabic and French was nothing. The merchants typically spoke at least one or two other languages, such as Armenian, Greek, or Russian. Lebanon was open to the world and embraced foreign influences with self-confident enthusiasm. A microcosm of the region, the country had seemingly found a formula for maintaining stability through a division of power along sectarian lines. All manner of political groups existed on campus: royalists, liberal secularists, Arab nationalists, supporters of various Palestinian movements, Lebanese nationalists, and leftists of all kinds, including Communists. Islamists, though, were a distinct minority at the time.

After the summer term, I enrolled as a full-time undergraduate in the political science and public administration department. Founded in 1866 as the Syrian Protestant College, the school became the American University of Beirut in 1920. AUB became deeply rooted in the country and the community. The university was a catalyst for bringing modern science and learning to the Middle East. AUB offered an array of excellent courses covering the history of civilization, the philosophy of the West and the East, and specialized courses on the region. In the many wars in Lebanon's recent history, the campus had been spared systematic attack, and there was never a push to shut it down, principally because all factions knew that they, too, would suffer without the medical facilities AUB provided.

I could sense, however, that storm clouds were gathering. The country was becoming more polarized. A large influx of Palestinians, including many fighters, had arrived after the so-called Black September, when a Palestinian attempt to become a state within a state in Jordan was suppressed by the military. Beyond threatening the careful demographic balance that kept Lebanon stable, the presence of so many combatants moved the Israeli-Arab battleground into Lebanon. The Shia were the poorest of the major communities and generally had larger families. The Shia, with their increasing numbers, and the Palestinians, with their deeply felt political cause, were both pressing for more influence. The Christians and Sunnis were trying to defend the status quo. The

Christians tended to be Lebanese nationalists, and the militant Christian student organization called the Phalange had as its slogan "Lebanon—Love It or Leave It." Sunnis leaned more toward Arab nationalism and were sympathetic to the Palestinians, who were mostly Sunni but quite secular in their ideology.

Lebanon proved too weak to protect itself against its adversaries or to prevent itself from becoming a proxy battleground for others. It could not prevent militant Palestinians from flooding in and operating from its territory, nor could it stop the Syrians or the Israelis. Everything came to a head in the 1973 war. I well remember Israeli jets buzzing over Beirut, flying over the AUB campus. For several weeks, the gates of the sprawling campus remained locked, with the curfew lifted for only a few hours a day so that students could go out and replenish their food supplies.

Lebanon had struck a successful balance between tolerance and piety, modernity and tradition, but it could not extract itself from the unfolding crisis of Islamic civilization. I started to see the nature of this crisis when I was in Beirut, and over the subsequent years I have thought a lot about the reasons for it. The overlap between secular power and religion, far more pronounced in Islam than in the other major religions, is certainly a big part of the problem. Muslims see Islam as the final and perfect religion, the one that ought to guide all of humanity and structure human society globally. Other religions have such concepts, too, but in the case of Islam, the emphasis on establishing a godly society in the temporal world and not just in the next life is arguably more pronounced. After Mohammed's death, the Islamic empire expanded rapidly and became home to the major centers of learning and science. But later, this dominance eroded and ultimately collapsed, both for internal reasons and because of the rise of stronger competitors.

From the nineteenth century onward, Muslim lands had been dominated by European colonial powers, particularly after the collapse of the Ottomans. It had been painful enough to lose their European foothold and be driven out of Spain; now Muslims were being dominated and even ruled by non-Muslims. The Europeans set about creating states and drawing borders with little regard to ethnic, historic, tribal, and other preexisting patterns. Indeed, tribal and sectarian rivalries were often deliberately exploited by the Europeans to make local populations easier to subdue.

I was part of a cohort of Middle Eastern intellectuals and young people who were grappling with the question of what had gone wrong and what path might lead us forward. Ataturk, the young leader who disbanded the Ottoman Caliphate and transformed Turkey into a modern state, articulated a secular philosophy that particularly resonated with me. I admired Ataturk's approach as compared with the creeping, sluggish modernization program of our own king in Afghanistan.

The more I learned about the broader Middle East, the more ashamed I became of Afghanistan's particular plight. AUB was a simmering mini-cauldron of the region's ideological and political turmoil. Arab nationalism was suffused with the impulse to modernize. The Egyptian leader Gamel Abdel Nasser was the lodestar, but there were other strains as well. Baathist parties and movements in Iraq and Syria were the spearheads of secular modernization. The enigmatic Qaddafi in Libya, who had toppled the country's monarchy in a coup, seemed to fit the same mold, albeit in an eccentric way. All across the region, impatient young men were frontally challenging traditional social and political structures. These leaders hoped that a shared Arab identity would inspire and energize the masses, but many were also quick to develop cults of personality to entrench their power rather than building for the public good.

A much smaller group of students saw Islam as the answer to the region's problems. Living strictly by religious precepts, they argued, would return the region to the glory days of the past. Though this current of thought had existed for well over a century, it seemed to be gathering fresh momentum. The Muslim Brotherhood, which had a significant social base in Egypt and reached into Sunni communities across the region, was the largest and most significant of these movements. In fact, when I was still at Kabul University, individuals and groups sympathetic to the Brotherhood had been trying to spread Islamist views in Afghanistan as well. The writings of Sayyid Qutb, which would inspire violent Islamist movements for decades, were making the rounds during those years. I was also aware of Jamaat Islami, the analogous fundamentalist movement in South Asia. Still, among the students at AUB, who had consciously made the choice to learn the modern sciences, Islamism had few adherents.

At another level, I began to see that the struggle to shape the Middle East had been a perpetual contest not just among major regional but also extra-regional powers. I became aware of the outsized influence of Iran, a country with an imperial tradition and significant economic and political weight among Shia communities in other Gulf countries. With the British withdrawal from the Gulf in 1971, a vacuum existed that Iran's shah sought to fill. But there were angry demonstrations against the shah by Iranian students at AUB, who considered him to be a Western puppet indifferent to the welfare of his people.

I was privileged to learn the history of the Middle East from world-class scholars. My professor Hanna Batatu, who wrote one of the most important books on Iraq's history, was a scholar of Arab politics and a historian of the creation of modern Arab states. In his class, I was struck by the enduring challenge of how to forge national unity in societies that had deep fault lines.

Some of our best professors were Palestinians. They were highly educated, well respected, and often from established but now displaced and disinherited families. I learned about the roots of the Palestinian conflict from Walid Khalidi, whose seminal book, *From Haven to Conquest,* presented a surprisingly empathetic narrative about the Jews' expulsion from fascist Europe and their desperate search for safe refuge. Khalidi, who looked and dressed like a British don from Oxford, spoke with a pronounced upper-class British accent and sweated profusely in his elegant tropical-weight suits, as if he were somehow unaccustomed to the heat of a Middle Eastern summer. He taught us about the convoluted diplomacy and the bitter military struggles leading to the Israeli-Arab standoff. He blamed the weakness of the Arab side and the cynical actions of the European powers for the plight of the Palestinians, far more in fact than he blamed the Jews, who, in his view, were simply and understandably trying to survive. He argued, however, that the search for a haven for the Jewish people had turned into a drive for domination.

From Batatu, Khalidi, and Yosuf Ibish, I learned about the decline and fall of the Ottoman Empire, the rise of the European colonial powers, and the division of the Middle East. They helped me understand, most deeply and consequentially, the despair and shame that the Arabs felt when their armies failed in their 1948 war against Israel and in their 1967 defeat in the Six Day War. Among my peers, the Israeli-Arab conflict was an ever-present and very emotional topic. Arab Palestinians were well represented within the AUB student body and had a prominent role in public debates and student government. I also had great sympathy for the Palestinian people, who, in my view, were being victimized not just by the Israelis but also by their own leaders and the region's Arab governments. Palestinian leaders had failed their own people by rejecting possible political settlements in 1947 and 1948, which entailed offers far better than what was on the table after the 1967 war. In the meantime, Palestinians continued to lose their land and homes, become refugees, or fall under Israeli occupation. I viewed the leaders of most Arab states as cynical actors, exploiting the issue to bolster their Arab nationalist credentials.

At AUB the two-state solution that seemed eminently sensible to me was not at all popular. Palestinian students and intellectuals were almost universally insistent on a one-state solution—a nonsectarian, multiethnic state in which the Arabs would have a demographic advantage over a Jewish minority community. I could not see how this kind of a polity would work—the divisions between the Arabs and Israelis seemed far too great.

While I still believe in a two-state solution, I have a far more nuanced attitude toward Israel today. As I have learned more about Israel's history and its vulnerability in the region, I have come to appreciate the strategic and moral case for supporting Israel, as well as seeking a just outcome for the Palestinians.

⟵   ⟶

EVEN WITHIN the struggling Muslim world, my country was especially under-developed. In 1971, to make matters worse, Afghanistan was struck by a severe drought. There were reports that Hazaras and desperately impoverished Afghans from other communities were selling their own children for food. During my summer visits to Kabul, I saw that the social elite in the capital were well off but that the country as a whole was stagnating.

At AUB, I joined the Association of Afghan Students and engaged in heated arguments about what should be done. I had concluded that while our king, Zahir Shah, was not moving fast enough, a Communist revolution was not a desirable alternative. Among the more reckless Afghan leftist groups were the so-called Parchami and Khalqi factions, who were aligned with the Soviet Union, and also some pro-China Maoists. I argued with their leaders and members, warning them that their success would spell doom for Afghanistan. Even if they managed to take over, I feared that Afghanistan would lose its independence to Moscow or Beijing.

Each year the Association of Afghan Students elected a president. I threw my hat into the ring. The anti-Communist Afghan students were mostly focused on their studies and social lives and did not care a great deal about politics, let alone student politics. This was the inert faction that I sought to mobilize. On Election Day, the candidates had to give a speech. Joneid Sharief, my leftist opponent, nervously accused me of being pro-American and unserious about politics. He was right on one count: I was pro-American. After I won the election, Sharief apologized for his remarks. I later learned that he had immigrated to the United States.

⟵   ⟶

BY 1972, as a third-year student in Beirut, I had a clear life plan. I would finish my degree, return to Afghanistan, and help reform my poor, belea-guered country. Somewhere along the way, I would get married to a nice Afghan girl. In the meantime, why not date and socialize at AUB? The annual launch of the student social year was a big dance held on the spacious tennis courts at the edge of the campus, between the women's dormitory, Bustani Hall, and the U.S. embassy, which at the time occupied prime real estate on the coastal highway but later would be bombed and rebuilt elsewhere. Of course, Arab girls are raised to be quite conservative, and persuading them to attend the dance required the social committee to create incentives. As an enticement, admission was free for women.

At the entrance sat a group of young ladies sternly collecting fees from the male students. I pretended to be outraged by this blatant discrimination. "What is this?" I demanded. "You talk about equality between men and women and here you are discriminating against men." They laughed but declined to admit me without the fee. But I had more arguments. Anyway, I continued, "Who said I am a man? Aren't you jumping to conclusions just because of my beard?" This was even less persuasive to them. Eventually I paid up, never guessing that I was about to meet my future wife.

I had noticed Cheryl while I was delivering my performance at the entrance; she had been directly behind me in the line. She had smiled mildly at my shenanigans, and I confess that I was smitten when I first saw that smile, the curly hair, and her purple suede miniskirt, the favored style of dress on campus at the time, even for the Arab girls. We danced for much of the evening. However, when she mostly wanted to talk about a paper she was writing on Arab nationalism and query me about the situation in my home country, I recognized that I was dealing with someone more formidable than her miniskirt suggested.

Cheryl was half European and half American. Her father had been a U.S. soldier in World War II and had met her Austrian mother in occupied Vienna. Once we started dating, we typically had lunch together almost every day on Bliss Street. Movie tickets were very inexpensive, and the theaters on Hamra Street were quite luxurious. So that and weekend dances hosted by student groups formed the bulk of our entertainment. And then there was shopping. Cheryl loved to go shopping, whether for gaudy trinkets in the souk, fresh loquat fruits from the vendor stalls, or just groceries for her dorm room. I was happy for any excuse to spend time with her, so I went along, even though I hated shopping. Accompanying her regularly confronted me with a dilemma. Obviously, I could not let her carry the shopping bags—I had to be a gentleman. However, if my fellow male students, particularly the Afghans, saw me doing so, I would be ridiculed. In their eyes, it was inappropriate for a proud Afghan male to tote bags for a woman. My infatuation won the day over my pride.

One of the great things about Beirut was that many regional destinations were within easy reach. Cheryl and I traveled together to Damascus and Aleppo. We went to Cairo and Moscow on student tours organized by the university. We also traveled around Lebanon. On one trip, we saw the Alvin Ailey dance troupe perform against the splendid backdrop of the historic ruins of Baalbek—the city that would later become a Hezbollah stronghold. We went to Tripoli and to the sparkling port city of Saida.

Cheryl loved to travel and was tirelessly curious about people and places. She had no problem with the crowded, communal taxis with terrible shock absorbers that would take you for a bumpy ride all the way from Beirut to Aleppo for a few dollars. She also did not believe in resting. The moment we arrived at whatever low-budget, flea-bitten hostel we could afford, she would be ready to go and see the local destinations, mosques, forts, souks, and other attractions that were on her researched list.

Like me, back then Cheryl had a soft spot for the Palestinians, whose undeserved misery was conspicuous in the camps surrounding the prosperous suburbs of Beirut. Some of our "dates" consisted of excursions organized by the student council to towns such as Nabatiya, where we would spend our weekend clearing the rubble left behind by Israeli air strikes, camp out at night in abandoned buildings, and join in lavish "solidarity picnics" put on by the local villagers.

Whether in Cairo, Damascus, or Aleppo, the dialogue with locals always followed the same pattern, with shopkeepers and waiters asking where this odd couple was from. Ironically, Cheryl was easier to explain. Everyone knew America, and thanks to Bruno Kreisky, the then-chancellor of Austria who supported Palestinian rights, they knew Austria, too. *"Ah, Autriche!"* they would exclaim approvingly.

Afghanistan was another matter. To my surprise, many of our interlocutors were hearing about the existence of my country for the very first time. "Where is that?" they would ask with great curiosity. At first, I drew elaborate maps on scraps of paper. After a while, I figured out that I could just say *"Baada* Iran," which meant, "We're down there right after Iran." The next question, invariably, was, "And the people there, are they Muslims?" When I answered in the affirmative, exclamations of *"al-hamdulillah!"* or "God be praised" would immediately follow. More than once, this discovery of a new land populated by fellow believers made some stranger so happy that, when we tried to pay our restaurant bill, we were told it had already been settled on our behalf.

Among the Afghan students at AUB was Ashraf Ghani, who had traveled with me to the United States as an AFS student. He was from a prominent Afghan family, and his father had held a senior post in the Afghan government. Ghani was ambitious and politically engaged. At the time, he was an Afghan nationalist, but considerably more to the left of the spectrum than I was. In 2014 he would become president of Afghanistan.

As I started to think about my next steps, several professors urged me to stay on to earn a master's degree in Middle East studies. I liked that idea, and the head of USAID in Beirut agreed to extend my scholarship for another two years.

In my graduate work, I focused on Egypt, specifically Nasser's interaction with the West. I was fascinated by Nasser, who struck me as the kind of modernizing leader the region needed. My optimism proved ill-founded. Nasser evolved from a patriotic and nationalist figure open to the West to an authoritarian leader pursuing socialist policies. Ultimately, he aligned with the Soviet bloc.

I was in Beirut when a coup led by Daoud Khan toppled King Zahir Shah in 1973. Thinking back to the ear-biting incident, I was grateful that the coup was at least carried out peacefully while the king was in Rome on holiday.

The instability in Afghanistan complicated my plans. The government of Afghanistan had supported my education in Beirut on the condition that I would return to the country. Given the changed political conditions, though, the USAID official asked the government of Afghanistan whether they objected to my pursuing a PhD, since I had received a scholarship to the University of Chicago. I am forever grateful to the bureaucrat in the Ministry of Planning who, a week later, allowed me to accept the offer.

In the fall, I was off to the United States. Cheryl and I had gotten engaged before she went back to Austria, where she was completing her PhD at the University of Vienna. We intended to finish our educations abroad and then move to Kabul, where I would work in politics and Cheryl on development issues and women's rights.

FOUR

ASPIRING STRATEGIST

CHICAGO AND NEW YORK CITY, 1974–1980

IT WAS GREAT TO BE BACK ON AMERICAN SOIL. THIS TIME, I ARRIVED WITH MORE self-confidence but also, perhaps, a bit of trepidation as I entered the University of Chicago's hallowed academic setting.

I moved into a large and imposing home for international students. The room assigned to me was on a co-ed floor, a novel concept to me. It was a surprise, therefore, when I went to the bathroom the next morning to take a shower, only to encounter a scantily clad young woman nonchalantly brushing her teeth at the sink. Adjusting the towel more firmly around my waist, I introduced myself.

I arrived two weeks before classes were to start, so I decided to get to know the area. Unfolding a map, the lady at the front desk explained that the university was like an island in the midst of a sea of "difficult" neighborhoods. If I wanted to go to downtown Chicago, she said, I should take the train or a taxi. Or I should head to the city's North Side for good restaurants. But this just piqued my curiosity more. I recruited a couple of fellow I-House residents, and we set off to explore the South Side.

The level of poverty and the sight of listless men on the street during the working day shocked me. We spoke to an older couple who shared their observations with us about crime, a brutal and unfeeling local police, rampant drugs, and unemployment. They complained that young people focused too much on sports—trying to make it big—and that naturally very few of them did. This segment of American society was nothing like the ones I had seen in my carefully curated tour across the United States with AFS.

DURING THE FIRST WEEK, I dutifully went to see my advisor Professor Morton Kaplan about what classes I should take. His assistant, a kind woman from Sweden, greeted me. Then she opened her desk drawer and pulled out a key chain with more than two dozen keys. She tried one key after another to unlock the nearby office door. Fortunately, she did not need to go through all of them; the third key worked. She waved me over. Peering inside, I saw Professor Kaplan at the end of a long, dark room, reading something by the light of a tiny desk lamp.

"Professor Kaplan?" I said softly, not wanting to disrupt whatever deep thoughts he was pursuing. He did not respond. I moved closer and repeated his name. Still no answer. Perhaps he had a hearing problem? I moved closer still and tried once more to get his attention.

Slowly looking up from what he was reading—a newspaper, I now saw—he uttered a sharp and unwelcoming "Yes?"

I barely had time to introduce myself before he cut me short. "This is the University of Chicago," he snapped. "If you don't know what courses you should take, you are in the wrong place."

In a sense, Kaplan had given me an appropriate introduction. I quickly learned that the University of Chicago favored an intense, even combative, approach to learning. I came to embrace it. As a young man in Afghanistan, I had enjoyed the sport of boxing. This was verbal and mental boxing.

Cheryl always says that my years at the University of Chicago transformed me—but she does not mean this as a compliment. She was very put off when she heard one of my professors, at a social gathering, regale the table with a tale of how he had "mopped the floor" with a debate opponent. She said she preferred me pre-Chicago, but I would point out that even without Chicago training, she herself was hardly timid and could pull off a take-no-prisoners style of argument when she cared about an issue.

I had a life-changing meeting on the first day of classes. I was on my way back home when I ran into two of my new friends. They were on a short break from a class that Professor Albert Wohlstetter was teaching. I was intrigued when they told me that Wohlstetter referred to Secretary of State Kissinger as

"Henry" and President Kennedy as "Jack." They suggested that I sit in on the rest of the class.

I found a seat in the back row. Wohlstetter was presenting a view common among some political science scholars of the period: At any given point in time, there was a probability of war breaking out. This year's probability would be compounded by next year's. Therefore, in this view, war was inevitable over time.

The theory made little sense to me. I raised my hand and said, "But at any given time, there is also a certain probability of permanent peace, so at some point permanent peace should occur." Amused, Wohlstetter asked me to meet him after class. He invited me to take his seminar.

Wohlstetter himself believed that war was avoidable but that peace required a persistent strategy of deterrence. He articulated his view most famously in a 1958 *Foreign Affairs* article entitled "The Delicate Balance of Terror."

Wohlstetter was larger than life. In addition to his position at Chicago, he had a company, Pan Heuristics, in California, that undertook research and consulting projects for the government. He lived in a beautiful house in Hollywood with a bamboo garden and swimming pool. He flew into Chicago in the mornings to teach and then left for California in the evenings. My most enduring memory is of seeing him in one of his sports cars, with his briefcase on the passenger seat, wearing his hat but not his seat belt, and dictating into a tape recorder while he raced to the airport, late as usual.

Wohlstetter also had an apartment on Chicago's North Shore, with a stunning view of Lake Michigan. This is where he held his seminar on nuclear proliferation. Class met over lunch, which he typically had catered by a fine restaurant.

Wohlstetter had unusual clarity of mind as a strategist. I learned a great deal from interacting with him as he worked through problems. He asked the basic questions, never taking a policy problem at face value. Before launching into analysis or developing policy prescriptions, he would devote a great deal of time to getting the question right.

He was never intimidated by the rank or status of his interlocutors in the policy world. When he did contract work for the government, his analysis was never skewed by who was paying the bills. And he was doggedly persistent. If he believed policy was going down the wrong path, he would engage at all levels of government, from cabinet officers to the most junior staffers.

Wohlstetter invited me to be his research assistant. Before long I was working for Pan Heuristics. Ironically, after a project I worked on was completed, I was no longer allowed to read my own work because the studies were classified by the U.S. Arms Control and Disarmament Agency, and I, as a foreign student, did not have security clearances.

Wohlstetter held to the maxim that you should identify and question your assumptions because it's not what you don't know that kills you but, rather, the things that you're sure you know but that turn out to be wrong. In any policy problem, you begin by questioning assumptions based on history, current realities, or conventional wisdom.

He urged me to think through and plan for contingencies. As I would frustratingly experience time and again in my later government positions, officials tend to view certain outcomes as inevitable. Wohlstetter taught me never to feel certain that policy will unfold according to plan.

He always reminded me that in strategy, you are dealing with human beings. You have to know your counterparts—discover what they value and how they see the world—in order to understand their actions and anticipate their responses. Mirror imaging—projecting our way of thinking onto others—was a surefire way to misread an opponent. And, whether dealing with adversaries or not, you need to empathize with other actors in order to understand them.

Wohlstetter emphasized the impact of changing technologies. He also pressed students to engage in what later would be called "alternative futures analysis." This involved describing a variety of possible future outcomes for a given issue or situation and then thinking through the necessary steps to move events down a path to the desired outcome.

Wohlstetter believed in the importance of analyzing the relative costs of pursuing a particular course of action—not just the costs of carrying it out but also those directly imposed on the other side and those the other side would have to bear to counter or defeat such action. This cost exchange, he believed, would shape decisions to escalate or deescalate.

Wohlstetter always encouraged me to think about all options before coming to a judgment on the "dominant solution"—the best of alternatives.

Wohlstetter chaired my dissertation committee, and I benefited from his personal network in the policy world. During the Ford administration, I briefed Secretary of Defense James Schlesinger. I was also asked to brief a number of Wohlstetter's former students and colleagues, now officials in Washington, including Paul Wolfowitz and Andrew Marshall, the director of the Pentagon's Office of Net Assessment, who always listened attentively in his Buddha-like way.

—◄   ►—

MEANWHILE, BACK IN VIENNA, Cheryl finished her doctorate in 1976 in stellar fashion, *sub auspiciis praesidentis*, an outcome that came with a gold ring from the Austrian president and the automatic offer of an assistant professorship. It was an offer too good to refuse. We faced a choice—conclude that our original plan had been made moot by the political upheavals in Afghanistan and our diverging career opportunities and call it a day, flip a coin to choose which of us would give up their opportunities for the sake of being together, or deal with the distance and devise a bicontinental arrangement. With youthful optimism, we chose Door Three.

In the summer of 1979, with the logistics more or less in place, it was time to make it official and get married. I was working for Wohlstetter in his L.A. office; Cheryl was with me, on her summer break. But persuading Cheryl to actually go through with the marriage meant that I had some ideological hurdles to overcome. This was the heyday of feminism, after all, and one couldn't risk any patriarchal anachronisms creeping into the ceremony, obedience not being Cheryl's strong suit. I found a minister identified by the Women's Book Store in Westwood, Los Angeles. Lucia Chapelle, a short, curly-haired African American woman, received us in the cavernous elegance of her Santa Monica church. We would be, she confided, her first wedding ceremony. "You look like you know what you're doing so you don't need to be lectured by me" was how she dealt with the premarital counseling. "But since you're my first married couple," she continued, "I'm going to need you to keep your vows and make a success of this. Stay together." If we didn't, she explained, it would be bad karma for her. "Promise me that if you ever run into trouble, you'll call me for counsel." We promised, and she proceeded to marry us, glancing down at her manual intermittently to make sure she got the ceremony right.

It was unconventional and certainly a long way from my Muslim upbringing, but there was something touching about our unlikely pastor's sincerity. It's been thirty-five years now and counting, so you can't argue with the outcome.

People sometimes ask how my family reacted to my marrying a Christian American. Actually, it created no difficulties. Perhaps my parents would have preferred that I marry an Afghan girl, but they never said anything. In fact, foreign brides were not uncommon in Afghanistan, and tended to be welcomed and warmly enfolded. Several of my fellow Afghan students also chose international brides. Ashraf Ghani married a Lebanese Christian woman, and other friends married Palestinians, Americans, and Europeans of various nationalities.

Things were more complicated with Cheryl's family. Her father knew me from his business trips to Beirut and we got along, but Cheryl's mother was not happy. She had nothing against me, personally; the problem was that German media, including the *Bild Zeitung* newspaper that was her daily reading, were filled with dramatic stories of the terrible things that happened to

Western girls who married Muslim men and returned with them to their homelands. Instead of the modern apartment that had been described to them, they would find themselves whisked away to a distant primitive village to be abused by their in-laws, kept locked up in seclusion, and forced to tolerate polygamy. Happily, we eventually developed a warm relationship of mutual fondness; we have a similar sense of humor, and I have learned a lot from her stories about civilian suffering during World War II and the rebuilding of Europe after that war.

IN APRIL 1978, during my last semester in Chicago, a coup toppled President Daoud Khan's regime in Afghanistan. The People's Democratic Party of Afghanistan assumed power. I was astonished to hear American experts argue that the leaders of the PDPA were just "agrarian reformers"—not Soviet-backed Communists.

I assumed that Afghans would resist the new regime. Afghans were too religiously devout to be ruled by committed atheists and too proud of their independence to become a Soviet satellite state.

I wanted to make my case in public, but I was worried about my family, who were still in Afghanistan. My teenage brother David had already been arrested for participating in an anti-Communist protest.

So in early 1979, I wrote an article in *Orbis* under the pseudonym Hannah Negaran, which, in Dari, translates to "be watchful."

I argued that Afghans were likely to rise up against the new Communist government and that the Soviet Union would eventually face a decision: letting the PDPA fall or intervening militarily. At the time, my views were considered alarmist.

In December 1979, I received an unexpected call from William Griffith, an advisor to President Carter's national security advisor, Zbigniew Brzezinski. I was by this time an assistant professor at Columbia University. He told me that I had been "outed" and that my articles had attracted notice at the White House. I might as well own up and help out with U.S. policy on the issue. I would like to contribute to policy deliberations, I told him, but still couldn't go public due to my family in Afghanistan.

FOR NEW YEAR'S EVE of 1978, Cheryl and I planned a trip to Paris. I was thinking more and more about the political turmoil that was spreading across the Middle East. In addition to the coup in Afghanistan, massive protests were challenging the shah of Iran. So I thought it would be interesting to meet with a principal leader of the Iranian opposition, Ayatollah Ruhollah Khomeini, who was living in exile in Neauphle-le-Chateau, a small town outside Paris.

A colleague gave me the name of one of Khomeini's aides, Ebrahim Yazdi. We didn't have a street address but it didn't matter. As soon as we stepped off the train in Neauphle-le-Chateau, all we had to do was follow a parade of Iranians streaming in the same direction. One of them, assuming I was Iranian and a fellow Khomeini enthusiast, started chatting with me in Farsi. Once we arrived at a nondescript little suburban house, I was led directly to Yazdi.

I introduced myself as a visiting academic, and we sat down to talk. I asked Yazdi why, as a technocrat and moderate, he was working for a religious figure. Yazdi assured me that Khomeini was only a symbolic figurehead. After the revolution, Iran would undergo a period of normalization, and the clerics would return to their own domain.

Yazdi showed me into a waiting room decorated with lush Iranian carpets, portraits of religious figures, and, on one wall, a European cuckoo clock seemingly left behind by a previous occupant. I was interviewed in what seemed to be an informal vetting process.

I came back the next day to see Khomeini in an adjacent villa. In full clerical robes, Khomeini sat cross-legged on the floor, polite but unsmiling. Not knowing that I understood Persian, one of his aides advised him, "Tell the American professor that we want democracy and rights for women—this is what Americans like to hear."

I asked Khomeini about his political vision for Iran and how he planned to govern the country. Khomeini maintained only fleeting eye contact, stroking his beard on occasion. But he still managed to appear engaged and interested, perhaps even charismatic.

The shah's regime, he began, was illegitimate, for it was not a government grounded in Islamic law. It did not matter how prosperous the nation became. Due to his secularism and domestic repression, the shah had lost touch with the people. He referred to Plato's *Republic* as a model. In the Islamic Republic, power would have to be exercised by those who knew Islamic law—the clerics.

I asked Khomeini how he reconciled a clerical-led concept with the practical demands of governing. Clerics, Khomeini maintained, would formulate the moral agenda of the state, while technocrats would provide the administrative skills necessary to implement the fundamentalist program. At the end of our conversation, Khomeini directed his aide to give me a large stack of books, papers, and tapes of his lectures. Once I had studied all of that, we could meet again.

I came away perturbed. I realized that Khomeini had a clear set of totalitarian ideas and an intricate plan to implement them. The reading material included vicious and sometimes bogus propaganda about the shah. One book, as evidence that the shah was an "agent of Zionism," printed a photograph of a cordial meeting with "Shimon Peres," the Israeli leader. Noting something odd about the photo, I looked more closely—it wasn't Shimon Peres of Israel at all but, rather, President Perez of Venezuela at an OPEC summit.

More problematic, though, was the ayatollah's conception of government. Until the twelfth Imam returned to earth to herald the end of time, Khomeini maintained, legitimate political power could belong only to a religious leader and his followers.

When I returned to Columbia, I related his words and my impressions to my Iranian colleagues and students. Incensed by the shah, they generally brushed my reactions aside in favor of their own rosy revolutionary narrative.

On February 1, 1979, a little over a month after my trip to France, Khomeini returned to Tehran and installed himself as Supreme Leader.

THE WINTER BREAK of 1979 was momentous for another reason: the Soviet Union invaded Afghanistan.

Several members of my family were seeking a way out of the country. The first to escape was my younger brother Tory. He obtained a U.S. visa a couple of days before the Soviet invasion and then got himself on a flight to Vienna, on the slender knowledge that Cheryl was often there. In an era before cell phones and email, he had no way to reach us. The first we learned of his arrival was when a representative of the Airport Information Desk called to tell us that somebody named Tory was looking for us.

In the ensuing years, other family members joined the refugee exodus to Pakistan. The move was traumatic as they adjusted to their new, more modest, and more tumultuous life. My father wanted to be buried in Afghanistan when he died. So he moved to Pakistan with the intention of returning home as soon as he could, and my sister Latifa remained to care for him. By 1983, all of my other relatives had settled in the U.S. and begun living together in a New Jersey suburb. Arriving with broken English and no possessions, they nonetheless hit the ground running. My brother-in-law Ehsan, who had been an engineer back home, embraced his new job as a taxi driver. In a proud tough-guy voice, he would declaim, "Don't mess with me, I am a New York cabbie." My son Alex looked forward to his visits, when he drove to Bethesda in his yellow cab and let Alex sit on his lap and steer the car around the driveway. His wife, my sister Malika, became a secretary at Leumi Bank. Only my mother was homesick, missing her roses, fruit trees, and friends.

I WAS SURPRISED by the unusual degree of consensus on the Afghanistan issue: Soviet success in Afghanistan was regrettable, but a done deal. Former Secretary of Defense James Schlesinger went even further when I discussed the issue with him in Washington. "I'm sorry, Zal," he said. "I know that with your background, it's a difficult thing to accept, but this is finished. Afghanistan is never going to be free again. Once the Soviets are in, they will not go out."

"You don't know the Afghans," I told him. History suggested to me that the Afghans would be willing to resist occupiers at a high price over long periods of time.

Schlesinger had an answer: "You don't know the Soviets."

I had to admit that the expectation of Soviet victory was not unreasonable. Afghanistan's location on the Soviet border meant that Moscow had substantial interests there. A Communist Party had taken over, and the Soviet record of defending allies and clients was unblemished at the time.

With my family in the relative safety of Pakistan, I was free to advocate more openly for the Afghan resistance. My writings caught the attention of the U.S. Information Agency (USIA). They arranged for me to travel around the world to lecture on the Soviet invasion and possible American responses. I also began to receive invitations from Washington think tanks. I felt hugely honored when the Wilson Center invited me to speak on a panel with Princeton University professor Bernard Lewis, an intellectual giant in the area of Middle East history.

Paul Wolfowitz, then the State Department's director of policy planning, approached me after that talk and invited me to work for him. I was flattered but had to decline. I still wasn't a U.S. citizen.

Becoming a U.S. citizen involved a massive amount of paperwork. The process had started through my employment at Pan Heuristics and was expedited after I married Cheryl, a U.S. citizen. But it was not until 1984 that I entered the Manhattan federal court building for my formal naturalization. As the last member of my group was sworn in, a solemn silence filled the courtroom. It occurred to me in that moment what a remarkable event had just occurred. Suddenly overcome with emotion, I began to clap. The large crowd then burst into a long, spontaneous applause.

IN THE DEBATE over Afghanistan, America's relationship with Pakistan emerged as a central question. President Zia ul-Haq had seized power in a July 1977 military coup and executed his civilian predecessor, Zulfikar Ali Bhutto, on trumped-up charges. Though I understood the risks of aligning with an Islamist dictator, I was concerned that Pakistan too could fall to Soviet influence. I thought the U.S. should take up Zia on his proposal that the U.S. provide security assistance, including sales of F-16 fighter jets, in exchange for Pakistan's facilitating American aid to the Afghan resistance—a view that I presented before the House Foreign Relations Committee.

After the testimony, I received a note from General Ejaz Azim, the Pakistani ambassador to the United States. He said that Zia had been impressed by my testimony and wanted me to visit Pakistan. When I told my Pakistani friends about the invitation, many of them implored me to decline. Under Zia, liberals and minorities were under siege by regime-backed religious parties and their allies in the military and Inter-Services Intelligence (ISI) directorate. Visiting Pakistan at Zia's behest, they argued, would be tantamount to siding with the dictator.

I was presented with a classic foreign policy dilemma. How should we balance tensions between competing interests? While I was generally more sympathetic to concerns over human rights and democracy than were my hard-line fellow travelers, I considered the Soviet threat to be the more urgent issue. Support for Pakistan's distasteful dictatorship struck me as a necessary tactical requirement for a strategically justifiable end.

Still, I did tell General Azim that I would come only on the condition that I would be allowed to visit democratic opposition figures in the country, including Benazir Bhutto, then under house arrest.

I came away from the Pakistan visit with a decidedly mixed view of the country. On the positive side, the human rights situation, while definitely worsening under Zia, remained better than in the rest of the region. Farooq Leghari, an imprisoned opposition leader, complained to me that things had become very bad in Pakistan. There were different classes of jails in Pakistan, he informed me. In Grade I prisons, inmates were allowed to keep servants, entertain guests, and enjoy other benefits such as fruit delivery. Zia, he lamented, was now sending his political opponents to Grade II prisons, where they were no longer allowed to have servants with them. I could not help but contrast their treatment with the fate of political prisoners in Hafez al-Assad's Syria and Saddam Hussein's Iraq, who were routinely tortured or summarily executed.

Still, my meetings with senior Pakistani leaders exposed me to a more troubling reality among Pakistan's political class. There is always a gap between declaratory policy and actual policy, but never had I seen officials tell flat-out lies to their American counterparts so frequently and with such impunity.

It was during this trip that I first met the Peshawar-based Afghan resistance leaders. Much of what they told me about Pakistani actions and objectives was at odds with the official Pakistani line. In discussions with the CIA and others in the American government, Pakistan vouched for Islamist leaders, such as Gulbuddin Hekmatyar of the Hezbe Islami faction, on the grounds that they were more tenacious fighters than the moderate and nationalist Afghan factions. In fact, Hekmatyar had not won any significant battles against the Communist forces. He was expending at least as much effort fighting rival resistance leaders as he was waging battle against the Soviets.

I could now see that Pakistan had several problematic motives for backing the Islamists. Zia wanted to control the Afghan resistance movement. The ISI had divided the Afghan resistance into seven organizations, three of which were moderate or nationalist and four of which were fundamentalist. This divide-and-rule approach facilitated Pakistani control. Zia also wanted to settle Pakistan's long-standing border dispute with Afghanistan. The Islamist elements of the resistance talked about creating a unified Islamic caliphate rather than consolidating a nation-state. This was closer to Zia's vision of a united confederation encompassing the lands of Pakistan, Afghanistan, and Central Asia than the robust independent state desired by Afghan nationalists. A confederation, he believed, infused with Islamist zealotry and funded by Saudi oil wealth, could provide "strategic depth" against India.

I left Pakistan with a negative view of the country's leadership. Even my gratitude for the fact that Pakistan had accepted so many Afghan refugees dimmed after the visit. I am still haunted by images of Panya camp in the northwest frontier province of Pakistan, where 80,000 Afghan refugees were making do with just 250 tents and 1,000 blankets. A sea of men, women, and children, some lightly dressed, were sitting on plastic sheets without tents. I was overwhelmed as people rushed toward me, begging for help that I could not provide.

Pakistan had won great international sympathy, not to mention aid and support, for taking in the refugees. Yet it became clear to me that Pakistan was exaggerating the cost and burden its government was bearing. In fact, Pakistan seemed actually to be profiting from the rise in real estate prices.

—◄   ►—

WHILE I WAS TEACHING at Columbia, our first son, Alexander, was born. We hadn't attended childbirth classes, but I had read several books and taken copious notes on the stages of childbirth and on how the father, as coach, could be helpful. All of that faded into abstraction once the time actually came. We were instructed to walk the halls of the rather bleak Roosevelt Hospital to speed up the process. After a few hours of that, we were ushered into a room for the serious part of the proceedings. Cheryl had opted for natural childbirth. It was the fashion of the day, but to me it seemed unnervingly similar to what women were forced to endure in my home country. If I had been in her place, my position would have been, "send in as many doctors as you have available and give me more drugs, please." Instead, we had two cheerful midwives who passed the time by betting on the child's likely gender (these were the days before routine ultrasounds provided that information beforehand). But immediately following the birth, their good mood shifted to serious, as complications arose. Unceremoniously, one of them shoved the newborn into my arms and directed me toward an armchair so they could urgently attend to his mother. As I sat there, slightly befuddled by this new little human package in my arms and trying to assess the gravity of what was happening, I was very glad to be in a modern Western hospital.

Having a child threw a much different and sharper light on the world. I now had to worry about the growing violence and uncertainty not just for strategic reasons, but because my Alex would have to live in whatever world resulted. I related this concern to Albert and Roberta Wohlstetter when I called to thank them for a baby gift they had sent. Albert immediately turned the issue around. He said that I should not worry about Alex's future. Instead, I should encourage him, as an adult, to shape a better future. It was, I agreed, the way to look at it.

FIVE

THE MUJAHEDEEN
AND THE HALLS
OF POWER

NEW YORK AND
WASHINGTON, D.C., 1980–1989

AN INVITATION TO VISIT THE WHITE HOUSE AND MEET WITH THE PRESIDENT OF THE United States is not usually a hard sell. But the fundamentalists of the Afghan resistance were cut from a different cloth. Gulbuddin Hekmatyar, the spokesman of the Afghan resistance who was in New York to participate in meetings at the United Nations, flatly refused the offer.

It was October 1985. At the request of National Security Council Senior Director Walt Raymond, I engaged Hekmatyar on the importance of meeting President Reagan.

"Why do you want me to come to the White House to be photographed with the president of the United States?" he asked. "That would undermine me throughout the Islamic world."

Realizing that our conversation was not going anywhere, I suggested a tour of New York instead. Hekmatyar refused that as well. My protestations that the city's attractions were of high cultural and educational quality fell on deaf ears. Hekmatyar insisted that there was nothing here but "houses of prostitution."

It was no great surprise to me when Hekmatyar went on to play a persistently troublesome role in Afghanistan. He was a central figure in triggering the civil war after the Soviet withdrawal, bombarding Kabul with rockets. After the overthrow of the Taliban government in 2001, Hekmatyar organized an insurgent group in Pakistan.

The leadership of the mujahedeen rotated to another fundamentalist, Younis Khalis, in 1987, presenting another opportunity for a meeting with the president. He, at least, agreed. But two days before the big moment, I found him in quite a nervous state. Almost wringing his hands with anxiety, he confided what, until now, he had kept to himself. Yes, his fellow fundamentalists among the resistance leaders had agreed that he could meet the American president. But they had imposed a condition: Khalis had to bring the message of Islam to Reagan. This, he reminded me, was in keeping with Islamic tradition—the Prophet Mohammed, too, had sent messengers to the capitals of non-Muslims in order to invite them to Islam. But tradition or not, Khalis was worried about how Reagan would react.

So was I, a bit. I urgently reached out to the White House. President Reagan, I heard back, wanted the meeting to go forward as planned. Khalis was free to follow his instructions.

I was not originally supposed to attend the meeting, but at the last minute, the White House discovered that their usual interpreter lacked a sufficiently high security clearance. I was rushed to the Oval Office and seated between President Reagan and Khalis. I had never served as an interpreter and did not know the protocol. When Khalis made his first remark, I whispered the translation quietly to the president. Reagan, however, asked that I say it loudly so everyone in the room could hear.

"Islam is a religion of righteousness and peace," I therefore heard myself announcing to the vice president, secretary of defense, secretary of state, and national security advisor, "and given its universal truth, Mr. Khalis would like to invite you, Mr. President, to accept the religion of Islam."

"Well, please tell Mr. Khalis that we have our own religion," the president replied smoothly, not missing a beat. "Furthermore, today, the struggle is between believers and non-believers. As fellow believers, we are on the same side. We are with you in your struggle against the Soviet Union."

Khalis was relieved.

At the follow-up press event in the Roosevelt Room, President Reagan gave an impassioned statement in support of the Afghan struggle. As Reagan spoke, I interpreted for Khalis. The Afghan leader, already elated by the president's support during the Oval Office meeting, was so moved that he asked for the text of Reagan's speech. To the horror of his aides, who generally keep the originals of such documents for the archives, Reagan casually shuffled together the note cards in front of him, scrawled in his own handwriting, and handed them to Khalis.

I learned later that Reagan, as he was leaving office, took with him his photo with Khalis. A tall, lanky man with a long graying beard streaked red with henna, Khalis, in his traditional Afghan garb, fit the romanticized image of the anti-Communist rebels that Reagan passionately supported.

—◄   ►—

I HAD TAKEN public service leave from Columbia University when I joined the State Department's policy planning staff in January 1986, but I did not expect to return to New York.

We moved to Bethesda, which at the time was a sleepy little suburb without the high-rises and bustling urban feel it has since acquired. The house, on Bradley Boulevard near Wilson Lane, was like the "before" version in those now-popular home remodeling shows—tiny bathrooms with 1950s tiles, narrow staircases, and small rooms. But it was light and bright, and it sat on a lot with a large backyard for Alex and his visiting cousins to run around in. We loved it and were enormously excited to actually own a house—well, sort of own it, if you discounted the mortgage.

Alex was three years old now and ready to have friends, so we signed him up in a "cooperative play group" at the nearby church. There was one professional teacher, and the rest of the "staff" consisted of the parents on a rotation system. Once a week, it was our turn to help with the lessons and keep watch over the playground. This was new to me. Afghan parents tended to be more serious and did not really play with their children. My father, I'm sure, would have found it very odd to hear me earnestly discussing Pokémon and Ninja Turtles with playgroup kids. Like me, my Afghan immigrant friends loosened up quite a bit in the United States. Many, for example, remained good Muslims but celebrated Christmas because it was fun for the kids.

Cheryl was pulling off an impressive "commute." She had published a sociology study that attracted the notice of the Austrian minister of science, and had been appointed research director of a government-funded research institute. She would organize the research for when she was in Europe, then write the corresponding books and reports in the U.S. Our friends joked that we held the long-distance commuter marriage record. That commute now included little Alex, who fortunately was a champion traveler. KLM airline had baby cradles that attached to the ceiling, and there, as if in a hammock, he would swing his way across the Atlantic. When they got older, both the kids attended the local American school for half of every school year, switching to their local Viennese kindergarten or school for the other half. It wasn't easy, but it made them effortlessly bilingual and very adaptable.

When our younger son, Max, was on the way, we joined the caravan of young Washington families moving out to the farther suburbs for space, safety, and better schools. We found a house between Potomac and Poolesville, off River Road on a cul-de-sac. As we had hoped, there were families with kids all around us. The French–South American family on one side had a son and daughter; when they moved, they gave way to a Korean-American extended family that contributed four kids, a set of grandparents, and a neighborhood supply of fresh kimchi to the mix. Our other neighbors were a family from New York and one from Puerto Rico. It was a Mr. Rogers setting of snow days, igloos, car pools, parent-coached softball leagues, paintball, basketball hoops on every doorframe, neighborhood BBQs, carved Halloween pumpkins, and block parties on the Fourth of July with sack races. Neither Cheryl—with her itinerant army brat upbringing and Austrian mother—nor I had experienced a classic picture-book American family life, and we enjoyed it as much as the kids did.

After intensive and skillful lobbying from which world-class diplomats could have learned a few tricks, Alex and Max persuaded us that what we really needed was a puppy. That is how a little Westie, Griffin, joined our family. It was a change for me, since I had never had a pet growing up, and certainly not a dog, an animal considered unclean by many Muslims. Griffin became friends with our Korean neighbors' dog, the poetically named Justice. When not making off with a softball or chasing around the neighborhood with their pack of human kids, Griffin and Justice would go off on daylong independent expeditions, causing regular panic and mass searches with high-pitched dog whistles if they were not back by nightfall.

I surprised myself by growing deeply attached to Griffin and learning to appreciate his qualities of loyalty, acceptance, happiness, and trust. The day I found myself racing to the supermarket before it closed, because we had run out of Beggin Strips, was the day I realized that I had left at least the anti-dog portion of my upbringing behind me.

Griffin later had a cameo appearance on an ABC news report about my U.N. assignment; he was described as diplo-dog, and indeed his gregarious nature, his little red-white-and-blue T-shirt, and his interest in finding and consuming fallen hors d'oeuvres made him an enthusiastic participant at embassy parties.

When Alex was a sophomore in high school, we began to rethink our commuter arrangement. He wanted to go to college in the U.S., so he needed to focus on the application process. Cheryl, too, was finding the continual moves, with two children and a dog, increasingly exhausting. It was time for a normal life, everyone together in one place. And it was just as wonderful as we hoped—while it lasted.

⏤◄   ►⏤

FROM MY PERCH on the policy planning staff, I had a front-row seat for the debate engulfing the Reagan administration: What should the U.S. make of the new Soviet leader, Mikhail Gorbachev? President Reagan had created a "steering group" to manage U.S. relations with the Soviet leadership. In addition to Secretary of State George Shultz, the regular meeting attendees included the secretary of defense, CIA director, and national security advisor. I was invited to the steering group's meeting on Afghanistan policy in January 1986, which included a few "outsiders," such as former secretaries of defense Donald Rumsfeld and Schlesinger.

On Afghanistan, everyone acknowledged Soviet difficulties, but the group was divided about Gorbachev's intentions. I weighed in. Hard realities on the ground would force a Soviet compromise, I insisted, if the resistance remained popular and the international community remained engaged. Gorbachev might seek a face-saving settlement if convinced that the alternatives were intractable war or a full-fledged defeat.

Schlesinger pushed back hard. The Soviets, he declared, wouldn't accept anything less than a total military victory. As we moved to another room for lunch, Shultz held me back. He was intrigued by my thoughts and wanted to hear more.

A consensus emerged within the Reagan administration that the United States should double down behind the Afghan resistance and provide more military assistance. A strong bipartisan consensus was forming more generally behind the Afghan resistance. The U.S. covert program dramatically increased the quantity and quality of arms sent to the Afghans, including the Stinger anti-aircraft system for targeting Soviet airpower. This, in turn, seemed to alter Soviet calculations. We did not know it at the time, but Gorbachev announced to his Politburo colleagues in October 1985 that it was time to disengage from Afghanistan. Soon thereafter, he informed Afghanistan's Communist leader that his regime would have to defend the revolution on its own. In February 1986, Gorbachev shocked the world with his public statement that Afghanistan was "a bleeding wound."

Seeing that the Soviets might indeed withdraw, I took a close look at the agreements that the State Department had been negotiating with Moscow. Under a U.N.-sponsored proposal, the United States had agreed to serve as a guarantor of an agreement in which Washington would recognize the Communist regime in Kabul as soon as the Soviet withdrawal began. It also required the United States and Pakistan to cease assistance to the resistance immediately, even before the Soviets were out. During this period, the Soviets would be permitted to provide continued assistance to their clients in Kabul.

Even worse, the cutoff of U.S. assistance would be an "act," while the Soviet withdrawal would be a "process" stretching out over time.

I thought the deal was far too favorable to the Soviets. When I raised concerns, however, supporters of the agreement questioned why I was even "wasting time" analyzing it. The United States, they claimed, could afford to give the Soviets generous terms. After all, the consensus at the State Department and CIA was that the Soviets would never actually withdraw. Once Moscow rejected this generous agreement, the United States would score propaganda points by demonstrating that the Soviet Union was recalcitrant.

I believed that it was imprudent to make offers without considering the possibility that the Soviets might actually accept them.

We were in a dangerous position. The terms were so lopsided in favor of Moscow that I thought the Soviets might consolidate their control over Afghanistan despite losing on the battlefield.

As late as 1987, I held the minority view within the Reagan administration. Fortunately, the president himself shared my view. After reviewing the draft of the deal, he refused to sign it. In the face of protests from the State Department, Reagan ordered the negotiators back to the drawing board. The Soviets felt double-crossed, and Shultz had a difficult time explaining to his Soviet counterparts why the United States was suddenly reneging on the earlier understanding.

The president's resolve was ultimately vindicated. During the last few weeks before the signing of what became known as the Geneva Accords, the Soviets were so desperate to leave Afghanistan that they caved on a number of lingering points of dispute and agreed to withdraw on a much more compressed timeline.

Even at this late stage, however, the Soviets insisted on an important condition. If they withdrew, the supporters of the resistance—the United States and Pakistan—would have to cut off arms transfers, which were flowing across the Afghanistan-Pakistan border. The Soviets, meanwhile, could still support the Communist regime unabated. President Reagan again rejected this provision.

Shultz sent a delegation to Islamabad to discuss this issue with President Muhammad Zia ul-Haq. The U.S. side explained to Zia that the United States needed a way to transfer arms to the resistance even if Pakistan signed an agreement of noninterference. Zia replied with characteristic cunning: "Who said we are providing arms to the Afghan resistance now?" The assistance program to the resistance, after all, was technically a covert operation. "Nothing will change," Zia promised.

Despite the implicit understanding with Pakistan, the Afghan resistance was furious. Under the terms of the agreement, the Communist regime in

Kabul and Pakistan were the principal signatories, while the Soviet Union and United States were "guarantors." The Afghan resistance—which had borne the brunt of the battle—did not have a representative at the negotiating table.

Under Secretary of State for Political Affairs Michael Armacost decided to travel to Pakistan to temper Afghan fears. Abdul Rasoul Sayyaf, a giant of a man with a quick temper, was the spokesman for the Afghan resistance. "The only reason I'm not killing you with my bare hands," he informed Armacost, "is that you are a senior American official on Pakistani territory."

Stunned, Armacost reported back: "God damn! They are very upset after all we have done to assist them. You need to go to Pakistan." Armacost also asked me to draw up a strategy for post-Soviet Afghanistan.

In August 1988, during one of my trips, the U.S. ambassador to Pakistan, Arnold Raphel, suggested that I meet Zia. I was supposed to join Raphel and Zia on a flight to a military base in Punjab. Just before the scheduled departure from Islamabad, however, Raphel changed his mind. Instead, he wanted me to go to Peshawar to meet with the Afghan leaders.

In the middle of my meeting with the resistance leaders, a young spokesman named Hamid Karzai received a call, abruptly stood up, and walked out. A few minutes later, I too got a phone call, ordering me to return to the consulate immediately. "Something has gone wrong with the president's plane," I was told.

Indeed. The plane carrying Zia and Raphel had crashed. There were no survivors.

There was initially some confusion in Washington about whether I was on the flight. The State Department had been told that Raphel was the only American diplomat on the plane. But given my appearance, they feared that the Pakistani officials sorting through the wreckage had taken me for a local and overlooked me. When the State Department finally tracked me down, Armacost asked me to stay behind and write an assessment of the situation for Shultz.

The atmosphere was tense. Conspiracy theories about the crash abounded. I shared the widespread fear that Zia's death would unravel Pakistan. However, with U.S. encouragement, elections were held, and Benazir Bhutto emerged victorious.

——— ⬅ ➡ ———

AT THIS POINT, with the Soviets on their way out of Afghanistan, the United States needed to plan for a new government in Kabul. I wanted to find a way to ensure that extremist leaders in the Afghan resistance, backed by Pakistan, would not become the dominant force in post-Soviet Afghanistan. I even argued that the United States and the Soviets could work together to empower moderate Afghans at a time when both had considerable influence with the resistance.

The Peshawar-based fundamentalists advocated the establishment of a "new" political system—a Sunni version of Iran's Shia theocratic regime. The largest Afghan fundamentalist groups were under the leadership of Hekmatyar, Khalis, Burhanuddin Rabbani, and Sayyaf. Khalis, Rabbani, and Hekmatyar looked to the ideology of the Muslim Brotherhood. Sayyaf was an adherent of the Wahhabi ideology centered in Saudi Arabia.

Traditionalists comprised the other major set of Pakistan-based anti-Soviet groups. They were drawn from the pre-war elite. Some advocated a role for the former king Zahir Shah, who was living in exile in Italy. They were Afghan nationalists and called openly for support from the West. At the domestic level, they favored a multiparty system.

I had previously pressed Afghan leaders to coalesce into a unified, coherent organization that would gain international recognition. I wanted Afghans to tell the story of what was happening in their country and what they wanted from the world. By and large, the Communist regime in Kabul continued to represent Afghanistan abroad, and there were worrying signs that the Communist government was gaining international legitimacy. My colleagues were skeptical. But given that the resistance groups had, at our urging, unified into a seven-party alliance, I believed there were possibilities for forming a transitional government.

I suggested that the United States help convene a *Loya Jirga*, or Grand Assembly. Tribes have used this kind of gathering, a uniquely Afghan process, for over 2,000 years to settle issues through consultation and consensus. Despite its Pashtun tribal origins, the *Loya Jirga* had won acceptance over the years as a national Afghan institution. I envisioned Zahir Shah playing a role in overseeing the political process. Many Afghans—even some who had favored his overthrow in the 1970s—now viewed his time in power as a golden age.

Armacost asked that I fly to Rome and propose a *Loya Jirga* to the king. In our meeting, the king was courteous but passive, preferring niceties to the more substantive discussion I was hoping to have. Though it would end his long exile, he was loath to assume responsibility for the transitional process. I concluded that Zahir Shah could play a symbolic role as the convener of whatever process was ultimately selected, but that he was not up to the task of serving as chief executive. I then shuttled between Rome and Islamabad to gauge the views of the resistance leaders.

As I was conducting meetings in Pakistan, the new U.S. ambassador, Robert Oakley, sent Armacost a cable. Oakley argued that the Pakistani military and its Islamist allies in the Afghan resistance were wary of forming an interim government. I believe that Oakley and the CIA station chief in Pakistan,

Milton Bearden, reached out to CIA director William Webster and argued that the U.S. relationship with Pakistan was too important to jeopardize over the issue of Afghanistan's political process. Shultz ordered me back to Washington.

I was very disappointed. We still had considerable influence with Pakistan and the Afghanistan resistance and could have shaped the Afghan transition by establishing a broad-based government. The Soviet-installed government and even Moscow were interested in such a transitional process. However, Shultz vetoed this option.

———— ◄ ► ————

IN EARLY 1989, during the first months of the George H. W. Bush administration, the Soviets were completing their withdrawal from Afghanistan. I was increasingly concerned about the role that Pakistan would play in post-Soviet Afghanistan.

I had decided not to pursue a position in the new administration, so was not officially involved with Afghanistan policy at this point. Instead, I accepted a position at the RAND Corporation. RAND had a policy of having its scholars work from Santa Monica to be "Randized," so I was expecting to settle down in Palisades. Armacost's replacement, Robert Kimmitt, however, wrote to RAND president Don Rice, asking him to let me commute to Washington so that I could consult on Afghanistan. I received permission to do so for a few months.

In meetings on Afghanistan, Oakley and I remained at odds. While he was sympathetic to the idea of an inclusive government in Kabul, he believed that conditions on the ground made it an unrealistic venture. Pakistan was determined to drive the Soviets out and overthrow the Communist regime militarily. Oakley cited the ISI's opposition and the CIA's unwillingness to break from the liaison relationship with Islamabad. We had defeated the Soviet Union by working with the Islamist groups, he reminded me. How could we suddenly abandon them and now say that they were the cause of the problem?

The Communist regime collapsed in 1992, a few months after the Soviet Union had disintegrated. Instead of working to stabilize the situation, the Bush and Clinton administrations watched passively as Afghanistan descended into civil war. It was from this civil war that the Taliban regime and its alliance with al Qaeda emerged.

———— ◄ ► ————

THE SOVIET-AFGHAN WAR was the last major struggle of the Cold War. It came at a monumental price for the Afghans. An estimated one million Afghans died, and one-third of the population became refugees in Pakistan and Iran, with even more displaced internally. Entire regions were depopulated, and the economy collapsed.

Afghanistan has yet to overcome the devastation of the Soviet-Afghan war. Almost all of the country's educated professionals either fled or were killed. The duration of the conflict ensured that those who emigrated never found a suitable moment to return. Later, when it came time to rebuild the country, the absence of an educated middle class would prove an immense obstacle.

The Soviet invasion and Moscow's brutal tactics created extreme circumstances that the Islamists exploited. Afghan fighters were radicalized, and militants throughout the Muslim world descended on the country. At that time, U.S. policymakers had a limited understanding of the rising Islamist threat. This blind spot enabled Pakistan to cultivate extremists as proxies. Inattentive to the longer-term risks, we went along.

I still think that it was the right decision to help the Afghans defeat the Soviet Union. Afghans would have taken up arms regardless of what we did, and I thought it was our moral duty to help. Strategically, the outcome of the conflict was a singular contribution to the victory in the Cold War.

I say this despite the fact that the conflict's tragic costs were more than an abstract matter to me. I witnessed the price of this conflict most vividly through my father. As we discussed plans for the rest of the family to leave for America, he began to cry in a rare show of emotion. Perhaps remembering his "funeral" when he left Laghman, he lamented that it was as if we were holding a funeral ceremony. He was sure he would never see his family again. After becoming a refugee in Pakistan, his mood and outlook on life darkened, and he soon began to suffer from a variety of physical ailments. I remembered him as a strong, sturdy man. Yet when I visited him, I noticed that he could barely pour himself tea because his hands were so shaky.

As I look back, I believe that the tragic aftermath of the Soviet-Afghan war was avoidable. Once it was clear that the Soviets might well withdraw, the United States did not adjust in a timely manner. We failed to form a broad-based transitional government, which could have empowered moderate forces and avoided Afghanistan's collapse into civil war. Instead, inertia led us to support Pakistan's preferred option of a military solution. Prolonged warfare and instability enabled the triumph of the Taliban, whose regime made Afghanistan a magnet for violent Islamists worldwide. These failures imposed an enormous cost and culminated in the attacks of 9/11.

SIX

CONTAINING
SADDAM

WASHINGTON, D.C., 1988–1992

I HAD WATCHED THE RISE OF SADDAM HUSSEIN SINCE MY DAYS AS A STUDENT AT AUB. My Arab peers tended to view him as a dynamic young leader intent on using his country's oil wealth to develop Iraq. However, by the time I arrived at the State Department, in 1986, Iraq's modernization had taken a backseat to the grueling war with Iran. I was tasked with developing ideas to manage the conflict.

Two upheavals of 1979—Khomeini's revolution in Iran and Saddam Hussein's ascendancy in Iraq—were the immediate catalysts of the Iran-Iraq war. However, the roots of the conflict lay much deeper, in centuries of competition among Arab, Turkish, and Persian empires. For much of antiquity, the areas of present-day Iran and Iraq had been contested by successive empires. Beginning in the seventh century, regional rivalries were further complicated by the Shia-Sunni split in Islam and by the emergence of a distinctly Persian identity in Iran. In Iraq, as in most areas that came under the Islamic caliphate, Islam's arrival meant the spread of Arab language, culture, and politics. Iran, however, in Bernard Lewis's words, was "Islamized, but it was not Arabized."

Saddam saw the Iranian upheaval as an opportunity. He believed that the Khomeini revolution and attendant disorder had weakened Iran's military power. In September 1980, he launched a surprise attack against Iran. Iraq had an initial advantage, but by 1982 the balance had shifted in favor of Iran. Rejecting Saddam's cease-fire offer, Khomeini vowed to continue the war until the regime in Baghdad collapsed.

The prospect of an Islamic revolution spreading into Iraq alarmed the Reagan administration. To maintain a balance of power between the historic adversaries, Washington tilted toward Iraq through a series of subtle but significant policy changes. It removed Iraq from its list of state sponsors of terrorism and began to provide Baghdad with agricultural loans and dual-use technology. The United States also launched Operation Staunch to press countries around the world to cease arms sales to Iran. In 1984 Washington restored diplomatic relations with Iraq for the first time since 1967.

DURING MY TIME in the Reagan administration, I made my first trip to Iraq. The official meetings were in Baghdad, but Ambassador David Newton also took me to Najaf and Karbala, two of the holiest cities to Shia Muslims.

The trip was eye-opening, showing me the diversity and complexity of the country. Saddam's regime was politically repressive, but I was surprised by the secular and liberal lifestyle prevailing in Baghdad. With relatively lax regulations on nightclubs and alcohol, the capital enjoyed a vibrant nightlife that seemed discordant in an Islamic city in the midst of a war. The cities of Karbala and Najaf to the south were different. Though they were located far from the battlefield, I felt close to the war there because of the unceasing mourning ceremonies for the fallen soldiers. On every corner, it seemed, groups of men were carrying bodies shrouded in white burial sheets.

Conducting official business in Baghdad felt like being in Moscow on the Euphrates, replete with staid government buildings, stodgy bureaucrats, and the suspicious glares of armed guards. Adornments celebrating the great and glorious Saddam served as a constant reminder that Iraq was a full-fledged dictatorship complete with a cult of personality. More than anything else, I was struck by the overwhelming aura of fear that permeated the ranks of the Baathist regime. Senior officials were unwilling to deviate even minimally from their talking points.

The only official I met who was willing to engage in frank discussions was Tariq Aziz. His association with Saddam went back three decades to their days as activists in underground Baathist circles. When Saddam took power a decade later, he chose Aziz as deputy prime minister to represent Iraqi interests abroad. With his white hair, signature horn-rimmed glasses, and bushy moustache, Aziz became a fixture on the diplomatic scene.

Aziz, dressed in military fatigues and carrying a pistol on his belt, greeted me warmly when I arrived at his office. Aziz conceded that the war was not going well and that Iraqi forces had seen unexpected setbacks. But in a departure from his urbane manner, Aziz made a determined fist, looked me squarely in the eye, and declared, "Iraq will not allow Iran to win. Yes, the Iranians are numerous—like mosquitoes. Saddam will deal with them as one deals with germs." The comment struck me as odd, but I chalked it up to bluster. Only later did it occur to me: Aziz may have been alluding to Saddam's plan to use chemical weapons against the Iranians.

Looking back, it is reasonable to criticize U.S. policy for playing a cynical game of realpolitik in supporting Iraq against Iran. Still, American assistance was not a decisive factor in the outcome of the war. Indeed, the most significant U.S. action was entirely accidental: the July 1988 downing of an Iranian civilian airliner over the Gulf. Although it was an error, Tehran believed that the strike was part of an intentional U.S. escalation. In my view, this had a powerful psychological effect that weakened Tehran's will to continue the conflict. With the balance clearly tipping in Iraq's favor, Khomeini reluctantly acquiesced to a cease-fire, calling the decision "deadlier than drinking from a poisoned chalice."

IN THE AFTERMATH of the cease-fire, a debate emerged within the U.S. government on how, if at all, to reorient U.S. policy toward Iraq. The regional bureaus in the State Department saw an opportunity to improve ties with Saddam. Iraq, they pointed out, had paid a terrible price for a victory that gained little in real terms. Estimates of Iraqi deaths in the war ran into the hundreds of thousands, with countless others injured and unable to reintegrate into society. Financially, the country was in shambles. Saddam would need outside help in rebuilding his country.

I disagreed. Iraq was now the dominant regional military power. I judged that Saddam would use Iraq's power position to push for hegemony in the Persian Gulf. This was bound to produce a clash, since the United States was committed to preventing regional hegemony by any power.

I wrote a memorandum for Secretary Shultz, offering three options. One, we could contain Iraq ourselves. This would require the United States to strengthen its posture in the Gulf.

Alternatively, we could tilt toward Iran and restore a balance of power between the two countries. We could ease economic sanctions against Iran and allow Tehran to import the technology it needed to build up its oil production and shipping capabilities. We could facilitate improved economic relations between Iran and the Gulf Cooperation Council states and stop using U.S. leverage to thwart arms sales to Iran.

Or, we could check the ambitions of both Iran and Iraq. This was the most difficult option. It would require the buildup of U.S. and allied forces in the region and continued enforcement of sanctions on both countries.

Before I had a chance to discuss the issue with Armacost or Shultz, my memo was leaked to the press. My suspicion is that someone in the Near East Affairs bureau wanted to squash the debate preemptively. In an article in the *New York Times*, Elaine Sciolino discussed my memo in the context of the Iraq policy review occurring within the State Department and suggested that the Reagan administration was weighing a tilt toward Iran.

It turned out that before reading the *Times* story, Shultz had not been informed that lower-level officials were revisiting our Iraq policy. Intrigued, he called me into his office along with Armacost, Assistant Secretary of State for Near East Affairs Richard Murphy, and Policy Planning Director Dick Solomon. He invited us into his small study adjacent to the secretary's main suite. Armacost began to brief Shultz on the Iraq debate within the building, but Shultz waved that off. "Where's *the* memo?" he wanted to know.

I handed Shultz my memo, and he sat down in his chair while the four of us stood around him. As he read, his face became redder and redder. Then he grabbed a marker and wrote a big "NO" across the first page. Cooling down a bit, he turned toward me. "Zal, this makes great geopolitical sense but no political sense!"

My response probably did not help the situation. "Mr. Secretary," I replied, "I'm being paid to advise you on geopolitics."

I suspect Shultz's outburst had more to do with Iran-Contra than with my memo. In that scandal, the Reagan administration had facilitated arms sales to Iran, partly to secure the release of hostages in Lebanon and partly to divert funds from the weapons sales to the Contras in Nicaragua, who were legally prohibited from receiving U.S. aid. It not only fell on Shultz to apologize to Baghdad for the sales to Iran, but also to testify under oath before Congress about the scandal. My proposal to facilitate arms sales to Iran may have struck him as another Iran-Contra drama in the making.

Later, Shultz apparently had a change of heart. In his memoir, published shortly after the Gulf War, he expressed support for my approach, specifically citing my memo in the footnotes: "By the end of the Reagan years . . . it was clear to me that no further reason existed for the United States to give Iraq the benefit of the doubt for balance-of-power purposes against Iran . . . and that a new and tougher policy toward Saddam Hussein's Iraq was now appropriate."

ONCE OUT OF GOVERNMENT, I began writing and speaking about the increasingly dangerous situation in the Gulf. Iraq was in a dominant position in the region, commanding the world's fourth-largest army. But despite growing signs of Saddam's aggressive intent, the Bush administration continued a policy of engagement with Iraq.

One Bush administration official, however, was receptive to my arguments. While I was at Chicago, Wohlstetter had introduced me to Henry Rowen, now the assistant secretary of defense for international security affairs. Rowen called General Norman Schwarzkopf, the new commander at Central Command, and suggested that he meet with me.

When I suggested to Schwarzkopf that Saddam needed to be viewed as a threat, his eyes widened. Schwarzkopf was working with senior leaders at the Pentagon—including Chairman of the Joint Chiefs of Staff Colin Powell and Under Secretary of Defense for Policy Paul Wolfowitz—to reorient CENTCOM's contingency planning away from Soviet threats toward potential regional flare-ups. "I want you to do a project on this right away," he instructed.

We organized a program at RAND that included a detailed threat assessment focused on Iraq. Intelligence analyst Patrick Lang, a longtime expert on Iraq, participated. By the end of July, Lang was one of the few analysts arguing that Saddam was likely to invade Kuwait. Journalist Bob Woodward later praised our July 1990 seminar as one of the few accurate intelligence estimates regarding Saddam's intentions toward Kuwait.

ON THE EVE of Operation Desert Storm, Wolfowitz and his deputy, Scooter Libby, invited me to return to government as director of policy planning at the Defense Department.

The move to the Pentagon, with its long hours, was not popular with our son Alex, who was seven years old at the time. "I'm working at the Pentagon, one of the pillars of American power," I explained.

He was not impressed.

Upset that I came home late and usually went to work on weekends, he now began to refer to my place of employment as the "Stupid Pentagon of Idiotic Power." You can be sure that years later, when he was a young Stanford-graduated lawyer doing an internship at that very Pentagon, I reminded him of his words.

In 1991, our second son, Max, was born. Cheryl's brother Charles took charge of Alex as we raced to Sibley Hospital for the event, hosting him for a Chuck E. Cheese pizza to distract him. The following morning, coming to view his brother for the very first time, Alex regarded the new little scrap of humanity in the plexiglass crib used by the maternity ward and suggested that we ought to wheel it out into the hallway. Why? Cheryl asked. "So people can admire him," Alex replied, in a tone of voice indicating that this was surely obvious. Sibling rivalry? No. It was the founding moment of a mutual admiration society. Later, during my increasingly long and frequent absences, Alex would prove to be a loving and reliable support for his younger brother. As for Max, when his first word was "hi," we understood that this was a very outgoing young man.

The rapid defeat of Saddam's armies opened a debate on how to end the war. At first, Schwarzkopf, and then President Bush, announced that the United States would not advance further into Iraq. Senior officials believed that the devastating defeat would lead to a coup against Saddam. Yet, by leaking statements to this effect, they only alleviated pressure on Saddam. Without the prospect of further U.S. action against Iraq, officers in the regime were less willing to move against Saddam. When it became clear that Saddam's security forces would stay loyal and intact, President Bush called on "the Iraqi people to take matters into their own hands and force Saddam Hussein, the dictator, to step aside."

Insurgents in Basra began to rebel against Saddam. Within weeks, armed revolts broke out across Iraq. Saddam believed that his regime had lost control of seventeen provinces, with only Anbar Province remaining loyal. In negotiating an armistice with Saddam's generals, however, Schwarzkopf permitted the Iraqi regime to fly helicopters over the south of the country because Iraqis argued that we had destroyed their bridges, making ground transportation impossible. Saddam deployed the helicopter gunships to mow down his opponents, slaughtering tens of thousands of civilians.

Wolfowitz emerged as the leading voice in the administration arguing that the United States should aid the Iraqis who were trying to topple Saddam. I agreed and suggested that the United States could overthrow the Baathist regime without sending large numbers of American troops to Baghdad. The United States already had F-15 pilots patrolling southern Iraq within one hundred kilometers of where the massacres were happening. They could prevent the gunship attacks and provide protection while we transferred arms to insurgents who were fighting Saddam's military with only small arms, machine guns, and grenades.

I was disturbed by the U.S. passivity in the face of Saddam's massacres. Building, in part, on my ideas, Wolfowitz advocated for three moves: shoot down Saddam's gunships, arm the Shia and Kurdish rebels, and create U.S.-protected enclaves in northern and southern Iraq.

Secretary of Defense Dick Cheney rejected these proposals.

I thought this issue was important enough to keep raising it within the government, even at the risk of irking the principals. Powell, however, called Wolfowitz to complain about "civilians in the Pentagon." At that point, Wolfowitz stood down.

Saddam retaliated ruthlessly. Iraqi forces moved into the Kurdish cities and slaughtered Saddam's opponents indiscriminately. Remembering Saddam's chemical weapons attacks against them in 1988, millions of Kurds began fleeing toward the Iranian and Turkish borders. The situation finally prompted an American response. Pursuant to UN Security Council Resolution 688, the United States began enforcing a no-fly zone in the north and provided humanitarian assistance to the Kurds under Operation Provide Comfort.

The United States was less responsive to atrocities in the Shia-dominated south of Iraq. Hundreds of thousands of civilians fled to the borders of Kuwait, Saudi Arabia, and Iran to escape Saddam's forces. Tens of thousands of other civilians sought refuge in the marshes of southern Iraq, where the Marsh Arabs had created a civilization and culture based on this unique environment. Unable to send tanks and artillery into the wetlands, Saddam drained over 1,000 square miles of marshes, killing 40,000 Marsh Arabs and devastating the area's ecology. Only much later, in August 1992, would the United States impose a no-fly zone in southern Iraq.

The events of 1991 planted seeds of distrust between the United States and Iraq's Shia, who accused the United States of indifference to and even complicity in Saddam's oppression. I would later hear the same refrain time and time again in my meetings with Shia leaders: *"Al-Amrikan mu jiddiyyin—The Americans are not serious."*

DURING THE UPRISING against Saddam, Lewis called me to say that he had just spent an evening with a group of "smart Iraqis" who opposed Saddam. A banker and mathematician named Ahmed Chalabi led these exiles. Lewis thought it was important for someone in the government to hear what Chalabi and his associates had to say.

I asked Paul Freeburg, a Marine detailed to my staff, to arrange a meeting. Freeburg returned with a surprising answer: it was against U.S. policy to meet with the Iraqi opposition. When he had tried to schedule the meeting, the State Department protested to the White House.

I was startled. We had just finished a war with Iraq, deploying everything short of nuclear weapons, yet we were not allowed even to meet with those who shared our objectives? The policy had been instituted in 1988 under entirely different circumstances. Yet officials at the State Department continued to enforce it due to their differences with the Iraqi opposition. Secretary of State James Baker had indicated in February that Saddam's ouster, while not a "war aim," was indeed a "political aim." But while amenable to a military coup, State Department officials were unwilling to allow meetings with political opponents of Saddam, whose goals, they feared, would destabilize Iraq.

Under pressure from Congress, the press, and advocates within the administration, the White House removed the ban in March 1991. Even then, I had to jump through multiple hoops to meet with the opposition. After I had scheduled a time for Kurdish leader Massoud Barzani to come to the Pentagon, the State Department pressured the White House to call it off at the last minute. Consultations between the Defense Department and the Iraqi opposition, they protested, would make people think that the United States was planning to arm Saddam's opponents. Still, I was able to meet with some of the Iraqi exiles. I initially invited Chalabi and Kurdish Democratic Party (KDP) representative Hoshyar Zebari to the Pentagon. Later I met with Barham Salih, the foreign representative of the Patriotic Union of Kurdistan (PUK).

I was moved by what the Iraqi opposition leaders had to say. They relayed harrowing stories about the torture, threats, and assassination attempts that they and other Iraqis had faced at the hands of Saddam's regime. Having focused on the geopolitical aspects of the conflict in the Gulf, I now became sensitized to the human rights dimension. I was convinced that the Iraqi opposition could be a strategic asset for the United States. Besides the moral authority that they brought to the issue, these leaders were knowledgeable and had access to important networks within the country. The opposition was also united behind a compelling message. While coming from varying backgrounds and different power bases, they advocated a free, peaceful Iraq aligned with the United States.

In June 1992, Chalabi formed the Iraqi National Congress—the name inspired by Gandhi's Indian National Congress and Mandela's African National Congress. The group included Shia, Sunnis, and Kurds. Chalabi built on that momentum with an opposition conference in October 1992. This time, the two largest Shia-majority factions—the Supreme Council for the Islamic Revolution in Iraq (SCIRI) and Islamic Dawa Party—also joined. Equally significant was the location of the conference—the protected area of northern Iraq—making it the first opposition conference convened on Iraqi territory.

I was disappointed that the United States opted against a more active policy of support for the Iraqi opposition. Though President Bush eventually authorized covert actions in Iraq, there was little interest within the Pentagon or the administration generally for the type of major program that we had provided to the Afghan opposition in the 1980s.

While we achieved our limited aim in the Gulf War, the outcome left unresolved the question of how to manage the continuing threat of a dangerous and unpredictable regime in Iraq. I was dissatisfied with the status quo and how it had left Iraqis with the worst of both worlds—Saddam and sanctions. Once I left government, I began to advocate publicly for regime change through greater support for the Iraqi opposition.

SEVEN

CRAFTING GRAND STRATEGY FOR A UNIPOLAR WORLD

WASHINGTON, D.C., 1991–1992

I WAS SURPRISED BY HOW MUTED THE RESPONSE WAS IN THE UNITED STATES WHEN the Soviet Union collapsed. The Cold War was over, and with it, the bipolar world of Soviet-American rivalry. Yet there were no celebrations commensurate with this monumental change. I expected, at a minimum, that a monument would be erected to celebrate freedom's triumph and communism's defeat, or that a museum would be built to document the struggle and remember the enormous sacrifices made by Americans, victims of the Gulag, and others who had resisted the Soviet Union.

As a Pentagon planner, I was concerned that the American people, and their leaders, did not appreciate the magnitude of this event. I feared that the United States would miss the extraordinary opportunities at hand.

Among the strategists who were thinking about the U.S. role in the world going forward, there was little consensus. "We need another X," the editor of *Foreign Affairs* remarked, referencing George Kennan's anonymously authored article from 1947. Written without attribution because Kennan was still at the State Department, the X article had analyzed the "sources of Soviet conduct" and prescribed in broad brushstrokes the containment strategy that guided U.S. foreign policy for the next four and a half decades.

I believed that the United States should exercise leadership and expand the liberal international order that the United States and its allies had built after World War II. The twentieth century had shown that the global security environment could change dramatically—with little warning.

The "new world order," as the president called it, presented a particular challenge for the Department of Defense. President Bush was committed to preserving a "base force" after the Cold War of no fewer than 1.6 million troops. But it was less clear what he believed the central goals of U.S. national security policy should be and why he wanted a force of that size. In the absence of a compelling strategy, there was no logical baseline to determine the appropriate level of defense capabilities and spending.

Doves, including many of the Democrats who controlled Congress, wanted to collect a bigger "peace dividend" and spend it on domestic priorities. Their opponents in Congress wanted to protect the defense budget but were struggling to do so in the absence of a clear rationale from the Bush administration. The toughest challenge was to break out of "threat-based thinking" and pursue opportunities to shape the world.

I was pleased that my office was assigned the task of developing a new defense strategy. For policy planners, periods of big change often provide the best opportunity to contribute.

Within the Pentagon, the traditional vehicle for providing strategic planning advice was the so-called Defense Policy Guidance (DPG). The 1992 DPG would inform choices for the 1994–1999 planning cycle. Given the epochal moment we were facing, I saw the DPG as an opportunity to outline a grand strategy for the post–Cold War world that would guide our force structure well beyond 1999.

The policy planning shop can only be effective if the secretary is receptive to new ideas and approaches. Luckily, Cheney was serious about developing a new strategy. He was drawn to conceptual thinking and blocked out time in his schedule to engage in long, substantive policy discussions.

In his reading of history, the United States had a record of demobilizing precipitously. After World War I, this enabled Germany and Japan to emerge as major threats. After World War II, Moscow took half of Europe, and Mao won power in China. In a speech on the fiftieth anniversary of the attack on Pearl Harbor, Cheney said, "The good news is that it's a safer world and we can probably . . . reduce the size of the force. The bad news is it's never been done successfully before. . . ."

I knew that large bureaucracies seldom produce sharp strategic insight. So I worked with a small team. At the same time, I wanted to cast the net wide for ideas and involve key officials so that they, too, would have a sense of ownership of the final product.

Throughout the winter of 1991 into early 1992, I convened discussions with a number of experts from both inside and outside the building. Our team developed a set of future contingencies that would be used to test the capabilities of proposed force structures.

The scenarios did not amount to predictions about the future, nor were they exhaustive of the possibilities. Rather, they were illustrative and, we thought, plausible. Some were based on recent or current threats, such as a conflict on the Korean peninsula or a reprise of Iraq's aggression against Kuwait. Others focused on an intervention in Panama or the Philippines to counter a coup attempt. One scenario raised the possibility of simultaneous wars against Iraq and North Korea. One contingency focused on a future, adversarial Russia seeking to reclaim territory in the former Soviet Union, which was viewed as unlikely in the near term but possible in the medium and long term. It involved crises in Ukraine, Eastern Europe, and the Baltic region.

The most foundational scenario involved the rise of a hostile global competitor. We feared that "a single nation or a coalition of nations" would coalesce behind "an adversarial security strategy" and develop "a military capability to threaten U.S. interests."

We were not arguing that the United States should necessarily get involved in these scenarios if they materialized. Instead, our job was to identify the kinds of forces and capabilities that would be relevant should the president decide to deal with such scenarios.

BY JANUARY 1992, I had a clear sense of the strategy I wanted the DPG to advance. With only 5 percent of the world's population, the United States could not be a global hegemon. Instead, I concluded that we needed a strategy of American leadership designed to preserve peace among the major world powers and galvanize collective action among allies as challenges arose.

I thought it was critical to expand what we called the democratic "zone of peace," which provided the basis for an open international system. This meant that we could not allow a hostile power to take control over key regions. These goals, I assumed, required the United States to preserve its military preeminence and forward presence as well as its economic strength.

While we believed that there had to be a floor beneath which defense spending could not fall, we understood how important it was to maintain the health of the economy at home. I did not see defense spending as a threat to the economy, but too large a budget would drag down economic growth. And even with a large military, I thought we had to be judicious in the use of force. Alliances were critical to share the burden of global leadership. Otherwise, public support in the United States would not permit American presidents to carry out this strategy.

The DPG went through multiple drafts and revisions. It was reviewed extensively within the Pentagon bureaucracy, particularly by the Joint Staff, which reported to Powell. The military services viewed all of these activities as a high-stakes game. For the most part, they were willing to concede the strategy development process to the civilians, but they were intensely interested in any decisions on force structure and resources that would affect their individual services. In the end, the civilian policy team produced the first strategy that guided America's post–Cold War policy, which fit well with the advice on forces and resources that Powell and his team were offering.

Though the draft DPG remains classified, important parts of the document have been published in the press and released by the Pentagon. The strategy reiterated U.S. intentions to uphold our alliances and multilateral collective security institutions. However, it also contained new, far-reaching strategic ideas.

Most importantly, the document argued that the United States must prevent the rise of a peer competitor. It stated, "Our first objective is to prevent the re-emergence of a new rival, either on the territory of the former Soviet Union or elsewhere, that poses a threat on the order of that posed formerly by the Soviet Union." The DPG wanted to preclude the emergence of bipolarity, another global rivalry like the Cold War, or multipolarity, a world of many great powers, as existed before the two world wars. To do so, the key was to prevent a hostile power from dominating a "critical region," defined as having the resources, industrial capabilities, and population that, if controlled by a hostile power, would pose a global challenge.

Values were an important part of the strategy. The DPG saw "increasing respect for international law" and "the spread of democratic forms of government" as critical factors in "deterring conflicts or threats in regions of security important to the United States."

Among the more challenging issues was how to establish criteria for sizing military forces. Some thought that sizing forces for one large contingency— a second Gulf War, for example—would be enough. But we argued that this was insufficient. What if a crisis were to erupt elsewhere or an adversary tried to take advantage of our preoccupation in one region? To be a credible global partner, I thought U.S. forces needed to be prepared for aggression in more than one region.

The military was ultimately directed to maintain sufficient forces for two major regional contingencies—or 2MRCs. This still represented a major peace dividend, but did not amount to the even larger downsizing that many were advocating.

◄ ►

INITIAL REVIEWS of the DPG inside the Pentagon were positive, so I was unprepared for the controversy that would soon erupt.

I was in Germany for a NATO security conference in early March 1992. My colleague, Assistant Secretary of Defense for International Security Policy (ISP) Hadley, approached me with a worried look. The French were wondering why the Pentagon was developing a strategy to "keep Europe down."

Later in the day, I learned that the source of the French outrage was an article on the front page of the *New York Times:* "U.S. Strategy Plan Calls for Insuring No Rivals Develop: A One-Superpower World." The *Times* reported that the Pentagon had a secret strategy document that advanced the "concept of benevolent domination by one power." It was the draft DPG.

When I returned home, I was surprised to see that the leak had generated an outcry in the United States as well. In fact, it had become an issue in the presidential campaign. Governor Bill Clinton's spokesman George Stephanopoulos—a former student of mine at Columbia—attacked the paper as "one more attempt" by the Defense Department "to find an excuse for big budgets instead of downsizing."

The leaked scenarios drew particular ire on Capitol Hill. Senator Joe Biden dismissed the strategy as "literally a Pax Americana." While he conceded that "American hegemony would be nice," he asserted with characteristic confidence, "It won't work." Senator Carl Levin quipped, "You have to have insurance against unlikely events. Having a fire in your house is an unlikely event but it's a plausible event. Some of these threats are implausible." Senator Ted Kennedy complained that the contingency planning was aimed "at finding new ways to justify Cold War levels of military spending."

Even inside the Bush administration, the draft DPG came under fire. National Security Advisor Brent Scowcroft considered the paper to be "nutty" and "kooky." At a staff meeting the morning after the leak, he made clear his unhappiness. Unnamed officials from State and the National Security Council lambasted the "dumb report," telling reporters that they wanted it to go "down in flames." One anonymously quoted State Department official likened a scenario involving a Russian attack on Lithuania to something in a "Tom Clancy novel."

As word got around the administration that I had drafted the leaked document, I began receiving phone calls from State Department and White House officials. My counterpart at the State Department protested that formulating a national security strategy was not "DoD's business."

"Of course it is not DoD business!" I replied. "It should be happening at the presidential level." Ideally, I believed, State would take the lead, and then the interagency process would review it. The State Department, however, had been missing in action in terms of formulating post–Cold War strategy.

A senior director on the NSC staff also reached out to tell me that the White House did not appreciate the document's provocative language and unilateralist theme. "Look," I responded, "I'd be more than happy to withdraw the text, but I need more material for a defense strategy. I need a strategy for force-sizing. Why don't you schedule an interagency review so we can agree on language?"

I had never before been the focus of a Washington policy tempest. While I told myself that this was exactly the kind of debate the country needed, I was disconcerted. I took solace in some of the positive reviews of the draft DPG. Charles Krauthammer, for one, praised the DPG in his *Washington Post* column. His was the minority view, however.

In light of this reaction, I felt demoralized when Cheney asked several of us who had worked on the DPG draft to come to his office. As the meeting was about to start, Libby leaned over and joked, "We're all in trouble with Cheney because of you."

In fact, Cheney was enthusiastic. "You've discovered a new rationale for our role in the world," he said, looking at me. "I read the document last night and I think it is brilliant." Startled, I thanked Cheney. Others jumped in and recommended that we change some of the more controversial wording before finalizing the draft. Cheney concurred but underscored that he wanted to keep the basic contours of the strategy.

When Cheney received a revised draft, he asked for a "sharper" rewrite. More of the original, assertive language returned to the draft. At the same time, Cheney published an op-ed in the *New York Times* in defense of the draft. "We can either sustain the forces we require and remain in a position to help shape things for the better, or we can throw our advantage away," he wrote. "That would only hasten the day when we face greater threats, at higher costs and further risk to American lives."

Even with Cheney's blessing, the DPG was not reviewed at senior levels of the interagency process. When Cheney realized that the rest of the administration did not want to conduct a full strategic review, he asked us to produce an unclassified version of the DPG with his name as the main author.

LOOKING BACK at the controversy, it seems oddly ironic. Many of the scenarios we mentioned in our document came to pass. President Clinton launched

Operation Desert Fox in December 1998 to destroy Saddam Hussein's weapons of mass destruction programs and considered going to war against North Korea to stop its nuclear weapons program. Entreaties by every post–Cold War president have failed to prevent the emergence of an aggressive Russia, which has launched wars against Georgia and Ukraine. Leaders in the Baltic states, including Lithuania, fear that they might be next, and today the United States has a treaty obligation to come to their defense. President Obama's "pivot to Asia" was based on the recognition that China's rise requires the United States to increase its presence in the region.

Though the DPG was prescient in some ways, the United States has been slow and uneven in taking the large muscle movements necessary to shape events rather than react to them. Europe, where NATO expanded the zone of peace, is a relative success story. However, even there, we missed the historic opportunity to bring Russia into the West in the years when President Boris Yeltsin led an avowedly reformist government. In East Asia and the Middle East, U.S. policy drifted, effectively allowing future challenges to develop. At a global level, we did not establish a political architecture in the way we did at the outset of the Cold War.

The DPG, however, created a conceptual foundation for future strategy, one that subsequent administrations carried out in large part.

⊸ ⊱

WHEN I LEFT the Pentagon in November 1992, I continued to think about grand strategy issues as a scholar at the RAND Corporation. In 1995 I wrote an article for the *Washington Quarterly* that reprised some of the key ideas from the DPG. I was surprised by how popular it became.

High school students still come up to me to discuss the article. Apparently, an excerpt is commonly cited on a card that debate teams use to prepare for their competitions. It is called the "Khalilzad 95" card and seems to have acquired iconic status in debate circles. I'm told by former debaters that in exchanges about how to preserve peace and prevent war, Khalilzad 95 was "gold" or provided a "decisive" argument. I'm glad to see that young people seem to have more strategic sense than some of my peers in government.

EIGHT

ONE NATION'S DISINTEGRATION, ONE MAN'S DESTINY

WASHINGTON, D.C., 1993–2001

I WAS AT THE PENTAGON WHEN THE COMMUNIST REGIME IN KABUL COLLAPSED IN 1992. As head of policy planning, I prepared a memo recommending greater U.S. engagement in Afghanistan to promote a political settlement. The senior leadership was uninterested. In the remaining few months of the Bush administration, other issues dominated my time. When I left government in December to return to RAND, I followed news reports on the civil war intently.

With the ouster of the Communist regime, a multi-headed civil war broke out in and around Kabul. The power struggle in Kabul soon took on an ethnic and sectarian character. Alliances shifted repeatedly, and temporary cease-fires and peace plans came and went virtually every month.

I was shocked and saddened when I saw pictures of my old high school in Kabul, the Ghazi Lycee. Only a few walls were left standing as testament to the once-boisterous institution.

Yet it was only after I went to Kabul after 9/11 that I realized the extent to which the war had taken a toll on ordinary Afghans. Over and over again, hardened men broke down as they relayed to me tragic episodes from the war. Street battles raged virtually every day. Gruesome mass killings became commonplace. Executions were carried out by driving nails into the heads of prisoners. Civilians fled from one neighborhood to the next as battle lines shifted week by week. At competing checkpoints, militia fighters routinely killed the women and children of rival parties or ethnic groups. Warring groups fired rockets indiscriminately at their adversaries' positions, not caring that these were also civilian neighborhoods, shrines, palaces, and ancient historic sites.

This horrendous, callous war over Kabul had a lasting effect on the psychology of the Afghan people, creating a profound sense of insecurity. Average Afghans felt that they had no one to lead them and no one to protect them. They focused on survival.

Amid this chaos, a new movement arose in southern Afghanistan: the Taliban. Its members portrayed themselves as young, idealistic students of Islam who would bring stability and order. That sounded good to the ordinary population, and initially, the movement attracted support.

I, like many, was optimistic about the Taliban. I saw the anarchy and pervasive violence that was ravaging the Afghan people. Warlords were abusing local communities, even abducting children. Militias set up checkpoints on roads and extorted money from travelers, no matter how poor. The economy had collapsed. It was a Hobbesian world.

The Taliban were saying all the right things. They promised to bring order, convene a *Loya Jirga*, and bring back the former king to oversee a political transition. Karzai, as well as other Afghans, saw the Taliban as a means to escape the catastrophe engulfing the country. The Gailani family, whose patriarch led one of the moderate resistance organizations during the Soviet occupation, went so far as to assist in buying suits and suitcases for the king in preparation for his return.

The Taliban at the time was a mysterious movement, largely in flux. But even so, I should have been more skeptical. I had seen firsthand what had happened in Iran when Khomeini seized power and imposed a totalitarian religious regime. In Afghanistan, the anarchy of civil war and warlordism had opened the door to an oppressive regime that could deliver order. I should have been more attuned to the possibility that the Taliban would take advantage of the situation to impose a harsh religious regime.

As the Taliban gained momentum, the movement began to receive support from Pakistan's security services, which had lost faith in Hekmatyar as its favored proxy. The Pakistani Interior Ministry and Inter-Services Intelligence directorate were soon funding, supplying, and training the Taliban. Backed by the ISI, the Taliban accelerated its military campaign, taking Kabul in mid-1996. By that point, the capital was in ruins.

The ISI was delighted with the Taliban's progress. When the Taliban captured the western Afghan city of Herat, an embedded ISI advisor to the Taliban, Colonel Imam, reportedly proclaimed, "Today Herat, tomorrow Tashkent"—an indication of the ISI's broader hopes to expand its influence all the way to Central Asia.

With the Taliban dominating the southern, eastern, and western parts of the country, several anti-Taliban fronts were opened. Rabbani's forces withdrew to the north. Abdul Rashid Dostum led Uzbek militias, and Iranian-backed groups were formed among the Hazaras. In exile, the king's supporters coalesced around the Rome Group.

Taliban forces turned their focus on offensives in the north, and Afghanistan settled into a protracted civil war. Eventually, the groups in the north coalesced into the so-called Northern Alliance.

AFTER I LEFT the Pentagon in 1992, I remained in close touch with Afghan leaders in the anti-Taliban opposition. During this period Karzai and I got to know each other better.

Like most Afghans, Karzai initially welcomed the Taliban as a force to end the civil war and combat warlordism. In fact, he took part in early Taliban gatherings and was in some ways instrumental in organizing the group. A decade later, even as the Taliban waged a merciless insurgency against his presidency, Karzai would stubbornly refer to the Taliban as "brothers" whom he hoped to bring back into the fold.

After the Taliban consolidated control in Kabul and other areas, their platform became clear. They banned secular education altogether. They publicly executed alleged adulterers in Kabul's sports stadium. They were collectively obsessed with making women invisible. The *chador*—the traditional garment covering Muslim women—had not previously been common in Kabul but was now obligatory. Windows had to be painted black so women could not be seen from the outside. If they wished to leave their homes—which was strongly discouraged—women now had to be accompanied by male "guardians." Aside from the offensiveness of the principle, this presented a huge practical problem for the hundreds of thousands of those widowed during the past decades of unrelenting war. The new regime also undertook systematic massacres against civilians as it battled the Northern Alliance. Prisoners were locked inside shipping containers and suffocated to death. Taliban militias razed homes and villages and destroyed orchards in contested areas in the north. The regime later withheld emergency food supplies from Shia areas, using mass starvation as a weapon.

If Internet bloggers are to be believed, Karzai and I spent the 1990s shilling for oil companies as they pursued business with the Taliban. The truth is not in the least bit scandalous. By late 1996, our initial hopes for the Taliban were waning. When Karzai and I met in Washington at this time, he confided to me that he was under consideration by the Taliban for the position of envoy to the United Nations. He asked for my advice.

"If you take the position," I said noncommittally, "you'll have to represent the Taliban in front of the world. Are you prepared to do that?"

"I know these men," Karzai replied. "They assure me that while things might be turbulent at the moment, their technocrats will ultimately govern."

I could tell from his tone, however, that he was skeptical and disinclined to identify with the Taliban so overtly. In the end, either the offer never came or he turned it down.

During the mid-1990s, Cambridge Energy Associates, which was assessing the feasibility of a UNOCAL oil pipeline in Afghanistan, asked me to participate in its research. Despite my growing distrust of the Taliban, I thought it was worth exploring whether the regime would welcome economic development for the war-torn country.

The project ended up hardening my views against the Taliban. I remember an exchange I had with the Taliban's minister of information, Amir Khan Muttaqi. Over dinner at the Four Seasons Hotel in Houston, I challenged him on the Taliban's fundamentalism.

"Show me where in the text of the Koran it says that women should be treated as second-class citizens," I demanded. "Where does it say that women have to be covered in a full burqa? Where does it say that they should not be educated?"

Muttaqi became visibly uncomfortable. He started to mumble a few passages from the Koran, but when I pushed back, he pleaded that he was not a cleric.

"The Taliban," he assured me, "is following the guidelines of the mullahs." Mullahs are a step above the Talibs in the Sunni Afghan religious hierarchy.

"Well, as you know," I replied, "Afghan mullahs in many cases are not very well educated. Their opinions on such an important matter cannot be accepted blindly." I asked him where the higher-level religious authorities—the Da-Mullahs, Maulanas, and Mawlawis—stood on the Taliban's edicts. And what about the rest of the Afghan society? He did not respond.

Conversations like this convinced me that the Taliban was headed in the wrong direction, and I became more active with the opposition to the regime. During the late 1990s, Karzai and I engaged in periodic discussions. We met in Washington and in Pakistan, where Karzai was actively organizing Afghan political and social leaders in Quetta. I encouraged Karzai to continue these activities but also to establish and unite a broad coalition of opposition factions.

I concluded that the coalition should include Zahir Shah. When I met with the king in Italy in 1996, he seemed more energetic than in the past, and he offered to act as a mediator between Afghanistan's various elements. Perhaps, he said, he might convene a *Loya Jirga* to promote a new constitution and a broad-based, representative government. Zahir Shah was one of the few Afghan exiles influential enough to spark a peace process for Afghanistan. His most unusual asset, in my assessment, was that he was unquestionably a Pashtun leader, yet enough of a national figure to enjoy popularity across ethnic lines. As such, he was well positioned to undercut the Taliban's base of support.

The Clinton administration was becoming more attentive to the threat posed by the Taliban. In 1996, after his expulsion by the Sudanese regime, Osama bin Laden moved to Afghanistan, taking up residence in Khalis's compound near the city of Jalalabad. He and Mullah Omar, the leader of the Taliban, struck a deal that allowed al Qaeda to build a base of operations in Afghanistan in return for the terrorist group's support of the Taliban regime.

This was an unusual development. The more common arrangement is for a state to sponsor a terrorist group. Here, by contrast, a terrorist group was sponsoring a state. Al Qaeda provided financing to the Taliban, as well as technical assistance in construction and other fields.

Al Qaeda brought thousands of extremists from across the Muslim world to learn paramilitary skills in Afghan training camps. Most were deployed against the Northern Alliance, a conflict in which they became known as especially vicious and fanatical fighters. The most skilled, however, were selected for al Qaeda's terrorist attacks abroad.

The base in Afghanistan allowed al Qaeda and other groups to train terrorists on an industrial scale. The U.S. intelligence community estimated that from 1996 through 2001, 10,000 to 20,000 recruits received such training. Militants made their way to these camps from across the Middle East. Bin Laden issued a series of fatwas proclaiming his intent to strike at Americans. In February 1998, he declared that killing Americans was the "individual duty for any Muslim who can do it in any country in which it is possible to do it." Three months later, he said in an interview, "We do not have to differentiate between military and civilians. As far as we are concerned, they are all targets." During this period, bin Laden began planning the 9/11 attacks.

In later years, senior officials in the Clinton administration claimed that they "declared war" on al Qaeda. The effort did not match the rhetoric. For the most part, the administration treated terrorism as a law enforcement problem, never even asking Congress for an authorization for use of force. A small cell in the CIA tracked al Qaeda's activities. Senior officials used a variety of indirect diplomatic approaches. Through Pakistani leaders, they tried to influence the Taliban to curb al Qaeda. The NSC, in cooperation with the CIA, came up with a variety of covert action schemes, most involving the use of Afghan tribal forces to conduct ambushes or raids aimed at capturing or killing bin Laden. After the bombings of the U.S. embassies in East Africa in August 1998, the Clinton administration launched cruise missile attacks at al Qaeda camps in Afghanistan, but bin Laden had moved to a different location prior to the strikes. There was a great deal of churning in the interagency process, but it never provided President Clinton with a credible strategy to eliminate the terrorist safe haven in Afghanistan, as this would have required supporting some kind of an Afghan military force to challenge the Taliban.

IN EARLY SUMMER of 1999, I again went to Rome to meet Zahir Shah. I encouraged him to become the *patragar* of Afghanistan. *Patragar* is an Afghan term for a craftsman who repairs broken metal objects such as pots and dishes. Given the poverty of the country, *patragars* performed a valued service; ordinary Afghans could not afford to throw away old possessions. Afghanistan was like a broken dish, I explained, and needed a *patragar* to patch it back together.

The king did not appreciate my analogy at first, resisting comparisons between his role and that of a menial, low-class peddler. He eventually embraced the concept, agreeing to chair a conference of Afghan exiles in Rome.

Still, the king continued to be a reluctant actor. Shouldn't we wait, he protested at one point, for the U.S. to back his enterprise?

I was exasperated. "The U.S. government does not take you seriously," I told him, with unusual bluntness. "They think you are an old man who has been gone since 1973. Insofar as they are paying attention to Afghanistan, they see the Taliban, al Qaeda, and Pakistan." I encouraged him to move forward on his own, soliciting private donations from Afghan exiles.

The conversation got heated. I was increasingly frustrated that the king, who loved to sip Italian espresso and wear expensive leather shoes, was so passive in helping his country. "How can you sleep at night when your people are in this situation?" I asked.

Karzai and other exiles, meanwhile, were generating momentum for an opposition gathering in Frankfurt.

Concerned about the growing opposition efforts, the Taliban retaliated savagely. In July 1999, the Taliban murdered Karzai's elderly father in broad daylight as he exited a mosque in the Pakistani city of Quetta. Instead of being intimidated, Karzai was emboldened. He became infused with a newfound sense of purpose, his zeal overcoming any caution. He contacted friends and associates of his father and before long arranged for a 300-vehicle convoy to accompany him as he drove into Kandahar to bury his father in the family graveyard. The Taliban let him pass unharmed. This courageous act of filial piety bolstered his standing among the Afghan opposition.

I was, at the time, working on a piece for the *Washington Quarterly* that called for confronting the Taliban. I contacted several Afghan exiles, asking them to get involved. Ishaq Shahryar, a California-based solar engineer, was particularly helpful in providing funds. He would later show the same generosity as the first Afghan ambassador to the United States, serving pro bono while contributing his own resources to refurbish the Afghan embassy in Washington, which was in a state of serious disrepair after standing empty for so many years. Dozens of prominent delegates—technocrats, former government officials, commanders, intellectuals, and other exiles—eventually participated in the November 1999 conference.

When Zahir Shah stepped to the podium, he announced that he was not seeking any role for himself. He simply wanted to serve as the orchestrator to make sure that the meeting succeeded. At that point, one of the female delegates stood up and threw her *chador*—the scarf covering her head—at the king. I had been away from Afghanistan for so long that I had forgotten this custom. In Pashtun tradition, this gesture was meant to shame a man into action. It signified that the king should "be a man, be brave and fight, or else put on this *chador* and just be a woman."

In the end, the conference participants agreed on a plan. They would convene a *Loya Jirga*, which in turn would build a national, elected government. To advance this objective and gain international backing, delegations would travel to various world capitals. I followed up by helping Karzai and other opposition leaders arrange meetings in Washington.

Though momentous for Afghans, the conference attracted little notice in the United States. The State Department issued a routine statement acknowledging the event. The American press ignored it. Karzai's delegation was having a hard time securing meetings at the State Department. Even as the Clinton administration embraced a harder line against the Taliban in its last years, the United States officially remained neutral in the Afghan civil war. It reached out diplomatically to the Taliban regime in a naïve effort to elicit cooperation against al Qaeda.

Nevertheless, in hindsight, it is clear that the Rome meeting was a pivotal event. By including many prominent Pashtuns, the Rome Group created a competing force that could undercut the Taliban in the country's south and east. The group went on to play a vital role in the post-Taliban transition, articulating a political plan that mirrored the one implemented after 9/11. Importantly, the conference helped bridge divides created by the earlier civil war.

Despite their shared interest in ousting the Taliban, relations between the Northern Alliance and mostly Pashtun exiles were uneasy. The Northern Alliance resented the fact that many Pashtuns had either joined the Taliban or fled the country while the Northern Alliance had stayed and fought the Taliban. Pashtun exiles were critical of the Northern Alliance factions for their roles in the civil war.

Even though the Northern Alliance was not a direct participant in the conference, Ahmad Shah Massoud, the group's principal commander, and its foreign minister, Abdullah Abdullah, voiced support for the initiative. I helped Karzai and his team engage the Northern Alliance by facilitating visas to travel to Uzbekistan. From Central Asia the group went into Afghanistan and visited Massoud at his base in the north. Karzai and Massoud subsequently held direct talks with the idea of organizing a unified anti-Taliban alliance.

When he was president, Karzai told me that, during this period, he had arrived at what seemed to be a presumptuous belief: "One day, I will be the leader of Afghanistan. It is my destiny."

Karzai explained that after the fall of the Communist regime but before the outbreak of full-scale civil war, he was deputy foreign minister. One day, he was arrested for allegedly aiding an enemy of President Rabbani and hauled into the KHAD intelligence headquarters, run by Mohammed Fahim.

"I didn't expect to leave alive," Karzai told me. "After all, most arrested there did not. Then, just as the interrogation began, a savior arrived. A missile landed in my prison cell. At first, I was stunned. Then I saw that my interrogator was bleeding to death on the floor. The walls that once confined me had collapsed. And there I stood—barely even injured. I ran for my life."

He explained that former colleagues from the Foreign Ministry helped him escape Kabul. "I had only been back to Afghanistan once since then," he continued, "to bury my martyred father. From that day, I was convinced that, mark my words, I would return, not at the head of a funeral train, but as the head of Afghanistan."

PART II

BUSH ADMINISTRATION

NINE

THE CALM BEFORE
THE STORM

WASHINGTON, D.C.,
JANUARY–SEPTEMBER 2001

I ARRIVED AT THE OLD EXECUTIVE OFFICE BUILDING ON MAY 23, 2001, WITH A SENSE of great anticipation. I was about to start my new job as a special assistant to the president and a senior director on the National Security Council staff. Like all offices in the Old EOB, mine had high ceilings and historic moldings, and enough room for both my government-issued desk and a sitting area. Multiple computers gave me access to unclassified, secret, and top-secret networks. I had a classified phone as well.

I was happy to be back in government. I had served at lower levels in the State Department and Defense Department, where I learned about political and military instruments of power. Now, at the White House, I saw an opportunity to integrate the work of the different agencies into strategies for the president.

At the beginning of every new administration, there is a period of intense political maneuvering for positions. At the more senior level, the contest focuses on who will secure the cabinet-level or principal-level appointments. At the middle level, the competition involves policy experts affiliated with the president-elect's party, former mid-level officials, and staffers on the campaign.

It is a byzantine and sometimes ruthless process because all factions understand that "personnel is policy."

I landed on the NSC staff through a circuitous route. The morning after Vice President Gore conceded defeat after the Florida recount, I was called to the temporary Bush-Cheney transition headquarters. I met Vice President elect Cheney and Libby, now his chief of staff. They asked me to lead transition efforts for the Department of Defense. I did not have a formal role in the Bush campaign, but Cheney and I had stayed in touch.

My name surfaced on short lists for the position of undersecretary of defense for policy, the number-three civilian position in the department. I think I was considered for the position as a result of my eight years at the RAND Corporation, where I had helped establish a center for Middle East policy studies. Within RAND's Project Air Force, I focused a substantial part of my research on China's growing military and strategies.

I may have underestimated at first the status of my position as chief of the defense transition team. I arrived at the Pentagon on my first day in my son's old, beat-up Jeep, dressed in jeans and a casual shirt. At the River Entrance parking lot, I was puzzled when I received an escort car at the security checkpoint, then amused to see that I was given a choice parking spot near the front stairs. As I approached the building, I was startled to see a formal greeting party, which included a couple of generals, a group of colonels, and representatives of the Office of the Secretary of Defense. My new colleagues graciously looked past my casual attire and escorted me to the basement offices that would be the new team's transition headquarters.

A few days later, Libby asked me to come by and meet the "new boss" of the Pentagon. I had assumed that former senator Dan Coats was in line to become secretary of defense. But the president had instead selected Rumsfeld. I advised Rumsfeld to pick his own transition team—people whom he trusted. He told me that he did not intend to fire anyone on the team and that he wanted me to help him, assuming we could find a way to work together.

I soon began to wonder, however, whether I would have a role in the new administration. Right from the get-go, my relationship with Rumsfeld was bumpy.

This was not because of policy differences. In fact, I liked the way Rumsfeld thought. He was future-oriented, empirical, and deliberate about examining policy assumptions and courses of action. I appreciated "Rumsfeld's rules," my favorite being: "Weakness is provocative." He was committed to maintaining a robust U.S. military and believed that it needed to be transformed to meet future challenges. Cognizant that U.S. policymakers had a poor record of predicting threats, he favored military planning against the capabilities—rather than assumed intentions—of potential adversaries, a method with which I agreed. He also understood that adversaries would adopt asymmetric threats, such as ballistic missiles and anti-satellite systems, to avoid frontal challenges against the United States. He was wary about indefinite deployments of military forces in what he considered to be marginal engagements, such as Bosnia and the Sinai. He saw those deployments as frittering away U.S. power. I believed that I could help him undertake a strategic review that would reshape our forces for the coming era.

However, I was in the unfortunate position of fielding requests for meetings from people Rumsfeld did not wish to see before his confirmation hearing. Senior Pentagon officials, eager to brief Rumsfeld, were bombarding me with requests and venting their frustration that he would not respond to their invitations. When I raised the issue with him, he pushed back.

"Zal," he said, "you don't understand. If I go to the Pentagon, then senators will expect me to give substantive answers in the confirmation hearing. Now I can say, 'I haven't been to the building. I haven't been briefed. These are my ideas and priorities, but let me get acquainted with the situation and I'll be back to brief you after a few months.'"

I was also inundated with "snowflakes" from Rumsfeld—short memos with questions or thoughts on a wide variety of issues that wafted down into my inbox by the dozen.

Despite the disconnect in our working relationship, my strategic ideas tended to resonate with Rumsfeld. Perhaps for this reason, he asked me if I would like to stay at the Pentagon. I expressed interest in becoming the undersecretary for policy and offered thoughts on how to restructure the policy shop to reflect post–Cold War realities.

Rumsfeld ended up selecting Douglas Feith for the position instead, but he asked me to stay at the Defense Department as a counselor until his senior appointees were confirmed. I agreed.

After the inauguration, I received a call from Libby, who now held the dual titles of the vice president's chief of staff and national security advisor. He asked me whether I was interested in becoming the deputy national security advisor to the vice president. We had a good conversation about how the new system would work. He knew me well, though, and sensed that I was not interested.

I then received a call from Hadley, who had become the deputy national security advisor under Condoleezza Rice. He invited me to come to the White House to discuss a position on the staff of the National Security Council. I knew Hadley well from our days together in the Defense Department under Cheney. Given that Rice was on the RAND board of trustees, I imagine we may have met at some point, but the first time I recall even saying hello to her was when we met in the transition headquarters in December 2000.

Rice suggested that I join her staff to advise on Afghanistan. She gave me a brief synopsis of counterterrorism czar Richard Clarke's ongoing efforts. She wanted me to complement his efforts by formulating a strategy to address the larger problem of terrorism in the region.

We also discussed Iraq. The president and the principals agreed that the United States needed a policy review on how to deal with Saddam. But the Defense Department vetoed the idea of giving the State Department the lead, and neither Defense nor State would give the lead to the NSC's senior director on Iraq, who was detailed from the CIA. When my name came up, no one expressed opposition. My stock thus rose with Rice.

I suggested that my portfolio cover not only Afghanistan and Pakistan, but also a wider set of regional issues. Rice agreed, and I was appointed as the senior director at the NSC for the Gulf, Iraq, Iran, Afghanistan, and some Pakistan issues.

—< >—

BY MAY, I was deeply involved in two major policy reviews, one focused on Iraq and the other on al Qaeda and its sanctuaries in Afghanistan.

In managing the NSC, Rice and Hadley sought consensus among the principals on a single option, which would then be presented to the president. In meetings of the Deputies and Principals Committees, they did not seek to crystallize policy differences into a set of clear choices. Instead, they tried to forge a common outlook through discussions and papers prepared at lower levels. Hadley, in particular, was talented at developing bridging language that moved the process forward. However, I sensed that Rumsfeld, Cheney, and Secretary of State Powell would have preferred to present disagreements and multiple options to the president for decision. Without a clear-cut decision among distinct options, departments and agencies assumed that they were authorized to pursue their preferred courses of action, to the detriment of an integrated strategy. This was reinforced by the president's inclination to delegate and reluctance to micro-manage.

The principals had distinct ways of operating. Powell was not assertive in meetings. He articulated his views clearly and logically, but I don't recall him being confrontational, even on important issues. Rumsfeld always came to meetings with a set of crisp points and was more assertive than Powell in making them. When he was opposed to an action, he raised questions in a way that ensured further deliberation. In debates, he counterpunched effectively. He skillfully kept issues out of the interagency process when he believed that they were the exclusive domain of the Defense Department. This preserved his freedom of action but left some policies without sufficient coordination.

Burh or. Rice

Rice had a unique source of influence—she had such a close relationship with the president that she carried his authority into every meeting. While it took her a little while to become confident in her position, she was fully an equal among more senior and experienced members of the Principals Committee. She had presence and command in these meetings, often announcing at the outset whether a particular session was for "discussion" or "decision." At its conclusion, she would often crystallize in a few points what consensus had emerged, what next steps were needed, and what decisions had been made.

I SAW IN THE Iraq policy review how difficult it was for the United States, even under a new administration, to undertake a bold policy departure in the absence of a crisis or major policy failure. Policymakers tend to live within existing constraints rather than challenging them. Policy reviews tend to conclude with minor revisions of the status quo. This was the story of the Iraq review in 2000.

The situation was troubling. Saddam had been throttled in the Gulf War and Operation Desert Fox but remained belligerent and dangerous. The consensus in the intelligence community was that he had retained stockpiles of chemical weapons and preserved the capability to restart his weapons programs if and when international pressure relented. Support for the sanctions was waning, even among U.S. allies, and Iraq had developed ways to skirt their constraints. U.S. forces continued to enforce no-fly zones in the north and south of Iraq. Efforts to orchestrate a military coup had failed, and the United States was providing only minimal support to Iraqi opposition groups. It was increasingly difficult to keep Saddam "in a box."

The principals brought different concerns to the table. Rumsfeld was concerned about the no-fly zones, given the way they exposed U.S. pilots and aircraft to Iraqi fire. He was troubled by the fact that Iraq was the only country in the world that regularly shot at U.S. forces without suffering significant repercussions. "There's no value from what we're doing," he argued. Rumsfeld was worried that Saddam might surprise us again, perhaps in Kuwait or by developing nuclear weapons. He described options for more extensive air strikes on radar systems and targets nearer to Baghdad, noting that there was never a good time to take stronger action.

Rice raised the possibility of training and arming the Iraqi opposition. All seemed to agree that the Defense Department and the CIA should identify the right people and develop a training plan. Powell said that the Saudis would support direct U.S. action to topple Saddam, but were unlikely to support regime change via an armed Iraqi opposition. Cheney seemed supportive of engaging the Iraqi opposition groups. When Cheney argued that we needed to articulate a policy on the Iraqi opposition, however, Rumsfeld observed that we did not know what was happening internally in Iraq and that "things can fall apart fast." Ultimately, differences over which opposition groups to support were left unaddressed.

Cheney, more generally, argued for making preparations in case Saddam miscalculated. He did not believe that the United States should wait on the world to act. Cheney asked if the only reason to fly aircraft over Iraq was to get intelligence and warning of Iraqi action. If so, why not use other means, such as satellites or U-2s? In the ensuing discussion, military and CIA representatives argued that overflights were still needed and that the intelligence and warning picture was more accurate if drawn from multiple sources. Powell said that we had started the no-fly zones to protect civilians, not to gather intelligence, and that satellites and signals intelligence could keep track of Republican Guard movements. No one would notice if we reduced our flights, he added.

Powell urged the adoption of "smart sanctions"—a narrower list of prohibited weapons and technologies. He believed that Saddam could not restock his conventional weapons in the near future and pointed out that our own intelligence community had assessed that Iraq was five to seven years away from developing nuclear weapons. He did concede, though, that the nuclear time frame would drop to one year if Iraq got fissile material. Powell argued that sanctions were not perfect but that the United States could maintain Russian and regional support with the smart sanctions option.

Early discussions on Iraq left me with the impression that the principals were unsatisfied with the tit-for-tat engagements that currently characterized our Iraq policy but, in terms of adopting a new strategy, were not even united on the goals we should be prioritizing. Did we want to contain Saddam or press for regime change? Did we want to increase pressure or reduce it through narrower sanctions and less activity in the no-fly zones? I knew that, in the absence of clear guidance from the principals, it would be difficult to develop robust policy recommendations at my level.

In the Deputies Committee, the State Department pressed for smart sanctions. State argued that the costs of pursuing regime change outweighed the benefits. Instead, the United States should modify the existing containment regime.

The Defense Department and vice president's office viewed the issue differently. They argued that Iraq was a looming threat—one that continued to grow as the containment regime against Saddam weakened. They doubted that the international community had the desire or will to keep pressure on

Saddam. That the Iraqi regime continued to seek weapons of mass destruction and support terrorism, they warned, only exacerbated the threat.

Representatives of the Pentagon and the vice president argued for an invigorated policy of regime change, though not a full-scale invasion. Instead, they urged that the United States increase support for the Iraqi opposition, create U.S.-enforced safe havens in Shia-dominated southern Iraq similar to the ones in the Kurdish north, and recognize a provisional government for areas of Iraq outside of Saddam's control.

With no policy agreement among the major players—either on goals or strategy—my NSC colleagues and I drafted a tactical paper with an escalating three-step plan for liberating Iraq. As a starting point, it called for taking advantage of the Iraq Liberation Act by allocating all of the assistance to the Iraqi opposition that Congress had already made available. The next step would involve arming the opposition. The final measure would entail direct U.S. military action to protect southern Iraq, weaken Saddam, and foment an uprising.

When we first presented the proposal to Hadley, he was understandably reluctant to endorse it without a presidential decision on U.S. goals in Iraq. But the plan's key elements were eventually incorporated into an NSC paper entitled "A Liberation Strategy," which the principals received in early August 2001. The document laid out a series of options short of a full-scale invasion that the president could consider if he decided to topple Saddam's regime.

In the absence of a clear decision, however, the option of smart sanctions carried the day by default, and the enforcement of the no-fly zones continued largely unchanged.

◄ ►

ON THE AFGHANISTAN FRONT, it was clear by this point that al Qaeda posed a serious threat. Despite the link between the Taliban and al Qaeda, however, no consensus had emerged on how to handle the Taliban regime. The State Department had not even designated Afghanistan as a state sponsor of terrorism. The U.S. agenda toward the Taliban in the Clinton administration had largely revolved around disparate functional issues—drug production, women's rights, religious freedom, and other human rights concerns.

Rice assigned the issue to a working group led by Clarke, and I became a regular participant. A self-confident civil servant, Clarke approached the terrorism issue with an unusual level of urgency. He knew the subject thoroughly, recognized the gravity of the threat, and presented his side forcefully. Clarke offered good recommendations for increasing pressure on al Qaeda, principally by hitting targets in Afghanistan.

Clarke's working group discussed a wide variety of options: deploying intelligence and military assets to Central Asia, using Predator drones to strike targets in Afghanistan, increasing pressure on the Taliban to separate from al Qaeda, and engaging the Northern Alliance. Our work was designed to produce two things: a draft national security presidential directive on al Qaeda and a multiyear strategy to address the terrorist sanctuary in Afghanistan.

As the process moved forward, I worked with Rice more closely, particularly when I sat in on her meetings with foreign leaders. I was impressed with her approach in these sessions. She conveyed her points with authority, and her interlocutors would have no doubt that she spoke for the president. I sometimes thought that her counterparts, who mostly came from male-dominated political systems, were taken aback by her confidence and directness. Unlike many senior officials I have known, Rice was effective in delivering a tough message. She generally had an ingratiating and positive disposition. As she prepared to make a tough point, her countenance changed—she leaned forward slightly and, while smiling, made clear her unhappiness. Her point made, she would then ease off or counterpunch as needed.

As part of the Afghanistan policy review, I sat in on a meeting between Rice and Pakistani foreign minister Abdul Sattar. Rice pointed out that Pakistan's Taliban allies were harboring al Qaeda and other dangerous groups. Incredibly, Sattar denied that any terrorist bases existed at all. I found it troubling, and revealing, that Sattar felt at liberty to speak not just for Pakistan but also for Afghanistan. Rice made clear that U.S. relations with Pakistan would depend in part on Islamabad's confronting this issue.

I followed up with Sattar over a private breakfast at the Omni Sheraton Hotel. I had developed a cordial relationship with Sattar, a sophisticated and worldly diplomat, during the 1990s. I hoped that he would be candid with me in a less formal meeting.

"What the hell are you doing denying all of this stuff?" I asked him. Sattar suggested that the United States should come to terms with "reality." The Taliban, he insisted, was here to stay. We should open a diplomatic channel with them and negotiate rather than pursuing a confrontational policy. Sattar didn't view the Taliban as a fundamentalist threat. Instead, he spoke of the regime with a mix of paternalism, condescension, and disdain, as if the Taliban were little more than a sorry, backward people in need of assistance.

As the policy review proceeded, I focused on formulating a political strategy to break the nexus among al Qaeda, the Taliban regime, and their sponsors in Pakistan. I agreed that counterterrorism should be an urgent priority, but argued that it should be one part of a broader strategy to address the Taliban's control over Afghanistan.

As a first step, I suggested that the United States help to forge a broad-based coalition of Afghan forces against the Taliban.

— ⟩

BY THE SUMMER of 2001 I was cautiously optimistic that a broad-based opposition was emerging against the Taliban. Massoud had dispatched his senior political advisor, Younus Qanooni, to open a dialogue with the king in Rome. Given the long, bitter rivalry between Massoud and Zahir Shah's entourage in Rome—one grounded in both personal and political animosities—I took Massoud's outreach as a sign of his seriousness.

I met with Abdullah Abdullah about the opposition's activities throughout the summer of 2001. Abdullah descended from a long line of high-ranking government officials dating back to the Emirate of Afghanistan, which ruled the country from the end of the Durrani Empire in 1823 until Amanullah seized power in 1926. His father split his distinguished career between Kandahar and Kabul, culminating in an appointment to the Senate by Zahir Shah. Abdullah, whose mother was Tajik, would later play up his mixed ethnic identity and his roots in both Kandahar and Kabul. Having spent the early phase of his career as an ophthalmologist, he fled Kabul in 1986 before resettling in Peshawar, where he continued to practice medicine in a hospital for Afghan refugees. During this period, he became a confidant of Massoud, forming a relationship that eventually catapulted him to the position of spokesman and then foreign minister of the Northern Alliance. After I left the Reagan administration, Abdullah and I became friends and stayed in close touch.

When he visited Washington, Abdullah was encouraged that senior Bush administration officials were receiving his delegation. The terms of the debate were changing in Washington more generally, with Congress passing nonbinding resolutions condemning the Taliban for its excesses against cultural sites, women, and minorities. Cheryl and I had become increasingly involved with these issues in the late 1990s. Alex, who had once written a fan letter to Jay Leno and had been excited to receive a signed photograph in return, was convinced that one of his cousins was playing a prank on him when Jay called our house to discuss his wife Mavis's campaign for Afghan women. They were halfway through what must have been quite a comical call when Alex finally realized that this truly was his idol on the line.

Abdullah was concerned about the administration's delays in formulating a comprehensive Afghanistan policy. He pushed for the United States to provide greater military assistance to the opposition and to distribute humanitarian assistance across the country. But what the opposition needed from the United States more than anything, Abdullah maintained, was political recognition as a legitimate resistance movement.

In the summer of 2001, Massoud agreed to get behind Zahir Shah's efforts to convene a *Loya Jirga*. This was noteworthy. Upon hearing about Massoud's commitment, the king approved the establishment of a *Loya Jirga* office at a neutral site outside Rome. Massoud and Karzai, meanwhile, were developing a framework for military cooperation.

Alarmed by Karzai's agitation against the Taliban, the Pakistani ISI demanded that he leave Pakistan by the end of September. With Karzai facing a deadline, Massoud offered to make arrangements for him in northern Afghanistan. Massoud hoped that he and Karzai could jointly launch anti-Taliban offensives from Northern Alliance territory while they developed a more robust Pashtun opposition in the south.

A concerted strategy between the United States and the anti-Taliban opposition was now coming into focus.

— ◄ ► —

AS THE SUMMER wore on, my counterparts at State and the CIA became increasingly concerned about the terrorist threat in Afghanistan. There was growing support for strengthening the Northern Alliance as an instrument against al Qaeda. However, I was still having trouble generating interest in my ideas on a broader political strategy against the Taliban.

We thought through various options. One was to pursue a deal with the Taliban in which the regime broke with al Qaeda and transformed to be more inclusive. If we went down this path, I thought we needed a stronger relationship with the Northern Alliance. We also needed to bolster the Rome Group or create a Pashtun alternative to the Taliban. Alternatively, if a deal proved infeasible, I believed the United States had to consider regime change, principally by working with the Northern Alliance and Pashtuns in exile.

I did not see my approach as coming at the expense of counterterrorism actions. An analogy was later made that compared Afghanistan to a swamp infested by mosquitoes. Those who wanted to focus on killing bugs favored counterterrorist policies. I also wanted to drain the swamp that was enabling the mosquitoes to breed. This required us to transform or replace the Taliban regime.

My reading of Afghan history told me that we had to create a broad-based opposition movement to succeed the Taliban. We could not rely on the Northern Alliance alone. Pashtuns, the largest ethnic group in Afghanistan, have been a dominant political force in the country since the seventh century. Nearly every Afghan leader in the last three centuries has been a Pashtun. I was concerned that too strong an American tilt toward the Northern Alliance could undermine efforts to mobilize the Pashtun opposition. That opposition was crucial, because the Taliban had come to power principally with Pashtun support.

Though Rice agreed with my preference for building a broad-based resistance to the Taliban, others in the interagency were less enthusiastic. It was not that they opposed Pashtun outreach. Rather, with the threat from al Qaeda growing, they viewed the Northern Alliance as the faction most capable of taking on bin Laden's network in Afghanistan. They doubted that the Pashtun opposition had the wherewithal and coherence to pose an effective challenge. They also feared that a sustained outreach effort aimed at the Pashtuns would hinder and delay American cooperation with the Northern Alliance.

Clarke's working group also discussed how to address Pakistan's role in the Afghanistan problem. Pakistan was the only country with an embassy in Kabul, and Pakistani military officers provided training, advice, and materiel to the Taliban regime. Embedded advisors helped frontline Taliban units fight the Northern Alliance. We had incontrovertible intelligence about al Qaeda camps near Kabul and Jalalabad.

ON SEPTEMBER 9 Abdullah called me. When I picked up the receiver, I knew immediately that Massoud had been killed. Abdullah's voice was quivering, a departure from his typical calm. He told me that two al Qaeda operatives, posing as reporters, had detonated a bomb hidden inside their camera. He said that Massoud was badly wounded but alive. He called again a short while later and confirmed that Massoud was dead.

I feared the worst. I was certain that, with Massoud out of the picture, the Taliban would wage a renewed offensive to destroy the Northern Alliance. Karzai was devastated by Massoud's death. He resolved to cross into Afghanistan and lead a Pashtun insurrection against the Taliban. With Karzai outgunned by the Taliban and in defiance of the ISI, I did not expect the mission to end well.

I was deeply concerned and wondered if the proposals we had developed in our extensive policy review were still viable. Clarke's working group had recently completed a draft national security presidential directive outlining a plan to "eliminate al Qaeda." It proposed a comprehensive multiyear strategy involving covert action, aid to anti-Taliban movements, and efforts to curtail terrorist financing.

We had also developed a three-phase strategy to deal with the Taliban. First, an American envoy would deliver an ultimatum to the regime demanding that it sever ties with al Qaeda. If the Taliban did not cooperate, the United States would increase covert aid to all anti-Taliban factions with an eye toward stalemating the Afghan civil war and using indigenous forces to attack al Qaeda bases. Meanwhile, the United States would take stronger steps to galvanize an international coalition to isolate the Taliban. If these two steps failed, the third phase called for overthrowing the Taliban through covert contacts within the regime's leadership structure.

The Deputies Committee approved the plan on September 10. On September 11, the national security presidential directive was undergoing final preparations for the president's signature.

TEN

AMERICA UNDER ATTACK

WASHINGTON, D.C., SEPTEMBER 2001

I WAS ALREADY DISCOURAGED WHEN I WALKED INTO THE SITUATION ROOM EARLY ON the morning of September 11. Losing Massoud was a devastating blow to the anti-Taliban effort, both in practical terms, because he was a gifted military strategist, and psychologically, because he was a revered and iconic figure. I had spent the previous evening on the phone with Abdullah and others in Afghanistan, seeking to understand the implications of Massoud's death for the anti-Taliban opposition.

Now, as I entered the Situation Room just after 9 a.m., the NSC senior staff was talking about some plane that had just crashed into the north tower of the World Trade Center. They assumed that a small plane had been involved in a freak accident. Rice entered and took her seat at the head of the table. I sat to her left, next to Clarke and across from Hadley.

As I was reporting on the situation in Afghanistan and what we knew about the Massoud assassination, an assistant from the White House Operations Center handed Rice a message. She abruptly closed the portfolio of papers in front of her, stood up, and announced, "We need to go." A second plane had crashed into the south tower of the World Trade Center, she told us. It was clear that we were under attack. She and Clarke left.

The rest of us hurried back to our respective offices to consult with our staffs and get more information. There had been a terror attack—that much seemed clear—but who was behind it? I phoned Cheryl, and we agreed to stay in touch as facts emerged.

Back in my office, the staff gathered anxiously around the TV, where smoke could now be seen coming out of both towers. I asked Philip Mudd, an expert on terrorism who was part of my staff, to check whether the CIA had any additional knowledge about this attack. Before he could reply, the loud-speaker rattled to life. "Evacuate the building immediately," the announcer said. Fearing that the White House might be the next target, we left through the Northwest Gate and congregated on the street between the White House and Lafayette Park. Rumors about additional possible attacks were circulating in the confused but surprisingly calm crowd of perhaps 100 White House employees. At about 9:45 a.m., we learned that a plane had struck the Pentagon. I had been working there until just a few months earlier, and I tried to reach my friends to find out if they were all right. Someone said that still another plane might be heading toward the White House or the Capitol.

Cheryl was now frantically trying to reach me. Having also figured out that the White House was a likely next target, she wanted to issue her own evacuation directive. But by this time the phone lines were completely over-loaded. Amid the uncertainty, the White House sent out instructions that we should all go home.

I was finally able to get through to Alex at Georgetown University to tell him I was okay and was coming to pick him up. I collected him from outside the gate of Georgetown. As we drove home, Alex remarked on how eerie the drive felt, with hardly a car on the road. Air traffic had also ceased by then, and the skies too were spookily silent.

At home, we all positioned ourselves in front of the television, and watched and rewatched the horrific scenes. We also compared notes on our respective days. I related how the White House staff had just milled about in the park, periodically ducking into nearby hotels to watch television and get updates. Everyone's cell phone had been out as we all fruitlessly dialed our families on hopelessly overburdened cell phone networks. There had been no proper emergency plan to tell the staff where to go and what to do, something that would change in spades in the months and years to come—in fact, Cheryl's brother Charlie would become a leading expert on "continuity of govern-ment." Cheryl had just dropped Max off at school when the news came over the car radio, and she had been so shocked and engrossed that she missed her exit and circled the Beltway aimlessly for the next half hour. Alex and some fellow students had stood disbelievingly at a window and watched the smoke billow from the Pentagon. In a sense the experience of Max, our youngest, was the most evocative. His first hint of something wrong, he told us, had come when he saw the older kids playing with unusual vigor during break, pretending to be a SWAT team and shouting that some building had been invaded in the city and they were going to go in on a rescue mission. It wasn't a game they usually played, and it seemed silly for their age. Then more signs had suggested something weird or wrong. The adults were whispering to each other and looking concerned, but still there had been no word on what happened, just a spreading sense of disorder. His next class was taught by Mrs. Heep, whose husband worked at the Pentagon, and she had been visibly distraught and had given her class the first real report on what had happened. It had been vague, either because that was all she knew or because it was all she felt comfortable telling such young children; she had just said that a plane had crashed into some government offices. This had been highly alarming for Max, who knew that my work took me to many of those exact buildings. But Cheryl had arrived shortly thereafter to pick him up, and had told him she had spoken to me and that I was fine. Now, at home, the full story of New York and the Twin Towers and the airplane brought down by passengers was unfolding.

In the early evening, I headed back to the office. I checked the intelligence traffic and forwarded what little was coming in to Rice. Most of the reports focused on how the attacks were being perceived abroad. There was an overwhelming outpouring of sympathy for the United States around the world. In the Middle East, the reaction was more mixed, but even in Iran, rallies were held to express support and sympathy for America.

Al Qaeda soon emerged as the prime suspect. That night on TV, President Bush laid out the administration's counterterrorism strategy. In what would become known as the first element of the Bush Doctrine, he vowed: "We will make no distinction between those who planned these acts and those who harbor them."

Cheryl and Max had watched the speech, sitting on the bed together with Griffin curled up at their feet. When Cheryl asked Max what he thought of the president's remarks, he thought for a moment and then answered: "It made me feel safe." That was quite a compliment.

———<   >———

EXHAUSTED BUT PROPELLED forward by adrenaline and determination, we gathered the next day with Rice, who set forth new divisions of responsibilities among the NSC staff. Every morning at 6:30, we would begin with a core group meeting, led by Rice and Hadley. We would review and discuss the war against al Qaeda, contacts made in the field by the CIA, and the morning briefing for the president.

I was grateful to be in a position where I could help come to terms with the threat. We all saw the response to the 9/11 attacks as a defining challenge for the United States. I wanted to contribute what I could to getting it right.

But as a senior NSC staffer, I also had to attend hours and hours of highly technical meetings, focusing on many issues outside my expertise, such as the vulnerabilities of chemical facilities, government agencies, and stock markets. I learned that even in a crisis of the first order, the bureaucratic process had an unbendable logic of its own: only senior staff could attend these meetings, so there was no delegating. Sitting at the conference table, I remember being envious of Josh Bolten. The deputy White House chief of staff also had to attend the meetings, but he sat in a chair along the back wall, where he was able to discreetly get other work done.

Rice asked me to review a memo on links between Iraq and al Qaeda. Based on the intelligence in front of me, I concurred with the analysts that there was only anecdotal evidence pointing to Iraqi connections with al Qaeda.

A week after 9/11, however, the delivery of anthrax-laden letters to U.S. media organizations and congressional offices underscored the myriad terrorist threats we faced.

While I did my best to support the president's immediate priorities, my mind was on longer-term issues. As the president had said during his remarks on September 11, a serious response to terrorism would have to address both terrorist networks and their state sponsors. With the most egregious state sponsors of terrorism in my NSC portfolio, I set to work on shaping this response. And though administration officials were reluctant to say so explicitly, the United States would have no choice but to confront the religious and ideological underpinnings of Islamist extremism. In this sense, the attacks of 9/11 had forced the United States to confront the crisis of Islamic civilization.

THE 9/11 ATTACKS naturally drew attention to the religion of Islam and to the country of Afghanistan. Attentive to the risks of an anti-Muslim backlash, the president praised Islam as a "religion of peace" and engaged Muslim American groups in well-publicized events. I was the highest-ranking Afghan American and Muslim American at the White House. Ironically, though, I did not get the impression that the president and his senior staff immediately recognized the significance of my background. Perhaps people wondered how I felt about the fact that terrorists of my faith had attacked the country and that the United States might go to war against the country of my birth. If they did, no one raised the issue with me. I certainly did not get the sense that people were more guarded with their thoughts around me. Most people, I believe, were of the same mind-set as Wolfowitz, who later told the *New York Times:* "We were a week into this crisis before it hit me that Zal was from Afghanistan."

The initial lack of attention to my background on the part of U.S. officials stood in marked contrast to the instincts of our foreign counterparts. My NSC colleague Torkel Patterson told me that in his conversations with diplomats in East Asia, there was a great deal of interest in my ethnic heritage. While they generally knew that I was a Sunni Muslim, they wondered whether I was Pashtun, Uzbek, Tajik, Hazara, or something else. They seemed to think that this knowledge would help them understand where my real loyalties stood.

President Bush feared a wave of anti-Muslim violence, so he decided to express solidarity with Muslim Americans at the main mosque in Washington on September 17. The president declared: "Islam is peace. These terrorists don't represent peace. They represent evil and war."

In later years, President Bush was criticized for sugarcoating the true nature of the Islamist challenge. In my interactions with the president, however, I never got the impression that he was under any illusions about the Islamist threat. Rather, my sense is that his statements had a political and strategic purpose. He did not conflate mainstream Muslims with extremists and their terrorist offshoots. In the tense climate after 9/11, he wanted to reassure Muslim Americans that they would not be scapegoated for the attacks. And in the global war, the president wanted to isolate Islamist terrorists from mainstream Muslims and encourage Muslim majorities to stand up against the extremists. Although I would have preferred for President Bush to speak with more precision about Islam's crisis of civilization, I think his rhetoric, given the context and climate, served its purpose.

AS THE ADMINISTRATION shifted from crisis management to developing a longer-term strategy for the region, the president began to consult me with greater frequency. Some in the press began referring to me as "Bush's favorite Afghan," even pointing to my earlier writing on Afghanistan as a harbinger of where U.S. policy was heading.

Within days of the attacks, the president and his advisors turned to me as they grappled with how to explain the threat to the American people. In his address to a joint session of Congress, President Bush wanted to help Americans understand the basics: Who is al Qaeda? Why did they attack us? What is the extent of the threat? How will we respond? Karen Hughes, the president's counselor, was not satisfied with early drafts. Having served as the Bush campaign's communications director, she had an acute sense of what message would resonate with the American people.

In seeking to describe an unknown enemy, she sensed that it would be helpful for the president to highlight its cruelty in vivid terms. At Rice's suggestion, Hughes asked me what life was like in Afghanistan under the Taliban. The president ultimately used some of my vignettes in his September 20 address: "In Afghanistan, we see al Qaeda's vision for the world. Afghanistan's people have been brutalized; many are starving and many have fled. Women are not allowed to attend school. You can be jailed for owning a television. Religion can be practiced only as their leaders dictate. A man can be jailed in Afghanistan if his beard is not long enough." The message let the American public see what life was like for ordinary Afghan citizens under the thumb of the Taliban. It resonated.

I became better acquainted with the president during this period and got to interact with him in a variety of contexts. I sensed that the enemy's brutality had affected him at a personal level. Even in the darkest moments of the war effort, President Bush never seemed to waver in his conviction that we held the moral high ground. The president's will to win the war against extremism never flagged, and it bolstered those of us around him.

THE PRESIDENT ALSO reached out to me as he worked to gain a better understanding of Afghanistan and the greater Middle East. For many in the Bush administration, it was a steep learning curve. While the president's foreign policy team collectively brought with them decades of experience, none of the principals and very few senior presidential appointees had a feel for the histories, cultures, and emotions that drove the politics of the broader Muslim world. This reality was compounded by the dearth of expertise within the permanent bureaucracy. As a general matter, promotion cycles among career professionals in the Foreign Service and military tend to discourage specialization. In the context of the war on terrorism, the problem was especially acute, since many veterans of the Soviet-Afghan period had retired, while a whole generation of South Asia experts had come of age during a period when the U.S. government had neither an embassy in Kabul nor deep bilateral relations with Pakistan and the Central Asian states.

A few weeks after his address to Congress, the president asked me to join him at Camp David over the weekend to discuss the Middle East. Rice and White House chief of staff Andrew Card were also there. When I arrived, I was shown into a big room with a card table to one side, where the president was sitting with his back toward me. He was looking at a map of Afghanistan spread out on a large oak table.

I sat down in the study area and began reading that morning's edition of the *Washington Post*, only to be jolted by a slap on the back. I should have expected it—it had become a source of amusement for the president to joggle me to attention. A few days earlier, I had been walking along a corridor in the West Wing, lost in thought, when the president snuck up from behind and grabbed my collar. "Hey, Zal, what are you doing?" he asked now. "Trying to find out what's going on in the world," I replied. He shot back, "You won't find that out by reading the *Washington Post!*"

We settled down in a plush and airy room with a comfortable couch and sitting area. The president asked me to give an overview of the challenges we faced in the region. For the next couple of hours, we discussed the history of Afghanistan and the problems of the wider Muslim world. The president's early briefings on Afghanistan had left him with a rather negative impression. As he recalls in his memoir, "Everything about the country screamed trouble." So he was surprised when I described the Afghan monarchy and told him about the relative progress and stability that Zahir Shah's government had achieved.

I could tell that he had been influenced by the prevailing wisdom at the CIA. The standard narrative from agency analysts essentially held that Afghanistan had never been a well-functioning state, that the country was generally a collection of tribes, and that its ethnic groups had little loyalty to the nation as a whole.

I told the president that the CIA's narrative was not quite right. I explained that even during periods when internal conflict had threatened to fragment the country, a strong sense of Afghan national identity had kept the diverse ethnic groups together. This was not another Yugoslavia, where communities wanted to live as separate countries. Afghan identity and nationalism were powerful.

I explained that over the nineteenth and twentieth centuries, Afghanistan had been governed from Kabul, sometimes by a relatively strong, centralized state and at other times by a national government that ruled through local leaders. The late nineteenth century was a high-water mark of central authority, when Abdur Rahman Khan, the "Iron Emir," pronounced himself the highest religious authority of the nation and deployed his army to impose order on recalcitrant clerical and tribal factions. I described Afghanistan's successful history of incremental state and nation building from 1929 until the Soviet invasion in 1979—a period Afghans now call the "Era of Tranquility." It was true that the country was poor and traditional, particularly in rural areas, but it had enjoyed a half century of internal peace, gradual economic growth, and democratic reforms. It had effective institutions, such as a national army, police, and civil administration. I told the president about the educational opportunities I had enjoyed as the Afghan government sought to strengthen ties with the industrialized world.

The president asked the overarching question on his mind. What had gone wrong in the Islamic world? Why the rise of terrorist groups like al Qaeda? Naturally drawn to big-picture thinking, he had zeroed in on the vital question. I was encouraged that he had conceptualized the magnitude of the crisis.

I took a stab at an answer by telling the president that the Islamic world was gripped by a crisis of civilization. Muslims could not understand how their civilization had fallen from its zenith in the fifteenth century, when Islamic empires ruled from Spain in the West to modern-day India in the East and when Islamic civilization led the world in education, development, science, and philosophy.

"It was a civilization on the march," I said.

"Now, come on, Zal!" the president interrupted teasingly, suspecting that I was exaggerating for effect.

Card intervened, "I think Zal is referring to the Ottoman Empire."

I gently noted that Ottoman rule came later and represented still another period of Islamic expansion under the Turks. The apex of Islamic civilization, I reminded them, had come earlier, under Arab leadership. The history of Muslim Spain was a glorious one—a thriving, multicultural society, with scholars translating the great works of the Greeks into Arabic. The civilization at the time welcomed learning. Baghdad, I mentioned, had been home to a major university over a thousand years ago.

But then, I continued, Islamic civilization had entered a period of rapid and cataclysmic decline. The West, supported by the achievements of the Renaissance and the rise of reason in the Enlightenment, overtook the Islamic world within a short period of time and had stayed in the lead ever since.

Reflecting on this fall, Islamic thinkers and leaders were polarized about what to do. Modernists argued that the Islamic world needed to imitate what worked for the West. Leaders in Turkey had gone so far as to embrace secularism, declaring Sunday the day of rest and adopting Western customs and dress. For this group, the key was to study why the West had prevailed, learn its lessons, and adopt them. Yet from Egypt to Syria to Iraq, modernist leaders largely failed to deliver progress or restore greatness.

These failures led to a search for new answers. Some claimed that Islamic civilization had declined due to impiety. Fundamentalists argued that Muslims had abandoned true Islam and that greatness could come only with a return to the faith. Traditionalists countered by contending that salvation required a blending of Islam and modernity. Islam was vital as a matter of personal faith, but society needed to be modern in the ways of the world.

I related how this debate among modernists, traditionalists, and fundamentalists had unfolded over time. In the latter half of the twentieth century, fundamentalism not only prevailed in its Shia form in the Iranian Revolution but also became the most dynamic political force in many Sunni societies. The Afghan victory over the Soviet Union further energized Islamist groups across the Middle East.

I concluded with a prediction: while fundamentalists were unlikely to deliver for their people, the period between their rise and eventual defeat would be long and bloody.

The United States was the unfortunate target of a great civilization's dysfunction and fallout. Something comparable had happened during the nineteenth and twentieth centuries, when the principal source of global problems emanated from Europe. Imperialism, fascism, and Marxism-Leninism resulted in violence around the world. It took two world wars and the Cold War to address the dysfunction of the region. In the beginning of the twenty-first century, the principal source of security problems had shifted to the greater Middle East.

For the Bush administration, Afghanistan was the immediate challenge. However, the wider and inescapable challenge involved working with moderates in Muslim-majority countries. The United States could not solve the problem alone, but we could help like-minded partners overcome the underlying crisis of civilization that had given rise to the attacks of 9/11.

The president was quiet. Whether he was lost in deep thought or shocked by the magnitude of the challenge ahead, I could not tell.

≼ ELEVEN ≽

A QUEST FOR LEADERS IN TYRANNY'S SHADOW

WASHINGTON, D.C., AND BONN, GERMANY, SEPTEMBER–DECEMBER 2001

ONCE IT BECAME CLEAR THAT TALIBAN LEADER MULLAH OMAR WOULD NOT BREAK with al Qaeda and cooperate with the United States, the Bush administration started to plan for post-Taliban Afghanistan. At the NSC, Rice divided postwar planning responsibilities between Frank Miller, the senior director for defense policy, and me.

Looking back, it is remarkable how seamlessly decisions were made. In deliberations over postwar Iraq, many of the same issues ended up producing contentious interagency debates even at a conceptual level.

Yet despite the lack of real philosophical disagreements, the administration produced a mixed record in planning for post-Taliban Afghanistan. On the positive side, the president and principals accepted the concept that we developed for a postwar transition—a U.N.-led political process to create a representative government. Though the principals were still reluctant to involve the United States in nation building, the deputies were more forward-looking. Hadley ensured that preparations were being made to organize an international donors conference, launch key infrastructure projects, and provide basic health and educational services.

The problem was that the president and principals were not pressing the departments to prepare for the actual logistics of installing and supporting a new government. In the absence of a concrete plan, they had different assumptions about the role we would play.

As the United States planned for military operations, I spoke with leaders of the Afghan opposition. I knew most of them from my time in the Reagan administration, though my relationships with some dated back to my days as a student. Amid the uncertainty after 9/11, many of my longtime Afghan acquaintances reached out to me proactively. For most of the opposition figures, I was the only connection they had to the Bush administration and the only one with whom they felt some rapport. I was also one of the few who could communicate with them without an interpreter.

The flurry of phone calls that I was receiving from Afghans drew notice within the administration. When President Bush saw me at the White House Christmas party later that year, his eyes lit up. "Zal!" he said, turning to Laura Bush. "This is the guy I was talking to you about. All the Afghans call him!"

Rice and Hadley were firmly against having NSC staff carrying out policy in an operational capacity. The lesson had been ingrained in them since the Iran-Contra scandal, when NSC staffers, handling military and diplomatic operations, nearly brought down the Reagan administration. Hadley and Rice believed in the Scowcroft model of NSC management, in which operations are left to the secretaries of state and defense.

Seeing my contacts, however, they made an exception in my case. It became my responsibility to help the president monitor the situation through a separate channel from the typical State Department, Pentagon, and CIA filters.

When Northern Alliance representative Haroon Amin arrived at the White House, I notified him that the United States would provide arms to the opposition. Amin was elated. As Massoud's ambassador in Washington, he had struggled to get U.S. attention. The issue of arms had been a particular source of frustration for the Northern Alliance. CIA officers had previously approached Massoud to request his help in tracking down bin Laden, yet they refused to provide the military assistance needed to carry out the mission.

─── ───

THE ATTACK AGAINST al Qaeda in Afghanistan and the Taliban regime started on October 7, 2001. As the war got under way, I essentially served as an additional check on our operations, ensuring that they were being implemented properly. In this context, my conversations with Afghan resistance leaders generally were not strategic or political. I was mostly helping to ensure that money and weapons were arriving as expected.

I remember one conversation I had with Dostum that demonstrated how effectively we were working with our Afghan partners. He and his fighters had cornered a large group of Taliban near the northeastern city of Kunduz. He told me that he had been using a megaphone to negotiate with enemy commanders, urging them to surrender. When the Taliban were unresponsive, he warned them that he would call in air strikes. He turned to the embedded Special Forces, who radioed bombers overhead. As they spoke with the U.S. pilots, Dostum noticed that the voices were female. He immediately asked the soldiers whether he could broadcast their voices to the enemy positions, which they proceeded to do. After the air strikes, Dostum shouted to the Taliban: "The bombing you just received was done by one of their women. Imagine what their men can do!"

Dostum told me the Taliban surrendered shortly thereafter.

By mid-November, Northern Alliance forces were closing in on Kabul. The Bush administration was now divided on whether the Northern Alliance should move on Kabul. Powell proposed two options: either the United States should turn the capital over to United Nations or Organization of the Islamic Conference peacekeepers; or it should fine-tune the war strategy such that the Northern Alliance and empowered Pashtun forces would liberate the city jointly. Militia commanders had looted the city when they entered Kabul in 1992, and Powell feared that a Northern Alliance occupation of the capital would alienate Pashtun opposition forces.

Cheney and Rumsfeld pushed back against the idea of restraining the Northern Alliance. They wanted to deliver a quick and devastating blow to the al Qaeda terrorist network in Afghanistan, overthrow the Taliban, and send a message of resolve to other state sponsors of terrorism around the world.

Eventually the principals reached a compromise. The United States would bomb Taliban front lines and aid the Northern Alliance's march toward Kabul. In return, Fahim, who had taken over the Northern Alliance after Massoud's death, promised that their forces would not take Kabul before international peacekeepers arrived. On November 10, President Bush told the press that the United States would not encourage the Northern Alliance to take Kabul.

I thought the compromise had missed the point. Concerns over the Northern Alliance seizing Kabul unilaterally were legitimate. Yet the State and CIA prescription—forestalling the liberation of Kabul—struck me as unrealistic and imprudent. It would take at least a few months to build up a United Nations and/or Pashtun force and deploy it near Kabul. In the meantime, I did not see how the United States, with limited troops on the ground, could pre-vent the Northern Alliance from capturing a target as enticing as the nation's capital. It would have been better, in my view, if the U.S. had secured early buy-in from the main factions on a political transition.

I was not surprised when events on the ground overtook the compromise. On November 13, the Taliban retreated from Kabul. Faced with the choice of leaving the city ungoverned or moving in to secure it, Northern Alliance forces peacefully descended into Kabul.

WHEN KABUL FELL, the Bush administration was still at an early phase in its postwar planning efforts. It was only in late October that Powell named James Dobbins as his special envoy with the task of negotiating a post-Taliban politi-cal compact. A Foreign Service officer who had served as an envoy to Kosovo, Bosnia, Haiti, and Somalia, Dobbins was perhaps the U.S. government's most knowledgeable expert on post-conflict stabilization and reconstruction. The rapid fall of the Taliban barely gave Dobbins a few weeks to get organized. But with his understanding of state and nation building and of bureaucratic poli-tics within our government, Dobbins made progress. As he made the rounds in Washington, I briefed him on Afghan politics and the key players with whom he would be working.

The United Nations proved useful in advancing the transition. Dobbins and I met with various officials in New York to get their buy-in for a transi-tional process. Lakhdar Brahimi, the United Nations special representative for Afghanistan, worked smoothly with his American counterparts. On Novem-ber 14, the Security Council adopted Resolution 1378. The resolution called for the convening of a United Nations–led political conference of Afghan leaders in late November to establish a transitional administration, which in turn would midwife a broad-based, representative government in Afghanistan.

I envisioned a compact between the main Afghan opposition groups. Above all, this would require an understanding between the Northern Alli-ance and the Pashtun elements of Afghanistan.

I pushed for a proactive U.S. effort to cultivate relationships with Pashtun groups. In the short term, I thought it would ease the war effort by under-cutting the Taliban's appeal to Pashtun nationalism. Pashtun fighters led by Karzai, Gul Agha Sherzai, and Abdul Rahim Wardak were liberating areas in the south and east. Gains against the Taliban, I thought, could be accelerated if Pashtuns were part of an inclusive political process.

Longer term, I did not think the United States could rely solely on the Northern Alliance to govern Afghanistan. As the largest ethnic group in the country, Pashtuns were the key power brokers of Afghanistan. No government had ever survived in Afghanistan without support among the Pashtuns—a historical pattern that the United States could not challenge with a light military footprint. At the same time, it was equally clear that the Pashtuns would not be able to govern alone as they had done in the past.

In my conversations with Northern Alliance leaders, I sought their buy-in for an inclusive political arrangement after the fall of the Taliban. My interlocutors, including Abdullah, Qanooni, and Fahim, emphasized that they had learned their lesson from the fighting in the 1990s. They understood that they could not govern alone and were prepared to support a broad-based government.

I approached Pashtun leaders with a different message. I told them that the United States wanted the Pashtuns to have a fair role in the post-Taliban transition. I suggested, however, that this could only happen if Pashtuns leaders earned the support of both the Afghan people and the international community. I reminded them that the Northern Alliance's stronger organization and consistent opposition to the Taliban had endeared them to the international community.

When I spoke to Zahir Shah, he reiterated that he was willing to assist in unifying the opposition and guiding the post-Taliban transition. But he disavowed any interest in serving as a head of state. I had been encouraged when, in early October, the king hosted a gathering that included key Northern Alliance figures such as Massoud's brother Ahmed Zia. The opposition at that time had created a joint council of anti-Taliban groups.

One of the obstacles to our plan for a broad-based government, however, was Rabbani. An ethnic Tajik from northern Afghanistan, Rabbani had risen to prominence as a leading scholar of Islam at Kabul University. In the course of his academic studies, he had developed ties to the Muslim Brotherhood in Egypt when he studied at Al Azhar. Rabbani helped spread the work of Sayyid Qutb—the intellectual godfather of Islamism—throughout Afghanistan. Since 9/11, Rabbani had been jockeying to reassert himself as president in Kabul, a position that he had held as the country descended into civil war in the early 1990s. When the Northern Alliance took Kabul, Rabbani resettled into the presidential palace.

At a Principals Committee meeting shortly after the fall of Kabul, we discussed how to deal with Rabbani. I interjected, "I can call Rabbani if you want." This turned heads. My colleagues were startled to learn that I had his phone number.

When I later called Rabbani, I told him that I was doing so at the behest of Powell and Rice. "We respect you for your contribution in the Soviet-Afghan War and for your recent assistance in the war against al Qaeda and the Taliban," I began. I reminded him that the United States—particularly our military strikes—had been decisive in recent Northern Alliance advances. Going forward, I requested his cooperation in establishing a new government. I made it clear, however, that it was unacceptable for him to remain president.

Rabbani was happy that we had noted his role in the war against the Soviets. He thanked the Bush administration for its decisive action against the Taliban and al Qaeda and pointed out that he had stood behind the U.S. when it continued its bombing campaign through Ramadan. Our bombs, he told his followers, were directed at terrorists—not the Afghan people. He was willing to cooperate with the U.N. and step down once there was an agreement on a political transition.

Rabbani closed by asking if he could use me as a conduit to communicate with the Bush administration. There were additional sensitive issues that he would like to discuss in person. I agreed that we should remain in touch.

—◄   ►—

ON NOVEMBER 24, I arrived in Bonn, Germany, for the United Nations conference to form the transitional government. The Germans had arranged for the gathering to be held at the Petersberg, an elegant guesthouse on a mountaintop overlooking the Rhine Valley. The site had been home to a number of historic diplomatic summits. After World War II, American, British, and French diplomats had convened at the Petersberg, where they created the German Federal Republic. More recently, negotiators had convened in Bonn to settle the Kosovo crisis.

Dobbins was leading the American delegation, and Rice asked me to join him as the NSC representative. In this capacity, I talked to Hadley every day to provide a report for Rice and the president.

The night before the conference, Dobbins received a phone call from the Iranian delegation. They asked whether Dobbins would meet them at their hotel to discuss the upcoming negotiations. The call was not entirely a surprise. Dobbins had secured Powell's permission in advance to talk to the Iranians. Brahimi, in turn, communicated Dobbins's desire to meet with Javad Zarif, Iran's deputy foreign minister, who was leading the delegation to Bonn.

Despite Iran's long record of sponsoring terrorism, the atmosphere between Washington and Tehran had actually improved since 9/11. When it came to Afghanistan, Washington and Tehran had some shared interests. Before 9/11, when the United States had been a reluctant supporter of the Northern Alliance, Iran was its primary backer. I thought it would be worthwhile to engage Iranian diplomats, who tended to be among the more moderate elements of the regime. I also thought the United States could benefit from their experience, knowledge, and insights related to Afghanistan.

On the evening of December 4, the day before the start of the Bonn conference, Dobbins and I drove to the Iranian delegation's hotel. Muhammad Ibrahim Taherian, the Iranian ambassador to the Northern Alliance, greeted us. We spent an hour discussing our goals for the conference. Taherian was well informed about Afghanistan. Despite their long-standing ties to the Northern Alliance, the Iranians recognized that it would be best for the new government in Afghanistan to include the other factions. Rabbani's remaining in power, they concurred, was not an acceptable option. The Iranians endorsed Karzai to lead the government.

The initial meeting with the Iranians set the stage for amicable and productive relations between the American and Iranian delegations throughout the conference. Every morning, Dobbins and I had coffee with Zarif and Taherian.

These informal get-togethers proved helpful. We shared stories about our backgrounds and built personal relationships, which eased our more formal discussions on the issues. Without these coffees, I never would have come to know the depth of Taherian's knowledge about Afghanistan. He had spent a great deal of time with Afghanistan's Communist leader. Mohammad Najibullah, he believed, had not been shot by Afghan Talibs, as the conventional history holds. According to Taherian, Pakistani officers shot the Communist leader before his body was hung from a pole on the streets of Kabul.

I saw our engagement with the Iranians as part of a larger effort to secure regional support for the post-Taliban government. Despite Afghanistan's long history as a battleground for competing outside powers, we had the benefit of general agreement among the regional states at the conference. Russia, India, and Iran had backed the Northern Alliance prior to 9/11. They welcomed the emergence of a new government so long as the Northern Alliance was assured a significant presence. At the same time, they accepted that power sharing with the Pashtuns was necessary to prevent a civil war. Pakistan was less sanguine, but with Northern Alliance forces in control of Kabul, the best Islamabad could reasonably hope for at this point was an agreement that ensured adequate Pashtun representation.

⤙   ⤚

THE TOUGHEST CHALLENGE at the Bonn conference was brokering a deal between the four main Afghan opposition factions—the Northern Alliance, Rome Group, Cyprus Group, and Peshawar Group. Of the four, the Northern Alliance and the Rome Group were the most important. The Northern

Alliance had a large number of forces on the ground and represented the Tajiks, Uzbeks, and Hazaras. The Rome Group spoke for the Pashtuns, the largest ethnic group.

The Northern Alliance delegation was led by Qanooni. Qanooni's limp—the consequence of a failed assassination attempt that he believed was orchestrated by Hekmatyar—betrayed a long association with Afghan opposition activities. He joined the Afghan resistance against the Soviets as an aide to Massoud, eventually becoming one of his senior political advisors. After Massoud's death, he was one of the trio, along with Fahim and Abdullah, who divided the leadership of the Northern Alliance.

Abdul Sattar Sirat, a former minister of justice during the rule of Zahir Shah, led the Rome Group. Sirat had relatively little control over the group. While nominally loyal to Zahir Shah, the Rome Group delegation was mostly a collection of émigrés and tribal leaders with their own constituencies and forces inside and outside the country. Karzai, who had remained in southern Afghanistan with his forces and with U.S. Special Forces and CIA advisors, was part of the Rome Group.

Despite their differences in identity and outlook, relations between the Rome Group and the Northern Alliance were remarkably civil. The conventional wisdom at the time was that Afghanistan was a country plagued by a variety of long-standing ethnic, religious, tribal, and sectarian divisions. This narrative discounted the searing and overarching hold that more recent events had on the Afghan people. The sorry experience of the past two decades bound the rival Afghan delegations together. Many among the American delegation were surprised when the Afghan delegates pointed to Soviet interference in Afghanistan, rather than more primordial differences, as the cause of factionalism.

Dobbins told me how difficult it had been to negotiate in the Balkans, where competing factions were quick to raise historic grievances. The Afghan delegates, by contrast, invoked earlier periods of the country's history, such as the reign of Zahir Shah, as eras of peace and national harmony. These recollections were of course tinged with romanticism and nostalgia, but they nevertheless revealed a sense of unity and determination to avoid mistakes of the past. As a symbol of their commitment to a new Afghanistan, each of the groups accepted the United Nations request that their delegations include women, who went on to make valuable contributions.

The one major Afghan faction not represented at Bonn was the Taliban, which was still putting up a determined fight. Kandahar had not yet fallen, and even at this late stage, the Taliban leadership had not broken with al Qaeda. I am skeptical that the international community could have lured the Taliban to the table at Bonn.

For the first few days, Dobbins urged the American delegation to keep a low profile. He asked us not to congregate with other Americans and even suggested that we leave the conference site to take a walk in the park if we could not find foreign delegates with whom to talk. Dobbins hoped that the Afghans would come to an agreement on their own and take ownership of it. Too prominent an American role, he thought, would undermine the United Nations' leadership of the conference and stir resentment against the United States.

This approach worked well at first. The delegates agreed in relatively short order on a phased transition. An interim government would convene an Emergency *Loya Jirga* to establish a transitional government. The transitional government would draft a constitution. A Constitutional *Loya Jirga* would ratify a new governing document. And national elections would be convened for president and parliament. All of this was to be accomplished over the course of two years after the seating of the interim government in Kabul.

Once the basic framework for the transition was settled, however, the conference came to a standstill. The major stumbling block was the king's role. While the royal family did not intend to reimpose the monarchy, it announced that the king would return to Afghanistan from Rome to take part in the new government. This was unacceptable to the Northern Alliance and its backers. Several days of indecision about the king started to jeopardize the conference.

Since our policy of benign neglect wasn't working, Dobbins decided to intervene. He proposed a compromise. Zahir Shah would not serve as head of state but would convene the Emergency *Loya Jirga*. His Rome Group would have the ability to nominate the interim leader of the government as long as that leader was acceptable to other delegations.

I played a relatively limited role in the conference at first. As the top political appointee on the American delegation, I was mainly responsible for giving the White House regular updates. Though I knew the Afghan leaders well and spoke to them regularly, I did so quietly and passively. But now Dobbins asked me to be more proactive. My relationships and language fluencies, he reasoned, could win the delegates over to our side. I warned Hadley to prepare for a big phone bill on my expense report when I returned. I would be calling Afghan leaders in Afghanistan on a daily basis, urging them to give Qanooni flexibility for a negotiated agreement in Bonn.

Dobbins asked me to get started by calling the king and soliciting his thoughts on our compromise proposal. I reached Zahir Shah at his home in Rome and explained our thinking. He agreed to the role we suggested for him and reiterated that he did not wish to lead the government. We were able to secure Northern Alliance agreement on this limited role for the king.

The next challenge was naming the head of the interim government. Going into the conference, we assumed that Karzai would easily emerge with the title. He was the only figure who enjoyed broad-based support both inside and outside the country. On a flight from Tashkent to Kabul before the Bonn conference, Abdullah told Dobbins that Karzai uniquely fit the bill of a Pashtun leader who was acceptable to the Northern Alliance. Surprisingly, the neighboring states, and even the Pakistani military, endorsed him.

On the first day of the conference, Karzai had addressed the Bonn delegates from his hideout in Tarin Kot—a small, damp hut with mud-baked walls in which a piece of parachute sufficed for a chair. Despite the primitive conditions, the CIA had managed to provide Karzai with a satellite phone. Fighting a cold, Karzai surprised the delegates with eloquent remarks that were broadcast over loudspeakers.

When it came time to nominate an interim leader, however, the Rome Group selected Sirat instead of Karzai by a vote of nine to two. As long-standing exile leaders, most of the delegates did not feel any sense of loyalty to the younger, less-experienced Karzai, who, in any case, was not at the conference to make his case. Some of them viewed Karzai as a threat to their own ambitions in the new Afghan government. Karzai had been part of the Rome Group during the 1990s but had focused more on mobilizing tribal and royalist Pashtuns in Afghanistan and Pakistan. Sirat, by contrast, had played an active role in the Rome Group throughout the 1990s. Besides serving as a senior advisor to Zahir Shah, he had headed an exile effort in support of the king's *Loya Jirga* initiative. But he was deeply divisive, even within the group he supposedly led.

Northern Alliance representatives insisted that I do whatever I could to block Sirat's candidacy. Qanooni explained that even if they did not object at Bonn, the Northern Alliance commanders were unlikely to respect Sirat's authority on the ground. Besides, he did not think that Rabbani would step down for Sirat. And since Sirat was ethnically Uzbek, he could not claim much of a following from the Pashtuns and would not be able to unite the country.

I observed that it might seem like outside interference if Dobbins or I pressured Sirat to step down. Qanooni agreed but admitted that he felt somewhat uncomfortable exercising a veto since Sirat was his brother-in-law.

The standoff threatened to unravel the Bonn conference. When Brahimi, Dobbins, and I informed the Rome Group that Sirat's nomination was unacceptable to other groups, Sirat remained obstinate.

The standoff was also testing the patience of the delegates. The Bonn meeting was taking place in the midst of Ramadan, which requires adherents to fast during the day. The delegates tried to cope with the restriction by waking up late and working into the night—an arrangement that was draining for even the most devout and committed of conference participants.

The German hosts were also calling for the conference to conclude quickly. We had already occupied the site for close to two weeks without finalizing an agreement. In the meantime, attendees for an upcoming dentists' conference had already begun to arrive.

Fearing that the conference would end in failure, I convened the full delegation of the Rome Group. "You have reneged on your earlier agreement," I said. I reminded them that they had agreed to nominate an interim head of government who would be acceptable to the other three groups. I warned them that unless they stuck with the agreement, we would blame the Rome Group for the failure of the conference. They would have to accept responsibility for such a development, with all its implications for Afghanistan.

I then called Zahir Shah again and explained the problem. He listened sympathetically before explaining that Sirat was not his choice either. He agreed with me that the Rome Group was being unreasonable and offered to make some phone calls to his followers. He encouraged me to consult closely with his grandson Mustafa Zahir—one of the delegates. Finally, under pressure from the king, the Rome Group reconvened and voted for Karzai.

A military accident almost upended our plans. On December 5, an American B-52 dropped a 2,000-pound bomb that came close to killing Karzai. One of the embedded Special Forces soldiers had been calling in an air strike with a laser designator that would give our aircraft the coordinates to hit. Seeing that his battery was low, he switched in a new one but did not realize that, when he did so, the device reset its GPS finder to its own location. As a result, when he transmitted the GPS coordinates to the bomber, he in effect called in an air strike on his own location. Karzai was nearby and was hit by flying shrapnel and debris. His CIA advisor, who would become the station chief during my time as ambassador, threw himself on top of Karzai, possibly saving his life. As he was wiping the blood from his head, Karzai received a call from Bonn. He was officially the new leader of the Afghan Interim Authority.

WITH KARZAI'S SELECTION RESOLVED, the final issue was to determine his cabinet. Here, the Northern Alliance, particularly Rabbani, was the obstacle. They were dragging their feet in proposing their own names for cabinet positions. The Northern Alliance knew that if the Bonn conference ended inconclusively, they had the inherent advantage, since they already controlled Kabul and occupied the ministries.

I began making phone calls to key figures in the Northern Alliance, circumventing Rabbani altogether. I urged them to release their list of candidates for cabinet positions. I reached Dostum in Mazar via satellite phone. Though he had been a key player in Afghan politics for nearly three decades, we had met for the first time in 1999. Back then Zahir Shah had asked me to fly to Turkey, hoping that I could persuade Dostum to rally Uzbeks behind the *Loya Jirga* initiative. As a "gift," I had presented him with a small statue of a crying Afghan girl, which I thought symbolized the destruction to which he had contributed as a Soviet-backed military commander and then as a warlord. The mission going forward, I told him, was to end the suffering of Afghan children and build a normal country for future generations of Afghans. Dostum would later recount this story to audiences as evidence that he was committed to a new Afghanistan.

When I connected with Dostum, I expressed sympathy for the fact that Uzbeks were underrepresented in the Northern Alliance delegation. Still, I encouraged Dostum to support the conference. Doing so, I pointed out, would give him greater influence later in the transition. If the Bonn conference failed, ties between the Northern Alliance and the United States would be jeopardized, and that would ultimately undermine his standing. Dostum concurred and promised to prod Rabbani to release the list of candidates.

I then called Ismail Khan, who had consolidated power in the western city of Herat. I knew him only slightly. His claim to Herat dated back to 1979, when, outmanned and outgunned, he had led a group of fighters to briefly liberate the city from Soviet forces. After the fall of the Najibullah regime, Ismail Khan took over as governor of the city until his defeat and capture by the Taliban. In 1999 he managed to escape prison. Two years later, he joined with the United States in liberating Herat for the second time.

As with Dostum, I appealed to Ismail Khan's self-interest. It was true, I conceded, that Heratis were not represented adequately at Bonn. But I told him that it would benefit him to make the Bonn conference a success. I knew he wanted to remain governor of Herat, so I warned that he would not be able to count on continued American support if he did not cooperate with the political transition. He assured me that he supported the effort at Bonn and would encourage Rabbani to issue the Northern Alliance's list of candidates.

Meanwhile, Dobbins touched base with Fahim and Abdullah. Both reiterated their support for the Bonn process.

Still, Rabbani would not budge.

Around midnight on December 5, I was in my room preparing to go to bed when there was a knock on my door. I was surprised to see that it was one of the Iranian delegates. He told me that Zarif and Taherian needed to see me urgently. Throughout the conference, the Iranian delegation had been very sympathetic to the Northern Alliance. On a number of occasions, the Iranians spoke up on the alliance's behalf when they thought we were pressing them too hard to make compromises. So I was surprised when they asked me to call Rabbani and pressure him to release the list.

In a less conciliatory tone than in our previous conversations, I reminded Rabbani of his earlier pledge to cooperate with the Bonn process. He insisted that he was still willing to leave but thought it would be best to suspend the conference and reconvene in Kabul for the final agreement. His government, he said, could help facilitate the transition.

"This is not acceptable," I said. I told him that the United States would refuse to carry out the transitional process under the auspices of his government. This meant that Afghanistan would not receive billions of dollars of American reconstruction aid until he resigned. I added that international peacekeeping forces would have to take over Kabul before the conference could begin again. This would mean that Northern Alliance militias would have to evacuate the city. One way or the other, I impressed upon him, he would have to go.

"Would you really do that?" Rabbani asked.

"You can count on it," I replied.

Rabbani promised to make a decision on the list of candidates shortly.

As a stroke of good luck, a U.S. plane accidentally fired a rocket near Rabbani's home the next day. No one was injured in the strike, but Rabbani concluded that we were sending him a signal. The Russians also helped by threatening to cut off aid to the Northern Alliance if it did not move forward on the list. Only then did Rabbani acquiesce.

Then began an all-night negotiating session over which leaders would receive which cabinet posts. The Northern Alliance was refusing to agree to a transitional government unless it controlled three-quarters of all the ministries. Fahim, Qanooni, and Abdullah wanted to head the three most important ministries—defense, interior, and foreign affairs. Dostum, meanwhile, was making a bid for the Ministry of Defense, a cause of further intra-delegation friction. Under instructions from Northern Alliance officials in Kabul to hold firm, Qanooni refused to compromise.

Dobbins convened a meeting with Brahimi and the top diplomats from India, Russia, Iran, and Germany in attendance. They summoned Qanooni. Although he was partly responsible for the impasse, I could not help but feel sorry for him as he stumbled into the room. It was clear that he had not slept for a long time, and I knew that he was suffering from high blood pressure. For the next two hours, each of us tried to explain to Qanooni that his demands would generate a government that was not sufficiently broad-based, representative, and inclusive. Qanooni replied that since the Northern Alliance had conceded the top position to Karzai, its proposals were reasonable.

The discussion continued until about 4 a.m. At that point, Zarif stood up, summoned Qanooni aside, and whispered something to him. *Newsweek* later reported that he said, "This is the best deal you're going to get." In any case, Zarif got Qanooni's attention.

"Okay, I give up!" Qanooni proclaimed as he returned to the table. He offered to relinquish two ministries and acquiesced to the creation of three others.

This meant that sixteen of the twenty-nine ministries in the interim government would be in Northern Alliance hands while Karzai would preside as head of government. Ethnically, the Pashtuns received eleven posts, Tajiks eight, Hazaras five, and Uzbeks three, with two going to smaller ethnic groups. However, the Northern Alliance did retain control over the ministries of Defense, Interior, and Foreign Affairs.

Hours before the end of the conference, we struck a deal. On December 6, the Security Council formalized the Bonn Agreement in Resolution 1383. The final deal had three main components.

First, it outlined a political transition. The Interim Authority was to take office on December 22, right after Eid, the end of Ramadan.

Second, the agreement set rules and guidelines relevant to the composition, procedures, and functions of the Afghan Interim Authority. The interim government consisted of Karzai and his cabinet; twenty-nine ministries of varying importance; a Supreme Court; and a special commission tasked with organizing the Emergency *Loya Jirga*. The Afghan Constitution of 1964, international law, Afghan custom, and *sharia* principles governed all aspects of the law not covered by the mandate of the Interim Authority. The Bonn Agreement also provided for broad United Nations involvement in Afghanistan.

Third, the Bonn Agreement established a basic scheme to maintain security in the country, mandating that all armed groups transfer power to the Interim Authority, which in turn would command these forces. This was critical because the new government depended on the willingness of the country's commanders and warlords to recognize its authority.

All in all, I was pleased with the outcome, though there was a tough and long road ahead. After decades of strife, the possibility of a free, stable Afghanistan was within reach.

TWELVE

RETURN TO KABUL

KABUL AND WASHINGTON, D.C., JANUARY–JUNE 2002

AS THE CIA PLANE DESCENDED, I CAUGHT MY FIRST GLIMPSE OF KABUL INTERNA-tional Airport; it looked nothing like the small, pleasant hub it had been when I'd left. Now it resembled a scrap yard. Surrounding the narrow landing strip was a wasteland of mines, broken tanks, armored vehicles, and airplane shells—casualties of unrelenting war. We hit the tarmac with a thud and tax-ied down the runway. As the door of the jet opened, I took in the air of Af-ghanistan for the first time in thirty years.

The Interim Authority had taken power in Kabul two weeks earlier, on December 22, and President Bush had appointed me as his special envoy. I had not expected to receive the appointment, but, as it turned out, others had seen it coming. In his last interview with Pakistani journalist Hamid Mir in November 2001, bin Laden predicted that I would "play the shots in Kabul." As Mir later recounted:

> After the interview, while we were sipping Arabian tea in his hideout near Kabul, he [bin Laden] asked me a question about Zalmay Khalilzad. I showed ignorance about the person. He informed me that they are going to vacate big cities of Afghanistan in coming days for a long guerrilla war and

after that Zalmay Khalilzad will play the shots in Kabul, Northern Alliance will get nothing.*

U.S. forces were operating out of Bagram Air Base, so the airport in Kabul had been left to the care of a lone elderly Afghan man with a long wispy beard and a few missing teeth. He rolled a stairway up to the door of the plane and welcomed me warmly.

Passing through the decimated terminal, Karzai's protocol people shepherded me into an incongruously luxurious Mercedes sedan. *Where in this desperate country*, I thought, *did they manage to find such a nice car?*

During the short drive into Kabul, I saw a quiet, almost dead city— a ghost town. The few pedestrians on the streets seemed fearful, hesitant, and traumatized. The poverty was overwhelming. Some people rode bikes, but there were almost no cars. The shops along the main road—many improvised from empty shipping containers—were deserted. The few shopkeepers who peered out were wrapped in layers of clothing to withstand the winter cold. It was a far cry from the lively, urbane city I remembered.

I asked the driver to detour into the neighborhoods from my childhood. The scenes were shocking. I knew that thousands of rockets had descended on the city in the 1990s. Yet nothing had prepared me for the destruction that now met my eyes. The restaurants I had frequented, the streets on which my friends had lived—they were all gone. Vast expanses of rubble had replaced entire districts of the city. Few buildings stood intact.

Our old house in the Karte Char district of Kabul was still there, though severely damaged. I wanted to knock on the door and say hello to the current residents, but refrained on the strong advice of my security detail.

Beyond this sad scene loomed the damaged and partially burned-out hulk of the Amanullah Khan Palace. It brought to mind scenes from Beirut after its civil war.

The Kabul River, which once flowed swift and strong through the center of the city, was now reduced to a filthy trickle of water. The riverbed had been converted into a garbage dump. To my horror, I saw women squatting there to wash laundry while children filled plastic containers from puddles to take home drinking water. The hillsides around the city, which had been made barren by years of war and drought, filled the air with dust when the wind blew, giving rise to the "Kabul cough."

---

*Hamid Mir, *Daily Jang*, 11 September 2002.

I took in these scenes in stoic silence, only to feel tears sting my eyes as we drove down Darulaman Road, one of the capital's main thoroughfares. For my entire life in Kabul, I had taken this stately boulevard, lined by ancient chinar trees, for granted. Now those trees, along with the forests that formerly covered the surrounding mountains, had been chopped down. During the 1980s, Soviet forces had razed them to prevent snipers from taking cover there. Later, ordinary Afghans chopped down the remainder for firewood.

The U.S. embassy compound was reasonably intact, aside from the broken windows and bullet holes in the walls. Inside, it looked like a weird time capsule. It had been abandoned during the Soviet withdrawal—temporarily, or so it was thought. The staff had departed in a hurry, expecting to return in short order once the Afghan resistance took control of the capital. When the first group of State Department employees reoccupied the embassy in December, they had found papers, telegrams, magazines, and ashtrays on the desks, covered with more than a decade's worth of dust. Portraits of Reagan and Shultz hung on the walls. Amazingly, the motor pool even boasted its full complement of vehicles—old Volkswagen Passats.

The embassy's custodian, Hassan, told me that as they were leaving, American officials had instructed him to "watch the place" until they returned. For the next thirteen years, he and a handful of unarmed attendants did exactly that. Through their determined presence, they managed to hold the compound even during the Taliban years. The toughest part, they said, was traveling to the U.S. embassy in Pakistan to collect their paychecks.

Unlike the embassy, however, the ambassador's residence, some distance away, had been destroyed. Before the Soviet invasion, the American ambassador had an elegant residence with a tennis court. At one point, other embassy officials had resided in spacious private homes in the upscale districts of the city. This time around, my team and I had to cope with more spartan conditions. The embassy compound was structurally intact, but the main building lacked electricity, heat, and water. The twelve-person security detail settled in an underground storage bunker about 200 yards outside the main building, where plumbing and electricity were functional. The staff prepared food in large pots on paraffin stoves.

As the senior diplomat, I was assigned a private room in the embassy. There was a desk, phone, and computer, but no bed. We had been warned about the living conditions only hours before our departure. I had managed to borrow a sleeping bag from our neighbors, the Goldbaums, whose children, Gena and Zach, were close friends with our boys. They had been excited that their camping equipment was headed to Afghanistan.

Most people had to bunk beside their desks in offices shared with two or three of their colleagues. In the morning, over a hundred of us would stand in a long line waiting to use one of the two bathrooms on the compound. We were still better off than the military officers and soldiers, who were camped in a nearby field with tents but no showers.

⟨ ⟩

AS I SAT in my room at the end of my first day, it was hard not to feel overwhelmed by what we were undertaking as a nation.

I soon discovered that there was a major fault line between the United States and Afghans on how to rebuild the state. It was one I had hardly expected. Afghanistan's legendary xenophobia had convinced the administration to pursue a light footprint strategy. What I now realized, however, was that Afghans wanted to see a much larger foreign role in stabilizing their country.

Assisting Afghans in the continuing political transition was another challenge. We would need to work with the dominant leaders in Afghanistan, most of whom had played important roles in the fighting of the last two decades. Some of these figures enjoyed political legitimacy in their communities, while others had achieved prominence primarily through coercion or threats from their militias. The trouble was that we had empowered, in the overthrow of the Taliban, some of the worst culprits responsible for the bloodshed of the 1990s. The next steps in the Bonn process—the Emergency *Loya Jirga,* the Constitutional *Loya Jirga,* and national elections—would give the Afghan people a greater voice in determining the country's direction.

⟨ ⟩

MY FIRST DAY in the country, I met Karzai for a working breakfast in the nearby palace compound. The compound, too, had taken a beating. In that formerly gracious complex of multiple palaces, a clock tower, and offices for the royal staff, about half of the structures were now uninhabitable, and some had been leveled altogether. The lower floor of the palace where Karzai had set up headquarters was relatively intact, albeit dilapidated. It still boasted ornately patterned walls, carved wooden chairs, and a large fireplace made of rare marble. As I walked up to the second floor, I could see the Taliban's signature. Any representation of life—human, animal, or plant—whether on the beautiful old carpets or on the paintings on the wall, had been chopped away or blackened. The Taliban believe that Islam forbids the representation of any living thing. In fact, one of the first acts of the Taliban was to decree the destruction not only of historical art but also of posters of athletes, actors, and other celebrities that adorned the walls of local shops.

Karzai was dressed in his signature combination of tribal and Western regalia—the striped green *chapan*, or overcoat, that would become his trademark, a Nehru-collar white shirt, loose trousers, a black jacket, and a *karukal* hat made from the fur of aborted lamb fetuses. Each article of clothing he wore was associated with a different region of the country—his way of delivering a message of national unity. The hat, a debatable item in a modern era that gives attention to the humane treatment of animals, has been popular in Central Asia since time immemorial. Several Afghan kings, such as the reformist Amanullah Khan, had worn them. In Karzai's case, the cold weather and lack of adequate heating inspired him to keep it on even when indoors, along with the additional layers of sweaters he was wearing. As we talked, the electricity in the palace went off and on repeatedly.

Karzai and I had become friends over the years, but now the dynamics of our relationship were more complicated. He was the head of state—a title that came with an enormous list of responsibilities but minimal resources. His authority depended on the protection and reliability of the United States. Conversely, despite the resources I had at my disposal as an American official, my influence was constrained. I could not make any decisions for Afghanistan; I could only support the Afghans as they, hopefully, built a functioning political system.

I decided that I would not try to impose any solution on Karzai or other Afghans. Instead, I would talk through issues and options and offer advice—forceful advice if need be. I would tell them, "If you can solve your problems among yourselves, I am happy to stay on the sidelines. However, failure is not an option."

Karzai was gripped by nostalgia. He spoke about Afghanistan's golden age. Like me, he remembered the Kabul of the 1960s and 1970s as a pleasant city with public services, comfortable suburban houses, and beautiful rose gardens. Personal security had never been an issue. Elders were respected. Restaurants and shops lined the streets.

Karzai wanted to restore this lost world but was oddly passive about doing so. He knew what needed to be done. The problem was that he wanted America and the rest of the world to do it. This was partially due to the sheer paucity of resources at Karzai's disposal as well as his awe of American capabilities. But I also came to realize that Karzai was channeling a broader cultural problem: the Afghan people had lost confidence in themselves.

As envoy, I spent hundreds of hours with Karzai. There were plenty of official meetings, but we would also attend ceremonies together and jointly greet visitors from around the country—dignitaries, warlords, tribal elders, activists, mourning parents, and anyone else who could get on his calendar. Karzai was always gracious and hospitable. I was impressed by how deftly and empathetically he conducted business with people from all walks of life. I learned a great deal simply by observing him. He seemed as comfortable with high-profile international dignitaries as he did with the average Afghan.

Karzai in turn appreciated that I was willing to spend time engaging Afghans. Eventually, he encouraged me to "hold court" on my own. When people came to discuss issues related to the United States, Karzai would direct them to me. A common complaint was how American forces would humiliate Afghans during raids by placing bags over their heads. It was difficult for Karzai to deal with these kinds of concerns since he had no say over our military operations. I understood his frustration, especially given that military excesses were undermining Afghan attitudes toward the new government. Having an American with him allowed him to be responsive to Afghan grievances without alienating the United States. He also hoped that, through these encounters, I would be more inclined to raise Afghan concerns with the U.S. military.

In meetings of Afghan officials, I was often the only foreigner in the room. Karzai liked to have me there. Perhaps the Northern Alliance leaders resented my presence at first, but over time, they came to see me as someone who could act as an honest broker and influence Karzai, provided that their demands were reasonable. They knew that I was the first and last person with whom Karzai would speak before making decisions.

Even on the busiest days, Karzai and I tried to meet and compare notes over dinner. Karzai's dinners were simple. He ate at exactly 7:30 p.m., with guests expected to arrive a half hour earlier. Guests were offered tea or juice upon arrival—fresh pomegranate was the favorite. The dinner itself consisted of one lamb or chicken dish, one or two kinds of rice, and one or two vegetable dishes. The menu seldom changed.

Without pressing time constraints, we could go in depth into our discussions, which helped me understand the intricacies of the Afghans' thinking. Karzai was deliberative and open-minded but indecisive.

He often invited ministers, relatives, or provincial visitors to dine with him. Karzai's wife, Zeenat, a gynecologist by profession, rarely joined the dinners. She wanted to be more active at least on issues of women's health, but Karzai was worried that this would irritate the mullahs and local leaders.

Within days of my arrival in the capital, Rumsfeld asked me to set up a phone call with Karzai. "We've just sent Zal to Kabul, as you know," Rumsfeld told Karzai, when they talked later that day. "Take care of him. He's a friend of the president and he's my friend."

Karzai joked back, "But, Mr. Secretary, we are expecting him to take care of us!"

From Kabul, I went on to visit Mazar. I met with Dostum and with Atta Mohammed Noor, a Tajik commander close to Fahim. I took note of Dostum's dominance in the north and of Atta's barely concealed hostility toward his rival.

I also met with U.S. Special Forces members deployed to work with Dostum. One of them opined that the United States should have made Dostum the president of Afghanistan because he had fought so well against the Taliban.

Herat was next. The city had more than 350 colleges, 12,000 shops, 6,000 bathhouses, and 440,000 homes. I was pleasantly surprised to see that it had survived the civil war.

From there, I went to Jalalabad and Kandahar, where I met with local power brokers Hazrat Ali and Sherzai. These visits drove home to me how challenging it would be to unify Afghanistan. I imagined it was almost like visiting medieval Germany and touring its principalities, each ruled by its own king or overlord.

Skyping was not yet an option in January 2002. But during my two-week trip, I called home once a day. Alex was eighteen and a freshman at Georgetown. Max was ten years old. Cheryl, whose background in political Islam and Middle Eastern studies was now a much-needed commodity, had been recruited to work for the RAND Corporation on its counterterrorism and nation-building programs. As an army brat, the notion of women holding the fort while the men went off to war zones (and vice versa) was familiar to her, even if it was not something she had ever hoped or planned to replicate in her own adult life. And none of us anticipated just how long my absence would be.

⸺◄   ►⸺

THE RAPPORT I developed with Karzai and his cabinet over meetings and dinners would prove useful as problems big and small arose. On one of my earliest visits to Afghanistan, a delegation of U.S. senators came to Kabul on a quick fact-finding tour. Senator Biden ended up extending his visit to spend more time getting to know the new Afghan leadership. Late one evening, Biden called my office and said that he needed to see me right away. He arrived with a sheepish look and confessed that things had gotten out of hand during his meeting with Qanooni. As their argument escalated, Biden confessed with considerable remorse that he had threatened to drop bombs from B-52s on Qanooni.

I wasn't sure whether to laugh or worry.

"Well, Senator," I told him, "I guess you'll have to fix this." Reaching for the phone, I dialed Qanooni's home number.

Qanooni's wife answered and said that her husband had already gone to bed. I assured her it was important and asked her to put him on the line.

"I heard you had an argument with someone from the U.S. . . ." I began.

"Oh!" Qanooni snapped. "Don't even mention that man to me!"

"Can you make some tea?" I said. "We're coming over."

When we got there, Biden apologized for the dispute and for losing his temper. Soon the two men were exchanging war stories like old friends. "Well," I finally said, excusing myself, "you seem to be getting along . . ." I learned later that they went on chatting for several hours into the night.

While subtlety was not Biden's diplomatic strongpoint, I give him credit for never expecting special treatment. He slept in a sleeping bag on the floor of the conference room, along with everyone on his staff, and shared our limited facilities without complaint. He stood in line every morning dressed only in a towel waiting for his turn to take a shower. One morning a young Marine, in line behind him, took his picture. When Biden heard the click of the camera, he turned and saw the Marine, who explained with some chagrin that he was taking the photo for his mom. Smiling, Biden pointed out that she would hardly recognize whose photo it was just from the back, and delighted the young man by posing from the front.

⟶   ⟵

IN THESE EARLY DAYS, it was a challenge even to keep Karzai alive. Within the first months of 2002, several senior members of his government were killed or nearly killed. Aviation and Tourism Minister Abdul Rahman was fatally attacked at Kabul Airport. Karzai suspected that this was a vendetta killing by the Northern Alliance dating back to their days in the opposition. A few months later, Fahim's convoy was nearly destroyed by a massive bomb. In July, Haji Qadir, a vice president of the Interim Authority, was gunned down on the street.

I was in my office at the NSC in July 2002 when I picked up the phone and was quickly connected to President Bush. "So," he asked, "what do you think of Karzai's security?" He had called on my open, not secure, line. "Mr. President . . ." I said with hesitation. "Can we talk about this in person?"

He understood right away. "Come on over," he said. As soon as I was in the Oval Office, the president became even more direct.

"Do you think Fahim might kill Karzai?" he asked.

I was shocked. Fahim was the first vice president and minister of defense. He and his men were in charge of protecting Karzai.

I had not seen any intelligence about threats to Karzai from Fahim. The president hadn't either but, like me, had been thinking about the recent assassination of Qadir.

I did not think it was likely that Fahim would kill Karzai or orchestrate a coup. Fahim had too much to lose. He was one of the principal beneficiaries of Afghanistan's cooperation with the United States.

The president observed that if we hadn't vetted the security people around Karzai, we couldn't be sure. If Karzai was killed, the president feared that everything we were trying to do in Afghanistan would be jeopardized. He asked me to see if Karzai would let us put our own security forces around him.

I called Karzai and guardedly relayed the president's message over an open line. "I have a message from your friend . . ." I began. He understood. After some hesitation, Karzai accepted about fifty U.S. Special Forces personnel—and not a moment too soon. During Karzai's first visit to his hometown of Kandahar for a family wedding, an Afghan police officer fired four shots at Karzai's car. The bullets barely missed him, with one instead striking Sherzai in the head. Karzai's security detail reacted quickly, killing the would-be assassin. The gunman was later identified as a Taliban sympathizer who had joined the Kandahar governor's security force a few weeks earlier.

By August, we were seeing a number of reports suggesting that Fahim might indeed be planning a coup. Alarmed, President Bush dispatched me to Kabul, where I immediately convened Karzai and Fahim. I told them that the president was concerned about reports of a rift between them. Turning to Fahim, I reminded him that President Bush remained skeptical that he was actually committed to a stable, unified Afghanistan. Fahim reacted angrily, denying that he intended Karzai or the new government any harm. But I could tell that I had struck a nerve. Fahim complained that neither Karzai nor I was adequately consulting him. After discussing his concerns, I suggested that he call a press conference and clarify that he remained loyal to Karzai and the Afghan government. He reluctantly agreed.

American security forces ended up guarding Karzai for two years until an American-trained cadre of Afghan security personnel was ready to take over.

⟵   ⟶

WARLORDISM WAS PERHAPS the most persistent challenge of this period. On a number of occasions, Karzai vented to me with great emotion about the threat. He worried that as people tired of insecurity or oppression by their local strongmen, they might again welcome the Taliban or others who promised them justice and peace.

In the absence of Afghan or international forces in the countryside, warlords were establishing, or reestablishing, their fiefdoms. Before I was on the ground in Afghanistan, I had sympathized with the idea of maintaining a light footprint, largely because of Afghans' historic xenophobia. But when

I spoke with ordinary Afghans in Mazar and Herat during an early trip in 2002, I began to see how mistaken I was. People confided that when they saw members of the local militia coming toward them on the street, they tensed up, expecting to be harassed, robbed, or beaten for no reason. By contrast, when they saw a soldier from a foreign country, they relaxed.

The difficulty was that the United States was working with the warlords. The warlords had carried the burden of the ground campaign against the Taliban and al Qaeda and, in the absence of anything like an effective national army, were still needed to take on the insurgents.

In the early months of the Interim Authority, Karzai was constantly at odds with various warlords. He vowed at times to arrest Dostum or demanded that we do so. Dostum's militia was looting communities to the point that many relief agencies would not operate in his territories. Thousands of Pashtun farmers were forced to flee from his forces. And along with other warlords, Dostum refused to cooperate with the U.N.'s Disarmament, Demobilization, and Reintegration (DDR) program.

In the spring of 2002, the Karzai government faced particularly brazen defiance from one militia commander, Pacha Khan Zadran. In an attempt to win his cooperation, Karzai appointed Pacha Khan governor of Paktia Province. The *shura*, or leadership council, of the provincial capital Gardez, however, voted to reject this appointment. In retaliation, Pacha Khan's forces shelled the city, accusing local authorities of being al Qaeda sympathizers.

Karzai is not confrontational by nature and was painfully aware of the limits of his power. For several months, he had made good-faith efforts to resolve the conflict peacefully.

Finally, he decided that he needed to act. Allowing a warlord to defy the central government so audaciously, he reasoned, would set a precedent for others to do the same. On April 30, Karzai issued an ultimatum to Pacha Khan to surrender. Fahim supported him.

When Karzai and Fahim broached the idea of arresting Pacha Khan, I asked whether they had enough forces to take on his militia. Pacha Khan's defiance was dangerous, I conceded, but if the Interim Authority took action and failed to control the situation swiftly, the central government's legitimacy would suffer irreparable damage. They said they were ready to act whether or not the U.S. supported them, but suggested that it would be best if U.S. forces provided air support in case the crisis spun out of control.

As Fahim's troops headed toward Gardez, I updated the Deputies Committee via teleconference. I explained that after several months of seeking a peaceful compromise, Karzai had issued an arrest warrant. We were at a critical juncture, and Washington had an interest in ensuring that the Karzai government prevailed in the showdown. Hadley, Deputy Secretary of State Richard Armitage, and Deputy CIA Director John McLaughlin echoed my sentiments. Generals Peter Pace and Tommy Franks were careful to note that U.S. forces were not providing support to Fahim, since Rumsfeld had not given the order to do so. Yet they seemed comfortable with a gradual escalation in which U.S. forces might clear roadblocks for Afghan forces while encouraging a negotiated settlement. McLaughlin pushed for more assertive measures aimed at removing Pacha Khan. The CIA, he offered, could provide Karzai with intelligence to help carry out the mission.

The only opposition came from the Pentagon's Wolfowitz and Feith. Backing Karzai, they argued, would effectively make him a warlord who could rely on the U.S. military to settle his local disputes. He should resolve the situation peacefully.

The issue went up to the Principals Committee. Cheney, Powell, Rice, and CIA Director George Tenet all agreed on the importance of standing with Karzai. Rumsfeld, however, pushed back with unusual force. We were about to make the "most significant war-related call" of the Afghan campaign, he argued, since it would determine whether Karzai would take responsibility or become dependent on the U.S. military.

I argued that inaction, too, could create poor incentives. Our strategy in Afghanistan, at least in the short term, relied on the success of the Karzai government.

My argument did not resonate with Rumsfeld, so I offered a compromise: What if we told Karzai that we were not ready to get involved now, but would step in if he found himself in a truly dire position?

Rumsfeld still would not budge.

We were at loggerheads, so the decision was elevated to the president. President Bush sided with Rumsfeld against the rest of his national security team.

While the Pacha Khan problem festered, the anticlimactic showdown that ensued reinforced to the Pentagon that the United States should not mire itself in Afghanistan's internal conflicts.

Against this backdrop, I advised Karzai to bide his time with the warlords. The U.N.-sponsored DDR program would gradually weaken them, and the national police and army loyal to the Kabul government would get stronger. As the balance of power shifted, Karzai could encourage the warlords to join the central government. For now, he should capitalize on his popularity and pressure the warlords in more subtle ways.

⟵   ⟶

AS I REFLECTED on the challenges in those early months, I began to rethink the central question informing our efforts: What precisely were U.S. objectives in Afghanistan?

In initial deliberations after 9/11, President Bush had opted for narrow war aims. Two weeks after 9/11, he had declared, "We're not into nation building; we're focusing on justice." To avoid an occupation or extended state- and nation-building effort, the president decided to maintain a light footprint.

In early 2002, the president articulated a broader goal: preventing Afghanistan's territory from becoming a safe haven for terrorists. In a landmark address at the Virginia Military Institute in April 2002, he even seemed to call for the equivalent of a Marshall Plan for Afghanistan. The speech, however, was not accompanied by a fundamental shift in policy.

Initially, I was encouraged that a light American presence would underscore our objective: we were there to liberate the country and empower local actors, not to colonize Afghanistan like past invaders.

Increasingly, though, I had concerns. In light of the miserable conditions that unrelenting war and tyranny had inflicted—a consequence, in part, of the international community's neglect—I saw that the overwhelming majority of Afghans welcomed American initiatives aimed at providing security, facilitating democracy, jump-starting the economy, and preventing meddling from regional neighbors.

I was skeptical that we could prevent the reemergence of terrorist safe havens in Afghanistan without rebuilding the country's institutions. The long-term solution was to enable Afghans to defend and police their own territory, thereby preventing the infiltration of terrorist groups from Pakistan. Otherwise, Americans, rather than Afghan troops and police, would have to stand watch. In order to steer Afghan leaders in the right direction, we had to convince them that we would not abandon the country again and that we would make the necessary investments to create a functioning Afghan state.

I came to see that a significant, long-term role in rebuilding Afghanistan would advance our efforts in the wider ideological competition with Islamic extremists. If we neglected the aspirations of the Afghan people, we would miss an opportunity to encourage others in the broader Muslim world to align with us in the ideological competition with extremists. Afghanistan was our first critical test.

I remember a conversation I had with President Bush at one point during my envoyship. I argued that we would need to help Afghans stabilize their country to prevent terrorist attacks down the road.

President Bush interjected, "Zal, we're not there to fix their problems!"

"We can't fix our problems without helping them fix their problems," I countered.

I had a similar exchange with Rumsfeld over a video teleconference. I was explaining the steps I was taking politically and the need for more robust institution building and development programs.

Rumsfeld, trying to cut off my argument, replied, "Zal, you have to take your hand off the bicycle seat!" Rumsfeld was suggesting that we had to allow the Afghans to succeed or fail on their own.

Having heard Rumsfeld's bicycle analogy one too many times, I was exasperated. I had seen actual conditions on the ground in Afghanistan—the complete devastation produced by a quarter century of war. I recounted the abysmal conditions in Afghanistan point by point. "Mr. Secretary," I concluded, "there is no bicycle!"

By this time, Rumsfeld had had it with me, too. On the screen, I could see he was waving his arms back and forth in a vain attempt to quiet me.

I may not have persuaded the president or Rumsfeld in those exchanges, but I think they played a role in the administration's evolution on the issue. Rhetoric assailing "nation building" gradually fell by the wayside as the administration came to see the importance of a strong Afghan partner to protect our own interests.

THIRTEEN

LOYA JIRGA

KABUL, JUNE–JULY 2002

THE *LOYA JIRGA* WAS BOTH COLORFUL AND MOMENTOUS. AS THE DELEGATES ARRIVED, a pulse of excitement and anticipation filled Kabul. Every manner of Afghan was present. From afar, the crowd of delegates were a swirl of yellow, white, and gray turbans. Mullahs with long beards. Former mujahedeen commanders with their flat wool *pakols*. Uzbeks with their *chapans*. Many other men wearing no hats or karakul ones. Women wore colorful outfits mixing traditional and Western clothes. Some covered their heads; others did not. Some men wore traditional Afghan clothes, while others sported Western suits. The delegates exhibited a pride in their distinct ethnic and tribal identities as well as their sense of national identity as Afghans. It was at times very noisy and other times very solemn.

In the twentieth century, Afghan leaders had convened *Loya Jirgas* with mixed success. Amanullah had asked Queen Soraya to remove her veil at the 1928 *Loya Jirga* in an effort to win support for modernizing Afghanistan. The move instead provoked a severe backlash from conservative delegates. Zahir Shah was the last leader of Afghanistan to preside over a representative *Loya Jirga*. In 1941 the assembly ratified his policy of neutrality in World War II. And his 1964 *Loya Jirga* created a parliament, called for direct elections, and integrated women into the political process.

In the *Loya Jirga* of June 2002, Afghans saw a way out of their suffering.

The assembly site resembled a festival as much as a political convention. In the absence of a suitable conference center, the Germans erected a large

Oktoberfest tent for the main meeting and several smaller tents nearby for consultative meetings for the delegates. The *Loya Jirga* facilities spanned an area the size of three or four football fields, behind the Polytechnic University.

I saw the excitement and optimism among the Afghan people as a mixed blessing. I feared that even a successful *Loya Jirga* would foster disillusionment in a population that was placing undue hopes in the assembly. While Afghans expected the Emergency *Loya Jirga* to make far-reaching progress toward security, national unity, and democracy, the actual mandate and purpose of the gathering was decidedly less ambitious. The assembly was to appoint a new government that would preside over the drafting of the national constitution in 2003 and would hold elections in 2004.

The key, I thought, was resolving the two biggest points of contention—the role of Zahir Shah and the allocation of the ministries.

These points were so contentious that the *Loya Jirga* almost didn't happen. In fact, things were in turmoil on the evening before the assembly.

Given the reverence with which the country now regarded the aged king, Karzai was determined from the get-go to treat his return as a unifying moment. There was just one problem: Karzai was worried about the return of the king's grandson Mustafa Zahir, who Karzai thought might make a bid for president. He asked me to raise the issue with the former king. When I talked to Zahir Shah, the king agreed that it would be preferable for his grandson not to join the entourage. However, it would be awkward for him to deliver this message.

I met with Mustafa Zahir later that day and explained the situation. As a sweetener, I added that if he cooperated and voluntarily recused himself from the entourage, Karzai would arrange a diplomatic posting for him. He agreed and Karzai appointed him ambassador to Italy.

The king had intended to depart Rome a few days before March 21, hoping to be in Afghanistan for Nowruz. Fahim and Qanooni, however, had been sharing alarming intelligence with me, suggesting that Hekmatyar was plotting an attack against the king. I suspected that they were exaggerating the threats. Hekmatyar and his mostly Pashtun followers were archenemies of the Northern Alliance, and playing up the threats had the advantage of forestalling the king's arrival—an event that they knew would galvanize the country's Pashtuns. Still, I could not take the risk.

I explained the situation to President Bush and suggested that he call Italian Prime Minister Silvio Berlusconi and ask him to delay Zahir Shah's departure. Given all the death threats, he might also request Italian bodyguards rather than entrusting the king's security to the mostly Northern Alliance security forces in Kabul. President Bush agreed, though he could not resist the opportunity to tease me. "Zal, you work for a republic," he said. "What's this monarchy you're trying to create?"

It turned out that the threats against the king were credible. On April 4, Qanooni announced that the Interior Ministry had thwarted a bomb plot to kill Zahir Shah and overthrow the Karzai government. Afghan security forces detained several hundred alleged conspirators and confiscated heavy arms caches all across the city. The mastermind of the coup attempt appeared to be Hekmatyar, who had just returned to Afghanistan from Iran.

Notwithstanding the string of attacks that preceded the king's arrival, Zahir Shah's homecoming later that month was a grand affair. Throngs of Afghans from around the country came to Kabul to pay homage—even some who had helped orchestrate the 1973 coup against him.

≺   ≻

ZAHIR SHAH'S ARRIVAL in Kabul kicked off campaigning at the Emergency *Loya Jirga*. Of the 1,501 delegates, 300 were designated for key individuals and groups: members of the interim administration, prominent religious leaders, technocrats, civil society figures, nomads, refugees, and professionals from scientific and other technical organizations. An additional 10 percent were guaranteed for women. The rest of the delegates were chosen through elections in administrative districts around the country.

Besides security issues, the U.N. faced a number of obstacles in organizing the election of delegates. One was to figure out the demographic breakdown of the country. The last partial census in Afghanistan had been attempted over two decades ago. This problem was compounded by the return of refugees and displaced peoples from Iran and Pakistan—over a million by some estimates.

Despite these challenges, turnout was high, and the selection of the delegates proceeded apace.

It was the king's party that upended our preparations at the last minute. One of the king's closest aides, General Wali, publicly floated the idea of Zahir Shah heading the transitional government. Karzai and the Northern Alliance leaders were shocked. I, too, was surprised. The king had repeatedly told me and others that given his age and health, he had no such desire. Northern Alliance leaders were suddenly debating whether to run their own candidate against the king or simply boycott the *Loya Jirga* altogether. Fahim threatened to take military action against the king's supporters if Zahir Shah ran.

I went to see Karzai. He was visibly nervous and shaken. The second his aide shut the door, Karzai went on a tirade, the likes of which I hadn't seen before. Karzai had always shown deference to the king, even in private. He had even traveled to Rome to escort Zahir Shah back to Afghanistan. I was taken aback by his vitriol at being "double-crossed." I let him vent for some time before urging him to calm down. "I sympathize with your frustration," I said, "but be careful not to say anything negative about Zahir Shah to others." He listened. "Much of your credibility as a leader rests on the fact that you are close to the Rome Group. I doubt that Zahir Shah really wants to head the transitional government. Chances are the king's family is just trying to use him as a figurehead to push themselves into power."

Once Karzai cooled down, I half jokingly chastised him. "You know, you don't see an opportunity when it strikes you on the nose!"

"What do you mean?" he countered.

"Don't you want to persuade the Northern Alliance to give up one of the ministries?" I reminded him. The problem before was that Karzai did not have much leverage. Now the Northern Alliance was frantic about the king's alleged intentions. The Northern Alliance was likely to make concessions if, in exchange, we resolved the issue regarding the king's role. Karzai brightened.

I left the palace around 10 p.m. and called Zahir Shah's residence. His assistant granted me the soonest possible appointment to see the king.

The next morning at 11, I was escorted to the king's bedroom. The room, painted a light blue, was spacious, with windows overlooking a garden. Pictures of the king's family members sat on the table next to his elevated bed. The king had just woken up and was still in his pajamas. There were three comfortable armchairs in the room, but the king's assistant remained standing.

"Your Majesty," I began, "What's going on? Have you changed your mind?" I went over our discussion in Rome, when the king had expressed his strong preference for playing a symbolic role as "father of the nation." He had explicitly rejected the other two options: a citizen without any official title or an official role as head of state.

Zahir Shah reiterated calmly what he had said in Rome: that he was not seeking responsibility for heading the transitional government, adding that it would be impossible anyway in light of his age and health. He went on to blame the rumors on his family members, his tone betraying a sense of frustration. An honorary role as "father of the nation," he concluded, was a more appropriate role for him than head of state.

I suggested a joint press conference with Karzai to calm the situation and remove the uncertainty. He agreed.

I returned to the palace to find Karzai pacing anxiously. He was relieved to hear my news. We then brainstormed about how to proceed with the *Loya Jirga*. I suggested that we talk to the Northern Alliance. Until now, they had not been prepared to give up even one of the security ministries. I proposed that in exchange for the king's agreeing not to run, they ought to accept granting Zahir Shah the title of father of the nation and hand over one of the key ministries.

Then we focused on specifics. Abdullah did not control any real security assets as foreign minister, and Fahim was too powerful to remove from the defense post. We agreed that it made the most sense for Qanooni to step aside and allow a Pashtun to take over the Interior Ministry.

The Northern Alliance tentatively accepted this proposal.

Still, the controversy angered delegates. "Why don't you head over to the *Loya Jirga* site tonight and mingle with the delegates?" I asked Karzai, suggesting that it might smooth the way for tomorrow's vote.

Clearly unenthused by my suggestion, he offered a different idea: "Well, why don't you do it?"

To the chagrin of my security detail, I agreed. Despite the sizzling summertime temperatures during the daytime, Afghanistan had cool, dry nights at that time of the year. If nothing else, I figured it was a good time of the day to deal with inflamed tempers.

When my car pulled up at the *Loya Jirga* site, the delegates were startled to see me. They were sitting on the carpeted floor chatting over pots of tea, surrounded by a perimeter of two ten-foot-tall barbed-wire fences with mounted machine guns. They were not expecting the American envoy.

For the next few hours, I went from tent to tent, talking to delegates, explaining the issue with Zahir Shah, and trying to persuade them to stick with the political process. I had a few tense exchanges—especially with Pacha Khan Zadran. "Zahir Shah himself has declared that he is not a candidate," I finally told him. "But if you want to push for the king at the *Jirga*, feel free to do so."

Generally, by the time I left, near midnight, I sensed a clear change in sentiment. Most of the delegates were so positively disposed toward the United States that they were willing to give American officials the benefit of the doubt.

THE NEXT MORNING, I walked toward the front of the stage. From above the stage, two large monitors displayed the speakers.

The delegates represented Afghanistan's diversity, but the Taliban were not present. In retrospect, some have suggested that we erred in not encouraging the Taliban to participate in the Emergency *Loya Jirga*. While it's true that we underestimated the Taliban's resiliency at the time, I think, even in hindsight, that the United Nations and the Afghans made the right call: they did not invite the Taliban to participate, but the permissive rules of the *Loya Jirga* elections provided ample opportunity for former members of the Taliban to join the political process. It is doubtful that the more committed Taliban would have been cooperative. The Taliban made decisions via a *shura* of Islamic scholars. The very concept of a *Loya Jirga* was anathema to them, representing the democratic and national values they despised. Formally involving the Taliban, moreover, would have provoked the Northern Alliance's ire, jeopardizing the *Loya Jirga*'s broader success.

Zahir Shah presided over the *Loya Jirga*'s opening ceremonies. Divisions in the room seemed to fade as the king, dressed in a dark suit, slowly ascended onto the stage, supported by two aides. The delegates rose to their feet and applauded for several minutes as he made his way toward the front table, draped with newly minted Afghan flags. In a soft but invigorated voice, Zahir Shah pleaded for "the unity and independence of Afghanistan" and reiterated that his "only wish" was "to bring peace in the country."

Now it was time to start debating the issues. The lack of clear rules created organizational difficulties, but the free-for-all discussions had their own value. Speaker after speaker rose to discuss a wide range of subjects. Some were trivial—complaints about bad food in the *Loya Jirga* dining hall or the sorry state of camels in Afghanistan, among others. But most speakers raised important concerns.

Some delegates used the opportunity to denounce the warlords, including some of the mujahedeen leaders, in unusually harsh terms. In a widely broadcast exchange, an elderly delegate—his frail body shaking with emotion—won a rousing round of applause for lambasting "those whose hands were wet with the blood of our people." In response, Sayyaf appeared on stage to defend himself and others involved in the civil war of the 1990s. "Insulting the military and the mujahedeen is an insult to our country's history," he said. "Without the mujahedeen's sword and its defeat of the Russians, we would not have this meeting here today."

At this point, Karzai's election as head of state was basically a forgone conclusion. Rabbani was the only serious potential challenger, but he, too, decided not to step forward. Only two other candidates declared. The first was Masuda Jalal, a female doctor and U.N. official who had taught at Kabul University's medical school until the Taliban came to power. Though she had little chance of winning, her candidacy was symbolically powerful. Karzai and Fahim had offered her a cabinet post in exchange for not running. This would have avoided a clash with Islamist factions within the *Loya Jirga*, who were threatening her on the grounds that her candidacy, because she was a woman, violated Islam. Instead of acquiescing, she proceeded with her bid, delivering stirring remarks in favor of women's rights, security, and freedom from warlords. The other candidate was Mir Mohammed Mahfooz, a lesser-known physician. In a secret ballot election, Karzai won 1,295 of the 1,575 votes cast. When the tally was announced, the delegates erupted in cheers and shouts of *"Allahu Akbar."*

One of the most contentious debates concerned the role of Islam. A Shia cleric, Ayatollah Mohseni, warned Karzai to abide strictly by *sharia* law and proposed for good measure that the transitional government be named the Islamic Transitional Government of Afghanistan. Mohseni's proposal inspired passionate chants of *"Allahu Akbar"* from some in the audience. But Kandahar governor Sherzai pushed back. "The Islamic name should be omitted from the government because in the past it has been misused," he stated. Amid threats against Sherzai, the motion passed in favor of adding "Islamic."

I had told the Afghan leadership ahead of time that the United States and the international community would find it difficult to support Afghanistan if *sharia* were imposed and basic rights for women and minorities were not protected. But realistically, I knew we would end up with a system that accommodated *sharia* principles and also committed Afghanistan to international norms, principles, and laws regarding human rights. Even during the pre-war period, when Islamic fundamentalism was a far less influential force in the country, the Afghan legal system had been based on a mix of French law and principles from the Hanafi school of Islamic jurisprudence.

After further deliberations, the *Loya Jirga* managed to strike something of a compromise. Chief Justice Fazl Hadie Shinwari announced that *sharia* principles would help guide the judiciary's decisions. He clarified, however, that the new government would ensure basic liberties and that it would not condone stoning and other harsh punishments permitted under the Taliban.

On Sunday the delegates moved to establish a national assembly. One proposal would give each province the right to elect two representatives. The other would grant provinces one vote per ten delegates they had sent to the *Loya Jirga*. The debate mirrored America's early debates about equal versus proportional representation that ultimately led to the creation of a bicameral legislature. The issue sharply divided the delegates along ethnic lines. With the assembly unable to reach a conclusion, Karzai asked the delegates from each of the country's nine regions to have a few representatives stay in Kabul after the *Loya Jirga* and form a commission tasked with creating a legislature.

After several days, we still had not been able to reach an arrangement on the most important issue—the allocation of ministries. Karzai did not help the situation when he announced that he would simply name his own cabinet at a later date. This prompted sharp objections by both Northern Alliance and Pashtun delegates, who insisted that the *Loya Jirga* had the prerogative of confirming his picks.

Particularly in light of the decision to postpone debate on the national assembly, I was becoming worried that the delegates would walk away from the *Loya Jirga* disgruntled and disillusioned. Dozens of frustrated participants were already leaving to protest the disarray and lack of progress.

I advised Karzai against ending the *Loya Jirga* without securing delegate support for at least some of his cabinet picks. Neither the United States nor our European allies, I reminded him, were likely to support his government financially if he did not stick to the Bonn Agreement.

When Karzai tried again to strike a deal with the Northern Alliance, negotiations came to a standstill, this time over Qanooni's role. On the first day of the *Loya Jirga*, Qanooni had delivered a gracious statement offering his resignation as interior minister for the sake of "national unity." Privately, though, he was furious that he was the one who had to take the fall.

Qanooni was bright, hardworking, and a recognized leader in the country, so it was understood that he would play a significant role in the transitional administration. A suitable position needed to be found.

On the final day of the *Loya Jirga*, Karzai announced to the delegates that he had selected thirteen cabinet ministers. Six were Pashtun, including the new interior minister, Taj Mohammed Wardak. In a nod toward women, Karzai retained the formidable Sohaila Sediq, a military doctor, to head the health ministry.

As Karzai wrapped up the announcements, the delegates began shouting, "What about Qanooni?" Karzai was supposed to reply vaguely. Perhaps overwhelmed by the moment, he instead told the delegates, "Well, I think he should be minister of education!"

Qanooni was sitting in the front row when Karzai blurted this out. He looked up at Karzai and protested that education was not his expertise and that he did not want that ministry. Whether Karzai could actually hear Qanooni amid the unruly crowd was unclear. Either way, Karzai announced the "good news" to the audience that Qanooni had accepted the appointment.

Furious, Qanooni tried to leap from his chair, seemingly ready to attack Karzai physically. Fortunately, Abdullah was sitting next to him. Given his limp, Qanooni's movements, even in a state of fury, were a bit slow, enabling Abdullah to grab hold of Qanooni's arm, maneuver, and sit on it. Trapped in his oversized chair, Qanooni yelled at Karzai, insulting his clothing, calling him a disgrace to Afghanistan, and reminding him that he was nothing without the Northern Alliance. Karzai quickly closed the session.

Qanooni dashed ominously toward me. "You think Fahim is a *baadmash* [troublemaker]?" he quivered, waving his finger in my face. "Well, I will show you who the real *baadmash* is . . ."

I warned him to be judicious. "Do you think I'm a potted plant?" I asked. "Any action you take will have consequences."

The next day, Kabul was abuzz with rumors of an imminent coup. Qanooni, still commanding the loyalty of the Tajik-dominated Interior Ministry, may have ordered security forces to block roads in the city. Soldiers armed with grenade launchers and police in full riot gear stood by the ministry, preventing Wardak, the new minister, from assuming office. U.S. aircraft and international forces were deployed to prevent the standoff from erupting into violence.

Brahimi and I headed over to talk with Qanooni. Still smarting from the *Loya Jirga*, Qanooni demanded that we prevent Wardak from sweeping into the Interior Ministry and replacing all of his staff. We assured Qanooni that we would not allow this to happen. "But you cannot get away with extra-legal power grabs," we warned. After some more discussion, Qanooni relented. He agreed to accept the post at the Ministry of Education so long as he could still serve as a security advisor in Karzai's cabinet.

To his credit, Qanooni stood down. He remained a loyal member of the Karzai government and served competently as minister of education. Eventually, he made light of the ordeal. In the middle of contentious meetings, Qanooni would sometimes lighten the mood by interjecting jokingly, "Do you think I'm a potted plant?"

◄   ►

DURING THE EMERGENCY *Loya Jirga*, a significant tension between American and Afghan perspectives arose that I had previously underestimated.

Bush administration officials took it as a given that liberal democracy was the best form of government for Afghanistan and that elections were the most legitimate way to work out differences among Afghans. The president and his principals seemed to believe that these goals were achievable, at least in broad outlines, without a significant U.S. investment in state and nation building.

Afghans were more divided on how the country should navigate the post-Taliban transition. One school of thought was optimistic about Afghan democracy. Adherents of this view threw themselves into forming issue-based civil society organizations and developing modern news-and-entertainment media. Another school of thought, based in the more traditional sectors of society, believed that the *jirga* was the best way to form a participatory political system. For them, elders and other social leaders would best represent and refine the popular will. They worried that elections would be divisive and could be manipulated. A third school of thought argued that Afghans were not ready for democracy and needed a strong but benevolent leader to rule for a number of years. In essence, adherents of this school wanted to find an Afghan version of Singapore's Lee Kuan Yew, and give him the authority to build Afghan institutions and decide when to open up the political system.

I might have supported the Lee Kuan Yew model had we identified a figure behind whom Afghans would rally. None existed. And even if we had found such a figure, the United States was not prepared to invest enough of its own credibility and resources to ensure that a benevolent strongman succeeded. Nor is it clear that an Afghan strongman would have remained benevolent.

I shared President Bush's aspirations for a democratic Afghanistan but believed that Afghan traditionalists were raising reasonable concerns about the challenges ahead. The right formula, I thought, was to create a broad-based governing coalition of Afghan leaders that was committed to building national institutions, curbing warlordism, and jump-starting economic development. Without enough progress on these fronts, I did not see how the country could convene free and fair national elections in which Afghans could go to the polls without facing intimidation from warlords. The Bonn Agreement's goal of holding national elections, I thought, was doable—Afghan leaders had shown a remarkable degree of political maturity and commitment to the democratic process—but only if the United States laid the groundwork with sizable investments in state- and nation-building programs.

FOURTEEN

EYES ELSEWHERE

WASHINGTON, D.C., DECEMBER 2002–FEBRUARY 2003

ON DECEMBER 2, 2002, PRESIDENT BUSH APPOINTED ME AS HIS "SPECIAL PRESIDENTIAL envoy to the Free Iraqis." I was to work with the Iraqi opposition to prepare for a post-Saddam Iraq. I concluded that the president had decided to invade Iraq.

Although I had been focused on Afghanistan, I had also participated in the Bush administration's deliberations over Iraq. I was a member of Hadley's Deputies Committee meetings on Iraq, comprised of a small group of senior officials. Attendees could not reveal even the existence of the meetings, and we processed papers through special channels to avoid press leaks.

At the deputies level, a consensus existed on three points. First, Iraq needed to be disarmed. Second, if Saddam refused to disarm, the United States would pursue a serious policy of regime change in Iraq. Containment was no longer a viable alternative. Third, our policy of regime change would seek a broad-based representative government in Iraq, even if a coup ousted Saddam during our planning.

Still, difficult questions remained unresolved.

The primary clash was between the Pentagon and the State Department. The Pentagon, backed by the vice president's office, proposed various plans to empower the Iraqi opposition. Among the opposition leaders, the Pentagon and vice president's office were closest to Chalabi.

The State Department and CIA were more skeptical of the Iraqi opposition. They argued that Iraqi "internals"—those Iraqis still living under Saddam—would not accept a government led by those who had fled Saddam's Iraq. State and CIA were particularly hostile to Chalabi.

Rice wanted a consensus. While the underlying disagreement was never resolved, a compromise was brokered in early 2002 on next steps. The State Department would convene a group of opposition leaders. Chalabi would be included, but so, too, would his rivals in the opposition.

The State Department, however, stalled in actually convening the opposition meeting. By July, State was pushing a plan with a relatively passive role for the opposition. In the State Department's proposal, a U.S. "transitional civil authority" would assume control after Saddam's ouster for an undefined period.

The Pentagon, the vice president's office, and Hadley resisted this idea.

Eventually, the principals agreed to convene an opposition conference in London in mid-December. I was chosen as envoy, again, by default—the principals could not agree on anyone else.

My mission was to unite the various Iraqi opposition groups and help them develop an inclusive plan for the post-Saddam political transition. During a videoconference from London, Powell joked that if I succeeded, he would nominate me for a Nobel Peace Prize.

I began working out the possibilities for post-Saddam Iraq. I was convinced that most Iraqis wanted Saddam removed from power. However, an abrupt overthrow by the U.S. military could lead Iraqis in one of two directions. They might move toward democracy, federalism, and, perhaps, even a partnership with the United States. Or, they might see the toppling of Saddam as an opportunity to fight for power among themselves. I knew that the political culture of Iraq had been quite violent throughout history and feared the country's fragmentation. At the same time, the idea of resurrecting Iraq after Saddam's tyrannical rule and recapturing glorious periods of Iraqi history could provide a powerful, unifying vision.

The United States, I concluded, could improve the odds of a good outcome by avoiding a Western occupation, which, I feared, might create a scapegoat and a common enemy for Iraqis.

I worked with the main opposition leaders to come up with a list of 300 Iraqis to invite to the London conference. The tumultuous process produced a solid mix of Shia Arabs, Kurds, and independent figures, but I was concerned that Sunni Arabs were underrepresented.

One major opposition group—the predominantly Shia-Arab Dawa Party—decided to boycott the conference. Some on the U.S. side never wanted to invite Dawa in the first place, given that it was allegedly involved in the bombing of the U.S. embassy in Kuwait in the 1980s.

I flew to London in early December to meet with the conference preparatory committee. While the Iraqis welcomed increased U.S. engagement with the opposition, they remained suspicious about whether the United States would really help overthrow Saddam's regime. Shia Arabs in particular were concerned about a repeat of 1991, when the president encouraged them to rise against Saddam before leaving them to be massacred by the thousands.

I was not in a position to confirm that President Bush had decided to invade Iraq. But I recommended as clearly as I could that Iraqis should prepare for the regime's overthrow.

◄   ►

I WAS FAMILIAR with the Iraqi opposition. But now, I had to take measure of them as future leaders of Iraq.

I had known Chalabi since he came to see me at the Pentagon during the first Bush administration. His wife was from the Osseiran family, an established clan based in Lebanon whom I knew from my days at AUB. One of the daughters, Zeina, had been Cheryl's neighbor and friend in the women's dormitory.

At the London conference, Chalabi mediated between the U.S. team and the Iran-backed religious Shia parties, notably SCIRI leader Abdul Aziz al-Hakim. He worked the phones to keep his friends back in the U.S. and Iran informed. Using his excellent contacts with the U.S. media, Chalabi ensured that his perspectives got press.

Ayad Allawi, the leader of the Iraqi National Accord (INA), was also a secular Shia Arab. Politically, though, he had little in common with Chalabi. Allawi continued to feel that a coup was the most promising approach to regime change in Iraq. He shared reports about restlessness in the Iraqi military and asked me to signal to the military, in my public statements, that they should side with the people of Iraq rather than with Saddam.

I took his advice.

The two principal Kurdish leaders, Massoud Barzani of the KDP and Jalal Talabani of the PUK, headed parties that had essentially divided the governance of Iraqi Kurdistan between themselves. The U.S.-protected safe haven in the north had allowed the KDP and the PUK to establish quasi-states in their respective territories. Though rivals and even warring enemies at times, the Kurdish parties shared a similar vision for post-Saddam Iraq: autonomy for their regions inside Iraq and the right to declare independence for Kurdistan.

Barzani was a strong leader. His father, Mullah Mustapha, had played a historic role in the Kurdish struggle. With a serious demeanor—a combination of a tough labor activist and a traditional Middle Eastern pasha—Barzani was a sharp and persistent negotiator, but would stick by any deal he struck. I sought his help in getting the opposition groups to come together on a strong statement of principles and plan of action.

I was also impressed with Talabani. Good-natured and ebullient, he was a natural mediator and conciliator who worked well with all sides. I immediately sensed that he could be a good president of post-Saddam Iraq. Although both Kurdish leaders had strong relations with the Shia Arabs, Talabani had the benefit of excellent ties with Iran. The Shia-Kurdish axis would be a powerful bloc, I believed, and he could be its leader. I could also see him reaching out to the Sunni Arabs. When I hypothetically broached with Talibani the possibility of his becoming president after the overthrow, he was both interested and pleased. "And you would make a good U.S. ambassador to Iraq," he added.

In London, I met for the first time with Abdul Aziz al-Hakim. The head delegate of SCIRI, he was the scion of a venerable Shia Arab clerical family. In the early days of the Baathist regime, the Hakim family, based in the city of Najaf, had been a particular target of Saddam's crackdown against Iraq's religious Shia community. Hakim himself fled to Iran in the late 1970s, along with his brother Mohammed Baqir al-Hakim. Shortly after the start of the Iran-Iraq war, Hakim's brother formed SCIRI, which organized military units called the Badr Corps to fight alongside the Iranians.

A thin, soft-spoken man with tinted glasses and the nicotine aura of a chain-smoker, Abdul Aziz al-Hakim wore flowing robes and a black turban that signified his status as a *sayyid*, a descendant of the Prophet Mohammed. But unlike his more prominent father and older brother, Hakim had spent most of his life not as a cleric but as an operative and military commander of the Badr Corps.

When we met, Hakim minced no words: there would be problems if the United States did not cooperate with SCIRI. SCIRI had worked closely with the Iranian Revolutionary Guard Corps, and the Badr Corps still received financial and military support from Iran. In preparation for a U.S. strike, Iran was helping SCIRI to establish secret operational centers in Iraq.

With SCIRI's long-standing sectarianism in mind, I made it clear to Hakim that the most important U.S. goal was to produce a unified statement of principles that guaranteed the rights of all of Iraq's responsible ethnic, religious, and political groups. I warned Hakim that there was still a debate within the U.S. government about whether the opposition was ready to assume power after Saddam. Unless SCIRI and other opposition groups demonstrated unity, I observed, the United States might pursue options that he would find unpalatable.

I shared with Hakim some of the lessons that I had drawn from the Afghan experience. Many of the groups that had been most effective in resisting the Soviets had subsequently inflicted civil war and destruction on their people. The U.S. had made mistakes, but those errors paled in comparison to what the Afghans had done to their own country. Could the Iraqi opposition rise to the occasion and find ways to cooperate?

Skilled at the rhetorical counterpunch, Hakim responded that the real question was whether the United States was ready to allow the Iraqis to form their own government.

Though I had some doubts about SCIRI, I thought the Iraqi opposition as a whole could potentially appeal to the Iraqi people. Saddam had thoroughly alienated the majority of Iraqis, particularly the Shia Arab and Kurdish communities.

Still, I knew that apart from the Kurdish leaders, the Iraqi opposition had had limited opportunity to govern. Our modest goals for the London conference would be a meaningful political test for them.

──◄ ►──

ON DECEMBER 11, I set up shop in a large fourteenth-floor suite at the Hilton Metropole Hotel. Located in a North London neighborhood marked by Arab storefront signs, the Metropole was an ideal place for the conference.

Critical issues remained unresolved, and I held "listening sessions" with dozens of Iraqis. I pressed the leaders to make sure that women were well represented at the conference. Observance of women's rights was one of the few positives in the Baath Party's otherwise oppressive legacy in Iraq.

The conference officially began the next morning. Beyond the 330 invited delegates, many other Iraqis simply showed up. After the morning session, I retreated to my suite and asked the rest of the U.S. delegation—a dozen or so officials from State, Defense, the vice president's office, and NSC—to leave the plenary as well. The Iraqis were sensitive to perceptions that they were not acting independently. So for most of the conference, Iraqis delivered speeches in the absence of the U.S. officials.

The next day I spoke to the full assembly. Surveying the delegates, I noticed that even the younger attendees appeared to be well into their forties. What did this mean, I wondered, for a country in which 75 percent of the population was under the age of twenty-five?

No line of my speech earned as much applause as the simple pledge I made to the "many old friends" and "committed Iraqi patriots" in the room: "We don't want half measures for Iraq. No Saddamism without Saddam. No dictatorship." The meaning of my words was clear: the United States would pursue genuine democracy in Iraq. We would not, as some in the CIA and State Department preferred, seek to install another Sunni Arab dictator in Iraq.

The toughest negotiations concerned the way seats would be allocated at the next opposition conference. SCIRI had already negotiated a larger percentage of seats than they objectively deserved. Yet Hakim was still holding out. Throughout the conference, Hakim had allowed Chalabi to act as his lawyer of sorts. Lacking confidence in his ability to deal with the United States, Hakim seemed to believe that Chalabi knew the psychological dimensions of selling a deal to the United States. Chalabi's willingness to mediate effectively gave Hakim two bites at the apple—he would state his own position, then Chalabi would reinforce his line.

After a series of interminable discussions, I decided to bring the matter to a head. I knew from my own sources that Hakim, for all his recalcitrance, did not want to be blamed for the conference's failure. I looked straight at Hakim and gave him an ultimatum: "If you are not willing to accept reasonable terms, I will walk out, declare the conference a failure, and tell the world that the only thing standing in the way of a deal was SCIRI."

Chalabi tried to intervene, but this time, I stopped him. I wanted to hear directly from Hakim.

William Luti, the Pentagon's representative in the delegation, became uncomfortable as I confronted Chalabi. Luti tended to defend Chalabi against his State and CIA critics and perhaps did not want me to pile on. Seeing that Luti was about to intervene on Chalabi's behalf, I subtly signaled to him not to do so. Throughout the conference, the Iraqis, well aware of interagency divisions in the Bush administration, had tried to play State and Defense officials off each other. I didn't want our interagency squabbles to let Hakim off the hook at this sensitive juncture. Luti immediately understood my message and stayed silent.

Hakim was now cornered. A little after midnight, he left the meeting to make some phone calls to Tehran. He returned in a much more cooperative mood and agreed to the deal.

The final statement approved at the London conference expressed the opposition's intent to build a democratic, pluralist, inclusive nation governed by the rule of law. Notably, the Iraqis affirmed that they opposed any form of foreign occupation after Saddam.

I came away from the London conference with a better understanding of Iraqi politics. I saw that the cleavages in Iraqi society were profound—much deeper than those in Afghanistan. Iraqis were divided about the role of religion in politics, the aspirations of the Kurds, their views on Iran, the right way to handle the crimes of Saddam's regime, and many other issues.

—◄   ►—

IN JANUARY 2003, I blocked out time to do some research. Could Iraq's historical dynamics shed light on what awaited us in Baghdad? My former professor at AUB, Hannah Batatu, had written a book entitled *The Old So-cial Classes and the Revolutionary Movements of Iraq: A Study of Iraq's Old Landed and Commercial Classes and of its Communists, Ba'thists, and Free Officers.* In 1,283 pages, the book analyzed Iraq's revolutionary movements from 1917 to 1958.

Batatu's book describes an Iraqi society that was utterly fractured along ethnic, sectarian, and class lines. The Hashemite monarchy may have created some cohesiveness, but Batatu assessed that even in 1978, "the psychology and ways of the old order—the work of long centuries—are still embedded in the life of broad strata of the people, and will not easily wither away."

Despite this research, the complexities and divisions that ultimately awaited us inside Iraq exceeded even my grimmest expectations.

IN EARLY 2003, President Bush began to reach out personally to the Iraqi op-position. In an Oval Office meeting in early January with three exiled Iraqi opposition figures, he was very clear, vowing that the United States would remove Saddam from power one way or the other. He then asked each of the three to share their personal stories. The president was clearly moved as they spoke of the suffering their families and communities had endured.

Brandeis University professor Kanan Makiya told President Bush that he was conducting research into Saddam's war crimes. Using his own biography as a segue, he told the president that the United States had a transformative opportunity in Iraq. Regime change, Makiya predicted, would "break the mold" and establish a new Iraq in which the United States would be liked and respected. The other Iraqi participants echoed Makiya's sentiments.

The president then peppered the Iraqis with questions. The press has covered this exchange extensively. Journalists have reported that the president asked the exiles to explain to him the difference between Shias and Sunnis in Iraq. This is not true. What I remember is that the president asked whether there was a sharp divide between the Sunnis and Shias and how these dynamics would play out after Saddam's downfall. Would sectarian differences instigate "hatred, civil conflicts, and more disasters?" He also asked whether the elite in the country was well educated or whether Saddam had purged the educated classes "like in China."

A Sunni Arab physician from Saddam's hometown of Tikrit, Hatem Mukhlis, assured the president that Sunnis, too, were eager to depose Saddam. Once the dictator was gone, Shias and Sunnis would work together in a new democratic government. The point clearly resonated with the president.

The other part of the meeting that has been reported widely is Makiya's assessment of how the Iraqi people would greet U.S. forces. Makiya, it is true, did tell the president that the United States would be welcomed "with sweets and flowers." As evidence, Makiya cited Iraqi reactions to the Gulf War, when people cheered from the rooftops as coalition forces waged air strikes against the regime. Makiya's optimistic statement was tempered by Mukhlis, who said that the United States would be well received, but only if it delivered for the Iraqi people within the first two months. After that, he stated, "you could see Mogadishu in Baghdad."

President Bush seemed to share the opposition's assumption that the Iraqi people would welcome a U.S. military intervention. But he was concerned about collateral damage from the war. What if the country sustained heavy damage during the campaign against Saddam's forces? All three Iraqis replied that the regime was fragile and would fall quickly.

The president then asked the Iraqis about postwar plans. Cheney, who had hardly said a word, interrupted at this point. The U.S. would have a "light hand in the postwar phase." This pleased them.

However, the group differed on how to establish a postwar government. Mukhlis suggested that the United States should wait until Saddam was overthrown and then work with Iraqis inside the country. Makiya and Rend Rahim Francke, a human rights activist, were equally adamant in urging the president to create a provisional government-in-exile that could step in to fill the vacuum.

The president replied in a noncommittal way. He agreed that democracy in Iraq was more likely to emerge if "the diaspora"—which had lived in Western democracies—returned. But he wanted to avoid "the impression" that the U.S. was "imposing" a leader on the Iraqis. Makiya pointed out that the U.S. had promoted Karzai in Afghanistan, but the analogy did not seem to jibe with the president.

The president was more decisive when it came to reconstruction assistance. What would the Iraqi people need? The exiles responded that delivering humanitarian relief would be the immediate challenge, but that the U.S. military likely would need to remain in Iraq for two to three years to ensure stability. "We're planning for the worst," the president assured them.

—<   >—

MY TAKEAWAY from the meeting was that President Bush was ambivalent. He wanted to work with the Iraqi opposition but did not want to anoint Iraq's new leaders. Thus, the president made important decisions on some matters in the weeks after the meeting but allowed others to remain unsettled.

On the one hand, he formally assigned the Pentagon responsibility for post-invasion planning, as Rumsfeld had hoped.

The defense secretary created an office for postwar planning known as the Office of Reconstruction and Humanitarian Assistance (ORHA). Once in the field, ORHA would serve as CENTCOM's civilian arm to tackle "humanitarian, reconstruction, and administrative challenges."

ORHA was not tasked with governing Iraq after Saddam's ouster but, rather, with aiding the transition to an Iraqi-led government. Until an Iraqi government was established, CENTCOM, under General Tommy Franks's command, had responsibility for providing security and establishing institutions.

At the same time, the president decided not to recognize a provisional government of Iraqi opposition leaders before Saddam's ouster.

Yet important interagency divisions remained with regard to how much support the United States should provide the opposition groups.

In a Principals Committee meeting, Cheney, alluding to the interagency divisions over Chalabi and the other opposition figures, suggested that the administration needed to decide on which Iraqi externals to support. Rumsfeld, by contrast, indicated that he was not interested in the particulars of opposition factions. "Let's make the decision on a postwar government later," he advised. Rumsfeld worried that if we "gave the keys to the car" too quickly to people who turned out to be corrupt, incompetent, or unpopular with the Iraqi people, we would damage our credibility.

My own view was that we should not occupy and govern Iraq for an extended period. At the same time, negotiations over a provisional government would be difficult and divisive; I doubted that they could be completed before the start of combat operations. The better path, in my mind, was the Afghan model, except that we should have the equivalent of the Bonn conference inside Iraq after liberation.

After a discussion with the principals on Iraq, Rice asked to meet with me separately in her office. In the aftermath of the London conference, the Iraqi opposition was intent on hosting its next conference in the U.S.-protected area of northern Iraq. Rice was concerned about the U.S. government's ability to provide adequate security. Recent history supplied ample cause for concern. Saddam's incursion in the north in 1996 had succeeded in dislodging the Kurds from some areas. In speeches throughout 2001, Saddam had threatened the Kurds with another attack if they refused to abandon their relationship with "foreigners." When Saddam learned that the opposition planned to meet in Iraq, he cut off fuel supplies to Kurdistan for a few days.

Rice suggested that I try to persuade the opposition leaders to have the conference in Qatar instead of northern Iraq. I told Rice that security of course was an important concern, but that I had already promised the Iraqis that I would join them in Salahuddin, Iraq. Rice persisted, asking that I just tell them new security issues had arisen. I argued that it was important to the opposition leaders to meet on Iraqi territory. It was the first opportunity in years for the exiles to return home and demonstrate their commitment to the Iraqi people. She then acquiesced.

FIFTEEN

PLANNING POSTWAR IRAQ INSIDE IRAQ

ANKARA, TURKEY, AND SALAHUDDIN, IRAQ, FEBRUARY 2002

THE IRAQI OPPOSITION CONFERENCE WAS SCHEDULED TO BEGIN ON FEBRUARY 10. Originally, I was to fly from Ankara, Turkey, to Iraqi Kurdistan along with a State Department security team and sixty Special Forces personnel who were supposed to stay behind in Iraq in preparation for the impending invasion.

Once in Ankara, however, we got stuck for almost a week. Each day we would prepare to leave, only to be told that Turkey had denied us permission to fly into northern Iraq. Hoshyar Zebari, who was calling me at least once a day on behalf of his boss, Massoud Barzani, was suspicious. Were we really being delayed by the Turks, or were we using this as a pretext to avoid attending the opposition meeting?

After what seemed like an eternity in Ankara, I received a phone call from Hadley. "Zal," he said, "your country has come through for you." Rice had called Abdullah Gul, the Turkish prime minister, and relayed, on the president's behalf, that I had been waiting for several days in Ankara. Gul assured Rice that we would receive permission to fly to Erbil.

A few hours later, we took off in a C-130. More than an hour into the flight, General Colby Broadwater delivered bad news. The Turkish military had overruled the prime minister, and we no longer had permission to fly into Iraqi airspace.

We now had two options. We could land at Incirlik Air Base, spend the night there, and then have the Turks bus us the following day to the Kurdish-Iraqi border. Once at the border, the Kurds would drive us for 300 miles along Iraqi military lines of control to Salahuddin. This would mean driving along the dividing line separating Saddam's forces and the Kurdish Peshmerga. The second option was to return to the United States.

The White House left the decision to me.

We held a quick inflight discussion. My State Department security team was strongly opposed to our traveling to Salahuddin by land. They were not familiar with the area and would not be able to do much in the event of an attack by Saddam's forces.

The members of my team from the military including the Special Forces, the NSC, and the State Department wanted to take the risk and head to northern Iraq anyway.

I considered the consequences of not going, especially for Barzani and the Iraqi opposition leaders he was hosting. If we failed to attend, we would severely damage our credibility and make it harder for me to deal with the opposition later on. With trepidation, I decided that we would proceed.

As we headed for Incirlik, Broadwater directed me to look out the window. A Turkish fighter jet flew close to our plane. He informed me that there was a jet on the other side as well. They were there, he said, to make sure that we went to Incirlik and not to Iraq.

"Would they shoot us down if they believed we are heading to Iraq?" I asked.

"They might," he replied.

Incirlik had a tidy dormitory which Turkish officers had made available for us. We arrived quite late but found the cafeteria open for breakfast the next morning. The man running the cafeteria urged me to drink Shalgham juice. The turnip juice, he assured me, was full of vitamin C and, therefore, would protect me against pneumonia. He did not convert me.

We boarded several buses and headed toward the border. As I gazed out the window, I was surprised to see how impoverished southeastern Turkey looked. In the distance were the beautiful peaks of the Taurus Mountains. On the ground were sights that had become all too familiar to me from Afghanistan—destroyed roads, barren farms, dilapidated homes, and tired, weather-beaten peasants. Broadwater tried to lighten the mood with a dark joke. "Just like a scene from *Sanford and Son*," he remarked as we passed a particularly ruinous junkyard.

Waiting across the border was the Kurdish greeting party and a convoy of forty-five Toyota Land Cruisers ready to take us to Salahuddin. The drive on the Iraqi side of the border was markedly more pleasant. The road was smoother and the countryside was prettier. Lining the highway were tall, broad cedar trees. Pleased that I took note of the scenery—and compared it favorably with the Turkish areas—Zebari became an ebullient tour guide. He explained that the cedars had been shipped to Iraq from Lebanon during the reign of Faisal II before his ouster in the July 14 Revolution of 1958.

The scenic route was blemished, however, by the sight of Iraqi infantry, missiles, and tanks just across the 36th parallel, where the no-fly zone ended. At times we were so close to Iraqi front lines that I could see the faces of the soldiers standing atop the tanks. If Saddam ordered a ground action, we were done for.

I learned later that President Bush was asking for updates about our group every half hour. I also was in touch with Hadley throughout the trip. The president was not the only anxious one. We kept asking Zebari how much longer the trip would take. "Thirty minutes!" he replied every time.

Finally, we trekked up a high mountaintop to Salahuddin. Barzani and Talabani were waiting to greet us, as were their hospitable staff, eager to care for our "small army," as a senior Turkish official had called it.

—◄   ►—

AS THE HOST, Barzani had delayed the conference until we arrived. The next morning, he delivered obligatory remarks on "unifying the work of the Iraqi opposition." His mind, however, was clearly on his northern neighbor Turkey: "Any regional intervention in the internal affairs of Iraq will cause instability. . . ."

Hakim warned against "foreign domination," rejected "colonialism," and asserted that "Iraq is able to administer itself."

Chalabi declared, "We are your friends, but not your agents." He added, "We fought Saddam Hussein before you knew of him."

Given the uncertainty regarding U.S. policy, my opening remarks were the most anticipated event of the day. With no clear guidance from Washington even at this late stage, I had to keep them ambiguous. "Should military action be necessary," I stated, "the U.S. has no desire to govern Iraq."

On de-Baathification, I indicated that "our quarrel is with Saddam Hussein and his inner circle." The implication was that the U.S. would not support a deep purge of Baath Party members. I also affirmed that the United States would not install another dictator. I called on the members of the Iraqi army to contribute to the "liberation" of their country.

Though I was not able to offer much in the way of detail, my concluding line seemed to satisfy much of the audience. "Help is on the way," I promised. Nechirvan Barzani, the nephew of Massoud Barzani, and Zebari later told me that this statement marked the first time that many in the opposition finally believed that the U.S. was serious about removing Saddam.

Still, the main point the opposition wanted to hear was that the United States would either recognize a provisional government now or an interim government immediately after the invasion. They heard neither.

The reason was that the Turkish parliament was debating whether to allow U.S. troops to enter into Iraq through Turkish territory. If the Iraqi opposition announced a provisional government, the Turkish parliament would almost certainly vote to deny U.S. forces permission.

In the end, the opposition refrained from announcing a provisional government. The Turkish parliament voted no anyway.

We had at last succeeded in unifying the Iraqi exiles: they were now against us. The prospect of an occupation government and the uncertainty surrounding our postwar plans were impeding our ability to enlist the opposition leaders as partners in the democratic transition.

I returned from Salahuddin to Turkey with a much smaller team. As planned, the Special Forces stayed behind, so my group now totaled fewer than ten. At the border, the Turks held us for over an hour, angrily demanding to know what had happened to our Special Forces colleagues. We said that they had not yet finished their business—which was true. They were part of the advance team for the initial phase of the impending invasion. After many phone calls, we were allowed to re-enter Turkey.

—◄   ►—

IN THE FIRST HALF of 2003, I held a series of talks with Iranian diplomats to discuss the future of Iraq. Ryan Crocker accompanied me from the State Department.

Zarif, now Tehran's ambassador to the United Nations, headed the Iranian side. They were always very hospitable, particularly in hosting us for lunch.

Interestingly, despite the sensitive nature of the discussions, neither the president nor the Principals Committee vetted my instructions going into the meeting.

In our two meetings before the war, I told Zarif that the United States intended to overthrow Saddam's regime, eliminate Iraq's weapons of mass destruction capabilities, and establish a democratic government that would be at peace with its neighbors. The important point here was unsaid: the United States, contrary to public accusations from Iran's supreme leader, Ayatollah Khamenei, had no plans to expand the war into Iran.

I said that if the United States intervened in Iraq, we expected Iran's cooperation in certain respects. We wanted a commitment that Iran would not fire on U.S. aircraft if they accidentally flew over Iranian territory. Zarif agreed.

We also hoped Iran would encourage Iraqi Shias to participate constructively in establishing a new government in Iraq. Zarif responded that Tehran strongly opposed a U.S. occupation and wanted an Iraqi government to be formed in exile as quickly as possible. Zarif also indicated that Iraqi security institutions would need to be rebuilt from the ground up—they could not be reformed. He advocated deep de-Baathification. I made a mental note that Zarif's points tracked with the arguments that Hakim and other Iraqi opposition leaders close to Iran were making.

We also discussed how Iraqis would react to the U.S. invasion. In the Iranian view, there was no question that Saddam would use weapons of mass destruction. While the Iranians were wrong on this front, I wish, in hindsight, that I had taken more seriously Zarif's warnings about the instability that would engulf Iraq in the postwar period.

Our final meeting in May focused on terrorism. Zarif requested that the United States turn over the leadership of the Mojahedin-e-Khalq (MEK), an Iranian opposition group based in Iraq. I told Zarif that the United States would disarm the MEK but would not hand them over to Iran. I brought up the fact that al Qaeda leaders, including bin Laden's son, were being harbored by Iran.

The Iranians were not forthcoming. Though they seemed at one point to air the possibility of a direct exchange—MEK leaders for al Qaeda operatives—the Bush administration was not willing to consider it.

Nine days after our meeting, truck bombs exploded at a housing compound in Riyadh, killing eight Americans. When the attacks were linked to al Qaeda in Iran, the principals decided to break off my channel with the Iranians.

⟵   ⟶

ON THE EVE of the invasion of Iraq, the diplomatic crisis with Turkey was escalating again. Turkey was now demanding the right to send its forces into Iraq. Turkey feared that Iraqi Kurds would exploit the war to declare independence, setting a troubling example to Turkey's own restive Kurdish population. Ankara also feared that the war would produce a flood of refugees into Turkey, as had happened during the Gulf War and its aftermath. Violent Kurdish separatists, who had bases in the Qandeel Mountains in Iraqi Kurdistan, might enter Turkey disguised as refugees.

In Salahuddin, in a private meeting in the wood-paneled conference room of his guesthouse, Barzani and I had discussed U.S. plans to have Turkish forces enter Kurdistan as part of the coalition. He startled me when he declared, with great emphasis, that was a serious mistake. "There would be a war within the war," he predicted, warning that the Turks would enter Iraq not to liberate Iraq from Saddam, but rather to disarm Kurdish forces and dismantle what the Kurds had built in northern Iraq.

Barzani said the Kurds would tolerate a small Turkish military presence on Kurdish territory so that Turkey could see for itself that Iraqi Kurds were not assisting Kurdish separatists. But on the question of whether the Turkish military should enter Kurdish areas as part of the coalition, Barzani was unambiguous: "We will fight them."

I reported Barzani's warning to Washington.

I was at Heathrow Airport on my way back to Washington from the Salahuddin conference when I got a call from Hadley and Armitage. Could I return to Ankara to make sure that the Turks did not send forces into Iraq?

"I didn't pack enough clothes," I protested, unsuccessfully.

My trip to Turkey turned into a two-week marathon. I decided that the best way to deal with the Turks was to engage them on why precisely they wanted to send their forces into Iraq. What were their end objectives, and how could we achieve them without the use of Turkish forces?

Turkey agreed to a three-way meeting with the U.S. and the Iraqi Kurds, represented by Talabani and Nichervan Barzani. We agreed to form a joint cell where representatives from all sides would share intelligence on the Kurdish separatist group, the PKK, and discuss how to respond to incidents near the border.

The stay in Ankara gave me an opportunity to meet individually with Iraqi opposition leaders.

I informed them that the Bush administration was still weighing plans but that our tentative concept was to organize a council of Iraqi advisors to assist the coalition on reconstruction and postwar administration. The United States was not prepared to transfer executive and legislative powers to the advisory body in the first phase. Instead, the path to full Iraqi sovereignty would begin with local, municipal, and provincial elections, ideally within a year.

This would give the U.N. time to conduct a proper census and the advisory council time to organize a constitutional convention to decide the precise nature of the new Iraqi government. Iraq's civil society, meanwhile, would need to organize quickly to facilitate a peaceful transfer.

Hakim was most hostile. In Afghanistan, he reminded us, the United States had immediately established a sovereign Afghan government led by officials from the Afghan opposition. Why was the U.S. unwilling to do the same in Iraq?

This was the question on the minds of all the opposition factions. Chalabi, incensed by the U.S. decision not to support an immediate transfer of sovereignty to Iraq, had even refused my invitation to meet in Turkey.

I tried to explain. In Afghanistan, the United States had only deployed Special Forces and a small number of troops to overthrow the Taliban. In Iraq, the United States would be invading with a larger footprint and would be undertaking a more involved mission.

Hakim proceeded to lambaste U.S. policy. In London, the Iraqis had unanimously rejected the idea of a U.S. occupation government. Hakim argued that the Iraqi opposition should take the lead in liberating Iraq and establishing a new government. In the coming weeks, the Iraqi opposition leaders would be ready to declare a provisional government. If the Bush administration insisted on sidelining the Iraqi opposition, he warned, the United States would face problems in securing the country.

SIXTEEN

IRAQ: FROM LIBERATION TO OCCUPATION

WASHINGTON, D.C., AND BAGHDAD, MARCH–MAY 2003

I WAS IN ANKARA, TURKEY, ON MARCH 20, WHEN THE INVASION BEGAN. AS THE pointman in working with the Iraqi opposition on the post-Saddam transition, I strongly believed that the United States should transfer authority to an Iraqi interim government as quickly as possible. However, senior policymakers in Washington were schizophrenic on the question. Some wanted the United States to govern Iraq as an occupying power for a significant period. Others sought to hand over sovereignty to a provisional or interim Iraqi government immediately. Still others pressed for a blend of the two approaches, with a kind of joint U.S.-Iraqi administration taking power and either gradually transferring responsibility to the Iraqi leaders, or governing until elections could be held.

Despite this debate, I thought my instructions were clear. I was charged with organizing the process to enable Iraqis, both the external opposition and internal leaders, to form an interim government as soon as possible. I spoke of my mission as "organizing a Bonn conference in Baghdad." As coalition forces advanced toward Baghdad, we needed to determine the balance of representation between external and internal leaders, the selection process for the internals, and the plan for convening a conference to select an interim government. I believed that we could form provincial councils, composed of local leaders, to select internal delegates and find a formula to distribute representation by province, and between internal and external leaders.

I also seemed to have clear guidance on important postwar issues. Iraqi security forces, including the army, would be reformed, not disbanded. This meant that we would not have to build these institutions from scratch. De-Baathification would focus on the senior leadership complicit in Saddam's crimes rather than targeting lower-level party members who did not have blood on their hands.

The overall goal, as I understood it, was to liberate Iraq without destroying the country's institutions. This would enable a speedy drawdown of coalition forces.

In retrospect, while important elements of the postwar plans had been worked out, the concept for when and how to transfer power to the Iraqis remained unresolved.

◄   ►

I REMAINED IN ANKARA in the early days of the war, still mediating between Turkey and the Kurds. At midnight on March 23, I received an urgent call from Deputy CENTCOM Commander John Abizaid. He reported that the Iraqis were fighting harder than expected and were refusing to surrender. The United States was losing soldiers. Abizaid said it was urgent that I convene the Iraqi opposition groups in the southern port city of Um Qasr, which had already been liberated, and form a provisional government. Abizaid thought Iraqi soldiers might be more willing to surrender to an Iraqi authority than to the United States.

I began to explain to Abizaid the political and logistical challenges.

"Those are goddamn details," he replied. "It's about American lives. The president has already made the decision."

I was surprised that I had not heard from Rice. Had the president really changed his mind on a provisional government? I began frantically trying to plan the Um Qasr meeting.

However, within forty-eight hours, Saddam's army retreated. Washington's interest in forming a provisional government followed in short order.

◄   ►

WITH THE UM QASR meeting canceled, I headed to northern Iraq for another round of talks with the opposition. Turkey continued to impose logistical difficulties. My flight had to go from Turkey to Romania before heading to Iraq because the Turkish government would not allow a direct flight. The C-130 in which I was flying was designed to land on unimproved runways and it circled for an hour to make sure that we could safely land in Sulaymaniya. The Special Forces guided us onto a highway outlined with markers that could be seen only with night-vision equipment. In preparation for landing, the pilot turned out all the lights and then put the plane into a steep, corkscrew descent. After a while, it was difficult to tell which way was up or down. Then, suddenly, the pilot pulled the plane level, and we heard the landing gear make contact and felt the engines reverse.

Barham Salih, then prime minister of PUK-controlled Kurdistan, greeted me as I stepped off the plane. Salih was in shock. He had been standing with Special Forces personnel in the pitch dark on a deserted road. Appearing out of nowhere, a massive black aircraft had pulled up right in front of them.

In the car on the way to Salih's house, where I would be staying, he promised to build "the Dulles Airport of Sulaymaniya." He later made good on his pledge.

Unfortunately, I had bad news for the Kurds. U.S. policy was still in flux. Barzani and Talibani reported that the Iraqi opposition wanted what we were calling the Interim Iraqi Authority (IIA) to be recognized as the "government." The Kurds did not want to use the opposition leadership council as a vehicle to form the IIA. Talabani argued that the council would fill the transitional government with too many Islamists. They proposed instead that a "Baghdad conference" should form the the interim authority. The U.N. should play a role so that, as Salih put it, "the U.S. and U.K. don't take the inevitable blame all alone." This accorded with my thinking.

I also met with Chalabi. After a brief private meeting, he introduced me to a number of former Iraqi military officers who had joined the Iraqi National Congress. He claimed that he had an army of 4,000 INC forces that were ready to fight the Iraqi military from the north with U.S. support. Washington was less than eager to take them up on the offer—a mistake, I thought, given the enormous challenge that lay ahead in the post-Saddam transition.

⤙   ⤚

THROUGHOUT EARLY APRIL, President Bush, British Prime Minister Tony Blair, and the principals repeatedly told the press that the United States would transfer power to the Iraqis as early as possible. On the day Baghdad fell, Powell announced to the press that I would have the lead on government formation. I happened to be in Kabul as I watched CNN coverage of U.S. forces bringing down the statue of Saddam in Firdos Square. At a press conference in Kabul,

I pointed to Afghanistan as a model for how we could transition quickly to a sovereign government in Iraq.

The Pentagon decided to hold a conference in the southern city of Nasiriyah in mid-April. The United States had received overwhelming support in the area and now had an opportunity to integrate leaders of internal Iraqi groups into the process. I saw this as a good opportunity to start a dialogue with internal Iraqi leaders.

In Doha I linked up with Jay Garner, who had arrived to lead ORHA on the ground in Iraq. At this point he was anticipating at least a partial transition of sovereignty back to Iraqis within 90 to 120 days. At Powell's request, the deputy assistant secretary of state for Near East affairs, Ryan Crocker, also joined us. Crocker and I had worked together productively, first in Afghanistan, where he was chargé d'affaires, and then during the talks with Iran in the run-up to the war.

The Nasiriyah conference convened on April 15 in the shadow of a large ziggurat dating back 4,000 years. In the midst of the Iran-Iraq war, Saddam had reconstructed the façade to make it more imposing. Now it was riddled with bullet holes from the Gulf War.

Garner opened the conference and then turned the meeting over to me. I explained U.S. policy: the IIA would be formed as soon as possible and would rule on a temporary basis until elections could be held for a future democratic government. "This week is the beginning of the road toward democracy in Iraq," I told the delegates. "Our meeting here in Nasiriyah, with representatives of the Iraqi people, is the first in a series of consultations with Iraqis in different parts of the country. None of these meetings will choose a government for Iraq." I added that this process as a whole would lead to the creation of an interim authority.

The mostly Shia delegates were in wait-and-see mode. They were more reluctant than their Shia counterparts in the external opposition to criticize the United States. I tried various approaches to gauge their concerns. I divided the delegates at several tables and asked each table to designate a representative. Security, services, the economy, and health emerged as the top issues.

At the end of the conference, the participants endorsed a thirteen-point declaration calling for a democratic, federal state, based on the rule of law and respect for diversity and the rights of women.

── ➤

FROM NASIRIYAH I headed to Baghdad to convene the next conference of Iraqis, scheduled for April 28. Baghdad was more peaceful than I'd anticipated. The looting that occurred immediately after the toppling of Saddam's regime had subsided. One afternoon I strolled around a part of the city that would later become the Green Zone. The city was quiet, but I chatted with some Iraqis on the street and bought ice cream from a small shop.

The buildings were not in particularly bad shape, but public services were in disarray. Electricity was fleeting, and I could see sewage backed up on many streets. Garbage was piling up everywhere.

As I looked around, I wondered if we could take responsibility for fixing the myriad practical problems facing Iraq, even if we wanted to. The Iraqis certainly knew their electrical, water, and sewage systems better than we did.

I became even more convinced that we needed an Iraqi government to take over as soon as possible. We needed an Iraqi in charge—a Karzai—someone to whom the Iraqis could go with their problems. We would be there behind the scenes, helping to get things done, but without the burden of running the Iraqi government.

The principals apparently agreed, deciding that the United States would begin the process of forming an interim authority by the end of May.

All in all, I was generally optimistic, but the Baghdad conference gave me pause. Convened in a modern government building in the Green Zone, it was a noisy meeting with passionate outbursts and diatribes against the United States. The United States was failing to deliver security and services to the Iraqi people, delegates complained. "Why did you overthrow the system that existed if you didn't have a plan to replace it with something better?" Participants also worried that Iranian proxies were filling the void.

At one point, the conference was teetering on the edge of total disorder when Ayad Jamal al-Din, a moderate Islamist, saved the day. He stood up and gave an eloquent speech about Saddam's crimes and how badly the Iraqi people had suffered. Nostalgia for Saddam, he declared, was unacceptable. The mood calmed and a number of delegates rose to express gratitude for their liberation.

The United States, I sensed, had a narrowing window to establish security and advance the political process.

⟩⟨

SOON AFTER the Baghdad conference, Garner informed me that Ambassador Paul Bremer would be replacing him. I knew that Garner's appointment was temporary, but I was confused when Garner suggested that Bremer would be coming as presidential envoy—the same title as mine. Garner advised me to stick with the political process I was pursuing.

Having been away from Washington for so long, I had only a partial sense of the debate going on there. An incident shortly before my departure from Baghdad gave me my first hint of just how toxic things had become. Crocker and I were working well together without any interagency tensions. In fact, on several occasions I urged Crocker to take a more proactive role in engaging Iraqis. He demurred, saying that it would be best for the United States to speak with one voice.

We faced a daunting task in organizing an interim government after the Baghdad conference. Crocker recognized that we would need more assets on the ground—communications equipment, staff, secure cars, etc. He suggested that I ask the State Department to arrange for these things to be brought to Baghdad as soon as possible.

I sent a quick cable, considering it a routine, bureaucratic request. I was shocked to receive an angry call from Wolfowitz, who was apparently convinced that I had been taken in by the State Department. He suspected that State was seeking to undercut the Pentagon's authority by establishing an embassy. The thought hadn't even occurred to me.

"Paul, don't we work for the same government?" I asked. "Is the Pentagon going to provide all these capabilities we need? If Defense can make these resources available, by all means! But if you're not going to do it, why not take advantage of the assets that State can provide?"

In our long friendship, I do not remember a conversation as tense.

When I recounted the call to Crocker, he was astonished as well and apologized for getting me in trouble.

WHEN I RETURNED to Washington, I expected to get back to Baghdad quickly to continue forming an interim authority. I found that President Bush was deeply concerned by events in Iraq, particularly the state of security and services in Baghdad. When the president asked for my impressions, I confirmed that these were real problems. I mentioned the sewage on the street and lack of power, caused in part by U.S. military actions.

I regret, in hindsight, that I did not provide the president with more context. I did not realize it at the time, but looking back, my briefing may have contributed to his impression that Garner was not on top of things.

Garner's small team, which had been pulled together only a few weeks earlier, could not have been expected to impose law and order. That was the responsibility of coalition military forces. In my view, the coalition was simply unprepared to operate as a government once Baghdad fell. Garner was making a heroic effort in a tough situation.

Looking back, I suspect that the president's lack of confidence in Garner made him question the broader transitional plan that we were pursuing on the ground.

At the time, though, I had every reason to believe that the plan for a rapid transition to Iraqi rule was in place. The principals approved a plan to send nvoys. Bremer would head the Coalition Provisional Authority (CPA), ;h would take over from ORHA. I would work with the Iraqis to advance government formation. I saw this as a sound approach since it would allow me to focus on the political transition while the CPA administered services. In agreeing to this plan, the principals were reaffirming their support for a transfer of power to an interim Iraqi authority.

Events took a different course.

On May 6, after a private lunch between the president and Bremer, the White House announced that only Bremer would go to Baghdad. I was surprised. Powell and Rice were blindsided as well. Agitated, Powell called me to ask what had happened. Rice expressed surprise and displeasure. I was shocked that senior leaders were as out of the loop as I was.

Later in the day, Wolfowitz asked me to come over to his office in the Pentagon to meet with Bremer. I felt a degree of hostility in the room, which surprised me, since I had known both of them for many years. After some small talk, Bremer asked me to come to Baghdad to hand over "your Iraqis" to him.

I told him I would consult with Rice and get back to him. He said that he would be leaving for Iraq soon and observed that after splitting my time between Iraq and Afghanistan over the past months, I would be able to concentrate fully on Afghanistan.

When I met briefly with President Bush later that day, he explained that the decision to give the entire mission to Bremer had nothing to do with me. He said that he wanted the Department of Defense to be in command.

In his memoirs, Bremer recounts that in an earlier, one-on-one meeting with President Bush, he persuaded the president to put only one envoy on the ground. He also convinced President Bush that the Iraqis were not ready for self-government. If his account is correct, in that moment President Bush, without consulting the principals, reversed his earlier decision to establish an interim Iraqi authority.

I had deep concerns about this turn of events—concerns that were reinforced as U.S. policy veered away from the plan to transfer sovereignty to the Iraqis.

Upon arriving in Baghdad, Bremer told the Iraqi leaders that the original plan was off. The United States would no longer support the quick establishment of a transitional Iraqi government. The new policy was for Bremer to run Iraq indefinitely until the Iraqis were "ready" for self-government. Bremer told the Iraqis that he held the executive, legislative, and judicial authorities of the country. The Iraqi leaders could advise him, but he would not be obliged to take their advice.

The Iraqi leaders were stunned. We had given our word that the United States would quickly restore their country's sovereignty. Breaking this promise would call into question our motives for intervening in Iraq. I feared that we would alienate key leaders and communities and disrupt the delicate negotiations that were occurring among Iraqi factions.

I was sad and angry about the decision to abandon the political transition. It was not a matter of my personal role, though I had developed a rapport with my Iraqi counterparts. I was concerned, rather, about the consequences of an indefinite occupation, backed only by a light U.S. footprint.

In retrospect, it seems that the principals disengaged from close oversight of Iraq policy after the private lunch between the president and Bremer. They appeared to believe that the president had given his new envoy free rein to manage Iraq. The principals saw their job as supporting, not overseeing or questioning, Bremer's actions. Hadley later told me that he stopped convening Deputies Committee meetings on Iraq because all the departments were represented in Baghdad and Bremer in effect would perform the functions of the Deputies Committee in the field. Nor did the principals insist on being briefed ahead of time to consider the pros and cons of competing courses of action. Rumsfeld in particular, who had insisted on having the lead on Iraq policy in the run-up to the war, disengaged from day-to-day oversight of policy because, as he later told me, the White House had taken over that role. None of the principals, in my recent conversations with them, could recall a meeting in which they decided whether to disband the Iraqi army. Only Bremer had a different recollection. I cannot help but conclude that the principals failed in their responsibilities for oversight.

Bremer's deployment effectively marked the end of my involvement in major Iraq issues. In the ensuing months, I watched from the sidelines as Iraq became engulfed in conflict and violence.

SEVENTEEN

ACCELERATING SUCCESS IN AFGHANISTAN

WASHINGTON, D.C., MAY–NOVEMBER 2003

PRESIDENT BUSH ASKED TO SEE ME SOON AFTER THE BREMER DECISION. HE GOT straight to the point and, to my surprise, asked if I would be willing to go to Afghanistan as the next ambassador. This was the first time anyone had broached the subject with me. Caught off guard, I replied half jokingly, "Well, Mr. President, I actually left Afghanistan to live here. Why do you want to send me back?"

The president laughed and told me he thought Afghanistan needed more attention. Karzai had asked him to send me back to Kabul. Would I accept?

I told the president that I would need to think about it. I did not want to accept the assignment without assurances that I had the political support and resources to succeed. The Bush administration was still divided on how deeply the U.S. should be involved with state and nation building.

And then there was Pakistan. Could we succeed in Afghanistan without fixing the Pakistan problem? Washington's emphasis on targeting high-value al Qaeda targets in Pakistan was enabling Islamabad to play a double game.

While cooperating with the United States on counterterrorism, Pakistan continued to support the Taliban, Haqqani network, and other insurgents.

Pakistan's persistent efforts to destabilize Afghanistan were deeply rooted in Islamabad's paranoia about India. Pakistani leaders believed, wrongly, that India was gaining a dominant position in Kabul. The Pakistani military's imperial mindset vis-à-vis its Afghan neighbor was also a factor. As long as Pakistan was providing sanctuary and active support to the Taliban, it would be difficult to build security institutions or grow the economy at a fast enough rate to get ahead of the insurgent problem and meet the expectations of the Afghan people.

Until now, I had had little success in advocating for a different approach, both on the state- and nation-building front and in addressing the insurgent sanctuaries in Pakistan. Too often, I had seen officials accept assignments with the mistaken belief that senior officials would later give them the necessary backing. I resolved that I would accept the assignment only if a solid plan, approved by the president, was in place.

◄ ►

LAST BUT NOT LEAST, there was my family to consider. We had finally gotten our act together. Cheryl had decided to make the move to the U.S. to give us all a normal, less peripatetic family life, and we were enjoying this new life without the crazy commuting. The three-year period when we were all in Washington felt like a wonderful time, and to be the one who ended it was not a decision I took lightly. All of us understood what it would mean. The kids even wrote a poem trying to dissuade me from accepting the posting. "You are needed at home at the BBQ grill," they wrote—tongue-in-cheek and humorously at one level, but very seriously on another.

Already, my envoy assignments to Iraq and Afghanistan had disrupted things. Cheryl was working at RAND while taking care of basically all the family and household matters, a de facto single mom dealing with snow, clogged gutters, flooded basements, and power outages, not to mention PTA meetings, soccer travel teams, SAT preparations, two adolescent males, and a full-time job with a long commute. She was also not in agreement with everything the U.S. was doing in Iraq and Afghanistan.

Given these stresses, I was surprised by how lightly she took the outlandish personal attacks that came her way because of me. Islamist extremist websites, managing to get almost all of their facts wrong, creatively denounced her as "Khalilzad's Swiss-born Zionist Jewish wife" and made much of the fact that she worked for the RAND Corporation. Radical preachers attacked her in their Friday sermons. I thought she might be frightened or upset. Instead, she joked that since apparently she was now Jewish, someone ought to throw her a bat mitzvah party.

Alex had agreed to attend Georgetown University for a semester to stay close to home, but his actual wish was to enroll at Claremont-McKenna in southern California, where his offer of admission could not be deferred any longer. We had an old family car, a Jeep Wrangler, he had years earlier intervened to prevent us from selling, arguing that it would make the perfect first car for him one day. Now that day had arrived, and he loaded up the car for the cross-country journey. The little old Jeep ended up making this voyage three times, as Alex so much enjoyed traveling across America and seeing its different nooks and crannies that he chose to drive instead of fly every summer break.

Cheryl and I came up with a solution. Cheryl and Max could move to Doha, Qatar, where RAND had an office. Max was just entering middle school. There was an American school in Doha that he could attend. The flight from Kabul to Doha was only five hours, so I would be able to visit much more frequently than if they stayed in Maryland. Max vigorously protested this plan at first, before suddenly agreeing. We wondered why he changed his mind until Cheryl's mother confessed that she had advised him to try it for just two weeks. If he didn't like it, he could come back and live with her. We were appalled. Two weeks? Couldn't she have at least insisted on two months? It turned out that Grandma knew what she was doing. Within two weeks, our gregarious Max was on the soccer team and had a passel of new friends—American and Arab—with whom he roamed the residential compound and broader city.

⟵   ⟶

AS I THOUGHT about the situation in Afghanistan, I concluded that the United States needed to make a number of adjustments. Without stronger economic programs in areas such as agriculture, minerals, and mining, I was skeptical that Afghanistan could develop a sufficient revenue base for the government.

I also believed that the United States needed to treat Afghanistan as a hybrid security challenge. The Taliban had been scattered and pushed into Pakistan—but it had not been vanquished. The United States had not found a way to counter insurgent sanctuaries in western Pakistan. I had raised the issue repeatedly, as had Karzai. I wanted additional pressure on Pakistan—but was unsuccessful in convincing the president and the principals.

In advocating for a new policy, I was expecting resistance from the Pentagon. From the outset, Rumsfeld had been the most vocal opponent among the principals of U.S. involvement in state and nation building in Afghanistan.

I was pleased to learn that the Pentagon's views were evolving.

Marin Strmecki, Rumsfeld's special advisor on Afghanistan, had a hand in this. After traveling to Afghanistan and meeting with senior officials, Strmecki developed the outline of a plan that called for greater U.S. initiative on the state- and nation-building front. He argued that a redoubled U.S. effort was needed to help Afghans defend and police their country and to address warlordism. Strmecki's plan tracked with my own thinking. To my surprise, Strmecki had persuaded Rumsfeld. General Franks at CENTCOM was also supportive and recommended the use of force if warlords acted against the Afghan government.

At Rice's direction, I organized an informal interagency process—the "Zal small group," as it became known—to flesh out an action plan and develop a budget request. Starting in mid-May, we met every two or three days in my office in the Old Executive Office Building. In addition to my staff, I invited representatives from all relevant agencies. We reviewed every U.S. government program under way in Afghanistan and considered options for new programs.

I was struck by how poorly equipped the U.S. government was for the task at hand. I found that no organization possessed the expertise to do serious post-conflict planning and implementation.

In mid-June, I prepared an integrated plan. "Accelerating Success in Afghanistan" was a comprehensive strategy to work with Afghans in developing an enlightened constitution, curbing warlordism, building up the Afghan National Army and Afghan National Police, and countering the nascent insurgency in the south and east. The plan also called for stepped-up economic development programs. The goal was to lay the groundwork for free and fair national elections, the final milestone in the Bonn process.

I anticipated that Accelerating Success would create a virtuous circle. Stronger Afghan institutions would enable progress on the Bonn process, reconstruction, and security. Progress in those areas in turn would bolster cooperation among Afghan leaders in Kabul.

We determined that Accelerating Success required an additional $1.2 billion in resources. After we proposed the concept on Capitol Hill, Congress ultimately increased the funding to $1.6 billion.

I was sitting in the Situation Room in late June when the Principals Committee considered the plan. They agreed that this was the right course of action. Cheney, who had just returned from meetings on Capitol Hill, was confident that Republicans and Democrats would be supportive. In terms of the needed funding, Cheney said, "Success in Afghanistan is important, and if this is what needs to be done, let's go get the resources for it."

Rice then scheduled an NSC meeting with President Bush to discuss the plan. I was prepared to brief him on Accelerating Success but as the meeting proceeded, I sensed that he was not so interested in the programmatic details. Once he had decided that he wanted me in Kabul, it seemed that he was willing to go along with my proposed plan and provide the necessary resources.

As I proceeded through the slides, the president interrupted me. "Zal, I want you to turn Karzai into a great politician," he said. He asked me to take Karzai around the country, talk about the needs of the people, and reorganize the Afghan government to deliver results. Karzai had great potential as a national leader, the president said, but it was my job to help him succeed.

As I was leaving the Situation Room, the president stopped me. "Let me tell you about management," he advised. "Focus on two or three things when you initially get there. When you get those things done, focus on two or three more. If you focus on fifty things you won't do any of them well. Prioritize."

Then, the president suddenly sprang from his chair, gave me a hug, and offered me his best wishes for my new assignment.

Although the Pakistan problem remained unaddressed, I was generally pleased with the outcome of the NSC meeting. I viewed the president's approval of Accelerating Success as a shift toward supporting a robust state- and nation-building program. I also saw the document as a contract. Unless a major new issue emerged, I intended to execute the terms of the plan without seeking further approval from Washington.

⟣ ⟢

AS SOON AS President Bush approved the plan, I called Karzai. He was grateful that the United States intended to step up its role in Afghanistan and asked me to convey his thanks to the president.

I wanted to engage Karzai right from the outset. Accelerating Success was designed as a *joint* action plan in every sense of the term. Bringing Afghan leaders on board would be critical in making the plan a success.

I also saw my conversation with Karzai as a crucial step in securing the administration's support. With the leader of Afghanistan briefed and fully on board, I could check attempts to reverse Accelerating Success by citing our commitment to Karzai.

I still had to secure funding for Accelerating Success. In the normal state of affairs, the government operates on a two-year budget cycle. To fund Accelerating Success through that process, we would have had to formulate the plan several months *before* 9/11.

Funding something outside the regular cycle is possible, but it requires cutting something else. In this zero-sum environment, anyone whose programs will lose money typically resists the change. I was not prepared for just how difficult the funding fight would be.

In a Deputies Committee meeting shortly after the president appr
Accelerating Success, Robin Cleveland, a senior staffer in the Office of Management and Budget, launched a blistering attack. Accelerating Success was a
"process foul," a term she used for any plan that was not already authorized by
OMB to spend money outside the two-year budget cycle.

I scheduled a follow-up meeting with Cleveland in my office. She opened
the meeting by shouting, "How dare you take this plan to my president without telling me!"

I was taken aback. *Her president?*

"Look," I countered, "I can't produce results out of thin air. I need resources to implement the president's plan. This isn't OMB's decision to make
once the president has signed off. We have to find the money or we can't
achieve the president's goals."

I was struck by the asymmetry between the ways military and civilian departments funded their post-9/11 operations. The military could draw on its
general funding for operations and replenish these accounts with emergency
supplemental appropriations bills. Civilian agencies, by contrast, were largely
expected to live within the straitjackets of their regular budgets.

Ultimately, Hadley oversaw a process to coordinate and integrate the
policy and budget process. Funding for Accelerating Success was included in
the next supplemental appropriation bill for the wars in Afghanistan and Iraq.
This set an important precedent, allowing for significant funding of civilian
activities through emergency supplemental bills. Over time, after Cleveland
visited Afghanistan and saw the progress we were making, OMB became supportive, going so far as to proactively advocate on behalf of our programs in
subsequent years.

—< >—

IN JULY I traveled to Kabul to meet with Afghan officials about Accelerating
Success.

The most significant meeting of the trip was with the minister of defense. Fahim opened with a litany of complaints about Major General Karl
Eikenberry, who was heading the effort to build the Afghan National Army.
Eikenberry was demanding that Fahim reform the Ministry of Defense to
create ethnic and political balance in its leadership. "All Eikenberry does is
torture me and give me grief," he complained, half seriously. Fahim then accused me of coming to Afghanistan to "take apart the Northern Alliance."
"I am not interested in getting into disagreements with the United States,"
he offered. "Instead, I will just go back to live with my people in the Panjshir
Valley."

Fahim went on to give me some unsolicited career advice. "Don't accept the ambassadorship," he urged. Fahim, as well as other Afghans, was not impressed with the clout of Western ambassadors or diplomats. He saw my operations as envoy, with a direct connection to the president, as being far more significant.

"Don't worry," I assured him, "I'll make sure not to lose influence with the president."

I suggested that we step into his private office. Once we were alone, I told Fahim that he was not looking at the issue of ministry reform the right way. This was a unique opportunity for the country. The United States would not invest in the Afghan National Army unless the Ministry of Defense was reformed into a national institution. As long as a single faction controlled the ministry, Afghan families would not send their sons to volunteer for the army.

I tried a Socratic dialogue of sorts. In the new Afghanistan, wouldn't the political standing of individual leaders turn on their accomplishments? The United States was offering to help Fahim build a national army. This would be an enormous personal achievement and an enduring contribution to the Afghan nation.

"You've been spending all your time preserving militias and looking after your own people," I challenged, alluding to the fact that he was recruiting principally from Tajik communities.

We moved on to discuss the ultimate size of the ANA—a topic of contention. Fahim wanted at least 200,000 troops. However, other Afghans, including Ghani, who was the finance minister, countered that Afghanistan could not afford an army of that size. Meanwhile, Eikenberry was advocating for 60,000, the number that was approved at a June 2002 security-sector reform conference in Geneva.

I was sympathetic to Fahim's view. Sixty thousand was not a lot considering the size of neighboring states' forces. Pakistan had an army of over 500,000, while Iran's stood at over 300,000—and both states amplified their military power through terrorist proxies. I promised Fahim that I would push for a larger army but stressed that my leverage would depend on his pressing ahead with ministry reform.

Back in Washington, I argued that we should double Eikenberry's recommendation.

The Bush administration ultimately settled on a compromise: the U.S. would help build an army of "up to 70,000 troops," with a goal of training 10,000 troops for the Kabul Corps in time for the June 2004 presidential elections.

After I returned from my trip to Afghanistan, it became clear that Fahim had kept his promise and shifted his position on reforming the Ministry of

Defense. In Washington, updates from Kabul reported progress on various issues through a "traffic light" system. Formerly a persistent red light, defense reform now quickly turned green. The reform of the ministry's top leadership was implemented in September.

I may have made an impression on Fahim, but his personal history and outlook also made him amenable to these reforms. Even though Fahim had contributed to the horrors of Afghanistan's civil war, he genuinely did not wish to relive them.

Years later, Fahim told me a story that helped me understand his mindset. Well before 9/11, he and Massoud were discussing the future of Afghanistan. Massoud asked Fahim what kind of political arrangement would create a stable Afghanistan. Fahim waved off the question.

When pressed, Fahim finally said, "The reason we are not getting anywhere is that you want to be the leader of Afghanistan. Tajiks, Uzbeks, and Hazaras might accept you, but we need the Pashtuns to buy in. That means that a Pashtun will have to be the number-one leader. Only then will they join forces and share power. However, you don't want to do that—you don't want to be number two."

Massoud conceded that he wanted to be the top leader. But, he said, there was nothing to prevent Fahim from accepting a number-two role for the sake of the country. In effect, Fahim had later done just that when he deferred to Karzai.

Fahim's outlook also evolved over the course of a visit to the United States in early 2003. He traveled to West Point and talked to ordinary Americans. He was particularly struck by the prosperity here. Perhaps influenced by American action movies, he had expected the United States to be a dark and dangerous place. Instead, he found it to be clean and beautiful. When he returned, he met with his senior associates and told them, "I have been to America. In the United States, everyone lives in a large villa. We don't have anything that they want. I am convinced that the Americans are here to help us."

—< >—

BY THE SPRING of 2003, Pakistan's double game was undeniable. Insurgent leaders were ensconced in western Pakistan. We had credible reports that the ISI was providing money, arms, and training to insurgents who were crossing the border with impunity to carry out attacks in Afghanistan. Senior Afghan officials repeatedly warned President Bush and the principals about Pakistani aid to and sanctuary for the Taliban.

Even as the evidence mounted, neither the president nor any of the principals were willing to acknowledge, much less act on, evidence of Pakistan's double game. In light of Pakistan's initial cooperation against the Taliban, President Bush had a hard time believing that President Pervez Musharraf was backing the insurgents. Powell and Rumsfeld trusted Musharraf as well, especially since he was waging his own fight against extremists targeting his regime.

While administration officials were reluctant to deal with the sanctuary in Pakistan, the U.S. military and intelligence leaderships in Afghanistan were both quite concerned. In May 2003, Lieutenant General John Vines took over military headquarters in Kabul on a temporary basis. He recalled the enormous damage caused by sanctuaries in Cambodia and Laos during the Vietnam War.

When Vines and I discussed the issue, he agreed to commission an intelligence review to document connections between Islamabad and the Taliban. In September 2003, Vines became the first top U.S. commander to state publicly that the Taliban were using Pakistani sanctuaries to regroup. I raised the issue again with the principals, to no avail.

IN LATE JULY 2003, President Bush formally announced that he would nominate me as ambassador. We worked out an arrangement with Congress that would allow me to retain the title of special presidential envoy, thus reassuring the Afghans that I was not being downgraded.

As I waited in Washington for the confirmation process to proceed, Karzai was growing impatient with the warlords. Without consulting me, he decided to act against Sherzai, a long-standing rival of his Popalzai tribe. He appointed Sherzai minister of urban affairs and assigned the incumbent minister, Youssef Pashtun, to replace him as governor of Kandahar.

Karzai's decision provoked concern in Washington. Robert Blackwill, who had just joined the National Security Council staff, argued that we should not back him since he had acted without coordinating with us first. Some Defense Department officials were nervous as well, not because Karzai was acting against Sherzai, but because he had done so unilaterally.

However, Peter Rodman, the assistant secretary of defense for international security affairs, argued that Karzai's actions, while precipitous, were consistent with our strategy. The plan in Accelerating Success was to present the warlords, one by one, with a choice. Provided that they demobilized their militias and played by the rules of a democratic Afghanistan, we would offer them a role in the new political order. If some warlords proved to be recalcitrant, we would work with Karzai to outmaneuver and marginalize them.

While I was unhappy that Karzai had not coordinated with me, I was also reluctant to criticize Karzai for moving on the warlord front, which he was doing at great political risk. I concluded that it would be best to support

Karzai. I arranged another trip to Kabul to ensure that the transition proceeded smoothly.

In resolving the Sherzai matter, I was fortunate to have logistical difficulties appear at the right moment. Typically, I traveled on commercial planes to Frankfurt, Germany, and then caught a ride on a U.S. C-17 transport plane either directly to Kabul or to the military base at Karshi-Khanabad (K2) in Uzbekistan. From K2, I generally flew on a C-130 to Kabul. But this time, when I arrived at K2, the only flight available would take me to Kandahar rather than Kabul.

When I landed in Afghanistan, embassy officials informed me that Fahim had urged Sherzai to defy Karzai, saying, "If you come to Kabul, then they'll start moving against all of us."

So I immediately went to see the burly, bearish warlord. Sherzai was surprised that I had arrived so suddenly in Kandahar. I told him about my logistical difficulties, but I doubt he was persuaded by my account.

I looked directly into his eyes. "You've been a great warrior. You have earned the respect of the United States in helping to free Afghanistan. Now you need to become a great political figure. You need to create a record of accomplishments in rebuilding this country. I'm looking forward to working with you in Kabul when you're minister of urban affairs. I will arrange a meeting when we are both in Kabul. I can expect to see you there in a few days, right?"

Sherzai accepted my invitation grudgingly. But once reconciled to the decision, Sherzai, boisterous as ever, assembled a massive caravan to accompany him on his trip to Kabul. A throng of cheering supporters gathered for his departure.

Pentagon officials were elated by the success of the Sherzai move. The warlord problem, they concluded, could be handled without military force. I was gratified by their reaction but had no illusions that every case would be resolved so easily.

◄   ►

ON MY OCTOBER visit to Afghanistan, I learned that the principal warlords had been holding secret meetings late at night. The Sherzai move underscored to the warlords that they needed to unite against Karzai, lest all of their roles be diminished. Some at the U.S. embassy feared a coup.

One by one, I met with the putative conspirators.

"What kind of conspiracies are you up to?" I joked, before turning serious. I told them that undermining the Bonn process would be unacceptable.

"You are part of a coalition government and elections are coming up in a year," I reminded them. "This government has to establish a record of achievement if it wants to extend its rule. In the new Afghanistan, each member of the transitional government needs to prove to voters that he has a record of political achievement."

Atta instantly recognized the opportunity. Raised in a prominent family in Balkh Province, he had joined the Afghan resistance as a teenager and spent the next two decades fighting in the country's wars.

"I have thought about getting a degree in public administration," he confided to me, "maybe from India."

We could help with that, I assured him.

Other leaders were more recalcitrant.

I met with Karzai for several hours at the palace. We agreed that we should produce an agenda for the transitional government that all Afghan leaders—warlords included—would endorse. I suggested that it would be better if an Afghan leader brokered the agreement. We agreed to approach Karim Khalili, one of the vice presidents in the transitional government, and ask him to mediate.

Khalili had the air of a quiet, distinguished intellectual. He had worked with Iran to organize Shia Hazaras, first to fight the occupying Soviet army and then to combat other Afghan factions in the civil war in the 1990s—experiences that had left him with various cardiac impairments. I had called him a number of times from Washington and Bonn after 9/11 and visited him occasionally when I was in Kabul as the special envoy.

I stressed to Khalili that if he could work with the warlords to come up with an acceptable agreement, he would have a solid basis to serve as a vice president on Karzai's ticket in 2004. I gave him a list of items, drawn from Accelerating Success, that I wanted to see included in the agreement. Khalili took up the challenge.

Through long negotiations Khalili and I were able to forge consensus on what I called the October Governance Agreement. All of the principal warlords pledged that they would cooperate in building new national institutions and demobilizing their militias.

I made great use of the October Governance Agreement as we moved forward. More than once, I pointed to the agreement in meetings with a problematic leader, saying, "You have already agreed that you would demobilize your militia. The only thing we have to talk about now is when and how you will do so."

—◄ ►—

LIEUTENANT GENERAL DAVID BARNO had arrived in Kabul as the new U.S. military commander a few days before my October trip. I could not have asked for a more capable and impressive military partner.

Although he was the first member of his West Point class to become a three-star general, Barno exhibited none of the formality characteristic of distinguished military officials. He devoured books on military history and was eager both to explore ideas and take on practical problems. Barno and I were equally frustrated by the overly conformist ethos of the military, and I was encouraged by his eagerness to experiment with new approaches. We hit it off immediately.

Barno had conducted his own review. A September visit to Afghanistan had convinced him that civil-military coordination needed to be strengthened. The military, he believed, was too focused on targeting the enemy rather than protecting the Afghan people.

Barno recommended a modest troop increase but, more importantly, a shift in strategy from counterterrorism to counterinsurgency. Barno redeployed the bulk of coalition forces to small forward operating bases and Provincial Reconstruction Teams, where they could establish a presence in contested regions and develop relationships with local Afghans.

The army at the time did not have a counterinsurgency doctrine. Barno described the new approach as a shift from an enemy-centric to a population-centric strategy. He personally traveled to every small unit to explain what he wanted them to do. On one trip, he was gratified to find that his officers had ordered books on counterinsurgency. Barno eventually asked his officers to read Lewis Sorley's *A Better War*, a revisionist history arguing that the United States could have won the Vietnam War once General Creighton Abrams and the U.S. embassy coordinated efforts to engage the Vietnamese people at the village level. Barno saw parallels for what he was trying to do in Afghanistan.

Barno's counterinsurgency approach rested on two "overarching principles." First, "respect for Afghans" would be the new operating watchword. Second, unity of purpose was essential. Military power would be fused with all elements of U.S. power to advance shared political objectives. There would be no "white space" between the military and the embassy. As Barno liked to say, "Same goals, different uniforms."

As an initial step, Barno, despite having limited air mobility for his own purposes, asked the military to provide me with on-call helicopter support so that I could move around the country freely. In Accelerating Success, I had requested dedicated aircraft so that I could travel to meetings with leaders in outlying provinces. Congress had rejected that request even though every other element of the U.S. government in Afghanistan—the military, CIA, and even USAID—had air mobility. I was gratified that Barno signed a standing order indicating that my travel was "mission essential."

Barno also shifted the senior military headquarters from Bagram Air Base, which was over an hour's drive from the capital, to Kabul so that the military and embassy staffs could coordinate on a routine basis. He moved into a trailer on the embassy compound about fifty feet away from mine and set up his personal office two doors down from where I would be in the embassy.

— ⟩

MY NOMINATION as ambassador was unanimously confirmed in November 2003. Powell, who was presiding over the State Department's formal swearing-in ceremony, stopped in his tracks when he saw how many guests I had in the waiting room. "I've brought my whole tribe," I informed him. The kids, Cheryl, her brother Charlie, and his wife came. My mother couldn't make it, because of ill health, but all my siblings arrived, along with some of their spouses and children. It was especially touching that my AFS family, the Perras, traveled across the country to attend. Barno, briefly back from Afghanistan, and his wife, Susan, were there as well.

I recounted, in my remarks, a time in the late 1990s when I had watched a documentary about Afghanistan's civil war with Max, eight years old at the time. I tried to explain to him the different factions and why they were fighting for control of the country.

As I did so, Max just shook his head. Reacting to the footage of burned-out and destroyed buildings on the television screen, he remarked, "They're fighting over *that*? Why don't they focus on building it instead?"

My staff was less than thrilled when I announced to the press and to Congress that I wanted to leave Washington the day after my swearing-in ceremony. Usually, it takes at least a month for new ambassadors to depart.

But the president was impatient, too, remembering that he had offered me the ambassadorship back in May. Whenever Afghanistan came up in morning staff meetings, he would look around and raise the same question: "Why is Zal still here?"

My father in 1980

My mother in 1988

Departing Kabul, Afghanistan, to come to America for the first time in 1966 with other students, including Ashraf Ghani, the current President of Afghanistan

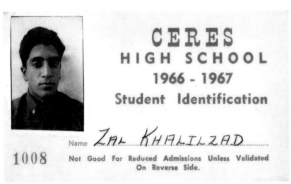

Ceres High School ID, 1966–1967

Graduating from Ceres High, 1967

With Cheryl at the American University of Beirut, 1972

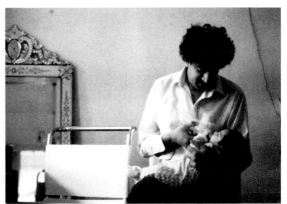

With infant Alex, 1983

University of Chicago, 1976

With three year old Max, 1994

With Alex and Max in Cairo, Egypt, 1997

With President Ronald Reagan and Afghan Resistance Leader Khalis, 1987
Ronald Reagan Library Archives

Road dedication between Kabul and Kandahar, December 2003

With my AFS family at my Ambassador swearing in, 2003

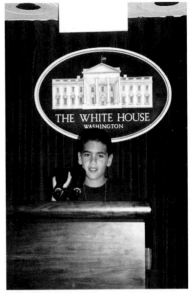

Max in the White House, 2004

Visiting Max at Claremont McKenna College, 2009

Nouruz holiday in Mazar-i-Sharif with President Karzai and General Dostum, March 21, 2004

With President Bush and Secretary Rice and Chief of Staff Andrew Card reviewing the official Afghan voting ballot. The ballot had a note to President Bush that said, "Who would you vote for?" signed Karzai, 2004

Laying the foundation of the American University of Iraq–Sulaimani with President Talabani, 2006

In the U.S. Mission in Baghdad with Presidents Bush and Talabani during President Bush's surprise visit, 2006
White House Photo by Eric Draper

Farewell photo with President Barzani of the Kurdistan Region, 2007
Reuters, Claudia Parsons

In Shindand near Harat with local leaders, 2004

Traveling in Baghdad, 2007
Ashley Gilbertson for the New York Times

EIGHTEEN

AMBASSADOR

KABUL,
NOVEMBER 2003–JANUARY 2004

THE BLADES WERE SPINNING, NOT AT FULL THROTTLE, BUT ENOUGH TO STRAIN THE ears. It was Thanksgiving Day, and I was at Bagram Air Base heading to Kabul as the new United States ambassador. Barno and I walked up the ramp and strapped ourselves into the fold-down mesh seats. I had long since learned that earplugs were essential. As the hydraulic system closed the back ramp, I felt the Chinook lumber upward and then turn toward the south.

When we landed at Kabul International Airport, my protective detail ushered me into an armored Suburban and we sped down the road, weaving and sometimes careening around traffic, to the embassy compound. The detail was led by a camouflaged Marine Humvee with a .50-caliber machine gun on top. A Marine gunner energetically waved Afghan civilian vehicles out of the way.

When I arrived at the embassy, I learned that a motorcade, sent earlier that day to pick up Senator Hillary Clinton from the airport, had accidentally struck a woman who was walking along the side of the road in a traditional full-body veil, the *chaddari*. Because of security concerns, the security protocol forbade the driver from stopping to check on the woman.

Barno and I, already unsettled by the blunt force displayed by our own motorcade, were appalled to learn of the incident involving Senator Clinton's. We decided to put into place new rules to make the protective detail less apt to ride roughshod over local civilians.

Senator Clinton, who was on her first congressional delegation trip since becoming the junior senator from New York, was waiting in my office to greet me. She was in Kabul to celebrate Thanksgiving with troops of Fort Drum's 10th Mountain Division, which is based in New York. She was accompanied by Senator Jack Reed. I was pleased to discover that she did not regard the trip as a mere photo-op, but rather as an opportunity to engage in substantive discussions with senior U.S. and Afghan officials.

Pakistan came up first. Senator Clinton had no illusions about the double game Pakistan was playing. When we went to see Karzai later that evening, she had a long discussion with him about Pakistan's role vis-à-vis the Taliban and other insurgents. Karzai was impressed with her.

I told Senator Clinton about my ideas for the "greening of Kabul," i.e., improving the environment around Kabul by planting trees. This idea resonated with her. She promised to connect the embassy to Cornell University, which had a renowned agriculture program, and followed through promptly once she was back in Washington.

After our meeting, I went to the presidential palace to present my credentials to Karzai. From there, I went to my new home. Unlike the grand residences enjoyed by many ambassadors, mine was a set of three metal trailers configured in the shape of the letter H. In one wing, I had a small office and a very narrow dining room. The other contained a minuscule bedroom, bathroom, and living room. In the middle section was the main entrance area and kitchen. I was happy to have a small patio and garden off to one side.

Barno and some of his staff, meanwhile, had chosen to live in even smaller accommodations because he believed that being on the embassy compound would allow us to better integrate our efforts. He liked to shock visitors by telling them that his prefab "hooch"—the slang term for the not-very-residential steel shipping containers—was a generous three steps by nine steps in size.

My staff, too, was quite small compared with that of most ambassadors. I had two personal employees. Both were ethnic Hazaras and had the same first name, so we came to refer to them collectively as "the two Hassans." "Big Hassan" had been the custodian of the embassy compound from 1989 until late 2001, when we had no diplomatic presence. Now he was the chef and did the shopping in the local market. At that time, the embassy was obtaining all of its foodstuffs from contractors who imported them from outside the country. Big Hassan disdained this practice and would sneak in produce from the local markets, which allowed me to enjoy Afghanistan's justly famous melons, grapes, and apples. "Little Hassan" was very shy. He did the laundry and the cleaning. As I got to know the two Hassans better, I found that they provided an interesting window into the mood on the street and how ordinary people perceived our actions.

I started every morning with a meeting of the country team. Barno was seated at my left while my deputy chief of mission, David Sedney—a wise China specialist—was on my right. The heads of all of the embassy sections, including USAID, gathered around a large conference table.

Next I would meet with the Security Core Group, which included Barno, the CIA station chief, Sedney, and Strmecki.

Barno and I looked for ways to support each other's objectives. I used my political influence with the Afghans to help him on military problems, and he made the military available to pursue political goals. More than once, when I described challenges I was facing, he would reply, "I can help you with that." I tried to do the same.

I worked with two CIA station chiefs during my time as ambassador. Though the CIA focused primarily on counterterrorism, the first station chief, who had served in Pakistan, helped me understand the sanctuary problem at a granular level. The second had worked side by side with Karzai when he was advancing on Kandahar during the effort to topple the Taliban. He was the one who had saved Karzai's life by throwing himself on the future Afghan president to shield him from an errant bomb. The two were so close that Karzai later recommended that the CIA station chief succeed me as ambassador.

I saw Karzai almost every day and then often circled back to the palace once more for discussions over dinner. It was often very late by the time I returned to the embassy and assembled my staff to draft one or more cables reporting the day's events to Washington.

I wanted to create a mission-oriented culture and a high operating tempo at the embassy. I was well aware that some diplomats believed they were there to "watch and report." In fact, shortly after my arrival, an embassy political officer asked someone on my staff, "Doesn't the ambassador know that we are here to report on events, not to shape them?" I was sure that this would not be a productive approach in the prevailing circumstances.

I was frustrated that a number of the Foreign Service slots at the embassy remained vacant. As a hardship post, Afghanistan attracted ambitious young officers as well as older diplomats looking for one last adventure at the end of their careers. But it was difficult to attract people at the prime of their careers, as many of them were just starting families. Those intrepid few who did volunteer for hardship posts generally opted for Iraq over Afghanistan, because it was more career-enhancing and at the time appeared to need more attention.

The secretary of state has the authority to deploy Foreign Service officers anywhere in the world. Like our military, our Foreign Service officers, in an earlier era, were expected to go where they were ordered. This was the norm until after the Vietnam War, when mores changed and the Foreign Service

egan to fight vociferously against directed assignments. I raised the
h Powell a number of times. He promised to deal with it, but did not
succeed.

Shortly after arriving in Kabul, I asked my staff to start planning for the
next funding request for Accelerating Success, only to encounter another of
those absurdities unique to government. OMB had instructed all departments
and agencies not to undertake any planning for future emergency supplemental appropriations. The policy, I suspect, was meant to obscure the costs of the
war and its impact on the deficit. Finally, I instructed my staff to undertake a
"planning exercise."

Accelerating Success required a larger embassy staff, and they would need
to work, live, and sleep somewhere. Already, the Bureau of Overseas Buildings
Operations (OBO) had packed the embassy grounds with hooches. Even this
was not enough.

The Afghans were thrilled when I told them that we needed more room.
A larger American presence, they reasoned, meant that the United States was
less likely to abandon them again. Karzai arranged for the Afghan government
to donate a large, valuable plot of land across the street from the U.S. embassy,
where we could create a medium-sized village. The Afghan government also
cleared a building across the street from the embassy, where members of a
Northern Alliance militia resided. The building was once the site of a firefight
in which the Marines killed several militia fighters. Within weeks, OBO was
on the scene preparing the ground for construction and planning an underground tunnel that would connect the new compound with the existing one.

MY FIRST DAYS in Afghanistan began with a terrible tragedy. Coalition military
forces had been tracking a suspected enemy commander and targeted him
with an air strike. Instead, they hit a group of children attending class in an
impoverished school under a nearby tree.

Karzai, Barno, and I felt the loss deeply. Barno sent Major General Lloyd
Austin, the operational commander of coalition forces in Bagram, to meet
with the parents of the children. At the end of the meeting, local elders were
so moved by his genuine grief that they spoke consoling words to him.

I was furious at Washington's reaction when I prepared a statement
about the tragedy. We could not, I was told, create even the appearance of
an apology for the actions of our military. It took hours of quibbling before
we could agree on the appropriate language. At a news conference near my
residence, I said that I was sorry to have to use my first meeting with the press

on such a sad matter. "Anyone who has children," I said, "empathizes with these parents."

Barno and I were determined to prevent this from happening again. This tragedy, we knew, was not a one-off accident. It was a symptom of broader problems with our military approach. We had a small number of troops, which prevented us from working closely enough on the ground with Afghan communities to develop good human intelligence. So we relied on other methods, such as signals intelligence, which inevitably led to targeting mistakes. In this particular instance, we had been tracking an individual who we believed was a high-value target. The individual was in fact near the identified location, but so were the children.

The problem was compounded by growing complaints about "night raids." Coalition forces would enter homes of suspected insurgents or terrorists, isolate the men, tie their hands, and put hoods over their heads before hauling them away to prisons. Afghan families then had no way to contact their detained husbands, fathers, and sons.

Karzai complained frequently that these raids were poorly targeted and humiliating to Afghan families.

I asked Barno to work with Defense Minister Fahim and Abdul Rahim Wardak, the deputy minister of defense, on an agreed approach to night raids. Short-term gains in capturing one or another terrorist in night raids, we knew, would be ephemeral if the operations undermined Afghan support for the United States. Barno and his Afghan counterparts drew up a "15 Point Agreement," to minimize mistakes and respect Afghan sensibilities. It foresaw closer consultation with the Afghan leadership before raids. Also, ANA forces would accompany coalition forces, and the coalition would coordinate with Afghan authorities to ensure that families knew about the detainees' status. We also accelerated the review process and released a large number of detainees after determining that they were innocent.

The 15 Point Agreement significantly reduced frictions. Barno's men implemented its terms, but we faced greater challenges in ensuring that Special Forces did so as well. After Barno and I left Afghanistan, our successors proved far less committed to the agreement. Night raids, along with greater civilian casualties from excessive U.S. firepower, were among the principal reasons why Karzai became so bitter toward the United States in later years.

The closer understanding we forged with the Afghans coincided with positive trends in the Afghan military. After the reform of the Ministry of Defense, the numbers of young Afghans volunteering for the ANA rose significantly. I had expected an increase in volunteers, but Barno told me that the new numbers even exceeded what the ANA could handle. We planned a further increase in ANA spending in our next funding request.

ONE OF THE LOOMING deadlines on my agenda was the Constitutional *Loya Jirga* (CLJ), set to convene in mid-December. I worked with Afghan leaders to shunt aside one draft that envisioned an Islamist government structure similar to Iran's. Afghans would have to make critical decisions on federalism and whether to adopt a presidential or parliamentary government. Emotional issues related to national symbols and languages would not be easy to resolve.

I developed and shared the U.S. "red lines" with Afghan leaders. I would work with them to reach an agreement on the major constitutional questions, but then stand aside so they could realize the *Loya Jirga* process. Only if they ran into obstacles—and requested my aid—would I become involved.

I met with Karzai and other Afghan leaders to develop a consensus on key issues. They eventually agreed to support a presidential system, with a two-term limit, and a unitary governmental structure inspired by the Afghan Constitution of 1964. With this agreement in hand, I was confident that the *Loya Jirga* would reach a reasonable outcome.

The CLJ was scheduled to begin on December 13. However, at the request of twenty-five delegates, who considered the 13th to be inauspicious, it was postponed until the following day.

As the delegates began to arrive, a pulse of excitement and anticipation filled Kabul. Never before had the Afghan people adopted the charter of their state. I thought about America's founding and wondered if this was what it felt like in Philadelphia at the time of the Constitutional Convention in 1787.

The delegates overwhelmingly favored a larger U.S. and international presence. I found hardly a trace of the xenophobia that had informed the Afghan national attitude of the past. I remember one exchange in particular that I had with an elderly delegate from eastern Afghanistan who didn't realize that I was the U.S. ambassador. "I want to visit this country of America someday," he told me. "Imagine what has happened. Their country was attacked from Afghanistan—many people were killed. America's military then knocked down the Taliban government. And what did they do next? They did not kill Afghans in vengeance. They did not force us to change our religion. Instead, they are helping us establish a new government and rebuild schools and even mosques. I have to see this America. It must be a very special place."

Confidence in the United States was sky-high. Afghans often commented that any military problem could be solved by "vitamin B-52."

I was also impressed by the importance delegates placed on addressing the problem of warlord militias. One delegate told me quite forcefully, "America should focus only on the problems that Afghans cannot solve on their own.

We can build schools, and we can rebuild our towns and cities. However, we cannot solve the problem of militias without your help."

Many delegates urged the United States to take swift and decisive action against the warlords. I had to explain the difficult trade-offs. The more rapidly we acted, I explained, the greater the risk of renewed conflict and violence.

I was surprised by how many requests I got from delegates to build girls' schools in their areas. One very traditional delegate from Paktika Province was quite insistent about educating girls in his tribe. This would have been unthinkable in the Afghanistan I knew growing up. I was proud to see this change.

Delegates were permitted to step to an open microphone. I was encouraged to see female delegates taking the stage to berate the militia commanders and warlords. A young Afghan woman named Malalai Joya made international headlines with a courageous critique of the warlords, calling for their prosecution in international courts. CLJ chairman Sibghatullah Mojaddedi initially moved to throw her out, but other delegates protested that she should remain.

I invited Joya for a meeting and later ensured that she and her family received police protection. I also met with Mojaddedi and reminded him that women had the right to be heard at the CLJ.

After a few days, I briefed President Bush from the CIA station. He listened with interest as I related the give-and-take of the sessions. "Zal," the president asked in his Texas drawl, "are the *ee-mams* and *moo-lahs* givin' you any trouble?" I assured him that the delegates with religious training were making sound contributions.

Debates about the form of government and ethnic issues, however, were vigorous and at times brought the CLJ to a standstill.

Northern Alliance leaders were determined to weaken Karzai's executive authority. At the outset, Qanooni threatened to resign from the government and lead a political movement demanding a parliamentary system. Proponents of a parliamentary system believed that Karzai had become too powerful and could become, as one leader put it, no different from the Middle East's other dictators. In most situations, I would have favored a stronger parliament. But after years of war and destruction, I believed that a strong executive structure was necessary to make decisions decisively and rebuild national institutions. The final compromise maintained a strong president, but with checks and balances for the parliament. Legislators would confirm cabinet ministers but not key presidential appointees.

On the issue of religion and human rights, the final deal specified the role of Islam as a source of law and promised protections for religious minorities. Islam became the official state religion, but broad religious freedoms were preserved through references to the U.N. Declaration of Human Rights and other conventions. Explicit protections of women's rights blunted any threat of "Talibanization." The constitution guaranteed "equal rights and duties before the law" for men and women.

The debates at the CLJ became most divisive over issues of national identity. Some Pashtun leaders wanted the constitution to affirm that Pashtu was the "national language." After much haggling, I helped broker a deal in which there would be no "national language" but an array of "official languages."

Pashtun delegates protested vehemently against the compromise, which they saw as yet another concession to the warlords from the north. As their criticisms turned to the United States, I stood up and spoke sternly. The country could not be built overnight after a quarter century of civil war, I reminded them. If the delegates were willing to compromise and quickly adopt the constitution, the world would stand with Afghanistan. Otherwise, the world would regard the CLJ as a failure and blame the Pashtuns for denying Afghanistan a constitution. Chastened, the recalcitrant delegates backed down and agreed to the compromise.

The CLJ then turned to what I thought was the last remaining issue: dual citizenships for ministers. The issue provoked ethnic divisions, since Pashtun technocrats like Ghani and Ali Jalali, who had emigrated after the Soviet invasion and who returned to serve as minister of interior, would be affected most directly. In a late-night meeting with Fahim, Karzai, and me, Abdullah promised that while he would not stand in the way of a deal at the CLJ, he would resign if ministers were allowed to retain dual nationality. Fahim also insisted to me in a private meeting that the dual-nationality issue was a red line for the Northern Alliance and threatened to join Abdullah in opposition over the issue. Karzai believed strongly that dual nationals should not be disqualified. In the end, however, the best deal we could get was one that Sayyaf and I helped broker. It gave the parliament the right to accept or reject any presidential appointee with dual citizenship. Since parliamentary elections were not to be held until 2005, this posed no obstacle to Karzai's appointments. In recent years, however, the parliament has insisted that President Ghani's cabinet nominees renounce their dual status.

I thought we now had clear sailing until I received an urgent appeal from an embassy colleague and a U.N. staffer. A group of women delegates had a set of unresolved issues. The group was frustrated that, after adhering to all the rules of the CLJ, they had failed to get a fair hearing for their agenda. They were crestfallen when Brahimi said that it was "too late" since the window for negotiations had closed. Brahimi had played an indispensable role in facilitating the Bonn process and assisting the interim authority afterward, earning the trust of his Afghan counterparts. Generally, I played "bad cop" to Brahimi's "good cop." This time, I switched roles. I argued that their ideas for increasing women's participation had merit and that they would raise the prestige of Afghanistan in the eyes of the international community. Brahimi shrugged and then acquiesced. I then met with key leaders at the CLJ and convinced them that the group's amendments should be accepted. As a result, the constitution provides that two women from each province shall be elected members of the parliament, amounting to some 25 percent of the lower house of parliament.

On January 4, 2004, the constitution was approved by acclamation. It stands as one of the most enlightened constitutions in the Islamic world.

The president and principals were elated. Even Rumsfeld, who believed that praising people would "ruin them," sent me a snowflake during the last days of the CLJ: "I am keeping posted on your activities. It sounds to me like you are doing a first-rate job and that it is going well. Congratulations in advance!"

⪻ NINETEEN ⪼

BUILDERS VERSUS SPOILERS

AFGHANISTAN, 2003–2005

I FOUND THAT THERE WERE BASICALLY THREE TYPES OF ACTORS IN AFGHANISTAN—builders, spoilers, and opportunists. The builders shared our aim of developing the country. The spoilers—warlords, drug traffickers, and the Pakistani military—were destabilizing Afghanistan in pursuit of parochial interests. And the opportunists, focused on their own survival, could go either way depending on how they perceived the balance of power.

Karzai was the most important builder. He was not a hands-on manager or institution builder, so I encouraged him to recruit a strong team. This was a challenge, since the country's protracted wars had forced technocrats out of the country. A number of expatriates returned home to help their country, including Daud Saba, Nadir Naderi, Akram Fazel, Mo Qayumi, and Ikleel Hakimi. Saba and Hakimi became important ministers in subsequent years.

Of Karzai's team, I was particularly impressed with Ghani, whom I had known for a long time. An academic and World Bank expert by background, Ghani joined the United Nations after 9/11, before leaving to work for the Afghan government, first as Karzai's advisor and subsequently as finance minister. Ghani could be gruff and impatient, but his achievements spoke for themselves. Within a short period, he established a trust fund for Afghan reconstruction, a modern finance ministry, a tax system, a new single currency, the country's first formal budget since the Rabbani government, and a national development plan.

Afghan leaders also achieved a great deal on reconstruction and development. Schools, under Qanooni, enrolled more children than at any point in the country's history. The Ministry of Public Health, led by Amin Fatemi, developed a national health program that decreased maternal mortality rates from 1,600 deaths per 100,000 live births in 2002 to 327 in 2010. Child mortality also decreased, from 165 deaths per 1,000 live births to 77. And the under-age-five mortality rate was down from 257 deaths per 1,000 to 97. Hanif Atmar, who led the Ministry of Reconstruction and Rural Development, created the National Solidarity Program, which provided small grants to support reconstruction by village-level councils. Interior Minister Ali Jalali played a critical role in building the national police force.

In the private sector, Afghan-American entrepreneur and philanthropist Ehsan Bayat created a mobile telecommunications business that enabled Afghanistan to leapfrog past landlines into a modern cellular system. With American support, Sharif Fayez was the lead Afghan advocate of the American University of Afghanistan, which we hoped would emerge as a local version of my alma mater in Beirut. Sima Samar and Nader Naderi played key roles in building the Afghan Independent Human Rights Commission.

Still, the problems were daunting. Physical infrastructure, for example, was an area that persistently needed improvement. Driving on Kabul's streets was like going over a washboard. I came away from every outing with lower back pains from the pounding we took. I sometimes quipped that we should either invest in roads or go into the car repair business.

When Karzai visited the United States in 2002, he asked President Bush to undertake a major reconstruction project to give the Afghan people a visible marker of progress. The 300-mile trip between Kabul and Kandahar, he explained, currently took forty-eight hours because the road was in such poor condition. In fact, for many stretches, the road did not exist at all. President Bush decided that the United States would lead a consortium of states to rebuild this highway.

However, there was a great deal of resistance within the U.S. government. When I called Andrew Natsios, the head of USAID, he protested that "USAID does not build roads." Its development strategies had "evolved," and building infrastructure was "not a priority." I reiterated that President Bush definitively wanted this road built and had made funds available. Still, it would take many interventions before Natsios grudgingly acquiesced.

When the United States eventually did build the Kabul-to-Kandahar highway, the project was marked by significant quality-control problems.

Even so, Afghans were in awe when we completed the first phase of the high-way in time for the Constitutional *Loya Jirga*. The road was soon bustling with commercial vehicles, private cars, buses, and occasional camel caravans.

Afghan security forces were another area where the United States could have moved faster. We struggled to build facilities for new units as the reformed ANA trained battalions. Deputy Defense Minister Wardak often complained to me that the planned ANA—sized at up to 70,000 troops—was too small and underequipped. A veteran of the Afghan resistance, he remarked that the United States had provided heavier weapons when the Afghans were fighting the Soviets. We had stepped up the ANA program and would continue to do so incrementally. Nevertheless, I sympathized with Wardak and raised the matter in Washington. Later, after the escalation of Taliban attacks in late 2005 and early 2006, the Bush and Obama administrations increased invest-ments in the ANA.

There were also persistent complications with international donors. Af-ghan officials complained that the international community was creating "parallel structures" by funding projects through NGOs or contractors in-stead of the Afghan state. NGOs could pay salaries many times higher than those offered by the Afghan government—a reality that drew talented tech-nocrats away from the government and depleted the already small supply of doctors, who would earn more as drivers or translators.

I understood the Afghans' frustration, but I also understood the perspec-tive of the donors. No Afghan ministry or organization, at this early stage, was capable of handling funds at Western levels of accountability, nor did they have the skills, human resources, or infrastructure needed to oversee or carry out much of the work. Still, I thought donors could have done a better job of using their programs to strengthen Afghan capabilities. We tried to do so, for example, by contracting with the Ministry of Public Works to pave roads and by using local contractors to build ANA facilities.

Afghans had a strong sense of community, but a far weaker sense of civic responsibility. My greatest frustration was an Afghan mind-set that led them to shirk responsibility for bettering their communities and country. In gen-eral, Afghans lacked initiative and a sense of urgency, and seemed to suffer from a culture of dependency. I was disheartened, for example, when I tried to recruit high school classes to water and care for seedlings as part of the "green-ing of Kabul" initiative. Many responded, "That is the responsibility of the government. Why should we do it?"

I tried to encourage a culture of civic responsibility by describing the volunteerism I had observed as a teenager in the United States. I relayed the history of how Americans on the frontier came together to raise schoolhouses and hire teachers. I also pointed to the great monuments at Bamiyan, Ghazni, and Mazar and Afghan cities like Herat and Balkh. These had been built at a time when the United States did not even exist. Yet today, the Afghans were looking to the United States to build simple structures such as schools.

Still, Afghans made remarkable progress. With support from the National Endowment for Democracy, civil society blossomed. A wide variety of groups were enlivening discussion on important issues such as women's rights, the rule of law, and economic reform. Civil society groups organized themselves to clean the streets of Kabul. Afghan media was flourishing as well. I was particularly gratified to see the success of Saad Mohseni's Tolo Television, an independent network that quickly became the most-viewed station. Its program *Afghan Star*, a local version of *American Idol*, is not only entertaining, but also is teaching participation and contributing to national unity as Afghans vote by text message for the singers they like best, regardless of ethnicity. Tolo TV has also been a pioneer in public affairs broadcasting, airing town hall–style discussions of political issues as well as high-quality documentaries.

At RAND, Cheryl worked on counterterrorism, de-radicalization, and how to strengthen Muslim moderates, but her favorite project involved a partnership with Sesame Workshop. The idea was to give Afghan children, who had been born into the grim era of the Taliban, a hopeful window into learning by creating a mini-version of *Sesame Street* for Afghanistan. One evening, randomly listening to Afghan radio, I was startled to hear her voice giving an interview from Kandahar. The program was well received and set the stage for Tolo TV to launch its own version of *Sesame Street* in 2011.

To encourage the Afghan people and keep them informed, I held regular news conferences in Dari. In interviews with the Afghan press, I discussed the programs we had under way and the approach the Afghan government and its international supporters were taking to demobilize militias.

◄ ►

UNFORTUNATELY, THERE WAS also a formidable group of spoilers. Besides the Taliban, these included warlords, narco-traffickers, and the Pakistani military and intelligence services.

No warlord irritated Karzai as much as Dostum. Karzai repeatedly vowed to arrest him. I advised Karzai to consider the balance of power in the north and to move with caution.

Dostum was refusing to disarm his militia. He complained that although he had done the bulk of the fighting in the north against the Taliban, he had not received an official position in the new government. Dostum wanted to be either the defense minister or the chief of staff of the armed forces. He also made the case that if he demobilized, Tajik warlords would dominate the entire north, from Badakhshan to Herat.

Atta was the strongest Tajik rival to Dostum in the north. When I asked Atta what I could do to end his repeated clashes with Dostum, he proposed two choices: facilitate an agreement between them or move them both to Kabul.

I went to see Dostum in Mazar-i-Sharif. Blaming the problems on his deputies, he promised to work with Atta to stop the fighting. I was skeptical, knowing how tightly Dostum controlled his subordinates.

When tensions flared in early April 2004, I saw an opportunity to address the Dostum-Atta problem once and for all. After Dostum deployed 600 fighters to invade Maimana, the capital of Faryab Province, the governor, who had been appointed by Karzai, fled and went into hiding near the border with Turkmenistan. Barno and I met with Karzai and supported his decision to deploy 750 ANA troops to restore order in the city. Dostum threatened to attack that battalion, and Jalali and Ghani argued that ANA forces should arrest Dostum.

It was a bold but risky proposition. We obviously could not allow Dostum to attack the ANA. Plus, with U.S. advisors embedded with the ANA battalion, Dostum was de facto threatening to attack American soldiers. But a clash between the ANA and Dostum's forces could end badly and open a new fault line inside a coalition that was cooperating against the Taliban.

My first phone call with Dostum did not go well. I tried to treat him with respect, communicating U.S. red lines while giving him a face-saving way out of the conflict. But no matter what I said, Dostum kept threatening to send the Americans home "in body bags." He was slurring his words. Perhaps he had had a bit too much to drink, a habit for which he was well known.

To give him time to reflect—or sober up—I said that I would call him again in two hours.

The second call did not go much better. "An attack on ANA units with embedded Americans is an attack on American forces," I warned. "If you assault them, you will cross a bridge from which there is no return."

Dostum's bluster went unabated. "It will be worse than Vietnam! It will be worse than Iraq! If you think those are bad, wait until you see what I will do to you in Afghanistan!"

Clearly, it was going to take more than words to get our message across to Dostum.

Barno and I discussed the options.

Late that night, a pair of B-1 bombers launched from the Diego Garcia. A sonic boom roared in the sky directly above Dostum's compound. One B-1 broke the sound barrier right as it passed over Dostum's palace.

Dostum showed a brave face in public. "My kids were frightened, but let me say that I am not the type of man to be afraid," he informed the *New York Times*.

However, I soon received a message from Homayoun Nadiri, his representative in the U.S., that Dostum had had enough and was ready to stand down.

On the phone the next day, Dostum was irate. "What kind of a war are you fighting here?" he demanded. "My kids cannot sleep because of your bomber planes!"

The B-1 and its sonic boom had sobered him. "You know," I told Dostum, "you're quite lucky. Imagine if it was some country other than the United States with this capability. Do you think they would have flown a bomber without dropping a bomb? Would *you* have flown a bomber without dropping a bomb?"

Dostum was silent. I could tell we had the upper hand. "Think about it, General," I said quietly. "You are still alive and your house is still standing because we have not come here to kill people. We want to build a better Afghanistan, and we want you to help, not to take it back to civil war like you did in the '90s. You fought over petty things. You lost a historic opportunity, and you are risking it again with your games, especially when you threaten U.S. forces after I warned you not to."

Dostum was quiet for a moment. "What do you want me to do?" he finally asked.

"Let the ANA battalion pass through," I replied. "If there is any shooting, if there is even so much as a traffic accident, you will be held responsible and there will be consequences. But if you show restraint, then in a few days I'll come and pay my respects to you. And your people will see that you are still a big boss in the north."

In subsequent negotiations, Dostum and Atta agreed to demobilize their militias. Dostum accepted an honorific position in the president's office even though it left him out of the military chain of command.

We won another victory against the warlords in Herat, where the governor, Ismail Khan, had a severe authoritarian streak. When Karzai attempted to strike a deal with him throughout 2003 and into early 2004, Ismail Khan responded by expelling Kabul-appointed officials in the region.

When I went to see him in Herat, he refused to disarm his commanders and fighters, claiming that such a move would destabilize Herat. I assured him that his men could be reintegrated into the ANA or ANP or take advantage of programs that reintegrated ex-militia soldiers and officers into the economy by providing vocational training.

In July 2004, Ismail Khan ordered a direct attack on the ANA, making clear that he had no intention of cooperating. In a three-hour firefight, Ismail Khan's men seized four ANA soldiers and five ANA vehicles.

I called Ismail Khan, and he flatly refused to order his men to stand down.

Karzai's cabinet was divided on how to handle Ismail Khan. The Northern Alliance leaders—Fahim, Qanooni, and Abdullah—favored accommodation with their longtime ally. Ghani and Jalali wanted him ousted immediately.

Karzai opted for continued engagement.

In August, another round of clashes broke out, this time between Ismail Khan and another warlord, Amanullah Khan. This local rivalry had an ethnic dimension. Ismail Khan considered Amanullah Khan and his Pashtun supporters to be "nothing better than Talibs."

I called Ismail Khan directly on his cell phone. He was belligerent, promising to march his forces into Amanullah Khan's territory and defeat him decisively.

Then Amanullah Khan launched a surprise attack against Ismail Khan's forces near the Shindand Air Field—a base with a 9,000-foot runway close to Iran. Ismail Khan's fighters performed badly. With the tables turned, I now had to help deter Amanullah Khan from advancing on Herat, fearing that his forces might loot the city. I sent a message to Amanullah Khan that his men should not cross a particular bridge near Shindand.

I worked with Barno to send units of the ANA, accompanied by U.S. advisors and Special Forces, by helicopter to Shindand, where they would set up blocking positions.

As these forces deployed, I called Ismail Khan, who was overseeing the airfield from nearby high ground. "The units are not here!" he complained. "Keep looking . . ." I replied. Soon I could hear the helicopter rotors over the phone.

Now that we had the upper hand, Karzai and I agreed that this was the time to move both Ismail Khan and Amanullah Khan out of western Afghanistan.

I instructed Amanullah Khan to surrender to Afghan authorities, and he was placed under house arrest. When it came time to transfer Ismail Khan, I personally traveled to Herat. In our one-on-one meeting, he tried to negotiate a deal in which he would become interior minister. This was no longer an option, but I relayed that Karzai would make him the minister of water and energy out of respect for his role in resisting the Soviets and the Taliban.

In the ensuing months, Ismail Khan's forces surrendered their heavy weapons and joined the disarmament, demobilization, and reintegration process.

By October 2004, I could write in the *Wall Street Journal* that we were "breaking the back of warlordism."

However, I was concerned that Washington would draw the wrong lessons from the successes against the warlords. The successful deployment of ANA and ANP personnel showed the gains that could be made by investing in Afghan security forces. The civil-military cooperation that Barno and I had developed was critical as well, enabling us to work in complementary ways to establish the credibility of the Kabul government.

The Pentagon was increasingly concerned about getting entrapped in conflicts with militias—understandable, except that failing to deal with the militias could jeopardize the entire venture. Developments in Iraq, at this point, were going quite badly, and Rumsfeld fretted that our warlord agenda might provoke a civil war in Afghanistan. He decided to rescind the language in Accelerating Success that permitted coalition forces to engage warlords. After I protested, we agreed that use of force remained an option but that such action would need to be approved case by case.

While we made a great deal of progress against the warlord problem at one level, we were not able to resolve it fully. Many militia members were admitted too quickly to the National Police, without proper vetting and training. Others turned their militias into "private security companies." Our strategy was undermined by lower-level coalition or CIA officers who formed relationships with local strongmen, for example, to protect reconstruction activities or provide logistical services. It was difficult to prevent these independent actions on the ground, which, in the aggregate, were empowering local militias and warlords. The U.N.-led program for reintegrating ex-militias, in which the Japanese had the lead, was the most important part of the demobilization, decommissioning, and reintegration program. Unfortunately, it was poorly executed in light of the severe resource limitations it faced.

— ⟨ ⟩ —

EFFORTS AGAINST drug trafficking had proved even less successful. By 2003, Afghanistan was the world's leading opium producer. I feared that drug money would corrupt Afghanistan's politics and burden the country with a large addict population.

The United Kingdom was in charge of counter narcotics, but its program was underpowered, underresourced, and conceptually misguided. The British initially had decided to pay poppy growers not to plant the illegal crop, which, of course, created perverse incentives to plant poppy in order to be paid to stop. At an April 2004 summit in Washington, President Bush agreed at Blair's request to involve the United States more actively on the counter-narcotics front.

When I discussed the issue with the president, his solution was straight-forward. "I am a spray man," he said, referring to a plan to destroy poppy fields by spraying herbicide from planes. He was close to Colombian president Álvaro Uribe, and attributed his friend's success in fighting coca production to this method. I reminded the president that Karzai adamantly opposed aerial spraying.

In developing Accelerating Success, I had purposely downplayed counter narcotics. It was not that I saw the issue as unimportant. Rather, I had calcu-lated at the time that other elements of our plan, such as police training and private-sector agricultural development, would help reduce opium produc-tion. In the meantime, as long as global demand for heroine remained strong, it would be difficult to suppress supply. Also, I did not want to diminish the U.K.'s responsibility to act.

Counter narcotics was a sensitive issue with the Afghan leadership. Karzai was rarely uncivil or short with me, even during tense periods. But counter-narcotics was a rare issue on which he would lash out. Typically, when I went to his residence, he offered chocolates from Switzerland, for which he had a weakness. One time, though, clearly in a cross mood, he summoned me to his residence and directed me to a bowl of dried figs on his coffee table, then showed me another bowl of figs.

"Do you see any difference?"

I looked carefully. "No, I don't."

"Take a closer look," he insisted.

Again, I did not see anything.

Karzai then pointed out that the color of the figs in one of the bowls was peculiar. Working himself into a rage, he proceeded to accuse the United States of spraying toxic chemicals on Afghan crops.

"Your chemicals are being used against our trees and water," he shouted. "You have no respect for us. You're no better than the Soviets."

"Excuse me, Mr. President," I replied. "Did I hear you correctly? Did you compare us to the Soviet Union?"

Karzai could tell how shocked I was at his hostility and cooled down a bit.

"We're not doing this," I told him truthfully. I knew the U.S. was not engaged in any spraying operations and to my knowledge the British were not doing so either.

We scheduled a meeting, this time with the British ambassador, Rosa-lind Marsdan. Cordial and professional as she was, Karzai tore into her. His diatribe on the narcotics issue soon turned into a broader lecture on how the British still held to an imperialistic and colonialist mentality. At first I was relieved that Karzai's anger had turned elsewhere, but eventually, I began to feel sorry for my British colleague and intervened.

Karzai's behavior initially struck me as entirely bizarre, but upon exploring further, I learned that his accusations were not without foundation. From then on, Karzai and I were on the same side. Unilateral chemical spraying by foreign countries was, indeed, unacceptable. I was not absolutely opposed to aerial spraying, but I had concerns about the lack of coordination with the Afghan government, as well as the environmental protection issues implicated in the practice. It struck me as an unduly reflexive—an overly "quick and dirty"—response to a complex problem. Counter narcotics deserved careful attention and a deliberate plan.

In a memo to the principals, I warned that the rapidly growing illegal drug industry could imperil all other things we were doing to rebuild Afghanistan. The 2004 opium crop was of record size. Money from the illegal drug industry was finding its way into coffers of Taliban and other terrorist groups.

And the problem was complicated. Many players were involved. Small farmers, with as little as two acres of land, might be planting opium to pay off debt or to cover costs of a family illness. Opium profits were ten times greater than profits for wheat, so a strategy aimed at encouraging alternative livelihoods by itself would not solve the problem.

Then there were the forty or so powerful drug lords who operated industrial-scale plantations and the domestic and foreign traffickers, well armed and with ties to some Afghan government officials and the Taliban. Taking on the drug lords was no simple matter. Security forces would be required, given the risks of violence and instability.

If farmers were nervous about the country's instability, they would opt for quick income from poppies rather than putting capital at risk for longer-term investments such as orchards. The more security we and the Afghan government could provide, the greater the likelihood that farmers would plant legal crops.

We also needed to be proactive in incentivizing a shift toward legal crops. Stronger agricultural programs could promote high value-added crops and food processing efforts. At the same time, we would need to deter poppy cultivation by strengthening eradication capabilities and reforming Afghanistan's weak and corrupt law enforcement system. Since the Pentagon did not want any part of this job, we had to embark on the slow process of bolstering Afghan law enforcement.

I worked with Karzai to develop a multipronged effort. We decided to target Nangarhar and Helmand provinces—the two main centers of opium production. We worked with OMB to move existing funds for this effort from other accounts. OMB promised to replenish those funds in the next emergency supplemental appropriations request. We now had a multilayered and sophisticated plan.

But when I briefed President Bush, he remained fixated on aerial spraying. I reiterated that chemicals would affect other crops and contaminate water supplies. And Karzai was vehemently opposed, warning that spraying would harm the legitimacy of his government. If he acquiesced to spraying, he had told me, he would be seen as a foreign agent—no better than Babrak Karmal, the puppet dictator the Soviets had imposed when they invaded Afghanistan. Afghans would believe that he was allowing a foreign power to wage chemical warfare on them. "I would sooner pull up my tent and leave," Karzai had said with absolute emphasis.

Only then did President Bush acquiesce, but not before repeating once more that he himself was a "spray man."

Karzai showed commitment and energy in implementing our strategy. He delivered one of his most powerful speeches to kick off the campaign. Appealing to Afghans' sense of honor, he warned that Afghanistan would become a pariah if it continued to export drugs. When foreign leaders raised the narcotics issue, Karzai said he would become emotional, calling it a "great shame on the nation." I traveled to Nangarhar, where the provincial leadership put great effort into implementing the plan.

Early in the fall, I was startled when the results came in. Opium planting had fallen to virtually zero in Nangarhar. The result in Nangarhar convinced me that the narcotics problem was treatable if the Afghan government and international community put resources behind a substantial and concerted effort. Progress in Helmand, where security was a greater problem, was less significant.

In the years after my departure, the narcotics problem ebbed and flowed. The Nangarhar operation was not extended nationwide. There were times when the number of poppy-free provinces, as assessed by the U.N. Drug Control Program, reached a majority. But the reality is that poppy production cannot be tackled without improvements in security, governance, and rural development. There are no shortcuts.

WARLORDS AND DRUG LORDS were a headache, but the biggest spoiler was Pakistan. I met regularly with ambassadors of key regional powers, including Reza Bahrami of Iran. But Pakistan's policies were most consequential for our efforts. At one point, the U.S. ambassador to Pakistan, Nancy Powell, and I sent dueling cables to Washington. I pointed to intelligence suggesting that the Pakistani military was playing a double game, tracking down certain al Qaeda operatives while aiding and abetting the Taliban, the Haqqani network, and Hezbe Islami. Areas of western Pakistan were becoming the type of terrorist sanctuaries that had existed in Afghanistan prior to 9/11. Afghan insurgents were comfortably ensconced in Pakistan, using camps to recover, train, and equip their fighters. Even al Qaeda appeared to have reconstituted camps. This was a growing threat to our mission and to our people in Afghanistan. If another terrorist attack reached the U.S. homeland, this time from Pakistani territory, the United States would have no choice but to respond in dramatic fashion. It would be far less costly and less risky to resolve the issue proactively.

Ambassador Powell countered that Pakistan was a trusted partner and was contributing more than was generally recognized. In her view, Islamabad could not control everything that took place in the ungoverned areas bordering Afghanistan. The Pakistani military had sent forces into the Federally Administered Tribal Areas, where some of the insurgents were operating. The United States needed to give Pakistan more support so the military could better secure those areas.

Even amid an open debate between the ambassadors to Afghanistan and Pakistan, administration policy did not change. The principals simply cited Pakistani successes in rounding up dozens of al Qaeda operatives.

Frustrated, I also spoke publicly about the sanctuary problem. At one point, Secretary Powell called me and told me outright to stop making public statements about these issues since they were causing problems in his dealings with Musharraf.

"What am I saying that's incorrect?" I countered. He didn't respond. If he conceded that the Pakistani military was providing sanctuary and support for insurgents, we would have to confront the issue head on and come up with a strategy. "Mr. Secretary," I pressed, "I read day in and day out the same intelligence that the rest of the government sees about the sanctuary problem. I do not know what your plan is to deal with the problem. I worry that you don't see the threat. If you do see it and have a strategy and a plan to address it—maybe not now but later—please explain it to me! I will support it."

Powell waved off my point and asked me not to make such comments in public. In the fall of 2004, President Bush hosted Musharraf during the United Nations General Assembly meeting in New York and, over the coming years, continued these outreach efforts. None made progress on the sanctuary issue.

I continued to press the issue, and in early 2005, President Bush gave me permission to meet with Musharraf in Islamabad. By this point, I had compared notes with Brahimi, who had met with Pakistani leaders on numerous occasions when he was still the U.N. special representative for Afghanistan. Brahimi, an ever-patient diplomat, was exasperated. Whenever he appealed to Musharraf to curb the insurgency, the Pakistani leader simply denied that the Taliban were present in his country at all.

Karzai called Musharraf prior to my meeting. "The American ambassador to Afghanistan is coming to see you with our understanding," Karzai told Musharraf. "I have full confidence in him. Whatever you and he agree upon will be fully acceptable to us. He is meeting with you with our blessing."

Karzai had also given me a box of Afghan pomegranates to give Musharraf as a gift.

When I met with the Pakistani president, he was not receptive. "I don't like pomegranates," Musharraf said coldly. He was bothered by the small seeds in the fruit, he explained.

Building on Karzai's message, I suggested that the United States would like to help Afghan and Pakistani leaders resolve their differences and establish a more constructive relationship.

Musharraf replied that India had set up consulates in Kandahar and Jalalabad to destabilize Pakistan. I told him that historically, India had consulates in those cities to facilitate exports of Afghan agricultural products. I suggested that the United States, Afghanistan, and Pakistan could monitor the consulates and determine whether India was in fact using them for hostile purposes. This was a great proposal, Musharraf said, and the United States and Pakistan should follow up on it.

Musharraf next complained about Afghanistan's construction of a dam on the Kunar River, which he believed would harm Pakistani agriculture downstream. Water issues had often arisen among the countries of the region, but Afghanistan and Pakistan and even India and Pakistan had worked out agreements in the past. I replied that I had not heard about any dam-building project in Kunar but that the two countries, perhaps assisted by the United States or World Bank experts, could study the dam project and propose a satisfactory solution.

Musharraf again approved of the idea.

I then said that I needed cooperation on a few things from Pakistan. It was unhelpful for him, as president of Pakistan, to state that Pashtuns were underrepresented in the Afghan government. "When Karzai takes steps to ensure ethnic and political balance, your statements make it seem as if the Afghan president is merely doing Pakistan's bidding."

Musharraf interrupted me and noted that he was impressed with our progress to date. He immediately agreed to stop complaining about Pashtun representation and promised to tell the ISI to cease doing so as well.

I then turned to the issue of the Taliban and insurgent sanctuaries. Just as we could work together on issues of concern to Pakistan, I offered, we needed to find a way to eliminate the sanctuaries.

Musharraf shifted in his chair, visibly uncomfortable with the turn in our conversation. "There are no Taliban in Pakistan," he said. Indian intelligence services were feeding misinformation to the Afghan government, and from there to the United States. He noted that there was a lot of movement back and forth across the border and that individual fighters might be mixed in with the others. "There are no Taliban sanctuaries here," he asserted. "If you have information about Taliban—phone numbers, locations, or addresses— we will move against them."

I did not relent. The Taliban's political leadership was in Pakistan, I said. Even journalists were able to find Taliban leaders and spokesmen in Pakistan.

Musharraf responded vaguely that with all the refugees crossing the border, it was difficult to tell who's who. "As far as our knowingly allowing leaders, commanders, and fighters to be in Pakistan, this is not the case."

What the U.S. needed to do, he told me, was to adjust its military strategy. Pashtuns had to be fought in a particular way. "If you want to stop them," he advised, "you have to use massive force, including tanks and artillery. You are too discriminating in your operations. That is why you are having problems. You have to act much more massively."

Noting that military strategy was "not in my lane," I refused to engage on his call to kill Afghans with greater abandon.

<hr />

IN THE COMPETITION between builders and spoilers, the Afghan government was ahead in 2004 and into 2005. Reconstruction and development were continuing and the economy had one of the highest growth rates in Asia.

To build on this progress, I put in another funding request. This time, my request was approved with little debate. The Bush administration was now in agreement that state and nation building in Afghanistan were worth the investment.

TWENTY

FRUITS OF
DEMOCRACY

KABUL, 2004–2005

ELECTION DAY—OCTOBER 9, 2004—SAW A HUGE SANDSTORM SWEEP ACROSS AF-
ghanistan. As I stepped outside into the eerie, yellowish hue, it felt like being
suspended in a mist of grit and dust. But this did not deter the Afghans from
voting. Long lines formed at every polling place, one for men and one for
women. Election officers checked voting cards and dipped each voter's finger
into blue ink to prevent repeat voting.

This turnout took real courage. No one knew whether the Taliban would
disrupt the voting with violence. There were many stories of Afghans writing
their wills or taking the equivalent of last rites in case they were killed at the
polling stations. Fortunately, though there were several shooting incidents,
violence was minimal.

Afghans were full of wonder that an election was actually happening in
their country and that they would choose the head of state for the first time
in Afghanistan's 5,000-year history. I saw evident pride and emotion at every
polling station I visited. More than 8.1 million Afghans voted, a number that
still stands as a record. One voter captured the national mood on Election
Day: "Finally, we are human again."

THE ELECTION was the product of enormous joint effort by the Afghan government, the U.N. mission, and the United States. By mid-March, six months before Election Day, only 1.5 million of Afghanistan's ten million eligible citizens had registered to vote. By early July, voter rolls surpassed six million, and Afghans were registering at a rate of over 100,000 per day. Barno and I worked hard to ensure security and provide the logistical capabilities needed to move ballots out to polling locations and into ballot-counting centers.

The politics of the election also required a great deal of maneuvering. I thought the best outcome for Afghanistan would be an election between two major candidates with distinct platforms and bases of support. Karzai was the only major figure with the capacity to reach across ethnic lines. Qanooni, who would likely get most of the Tajik vote and would have the backing of the Northern Alliance, represented a genuine alternative to Karzai.

The most consequential decision Karzai had to make was the selection of his two vice-presidential running mates. He quickly enlisted Khalili as his second vice president to appeal to Hazara voters but was not sure if he should give the first slot to Fahim, currently the first vice president and defense minister.

Fahim desperately wanted to be Karzai's running mate. For over a decade, he had fought in Massoud's militia, contending with a civil war, rivalries within the Northern Alliance, and limited international support. Massoud, charismatic and telegenic, had been an effective resistance leader. Fahim was different. Burly with a tightly trimmed beard and thinning hair, Fahim was an introvert with a stern demeanor. While intelligent, he lacked Massoud's warmth and natural skill in crafting political alliances. It was only because of Massoud's death and the Bonn process that he had emerged as a national figure.

Karzai had reservations. Fahim had been a central figure in the destructive civil war of the 1990s. More recently, he had become a liability for Karzai. Jean Arnault, Brahimi's successor as U.N. special representative for Afghanistan, encouraged Karzai to drop Fahim, remembering the heavy-handed threats Fahim had used at the *Loya Jirga*. Japan's ambassador, Kinichi Komano, who had to contend with Fahim's recalcitrance on militia-disarmament issues, was of a similar mind.

But who could replace Fahim? Zia Massoud, Ahmad Shah Massoud's brother, came from an honored Tajik family and did not have blood on his hands from the civil war. He was currently serving as ambassador in Moscow. The more we talked, the more Karzai gravitated toward Zia Massoud. He asked Massoud to return to Kabul.

As usual, Karzai waited until the last moment to make this decision. But finally he offered the position of first vice president to Zia. A few days later, he called a meeting of the Northern Alliance leaders, including Fahim, Qanooni, Abdullah, and Zia Massoud. Fahim was visibly anxious and stressed, perspiring profusely.

Karzai began by talking vaguely and meanderingly about the need for change. Abruptly, he closed by saying that he appreciated Fahim's service to the country, that they all would continue to be partners, but that he had decided to go in a different direction on the first vice-presidential slot. Fahim was out.

Signaling to his cohorts, Fahim rose to his feet and they all departed.

Fahim, though, was not done. He summoned Zia Massoud to a meeting with other Northern Alliance leaders. Over several hours, he made the case that there be a consensus among the Northern Alliance on which of their leaders should be Karzai's running mate. He succeeded, and Zia Massoud called Karzai to inform him that because of the Northern Alliance leaders' opposition, he could no longer be on the president's ticket.

Time was now running short. The deadline for filings was only a few hours away. Panicked, Karzai lamented that he had allowed Arnault to pressure him into dropping Fahim. "Look at what you internationals have gotten me into," he shouted. "I will never listen to you again!"

Abdullah arrived at the palace to insist that Karzai reappoint Fahim.

"That's not doable," I told him. "It's not realistic at this point." But I did see another possibility. "Would you be willing to serve?" Only if the Northern Alliance leaders agreed, Abdullah replied.

And he had a helpful suggestion: "Why don't you call Rabbani?" As Zia Massoud's father-in-law, Rabbani might be willing to urge him to join the ticket.

I went to see Rabbani. "I'll fix the problem," he promised. Soon, Zia Massoud recommitted to joining Karzai—and not a moment too soon. Karzai filed the paperwork within minutes of the deadline.

Each of the major ethnic communities had a candidate running: Karzai was a Pashtun; Qanooni, a Tajik; Dostum, an Uzbek; and Mohammad Mohaqqiq, a Hazara. I expected Afghans to vote largely on the basis of ethnic identity. Pashtuns, the largest group, viewed themselves as the founders and natural rulers of Afghanistan. The other communities would likely vote for their candidate out of ethnic pride—they had never before even had a chance to vote for one of their own.

With Afghanistan's two-round voting system, the key question was whether Karzai would secure 50 percent of the vote in the first round or whether he would have to go into a second round against the runner-up.

IN EARLY JUNE, four months before the scheduled election, I sent Powell a memo asking for guidance on what options were permissible and available in regard to electoral assistance for political groups and candidates. The general policy was that the United States could provide communications and organizational training to all interested political parties but would not provide funding or operational support to any preferred candidate or campaign.

The philosophical rationale for these restrictions made sense in general, but in practice they created an uneven playing field for liberal and moderate political groups. Candidates with links to foreign governments could get money through clandestine means. Those affiliated with criminal groups, such as drug kingpins, could secure needed funds from disreputable sources. Corrupt individuals could fund their own candidacies. Candidates who leaned toward liberal democratic principles and pro-American policies were at a disadvantage.

While the United States had an interest in staying out of Afghanistan's elections, we also had a stake in ensuring that candidates who shared our interests and values operated on a level playing field. I was sure that foreign money, certainly from Iran but possibly also from Turkey and Pakistan, would find its way to various candidates.

Nor did existing laws address an array of practical questions concerning Karzai and the line between his presidential and political activities. Could he, for example, campaign using U.S. helicopters? Should his U.S.-provided security detail accompany him to political events? Could Karzai take our helicopters and vehicles to attend presidential events, such as ribbon-cutting ceremonies, if they had political overtones? Karzai and I had developed plans for several presidential events, some—but not all—of which would include other candidates.

Powell replied that we were not permitted to provide any one candidate with financial support. We could, however, provide logistical support to Karzai since he was the president.

The campaign season was remarkably civil, particularly for a pool of candidates not exactly known for restraint. Lively posters adorned major cities and towns. Karzai, Qanooni, and Mohaqqiq addressed large rallies. Dostum organized parades in northern cities, riding down the street in an open car and waving to his supporters. The Afghan media arranged televised debates.

I made several appearances of my own during the election season, urging people to vote. I repeatedly explained how the election would be conducted via secret ballot. Many feared retaliation from local warlords. "How you vote,"

I stressed, "is just between you and your God." I continued, "Regardless of whether someone offered you money or tried to intimidate you to vote a certain way, once you are in the voting booth, your decision is up to you and your conscience."

As the election neared, Afghans were gaining confidence that the process was indeed free and fair. This increased the sense of excitement and anticipation.

My senior staff, other diplomats, and U.N. officials were getting excited, too, placing bets on the outcome. The chief of the MI6, the British intelligence service, declared that the bet was to be settled in a bottle of champagne. I predicted Karzai would receive 55 percent of the vote.

AROUND NOON on Election Day, I started to receive reports of technical problems. Qanooni was complaining that some polling stations in his area had run out of ink and that the ink at some polling stations could be washed off, thereby allowing people to vote more than once. He began calling for voting to halt and the elections to be suspended. A quick investigation showed that the problems were limited to a few voting sites. Election officials responded quickly, sending new supplies of ink to the sites to ensure that no one was deprived of the right to vote. They also extended the voting hours at the affected sites. The commission rejected Qanooni's demand to suspend the elections.

Nevertheless, Qanooni continued to assert that the election had been tainted and that he might not accept the result. His claims started to attract support from minor candidates.

I called a meeting with all of the candidates involved in the controversy, emphasizing the limited scope of the problems and the fact that they could not possibly affect the overall result. All quickly understood, except Qanooni. When we met one on one, Qanooni reiterated his threat to reject the outcome of the election.

"How many districts have had problems with the ink?" I asked.

He admitted that it was a small number.

I asked how many votes he would gain if all the ballots in those districts were counted in his favor.

He did not know, but conceded it would not mark a huge increase in his overall vote count.

"Do you really believe that will change the result of the election?" I knew, as did Qanooni, that the polls showed a big gap between Karzai's vote and those of the next tier of candidates.

He agreed that it would not.

I asked whether he really wanted to risk the future of the country by making an issue of these small technical difficulties. I described all the preparations that had been taken to hold the election. I urged him to announce that he would accept the official result when ballots were counted in a couple of weeks, but he continued to hedge.

We went back and forth about his future plans. I stressed that he was young and could run again in the future. He could seek a position in the cabinet or lead the opposition in the parliament, as major political figures in other countries had done. He had been one of the architects of the Bonn process and would always have an important place in Afghan politics.

Finally, Qanooni agreed to accept the election result and find another way to contribute to the political process. I sensed that he was disheartened—he did not like backing away from a fight—but also relieved. I had given him an honorable way out.

With the crisis abated, I departed for Washington, carrying a handful of extra ballots from the election. I delivered one, autographed by President Karzai, to President Bush. I unfolded it on the president's desk in the Oval Office and explained that each candidate was represented by a picture and a symbol to help illiterate Afghans find the right box. President Bush was in a solemn mood as he looked at the ballot. He smiled, though, when he read the inscription from Karzai: "Who would you have voted for?"

I also gave a ballot to Rumsfeld. He was impressed, indeed surprised, by how well the election had gone. He had always been skeptical about whether democracy could take root in countries like Afghanistan. He displayed the ballot prominently under the glass top of a circular table in his office.

It took several weeks for the ballot boxes to be collected and validated and for the votes to be counted. Karzai won 55.4 percent of the vote, comfortably avoiding a run-off. Qanooni received 16.3 percent, Mohaqqiq 11.7 percent, and Dostum 10.0 percent. Karzai received the most support from Afghans who voted across ethnic lines. Afghans recognized that Karzai enjoyed the confidence of the international community, so a vote for Karzai represented a vote for continued U.S. involvement in Afghanistan.

I soon started to receive bottles of champagne from the other election bettors. I noticed that intelligence officers all made good on their promises. The diplomats were less reliable in settling up.

On December 7, I was back in Kabul for Karzai's inauguration. Rumsfeld and Cheney also attended. Upon entering the gates of the Deljushah Palace—the "palace that pleases the heart"—we glanced at the clock on the large tower above. The minute hand ticked forward to show 8:20—precisely the time at which we were scheduled to arrive.

The meeting hall resembled a church, a long building with high ceilings, rows to seat 500 to 600 people, and a stage at the far end. It had been refurbished just for this event and the formal ceremony proceeded like clockwork.

As we were leaving, Cheney captured the moment with a characteristic compliment: "Zal, what have you done with Afghanistan? It feels like we're in Europe."

⤛   ⤜

WHEN I RETURNED to Washington a few weeks later, the president asked to see me.

Cheney, Powell, Rumsfeld, Rice, Director of Central Intelligence George Tenet, and others sat on the two couches to the side.

"I must be in serious trouble," I remarked.

Everyone laughed, and then the president asked me to take the seat next to him, giving me a high five as I approached him. And then he said, "I think you should go to Iraq. You have done a marvelous job in Afghanistan. The vice president has reported to me after his trip to Karzai's inauguration that things are going very well. We need you in Iraq. You get along well with the military, and they like working with you. General Casey is a good man. It's a very important mission for the country."

"After Afghanistan, don't I deserve an assignment to Rome or some other comfortable post?" I joked, taken aback.

The president bantered in response that he was going to make me a "household name." Then, more seriously, he leaned forward and stressed, "This is the most important thing facing us. It would help us a lot."

I replied that I was honored, but needed to think it over. And discuss it with my family.

To stem the violence, the president said, Iraqis needed to accelerate political progress. It would be my task to help the Iraqis complete a draft constitution quickly, so that they could hold elections under a new constitution in December 2005. Rumsfeld noted that Iraqi security forces were developing steadily, which would allow us to downsize our military presence.

As I left the meeting, my mind turned to Afghanistan. Karzai would not be happy. He was a courageous man, but not an effective state builder. I knew that his stature derived in large part from his relationship with the United States. We worked well as a team because I had the benefit of long-standing relationships with Afghan officials. They trusted me to bridge differences and overcome obstacles, in part because they knew I felt a real attachment to the people and culture, and also because I could help them build the institutions of the state.

I also worried about who might replace me. My relationships in Washington gave me a distinct advantage in securing resources and high-level attention for Afghanistan. In pressing for funding, I could make the case directly to President Bush and the Principals Committee. A successor might not have the clout to make such direct appeals, and programs in Afghanistan might be shortchanged in the budget process.

Still, I felt compelled to accept the assignment to Iraq. If the president believed that I could improve the outcome, I wanted to try.

IN THE MONTHS after the elections, the number of security incidents throughout Afghanistan plummeted to record lows.

There were also hopeful signs that Taliban leaders were considering abandoning the insurgency. The Afghan people had spoken in the election—and not in favor of the Taliban.

Karzai agreed that, in my remaining months as ambassador, it might make sense for me to reach out to the Taliban. I traveled to outlying provinces and made direct appeals to the insurgents to join the political process. I argued that it was time to stop the killing of Afghans by Afghans, that there had been too much bloodshed already, and that Afghans should come together to rebuild their country. Taliban fighters and supporters who did not have blood on their hands, I offered, should have no fears about returning to their villages. Those who had been part of the armed opposition, I added, should accept the new constitution and reconcile with the newly elected government. I emphasized that the votes of eight million Afghans had legitimized the government.

In the ensuing months, several Taliban commanders contacted me to discuss reconciliation. I worked with Mojaddedi, who headed the Afghan government's reconciliation and reintegration program, to follow up on each of these leads. Some lower- and middle-level commanders, as well as their fighters, decided to lay down their arms as a result.

I put a great deal of energy into this reconciliation effort. Ultimately, however, it proved unsuccessful. While there were some takers among the Taliban, the numbers were not enough to transform the situation. My sense is that the Pakistani leadership did not want the Taliban to make a deal on their own—they wanted negotiations to go through Islamabad.

More troubling, the successful election in Afghanistan produced a sense of complacency in some quarters of Washington. I saw the election as a milestone in a long road; others viewed it as the end of the road.

Throughout my time in Kabul, career officials at the State Department urged me to transition toward "normal embassy operations"—diplomatic code for a less energetic approach than the one I was taking. "When Afghanistan is a normal country," I would rebut, "we will become a normal embassy." As I prepared to depart, I was worried that calls for a "normal embassy" would win out.

In the final leg of my ambassadorship, I pushed hard for a strategic partnership agreement between the United States and Afghanistan. I wanted to signal to Afghans and to regional powers that the United States was committed to Afghanistan for the long haul. Uncertainty about the American role, particularly in light of the decision to transfer the security assistance mission to NATO in 2006, was causing many to hedge their bets.

I thought a strategic partnership agreement might encourage regional powers to cooperate in the stabilization of Afghanistan. Pakistani leaders were calculating that the United States would tire of Afghanistan or become distracted by other issues, giving regional powers another shot at dominating Afghanistan. Pakistan kept the Taliban and other insurgents ready as their horse for that race. Only if we convinced regional powers that we would not leave until the job was truly done would they accept the reality of a stable and independent Afghanistan.

In Washington, the president and the principals were supportive. Rice, now secretary of state, was in favor of a strategic partnership agreement. Rumsfeld also wanted an agreement that gave the United States access to Bagram and other military facilities. He saw the strategic partnership agreement as a bargain: the U.S. would commit to helping Afghanistan in exchange for an Afghan commitment to provide base access and military freedom of action. I collaborated with Karzai to form a group in Kabul to work on this issue.

I initially worked with lower-ranking State Department officials on the strategic partnership agreement. An ironclad security commitment to Afghanistan was not feasible, since a defense treaty would need to be ratified by the Senate. I knew that we would need a creative agreement that was responsive to the situation in Afghanistan without creating legal challenges. The mid-level bureaucracy in the State Department, however, was less than enthusiastic about the very concept of a strategic partnership agreement. When I asked the Bureau for South and Central Asian Affairs to prepare a draft, I was disappointed to receive a cut-and-paste document that simply took stock text from other agreements.

My team in Kabul tried to devise a better draft. But no matter how much I strengthened the language, I could not reassure Karzai and his colleagues. They had lived through the tragic consequences of the U.S. abandonment after the Soviet withdrawal and knew that a change in circumstances or a change in administrations could fundamentally alter U.S. policy toward their country.

Presidents Bush and Karzai signed the United States–Afghanistan Strategic Partnership declaration on May 23, 2005, in Washington, D.C.

While the declaration discussed political and economic cooperation, the security provisions were the most important part. The parties undertook to "consult with respect to taking appropriate measures in the event that Afghanistan perceives that its territorial integrity, independence, or security is threatened or at risk." U.S. military forces would "continue to have access to Bagram Air Base and its facilities, and facilities at other locations as may be mutually determined." It also affirmed freedom of action for U.S. forces—a controversial provision in human rights circles.

I saw the joint presidential declaration of the United States–Afghanistan Strategic Partnership as the capstone of Accelerating Success.

Despite the strategic partnership agreement, Karzai was unhappy that I was leaving and repeatedly tried to reverse the decision to send me to Iraq. During the summit meeting, he told Rice, in front of his cabinet officials, that it would be very difficult for him personally if I left Afghanistan. "How can I explain Ambassador Khalilzad's departure to the Afghan people?" Karzai asked Rice whether he should raise the issue directly with President Bush.

"Please don't," Rice replied. "It's a done deal." She explained that Afghanistan was in good shape and that I was needed in Iraq.

Karzai repeated that my transfer was a bad mistake and that Afghanistan was not out of the woods.

◄   ►

I RETURNED to Kabul after the signing of the strategic partnership agreement, but I had to cut short the farewell events. I had been confirmed as U.S. ambassador to Iraq, and President Bush was eager to get me to Baghdad. The last event on my final day in Afghanistan was a lunch hosted by President Karzai.

It was held at Gulkhana—"house of flowers"—Palace. Above the courtyard were beautiful, ancient chinar trees so massive that three or four people would need to lock hands together to reach all the way around them.

At the conclusion of the sumptuous lunch, Karzai awarded me the King Amanullah Ghazi Medal, the highest recognition bestowed by the government of Afghanistan. The medal was accompanied by a citation from Zahir Shah, which commended me as the "son of the soil," who had "achieved greatness overseas" yet had not spared any effort to help Afghanistan.

After the lunch, President Karzai and I went up to his office. We made small talk, as we had done in hundreds of previous meetings. It was emotional and a bit awkward. He told me to be safe in Iraq and said that he would stay in touch by phone.

We both had mixed feelings. On the one hand, Afghanistan was certainly on a much-improved trajectory. Since October 2003, more than 63,000 fighters had been disarmed, and over 10,000 heavy weapons had been removed safely. As the U.N. reported, major cities were "largely free of operational heavy weapons," a development that had "furthered the goal of ensuring military assets and weaponry belong to the State of Afghanistan alone, for the protection of national sovereignty." We had built up the Afghan army and police to preclude a vacuum of power.

On the other hand, we feared that the progress was reversible. As our conversation wound down, Karzai became visibly emotional, recollecting the suffering his people had endured for a quarter of a century.

I sensed that he was reluctant to have our meeting, and our time together, come to an end. It was a sentiment that I shared but could not indulge, given the C-17 waiting to ferry me to Baghdad. As we left his office, Karzai insisted on walking me not only to the door, but all the way to the motorcade in the parking lot. I was deeply touched.

—< >—

SINCE I LEFT Afghanistan as ambassador, I have reflected a great deal on why the situation deteriorated so dramatically in the years that followed.

Our principal failure, in my view, was our refusal to deal with Pakistan's double game. Even the accelerated drone attacks in western Pakistan under the Obama administration, which were somewhat effective in the fight against al Qaeda, failed to a large extent to target the Taliban, the Haqqani Group, or Hezbe Islami.

The United States also signaled a lack of military resolve. The Pentagon made incautious public statements about the reduction of U.S. military forces in Afghanistan. At one point, the combat power of the United States dropped to a single brigade, even as the insurgent threat was rising. The evident lack of U.S. commitment gave Pakistan a green light to step up the Taliban and insurgent offensive in late 2005 and early 2006.

As NATO-ISAF took over for the coalition, Afghans began to doubt the U.S. commitment. An unwieldy command structure, involving multiple combatant commands and countries operating under a bewildering array of "national caveats"—rules of engagement that could differ widely—undermined the capacity of international forces to pursue an integrated counterinsurgency strategy. Some non-U.S. NATO forces defined Afghanistan as a peacekeeping mission, and were not prepared to fight an insurgency.

In 2009 President Obama approved the deployment of only 30,000 of the 40,000 additional troops requested by Generals Stanley McChrystal and David Petraeus. More problematically, the president paired this escalation with an arbitrary deadline of one year, at which point the United States would start the withdrawal. As a result, the military could not carry out the campaign plan as designed by the generals in the field. The surge went a long way toward stabilizing the south, but commanders lacked the resources and time needed to do the same in the east.

Given that we were unwilling to deploy a large force, the decision to build a small Afghan National Army was misguided. The ANA totaled only 70,000 troops in 2007. Late in the Bush administration, an increase was approved, but Afghan National Security Forces were never large or capable enough to cope with the escalation of Taliban operations. The Obama administration increased the size of Afghan forces in its policy review but rejected the military's proposal for a combined ANA and ANP force of 400,000.

Our difficulties have resulted from reactive rather than anticipatory policies. We were always playing catch-up.

Karzai and the Afghan leadership failed to move quickly and energetically to extend the reach of the Afghan government into contested areas. Weak or nonexistent government in the provinces left areas vulnerable to the enemy. Other governance problems, notably corruption and poor delivery of services, went unaddressed. These difficulties were compounded by the way the United States mishandled the relationship with Karzai. He was mystified by our failure to address the sanctuary problem and incensed that U.S. officials wouldn't even discuss the issue with him honestly. Karzai eventually gravitated toward conspiracy theories: perhaps the United States wanted to perpetuate the insurgent threat in order to create an excuse for its continued military presence in Afghanistan?

U.S.-Afghan relations deteriorated. Though the relationship with Karzai worsened during the Bush administration, it became openly adversarial during the Obama administration. The United States was no longer cooperating actively with Karzai on warlordism and corruption, yet expected him to act decisively against these problems. Without U.S. support, Karzai reluctantly concluded that stability depended on his keeping all the problematic actors inside the tent, and that tolerating corruption was the unavoidable price he would have to pay for their cooperation.

A case in point is how Dostum has fared over the past few years. In 2005 Karzai moved against Dostum as part of a broader push against the warlords. In fact, he wished to press the warlords more aggressively than the United States. Yet when Karzai determined that Washington was against him, he concluded that his victory in the 2009 election depended on the warlords' support. That year he called for Dostum to return to Afghanistan from Turkey, where he had fled.

I do not think it was realistic for the Obama administration to expect Karzai, or any leader, to risk his political survival in an election year to take a stand against corruption or warlordism. The shortsightedness of the Obama administration's personal attacks on Karzai is illustrated again by Dostum's fate under the Ghani presidency. An unabashed reformer who was perhaps Dostum's fiercest critic in the 2002–2005 period, Ghani, in 2013, asked Dostum to serve as his running mate amid changed political circumstances. From marginalized warlord and a symbol of the bad old days of Afghanistan, Dostum has now emerged as the country's vice president.

These and other negative dynamics began to spin out of control over time. Karzai would complain. Washington would ignore his complaints. He would make critical statements about U.S. night raids and civilian casualties. We would denounce him. We would demand that he move against corrupt officials. He would ignore our demands. Ultimately, the United States alienated Karzai—a highly regrettable and unnecessary outcome, since he could be an extraordinarily constructive leader when we worked with him in the right way.

I believe that had the United States, in 2002 and 2003, forced Pakistan to eliminate the insurgent sanctuaries, sustained Accelerating Success or another initiative like it, and adopted a program to train Afghan forces along the lines of the McChrystal-Petraeus recommendation, positive dynamics in Afghanistan would have built upon each other. Many now view today's difficulties in Afghanistan as evidence that success was impossible in the first place. I disagree.

TWENTY-ONE

PREPARING
FOR IRAQ

WASHINGTON, D.C.,
NOVEMBER 2004–JULY 2005

I ALMOST DIDN'T BECOME THE U.S. AMBASSADOR TO IRAQ. IN LATE NOVEMBER 2004, Brahimi, who had become a close friend and had recently served as U.N. special representative to Iraq, called me. He had heard that I was going to Baghdad and wanted to offer some advice. Prime Minister Ayad Allawi wanted more time before elections were held in Iraq. If elections went forward as scheduled on January 30, 2005, Allawi believed that the Sunni Arabs would boycott. He was concerned that security conditions were not conducive to broad participation in the election or to wins by moderate and secular forces. Allawi had tried to explain these points to President Bush, but the president was insistent that the election take place on time. Brahimi shared Allawi's concerns.

I suggested to Brahimi that he might urge Allawi to try to make his case to President Bush again. The president obviously wanted Iraq to succeed as a nation. If the prime minister of Iraq, who was America's friend, thought that holding elections in January would undermine prospects for success, then he should ask the president for a chance to explain himself.

Allawi's arguments for delayed elections made sense. Shia Arabs were pushing for elections, knowing that Shias would then dominate the parliament and take the lead in writing Iraq's constitution. Sunni Arabs were boycotting the political process, some because they wanted to undermine the new political order and others because security threats from extremists made it too dangerous for their communities to vote.

I was traveling back to Kabul from Washington when, during my stopover in Dubai, I received an urgent message that Hadley wanted to talk to me. I rushed to the U.S. consulate and, on a secure line, reached an irritated Hadley. He said that the president was very angry with me, as he had learned that I had advised a foreign leader to "stand up" to him. Hadley said I should forget about going to Iraq and be glad that the president had not fired me.

I was taken aback. I urged Hadley to check his sources. I had not encouraged anyone to "stand up" to the president, though I did strongly feel that President Bush should give Allawi an opportunity to explain his thinking on the election.

Hadley replied that the decision on the timing of the election had been made, and the election would occur on schedule. The issue was not in my jurisdiction while I was still ambassador to Afghanistan. As for my role, Hadley advised me to lie low while he worked the issue.

The election was held on schedule on January 30. News reports focused on happy images of voters proudly displaying their blue ink-stained fingers as they streamed from the voting stations. The actual results, however, were troubling. Sunni Arabs boycotted en masse—at some polling stations in Sunni Arab areas, virtually no one showed up. The Shia Islamist parties gained a sweeping victory, winning 48.2 percent of the vote. The moderate and secular party of Allawi won only 13.8 percent.

I assumed that I would not be going to Iraq. But during my next visit to Washington, when Rice ushered me into the Oval Office, the president told me, "You have to go to Baghdad and solve the situation in Iraq." It was a brief, direct conversation. No reference was made to my conversation with Brahimi. He offered to talk to Cheryl, knowing the toll that back-to-back overseas tours in war zones were taking. I told him that this was something I needed to discuss with her myself.

My initial agreement with Cheryl had been that I would go to Afghanistan for six months, just to get things launched. That had turned into almost two years, and I was now proposing to go to Baghdad instead of coming home. Obviously, this was not something she was pleased about, either for herself or for the family. Friends had warned me that she might issue an ultimatum, but that wasn't her style. She could tell that I felt an obligation to take this assignment, and since she was my friend and colleague in addition to being my wife, she could not bring herself to hold me back.

When I accepted the offer, the president was gracious and invited my boys to the White House as a thank-you. "Cool sneakers!" Meghan O'Sullivan, the NSC senior director for Iraq, exclaimed as she noticed Max with his nice slacks, dress shirt, and LeBron James sneakers. Max had insisted that no one would notice his sneakers when he refused our offer to provide him with dress shoes.

"How are you dudes doing?" the president asked Alex and Max. When he learned that Alex had just been accepted to Stanford Law School, he looked playfully over at Hadley and Libby, both lawyers, and remarked that we had too many lawyers already. Having recently won re-election on a pledge to rein in tort lawyers, however, he appreciated Alex's response: "Don't worry, Mr. President. I won't be one of those lawyers driving up the costs of health care."

◄   ►

AS I READ UP on Iraq, consulted experts, and spoke to Iraqis, it did not take long for me to form a sobering first conclusion: we were facing an incipient sectarian conflict that could become an all-out civil war. The conflict was grounded in the histories and complex psychologies of the country's major communities. Each group was determined to advance its interests, by violent means if necessary. Al Qaeda in Iraq (AQI) was trying to provoke civil war between the Sunnis and the Shias. Iran was seeking influence in Iraq by supporting Shia Arab proxies, while the Sunni Arab states were equally intent on backing the Sunni Arab cause.

Iraq had long been dominated by the Sunnis. Many Sunni Arabs viewed the Shia Arabs and the Kurds as second-class citizens, even as subjects. Operation Iraqi Freedom overturned this long-standing order, leaving the Sunni Arabs disoriented and distraught. It was inconceivable to them that any other group should rule Iraq. Many even believed that Sunni Arabs constituted a majority of Iraqis, even though they actually accounted for only about 20 percent of the population. A powerful nostalgia and an acute sense of deprivation and grievance made them vulnerable to the appeals of armed extremists.

A key part of solving the puzzle in Iraq was to reconcile the Sunni Arab community with the new order.

The Shia Arabs had never ruled Iraq despite being the majority. When the coalition intervention propelled the Shia Islamist parties into power, they had difficulty believing their good fortune.

Shia Arab leaders were constrained by a powerful fear that all they had gained would suddenly be taken away from them. They were determined not to lose this unprecedented opportunity. Their greatest fear was that the Baathists, or the Sunni Arab community more generally, would engineer a coup d'état and cast the Shia Arabs back into subjugation. This fed a winner-take-all mentality. The Shia Arabs sought tight and exclusive control over as many institutions as possible, particularly those involving security, to prevent them from becoming bases for the clandestine conspiracies of their enemies, real or imagined.

Iraq would not succeed unless the Shia Arab community was reassured about its future or unless its leaders were willing to accept genuine power sharing.

The Kurds were interested observers in this intra-Arab conflict. Their interest was not merely in the future of Iraq—they were keeping their eyes on their own historic opportunity. The Kurds have often been described as the world's largest national group without a country: about thirty million live in Iraq, Turkey, Syria, and Iran.

Kurds were of mixed minds about the new Iraq. They chose not to secede after Operation Iraqi Freedom, fearing the Turkish reaction and the difficulties of being a landlocked country surrounded by potentially hostile neighbors. At the same time, they feared that a new government in Baghdad would emerge as a threat to their hard-won autonomy. They wanted to preserve the option of seeking independence if the new Iraq did not work out.

With their common history of opposing Saddam, the Kurds were much closer to the Shia Arabs than to the Sunni Arabs. The Kurds suspected that Sunni Arabs would oppose the federal structure that gave Kurdish areas autonomy. During the coalition occupation, the Kurds had skillfully played their hand in the negotiation of the Transitional Administrative Law (TAL), the quasi-constitution governing the Iraqi transition. They had effectively secured a veto over the future Iraqi constitution and established themselves as the decisive swing-vote bloc.

I also considered the motivations and strategies of the enemy. Al Qaeda in Iraq orchestrated bombings to kill innocent Shia and destroy symbols of Shia faith, both to punish the Shia Arabs and to provoke a wider Sunni-Shia war. They hoped that Shia would engage in reprisals against the Sunnis, which, in turn, would lead the Sunnis to join the insurgency. AQI wanted to pull the country apart through a paroxysm of violence that would not only defeat the United States, but also open up possibilities to take control amid the chaos.

The challenge for the United States was to defeat AQI's strategy by building a political coalition outward from the center to isolate and defeat the extremists.

Regional actors also had a hand in the violence. Both Syria and Iran had been shaken by the U.S. invasion, fearing they might be next. At first, they sought to avoid the wrath of the United States, but over time they concluded that their best strategy was to compound American difficulties.

Syria was allowing former Baathist leaders and insurgents to set up shop in Damascus. Young extremists would arrive at the Damascus airport carrying one-way tickets and no luggage. They would be met by representatives of insurgent organizations and moved through a series of safe houses until they were smuggled across the Iraqi border.

Iran supported several Shia Arab militias and allowed the movement of AQI operatives across their territory. At every turn, Iran sought to strengthen the Shia Islamist parties, all of which had been based in Iran during Saddam's rule. In the run-up to the January 2005 balloting, Iran did not believe that the United States would hold free and fair elections. Surely, the United States understood that the Shia majority would win power and that Shia leaders would maintain close relations with Tehran. The Iranians believed that the United States would put someone in power, perhaps a former military officer, who would do America's bidding and keep Iran at arm's length. Tehran was incredulous when the United States allowed the elections to go forward.

Iran exploited this opening, encouraging their Shia allies to dominate security institutions and establish militias. Iran's Quds Force engaged in targeted killings of political figures and former officers from the old regime. Tehran was not averse to the violence that was driving the Shia Arabs into its arms. Iran also seemed intent on keeping Iraq sufficiently unstable to deter or prevent any action by the United States against Iran.

—◄   ►—

PART OF MY CHALLENGE was to undo the consequences of poorly conceived U.S. policies. In 2003 the Coalition Provisional Authority had dismantled the Iraqi army, creating a vacuum of power that both the Sunni Arab insurgency and Shia Arab militias exploited. The CPA sought to build up a small force that would not be able to carry out a military coup. In the absence of Iraqi forces, coalition forces were the only ones available to maintain security.

Iraq was awash in angry, resentful ex-soldiers. Many former officers told me that they felt humiliated. Serving as an officer was prestigious. Now, however, they had lost face in their communities and could not feed their families. To be sure, many former Iraqi military personnel were complicit in the crimes of the Baathist regime and opposed the U.S. invasion. But what caused them to take up arms was their shame. By joining the insurgency, they were able to regain the respect of their friends and family.

Bremer has said that the president had authorized him to dissolve the Iraqi army. However, President Bush told me in a recent conversation that he had learned about this decision after the fact. Hadley also flatly stated to me that the White House was not involved in the decision.

De-Baathification multiplied the number of recruits for the insurgency. While I thought it was appropriate to ban the Baath Party, de-Baathification suffered from two serious problems. One, the criteria for excluding former Baath Party members from government jobs were too broad. Thousands of schoolteachers and technocrats in the ministries who knew how to run things lost their jobs. This decision affected more than 100,000 people directly—and many times more when one includes members of their families. The CPA provided exemptions, but those required an overly cumbersome bureaucratic process that involved finding sponsors who would vouch for the applicants.

A political committee headed by Chalabi was tasked with implementing de-Baathification. Many Iraqis involved in this process admitted to me that the political and sectarian tensions engulfing the country played a big role in the committee's decisions. Former Baathists joined the Sunni Arab insurgency. A few also joined the Shia militant groups.

Circumstances surrounding the January 2005 election of the Transitional National Assembly made things worse. After the election, the United States took a hands-off approach to the formation of the new Iraqi cabinet. We went from governing Iraq ourselves to practicing political detachment. In so doing, we forfeited the opportunity to help create an inclusive and evenhanded government.

━   ➤

I WORKED with my team to prepare a set of briefing slides with my diagnosis and prescription for Iraq.

President Eisenhower once said, "The plan is useless but planning is essential." While it is difficult to anticipate circumstances on the ground or the reactions of the adversary, the process of planning forces decision makers to grapple deeply with problems and think through an initial approach that can be adjusted over time. I wanted to present my plan for Iraq to senior policymakers, elicit their comments and incorporate their suggestions, and ultimately secure the president's approval for my overall approach. I would then view that strategy document as a kind of contract, giving me authority to pursue the approved course of action.

I spent a great deal of time thinking about how the Sunni Arab community could be reconciled to the new democratic political order in Iraq. Pulling segments of the Sunni Arab insurgency out of the fight would save American and Iraqi lives and make state building and economic development much easier. It would also allow us to focus military efforts on the smaller number of irreconcilable fighters.

One problem was that the Sunni Arabs had diverse outlooks and motivations. They did not seem to have a single leader or even a small number of leaders who could move the community politically. A large portion of the community was not involved in violence but was extremely hostile to the new government and sympathetic to varying degrees to the armed opposition. I thought that it might be possible to reconcile these elements, provided that the Shia Arabs and Kurds acceded to genuine power sharing and helped protect Sunni Arabs from reprisals by insurgents and terrorists.

Among the Sunni Arab armed opposition, some wanted to restore the Baathist order. Others rejected the new government and sought some kind of a Sunni Arab restoration but were not wedded to Baathism. Still others advocated an Islamist revolution and cooperated with al Qaeda in Iraq. I devised a variety of ways to categorize these groups. I finally settled on dividing the armed opposition into Saddamists, rejectionists, and terrorists. In my view, the rejectionists were the most viable target for reconciliation. If they could be turned, in whole or in part, they could help us defeat the other two groups of hard-liners.

Cables from the embassy in Baghdad described ongoing Sunni outreach efforts. However, the complete lack of trust between the Sunni Arabs and the Iraqi government thwarted any real progress. U.S. diplomats seemed reluctant to step into the role of mediator. I thought a more engaged approach might yield a better outcome.

I asked for intelligence assessments of Sunni Arab political groups and insurgent networks, as well as profiles of their leaders. I was dismayed by what I received. We had been at war in Iraq for two years, yet we still did not seem to have a clear idea of whom we were fighting. Whenever I asked analysts to describe the enemy, they told me that the insurgents operated as "a network of networks." Individual leaders headed discrete networks of clandestine cells and fighters, but these networks might share bomb-making factories, financiers, or logistics. Some insurgent groups would exist for a while and then disappear or regroup under other names. With one or two exceptions, when I pressed the analysts to name the most important networks and describe who led them and how they worked, I received vague and unsatisfactory responses. I needed names of specific groups and individuals, as well as assessments of their motivations, in order to develop a plan to engage and influence them. It became clear that I would not be able to get this in Washington.

Even with the limited information I received, however, I sensed that it was possible to reconcile with elements of the Sunni Arab community. I was given a sheaf of intelligence profiles of Sunni Arab leaders. Their goals, it seemed, were to expedite the withdrawal of coalition forces, prevent Shia Arab domination, and eliminate Iranian influence in Iraq. I quipped to my staff that we had no fundamental disagreements with these people. We did not want to remain in Iraq indefinitely, opposed domination of Iraq by any one group, and sought to contain Iranian influence. It was not so simple, of course, but this strengthened my belief that national reconciliation had to be part of the U.S. strategy.

My team and I then focused on how to categorize the reconcilable and irreconcilable political groups. I concluded that we should start with the Sunni Arab political figures who were not part of the armed opposition, move to tribal leaders who may or may not have been involved with the insurgents, and then attempt to pull the rejectionist insurgents out of the fight.

Through further discussions, I realized that Sunni Arab reconciliation needed to be part of a wider political construct. Otherwise, we would be attacked for pandering to the community that had caused the most trouble.

The way to deal with this dilemma, I decided, was to promote a "national compact" among Iraq's communities—a common vision and agreement on the rules of the game for the new democratic Iraq. Iraqis would have to come together around an inclusive narrative about their country's national identity. U.S. leadership would be necessary to galvanize a coalition that united the Kurds and the moderate forces in the Sunni Arab and Shia Arab communities. This moderate bloc could make common cause against the violent extremists who were tearing Iraq apart.

A common vision for Iraq had to be uplifting but realistic. I discussed this with Rend Rahim, who had become the Iraqi ambassador to the United States under Prime Minister Allawi. She agreed that I, as U.S. ambassador, could perform a valuable service by raising the sights of Iraqi leaders. The Iraqi people, she said, were beaten down emotionally. They were demoralized by the failure of their leaders to set aside parochial interests and capitalize on the historic opportunity presented by Saddam's fall.

My first opportunity to communicate to the Iraqis came at the formal announcement of my nomination at the State Department. I arrived from Kabul that very afternoon. I had worked on the text of my statement along the way, calling in changes to my staff at every transit stop. I was driven straight to the State Department from Dulles. My staff had to buy me a shirt because I did not have time to get my luggage. I went down to the locker rooms of the State Department and got cleaned up from the long flight. Back in my office, my team barely had time to hand me the final version of my statement before I was rushed to Rice's office.

I invoked Iraq's history as a great civilization. Acknowledging Sunni achievements, I noted that for centuries Baghdad had been a city that attracted scholars and innovators in every field. In a symmetrical signal to Shia Iraqis, I said that Najaf had been a seat of learning for centuries, giving rise to one of the world's first universities more than 1,000 years ago. To weave these appeals together, I observed that in the early twentieth century, as the Iraqi state reemerged, Iraq began recapturing its heritage. In the 1930s and 1940s, it had enjoyed multiparty elections for parliament. It had a free press and an independent judiciary. I pointed out that women had been active in the professions and in the workforce. Then, in the late 1960s, this progress had been cut short by the brutal regimes of the Baathists and Saddam Hussein.

I urged Iraqis to resume the national trajectory they were on before Saddam's reign and rise to new heights by embracing the universal ideals of representative government, individual rights, and the rule of law. I pledged that, if confirmed by the Senate, I would do everything in my power to help Iraqis achieve this vision in a manner consistent with local traditions.

As we walked away from the podium, Rice complimented my statement, then added: "Now, at least, you can't change your mind about going to Iraq."

My statement seemed to strike a chord with Iraqis. Some emotionally criticized their own leaders for failing to raise the sights of the people. Others sent me materials and facts about Iraq's past, suggesting that much more could be said about its golden eras. Many discussed the promise with which they or their parents had viewed the 1930s and 1940s, when Iraqis embraced modernity without abandoning their culture or religion.

ARTICULATING AN INCLUSIVE and unifying narrative was just the first step in forging a national compact among Iraqis. The United States would also need to bring Iraq's leaders together to negotiate a power-sharing deal. I faced three fast-approaching deadlines.

First, the drafting of the Iraqi constitution. The deadline was less than three months away.

Second, national elections, which would be held in December 2005. It was vital that Sunni Arabs participate in the elections this time to ensure a genuinely representative national assembly.

Third, the formation of a new Iraqi government. After the December elections, I intended to press Iraqi groups to form a government of national unity. Within this government, Iraqi leaders could address the issues that were driving the conflict. Security institutions needed to be reformed to ensure that all Iraqis could trust them. Revenues from hydrocarbons would need to be distributed more equitably. And the de-Baathification process would have to be modified.

I also examined the way we were fighting the war. The security situation was even worse than I had anticipated. Provinces in western Iraq, particularly

Al Anbar, were effectively controlled by the insurgents. Attacks in Baghdad made movement outside the heavily protected Green Zone exceptionally dangerous, limiting the embassy's ability to work with Iraqi officials and advance reconstruction programs.

The Pentagon presented me with a time series of colored maps, each showing the geospatial pattern of insurgent attacks in a particular month. The overwhelming share of incidents, depicted in areas of yellow and red, was concentrated in western Iraq and around Baghdad. I noticed that the geographic pattern of attacks did not change and that the intensity only increased over time. I could only conclude that our strategies to date had not worked.

I was dissatisfied with the quality of the discussion in the Bush administration on military strategy. When I asked one administration official who had spent time in Iraq for an assessment of military progress, he told me, "We are certainly killing a lot of young Sunni Salafis." I was taken aback, shocked by his cavalier attitude toward the taking of human life. "I hope that this killing is not an end in itself," I responded. I asked what political goals we were trying to achieve. I did not receive a clear answer.

I asked Strmecki to develop a briefing on counterinsurgency strategy. Earlier, he had worked on a book about the Vietnam War with former president Nixon and knew the literature on irregular warfare well. Strmecki contacted Andrew Krepinevich, a leading defense policy analyst who had written a highly regarded volume, *The Army and Vietnam*.

I sat down for an initial session with Krepinevich and Strmecki, over dinner in a small private dining room at the Jefferson Hotel. In their briefing, Strmecki and Krepinevich stated starkly that the United States did not have a strategy to defeat the insurgents. Success depended on adopting an approach based on classical counterinsurgency doctrine—securing the population, winning the people's cooperation against the insurgency, and building up the legitimacy and capacity of our local partners. They recommended an "oil spot" strategy: creating enduring security in one location and then expanding this zone into contiguous contested areas, much like a drop of oil spreads on the surface of water. Given Barno's success with a similar approach in Afghanistan, the briefing resonated with me.

With a better understanding of counterinsurgency, I began thinking about how to integrate political and military initiatives so that they would reinforce each other.

THE SENATE CONFIRMED my nomination by unanimous consent in June. Shortly thereafter, Rice directed me to speed up my departure from Kabul. I was formally sworn in at the embassy in Baghdad before returning to Washington to accompany Prime Minister Ibrahim al-Jaafari on an official visit. I was then scheduled to present my plan for Iraq to the National Security Council before returning to Baghdad.

Around three or four o'clock in the morning the evening before my presentation I woke up with such severe chills that my whole body was shaking. I had suffered from some cold sweats in Kabul in recent months, though the doctors at Bagram Air Base had not been able to identify the cause. These chills were much worse than any of those episodes. Additional blankets did little good. I phoned Cheryl overseas at a conference, who, half asleep, suggested that I take a hot bath. A few minutes later, properly awake and recognizing that this was probably not enough, she phoned a friend, Dr. Abdullah Riar, who lived near our house. He came over right away and quickly decided that I needed to go posthaste to Shady Grove Hospital for tests. In the emergency room, the doctors took blood samples but were unable to diagnose the problem immediately.

Even though I felt terrible, I asked the doctors whether I could go to the White House for the planned meetings and then return to the hospital. It was too risky. The day's schedule was canceled.

Once I was checked in and taken to a room, the doctors concluded that I had an infected gallbladder that required surgery. When word about my condition got around the administration, I received calls expressing concern and wishing me a quick recovery. Always one to be empirical, Rumsfeld offered some advice: if I needed surgery, I should insist on a doctor who had done that particular procedure many times.

Because my doctors assessed the situation as precarious, the surgery was scheduled for the next day at Sibley Hospital. Afterward, I had to spend a couple of nights in the hospital to recuperate from the surgery but quickly felt much better.

During this period, Peter Saleh, an experienced physician whom I had recruited to serve as senior health policy advisor in Kabul, stopped by. After conferring with the doctor, he told me that my illness had been a very close call.

When I was preparing to be discharged, my doctor told me that he would need to see me a week later for a follow-up and to discuss the results of additional tests.

I told him that this was not feasible: I was already late in getting to Iraq.

He insisted that I could not go without further blood tests to ensure that the infection had not spread.

We negotiated for a while before reaching a deal. He would get the hospital to process the test results later that day. If the tests came back negative,

I would be free to leave for Iraq, though I would have to schedule a follow-up appointment on my next trip to Washington.

WITH THAT, it was wheels up for Baghdad in twenty-four hours. Before I departed, President Bush received me in the Oval Office for a last conversation. I took him through the briefing slides on my strategy, before he signed on to my approach. Above all, he tried to be supportive, assuring me that I would do a great job in Iraq. He would defer to my judgment on the intricacies of Iraqi politics. I thanked him for his confidence in me. I was pleased with the situation as I left the White House. We had a plan.

TWENTY-TWO

REPAIRING IRAQ

BAGHDAD, JULY–DECEMBER 2005

I LANDED IN BAGHDAD CLOSE TO MIDNIGHT. I WAS ACCUSTOMED TO SPARTAN CONDI-tions in Afghanistan and was not expecting much of an upgrade in my new residence. I was in for a surprise. Here, the ambassador's residence was a three-story house formerly occupied by Saddam's mother-in-law. The residence was quite luxurious, with her ornate baroque and gold-embellished furniture still in place. The protocol officer had made additional adjustments to make it suitable for our purposes. The first floor had a large entrance area, kitchen, and dining and living rooms that could entertain up to one hundred guests. The second floor had a master bedroom and guest bedroom for visiting dig-nitaries such as the secretary of state. It also had an office with secure com-munications and a small workout room. On the negative side, except during Baghdad's brief winter, it was impossible to get the water temperature in the shower to an acceptable level. The water was always too hot, because the water tanks on top of the building reached near-boiling temperatures.

On that first night, even given the lateness of the hour, a staff of private chefs directed me to an elegant table set with fine china and, moments later, brought me a cup of freshly prepared gazpacho followed by steamed fish, veg-etables, and dessert. The food only got better when, a few weeks later, the embassy hired a Lebanese chef to replace the contractors previously in charge of preparing meals.

The contrast between the opulence of the residence and the broader at-mosphere of a mass encampment under siege was stark. Our compound was encircled by high concrete "T Walls" to obstruct direct fire. As in Afghanistan, most of the staff lived in hooches. Though reinforced with sandbags, these hooches were vulnerable to attack, offering only a thin shell of metal to hold off incoming mortars. Even inside the actual buildings, my security detail would rush me to the inner corridors when they feared an incoming attack. And the windows of my office were no more, having been plastered shut for greater safety against mortar shells or snipers.

All this posed enormous challenges to my security team. When I left the Green Zone, travel by ground was extremely complicated. The route had to be cleared and secured. I rode in an armored SUV, with additional cars leading and following. Among these was a Humvee equipped with a heavy machine gun. Often, above the motorcade, a helicopter would surveil our journey, watching for threatening movements that might indicate an approaching so-called VBIED, a vehicle-borne improvised explosive device that could ram into my motorcade in a suicide attack. My security detail could also move me by air, either in what I called a VW helicopter—a tiny round helicopter that was able to land in the backyards of Iraqi leaders' compounds—or in larger helicopters that could accommodate more than one passenger.

I remain deeply indebted to the men and women who served on my security detail, both in Kabul and in Baghdad. We came to be not just colleagues but also friends. Tragically, several lost their lives in Iraq when one of the surveillance helicopters was shot down. I was heartbroken when I learned of it. Hours before, we had joked and laughed as usual; now I was saying a final farewell to them in the embassy morgue. Calling their families to express my condolences was among the most difficult things I have ever had to do. To vindicate their sacrifice, I vowed to redouble my efforts in Iraq.

≺   ≻

BY THE TIME I arrived in Baghdad, the countdown was on: there were just three weeks to go before the August 15 deadline to submit a draft constitution to the Transitional National Assembly (TNA). But even with the clock ticking, I wanted to avoid injecting myself into the talks too crudely. Ideally, Iraqis would solve the problems on their own. If I was going to get involved, I wanted the Iraqis to remember that they had actively requested my help.

Things started well. Iraqi leaders had formed the Constitutional Drafting Commission (CDC) headed by Humam Hamoudi, a SCIRI delegate. In an encouraging move, Iraqi leaders negotiated an agreement to include twenty-five Sunni Arab delegates from outside the TNA, the formation of which they had boycotted. And they had agreed to make decisions on the basis of consensus. This meant that when a draft constitution was presented to the TNA, all of Iraq's major political groups would stand behind it.

I knew from Afghanistan that constitutional negotiations bring to the surface people's fundamental hopes, fears, and psychologies. Issues that strike outsiders as symbolic—the official language, the design of the flag—strike deep emotional chords and inspire desperate battles. Discussions about the form of government touch on a society's conception of the role of the individual versus the group, the appropriate extent of the state's reach, and the relationship of religious to civil authority. Such discussions revive fundamental political cleavages. Because a constitution defines the distribution of powers, negotiations reveal how little or how much competing groups trust each other, how many checks and balances will be needed, and what promises and compromises will induce cooperation. Historic memories—particularly the traumatic ones—inspire constitutional provisions to guard against one or another group's nightmare scenario.

In Afghanistan, leaders had opted for a unitary state because the country had suffered from anarchy in the absence of an effective government. Iraq, by contrast, had suffered from an excessively strong and oppressive state under Saddam. For those who had suffered most under that regime—the Shia Arabs and the Kurds—the principal constitutional goal was to limit the power the central government could exert over their communities. For the Sunni Arabs, who felt entitled to ownership of Iraq, the issue was how to establish a strong state and keep Iraq together—under their control.

Each community had staked out maximalist positions on key issues. The Shia Islamists called for the creation, in effect, of an Islamic republic, with elements eerily similar to Iran's constitution. The Kurds wanted to bolster the autonomy and resources available to the Kurdish Regional Government (KRG) and guarantee their right to secede from Iraq. The Sunni Arabs opposed most of the key demands of the Shia Islamists and Kurds. Mahmoud Mashhadani, a prominent Sunni Arab leader, insisted that federalism—sought by the Shia Islamists—posed a mortal threat to his community: if the Kurds took the land and resources of the north and the Shia Arabs did the same in the south, the Sunnis would be left with the barren and resource-poor tracts of western Iraq. Symbolic issues of national identity—particularly whether Iraq was an "Arab state" or a "part of the Arab world"—were high priorities for the Sunni Arabs and were guaranteed to produce clashes with the Kurds, who were not Arabs and who wanted Iraqi identity to encompass the country's minorities.

Still, I sensed that with help, negotiations could move to a successful end game.

◄   ►

I STARTED TO MAKE the rounds, reestablishing old friendships and taking the overall temperature. One of the things I soon realized was how important it was to speak the right language at the right time. Some preferred to speak in Farsi in private but quickly shifted to English or Arabic in larger meetings lest they draw attention to their Iranian roots. Though I had studied Arabic for a year at AUB and had refreshed my knowledge with a tutor before leaving for Baghdad, I was far less fluent in Arabic than in Farsi. So with my counterparts who spoke only Arabic, I used an embassy interpreter. I understood Arabic for the most part but wanted to make sure, in sensitive negotiations, that I was delivering precise points. I was cognizant, however, that speaking through an interpreter made it harder to establish rapport, so I tried to speak in Arabic whenever possible. I would also speak in Arabic when I wanted to put my counterparts on the spot, to deny them the excuse of waiting for the translator before formulating a response.

President Talabani suggested that I convene the key Iraqi leaders for a summit meeting in Baghdad to finalize the discussions. Since we both knew that Barzani did not like to come to Baghdad, this entailed going to Erbil to request his presence in Baghdad personally. I asked Talabani to weigh in during the constitutional negotiations to ensure protections for human rights generally and women's rights in particular, and he agreed, pledging that he would not allow Iraq to become an Islamic republic.

With Tariq Hashimi, a prominent Sunni Arab leader, I raised the issue of federalism. Not surprisingly, he opposed Hakim's proposal to create one or more federal regions in southern Iraq. He did not oppose federalism in principle but believed that the National Assembly should delay the process for at least the next four years. I saw promise in the idea of phasing in federalism provisions.

My meeting with Mowaffak al-Ruba'i proved to be important. Ruba'i had a message to relay from Grand Ayatollah Ali al Sistani. Sistani was one of the most senior and revered ayatollahs of Twelver Shiism, enjoying the status of *marja*, or "source of emulation." This was the title for someone considered to be so virtuous and holy that others should try to be like him in their thoughts and actions.

Ruba'i said that Sistani had studied my background and expressed great respect for what I had done in Afghanistan. He had read the new constitution of Afghanistan—twice in fact—and was willing to accept for the Iraqi constitution the formula in the Afghan document on the role of Islam "word for word."

Actually I could not recall precisely what the Afghan constitution stated on the relationship of religious and civil law. In a break in the meeting, I called Karzai and asked him to remind me of the exact language. He read the text to me. Article 2 made Islam the official religion of Afghanistan but also guaranteed the rights of non-Muslims. Articles 3 and 7 required courts to integrate the tenets of Islam and universal human rights. Articles 130 and 131 allowed courts to use Sunni and Shia jurisprudence to fill gaps in the constitutional or statutory law, which was not a significant concession because Afghanistan had well-developed and comprehensive legal codes.

I told Ruba'i to thank Ayatollah Sistani and also asked him to bring to Sistani's attention another part of the Afghan constitution that I believed merited replication: that women were guaranteed two parliamentary seats for every province.

I had already discovered that both Shia and Sunni Arabs were largely indifferent to women's rights, and that the Islamists within both groups were willing to protect those rights only on the condition that they were in accordance with religious law. The generally more progressive Kurds, who knew the rights of Kurdish women were well protected under the KRG's laws, were willing to support my efforts on behalf of other Iraqi women but would not take the lead themselves.

In my meetings with women's leaders, they not only pressed for basic equality before the law but also wanted to see personal status law—laws regulating marriage, divorce, custody, and inheritance—regulated by civil, not religious, law. They insisted that Islam not be cited by the constitution as "the" source of law, which would allow Islamists to impose *sharia* through the courts, but rather as "a" source of law, leaving room for more secular legal provisions. And they pressed for language in the constitution to guarantee universal human rights.

When I went to see Barzani in Erbil, I knew not to move to business too quickly. That was not his style. We discussed our families, world events, the weather, and so forth. As the meeting drew to a close, we stood and walked to the door. I then turned to him and asked, "I would like you to join us at the summit meeting in Baghdad. You will be there. Right?"

"Of course, I'll be there," he replied. He also made clear the Kurdish red lines: preserve the status of the Peshmerga as an independent military force, give the Kurds control over natural resources in KRG territories, and ensure for Kurds an equitable share of revenues from Iraq's hydrocarbon revenues. These were reasonable and should not be deal-breakers, I thought.

―< ―>

ON THE DAY the summit was scheduled to begin, a massive sandstorm enveloped Baghdad in an orange haze. The storm prevented Barzani from flying in from the north. This was only the first bump in the road.

Negotiations began in a large hall holding perhaps 150 people. I soon saw that this was not going to work. There was constant distraction as the delegates were served tea, snacks, and meals. Whenever a leader entered the room, he would proclaim, *"Allah bel khair,"* "May God bless this meeting." This would then touch off a round of protocol rituals, as others paid their respects to the new arrival. The sessions could be excruciatingly long, lasting from 2 p.m. to 10 p.m. In the presence of their supporters, senior party leaders were reluctant to strike compromises or make concessions.

After consulting with the principal Iraqi leaders, we agreed to conduct real negotiations in small meetings over lunch and dinner.

As the summit progressed, I noticed that I could pick out who was a Shia by certain tells. Among Shia it was common to wear a ring with a blue or brown stone on the ring finger of the right hand. Many Shia also had marks on their foreheads. When kneeling to pray, they would put a small stone—made from the sand of Karbala—in front of them on the floor. The repeated impact of their forehead striking against the stone over time left them with an indentation.

I noticed that many more delegates carried "worry beads" than in Afghanistan. Iraqi worry beads were fancier and more diverse; Afghans were attached to their more simple green Shah Maqsud worry beads. During the summit, Iraqi leaders exchanged worry beads with each other as a sign of friendship and camaraderie. Admiring another's worry beads and inquiring about their origin was an ice-breaker. Usually, at the end of the meeting, everyone would end up with their own strand of beads back, but not before "insisting" that they wanted to gift them to their new friend.

I received much advice from the delegates about what the United States was doing right and wrong. The Shia delegates, in particular, relished critiquing our policies and took special pleasure in eliciting admissions of fault. In their comments, I saw an association with Shia rituals of self-flagellation at the holiday of Ashura, when they relived the community's feelings of guilt for not saving Hussein at the battle of Karbala many hundreds of years ago.

"Self-flagellation is not an American cultural characteristic," I joked. "That's your department."

I was surprised to see how difficult it was for Iraqi leaders to work together. Sometimes they did not even want to sit in the same room. I was struck by how uncivil, personally, the Sunni and Shia Arabs were to each other at times. Shia Arab and Kurdish leaders would consult for hours, knowing that their Sunni Arab counterparts were waiting outside. Such disrespect would never have been tolerated in Afghanistan.

It was obvious that Shia leaders were determined to marginalize the Sunni Arabs. As the largest group in the TNA, the Shia Islamists aimed first to reach an agreement among themselves. Their next step was to bring in the Kurds and arrive at a joint position. If that was successful, they had a strong majority and saw no reason for further compromises to accommodate the Sunni Arabs.

The only way to break that dynamic was for me to be in the room, reviewing constitutional language provision by provision and personally developing bridging language.

Sistani's role also presented a challenge. Though privately cooperative, Sistani refused to meet with American officials as a matter of principle, since they represented the "occupying powers." When I tried to arrange direct meetings with Sistani, he responded through third parties that while he respected me, he would not meet so long as U.S. forces were fighting in Iraq.

I thus had to communicate with Sistani through intermediaries. More than once, a delegate from a Shia Islamist party would say that "Najaf" wanted this or that outcome. It was unclear whether this was just an attempt to play the "Sistani card" or an actual expression of his view.

This sometimes led the Shia Islamists to get two bites at the apple. Their delegates would drive a hard bargain with other Iraqis before we would seem to have an agreement. Then Hakim, who led the Shia Islamist delegates, or one of his people, often Adel Abdul Mehdi, would say, "We have to check this with Najaf." When the meeting reconvened, they sometimes insisted on another round of concessions from their colleagues.

⟵   ⟶

AS THE LEADERS of the Iraqi blocs realized that they could not reach agreement on their own, they asked for my mediation.

The only major question that was settled quickly was the basic structure of the Iraqi government. All of the major blocs conceded that the KRG should retain its autonomy, from which it followed that Iraq would be a federal state. They also agreed on a parliamentary system in which the president and prime minister would be elected by the national assembly with a two-thirds majority. This supermajority provision was a good rule, because it would require Iraqis to work toward inclusive politics.

Hakim fought a rearguard action on this point for a time. He claimed that this provision was anti-democratic and was designed to thwart the will of the majority. At one point he accused me of seeking to nullify the result of elections and instead promote "consensus democracy," which he considered a contradiction in terms.

Iraqis, I responded, were divided by identity, more so than by views on specific issues. They needed a system that would help them build trust and habits of cooperation. The two-thirds rule, I argued, was rational at this point in Iraq's history. Hakim reluctantly acquiesced.

When it came to the other major issues, though, the process was a slog. As the summit meeting crept along toward the August 15 deadline, Washington grew increasingly impatient. President Bush insisted on meeting the timeline, and I had to provide ever more frequent updates. While deadlines created discipline and could force Iraqis to make decisions, I feared that they could also lead to suboptimal outcomes.

Because the Shia Islamists and Kurds had the numbers in the TNA to impose an outcome, I had to use the element of time to wrest the concessions necessary to win over the Sunni Arabs. If I let the Shia Islamists and Kurds use the pressure of time against me, we would lose the opportunity to achieve a national compact. It was never good to be more eager for an agreement than were the actual parties to the talks.

On August 15, the Iraqis completed a draft just as we hit the deadline. However, it represented a Shia Arab–Kurd consensus. More work was needed to ensure that Sunni Arabs bought into the document. To accomplish that, I worked out a way to submit a complete draft while leaving the process open for further negotiations before the TNA acted on it. This satisfied Washington.

President Talabani insisted that I accompany him to the TNA on the evening he presented the draft. As I entered the hall and walked down the aisle, I felt as if I were in Iran. The delegates from the Shia Islamist parties, who controlled many of the seats, were chanting "*Allah Akbar*" and raising their hands in the manner of Iranians.

Talabani, as president, had an assigned seat in the place of honor in the front row. Naturally, since protocol officers did not expect him to bring a guest, there was no seat for me. So he found a place for both of us in chairs along the side of the room, and there we sat, with him holding my hand. Hurriedly, senior Iraqi leaders shuffled around to make room for me next to Talabani's seat, and we were moved to the front row.

When Talabani spoke from the podium, he explained the procedure for continued deliberations on the draft constitution. In doing so, he recognized my contribution to the negotiations and referred to me warmly as his "brother." He then shot me a quick, mischievous look; it was a private joke. Usually, he referred to me as his "friend," because—as he liked to say—"We choose our friends, but our brothers are imposed on us." In this instance, his use of the word "brother" was a reference to my Muslim faith, aimed at silencing the Islamists who might object to my presence.

In the midst of this drama, my phone was vibrating nonstop in my pocket. I took it out at one point and saw that the call was coming from the Operations Center at the State Department. Rice was trying to reach me. I had to ignore the call, since I could not, of course, answer in the middle of the National Assembly. When I later spoke to Rice, she was quite upset: "Zal, you have to take my calls." The president wanted frequent updates and was not satisfied to hear them from my deputy. I explained the circumstances.

DURING THE FINAL PHASE, I presided over a series of protracted sessions. Iraqis were serious, take-no-prisoners negotiators. At one point, Allawi became so upset that he stormed out, declaring that he was going to the airport to fly to Jordan. I made a call and instructed that no airplanes be allowed to take off. I then implored Allawi to return, and the negotiations resumed.

I tried to build consensus step by step, with individual blocs or parties, before bringing the language into a session with all of the main Iraqi leaders. I first sought to reach agreement on key provisions between the Kurds and Al- lawi's cross-sectarian Iraqiyya coalition. Then I would take that agreed-upon language and work out the compromises necessary to secure support from the Shia Islamists. Finally, I would engage the Sunni Arab leaders.

I was able to wrap up some of the women's rights issues quickly. There was not a great deal of controversy over ensuring fundamental equality before the law, including all political rights. The Iraqis agreed to allocate not less than a quarter of seats in parliament to women. We were able to secure a pro- vision that gave Iraqi citizenship to any child born not just to an Iraqi father but also to an Iraqi mother, a very progressive provision in the context of the Middle East. At the request of women's groups, I also persuaded Iraqi leaders to add a sentence: "The State shall prohibit the tribal traditions that are in contradiction to human rights."

Still, the women's groups were concerned with language suggesting that clerics would be appointed to the Federal Supreme Court. After much back- and-forth among Iraqi leaders, the final language stated that the court would be composed of "judges, experts in Islamic jurisprudence, and legal scholars," whose selection would be determined by parliament. I ensured that this law required a two-thirds majority for enactment, which would give substantial leverage to non-Islamist parties and women.

It was far more difficult to settle the personal status provision. Women's leaders wanted individuals to have a choice between religious or civil law. They feared that religious judges would be reactionary and would favor men over women in settling cases.

Hakim was entirely obstinate on the issue. I thought I understood his zeal. In imposing secular law, Saddam had cracked down ruthlessly against the Hakim family, which believed that personal status should be governed by religious law.

I was largely on my own on this issue. I argued that the constitution should not force people to go before a court in which they did not believe. I pressed for an "à la carte" solution, which would allow an individual to settle personal status issues before either a civil or a religious court.

Even after Hakim accepted the "à la carte" option, he continued to oppose language about "choices" in this section of the constitution. At a break, I approached Hakim, asking him, in Farsi, why he was so opposed to Iraqis choosing how to determine their personal status. I added that Iraq had many secular men and women who should not be forced to live under religious law.

His eyes widened with surprise. "I did not think that this was the purpose of the language!" he exclaimed. He thought the United States was trying to establish a right to gay marriage in Iraq through the inclusion of the word "choices." With the issue clarified, he quickly accepted the text.

OTHER ISSUES were settled over contentious dinners either at my residence or the Baghdad homes of Iraqi leaders. I did my best to avoid sessions at Barzani's house because Barzani opposed the "terrible American institution" of working dinners. "When we eat," he argued, "we should eat, not work."

Talabani loved to host these dinners at his house, which was in the Red Zone, just across the river from the U.S. embassy. Like many Iraqi homes, this one had a reception room with several couches and large chairs that could accommodate a big party. He particularly loved to hold court at his long dining table. As he passed a plate of roasted turkey, he always quipped to new guests, "Have a piece of Turkey." When his guest caught the geopolitical double entendre, he added, "I will take the southeast."

At a negotiating session at my residence, we settled the hydrocarbon provision. In the final agreed-upon text, the draft constitution stated, "Oil and gas are owned by all the people of Iraq in all the regions and governorates [i.e., provinces]." This satisfied the Sunni and Shia Arabs, who did not want to relinquish resources in the Kurdish areas. The concession was painful for the Kurds, who wanted to secure a revenue flow of their own. However, it was balanced by language ensuring that oil revenues would be allocated to regional governments and provinces on the basis of population.

At Hakim's house, appropriately, we settled on final language defining the role of Islam under the constitution. Hakim's compound had the feel of a mosque. In the center of the yard to one side was a large tent, which he used for religious services. I had attended remembrances in that tent for Hakim's brother, who was killed in a terrorist bombing.

The language we agreed upon read, "Islam is the official religion of the State and is a foundational source of legislation." As the official religion, Islam would be incorporated into state ceremonies. I was able to wrest a concession from the Islamists to make the religion "a" source but not "the" source of law. This language was further modified by provisions stating that no law may be enacted that "contradicts the principles of democracy" or "freedom of thought, conscience, and belief" and "freedom of worship." The constitution also committed Iraq to respect international human rights treaties.

Taken together, these provisions required the Iraqi government to reconcile Islam and respect for human rights. Shia Islamists cleared the language with Sistani, who had to see that it mirrored the balanced formulation in the Afghan constitution.

I felt that I had protected the interests of civil society and women's groups but I was still criticized in the press for accepting this provision. One prominent Kurdish delegate, Mahmoud Osman, accused me of creating an Islamic state. After I challenged him to show me the language that had this effect, he desisted in his criticism. Still, while I believed that the constitution, if fairly interpreted, would protect the rights of Iraqis, I knew that the interpretation of these provisions would depend a great deal on future election results. It would be Iraqi's elected leaders who would ultimately appoint the justices and interpret the language of the constitution.

◄ ►

THE MOST DIFFICULT ISSUE—the process for creating new federal regions—took the longest to resolve. Iraqi leaders came to terms on final language at Barzani's second home in the Green Zone. It was an idyllic setting for an intense battle. His house had a beautiful garden at the entry of the compound. Kurds, like Afghans, liked to care for their lawns and plant flowers around the perimeter.

As we settled in to negotiate, Barzani's house staff brought us a succession of drinks. It had taken me a while to adjust to Iraqi rituals in this respect. Unlike Afghans, who drink green tea with cardamom, Iraqis prefer strong black tea—typically with three or four bags of tea per cup and inordinate amounts of sugar to counteract the resultant bitterness. I covertly signaled the server to hold the sugar for my cup. As the discussions heated up, I was glad to see that Barzani's home was equipped with wall-mounted air conditioners.

In the run-up to this meeting, Hakim had been adamant that, like the KRG, the Shia Arab–dominated provinces of southern Iraq should have the right to form one or more federal regions. Sunni Arab leaders were equally insistent that this would lead either to the breakup of Iraq or to Iranian domination of these new federal regions. To add to the contentiousness, the Shia Islamist bloc wanted to form a new federal region during the current parliament since they enjoyed disproportionate strength due to the Sunni Arab boycott of the January 2005 election.

I was puzzled by the Shia Arab and Sunni Arab positions on federalism. Since the Shia Arabs were the largest community, it would have made more sense for them to defend a centralized state, which they, in all likelihood, would lead. Sunni Arabs, as a minority, should have seen federalism as a way to protect their rights, just as the Kurds had done in the north. I could only conclude that Shia and Sunni Arabs alike were bracing for a Sunni Arab restoration.

The climax of these negotiations came at Barzani's dinner table. The ultimate compromise recognized the right of one or more provinces to form a federal region under a future law that would define the procedures for forming regions. This law, which required a simple majority, would be enacted "in a period not to exceed six months" from the opening date of the next National Assembly, which effectively pushed off decisions on new regions until the next parliament.

As this compromise was crafted, Hakim became agitated, fearing that Shia Arabs in the south might be losing their opportunity to form a region. I tried to allay his concerns, noting that the simple-majority requirement for the law on region formation would put the Shia Arabs in a good position. This was not enough. Hakim asked that I draft a letter to him stating that the United States would not oppose Iraqi efforts to form a new federal region in the south.

I asked him why he needed such a letter. After all, he led the largest political party in Iraq, and I did not control any votes in the National Assembly.

He replied, "You have a lot of influence here. You can derail the process to form a new region."

Although Hakim agreed to the compromise language, Sunni Arab leaders held out. I was at this point exasperated with their obstinacy. As written, the language gave them the opportunity to rally their political power in the December 15 election and have a voice commensurate with their numbers in writing the law on region formation. I could not take away the right of other Iraqis to form federal regions along the lines of the KRG.

—◄   ►—

I DEPARTED IRAQ on September 6 to escort Talabani on a trip to the United States. While I was away, I received reports that Sunni Arab opposition to the draft constitution was growing. Several Sunni Arab leaders told embassy officials that they could not support the constitution without changes on federalism. They also wanted accommodations on Iraq's identity as an "Arab state" and references to de-Baathification. Talabani made a public statement that additional changes could still be made, offering to work with the Sunni Arabs.

I knew that getting broader Sunni Arab support was critical. If the referendum to ratify the draft constitution failed in three provinces by a two-thirds majority, the constitution would be rejected. This provision, which the Kurds had designed to ensure that their three provinces would effectively wield a veto, also empowered the Sunni Arabs. Two provinces, Al Anbar and Salah ad Din, were solidly Sunni Arab. Another, Ninewa, had a sufficient number of Sunni Arabs to make a two-thirds vote against the constitution conceivable.

To make matters worse, the consensus between the Kurds and the Shia Islamists had broken down over an issue raised by Ayatollah Sistani. He objected to a provision that gave regional governments control over water resources flowing through their territories, which he saw as a threat to the allocation of water from the Tigris River.

While I was able to broker a compromise on the water issue, I had less luck with the Sunni Arabs on federalism. Shia Islamists and Kurds went ahead and approved the draft constitution without much Sunni Arab support. I was disappointed with this outcome.

I returned to Baghdad on September 21 and took stock of the situation. We would have no problems winning support from the Shia Arab and Kurdish communities. Sistani issued a religious ruling telling his followers to vote for ratification while Muqtada al-Sadr, the militant Shia Islamist leader, told his people that the constitution "would be good for Shia." However, reports from the Sunni Arab front were overwhelmingly negative. I received troubling polling data: the vote in Al Anbar and Salah ad Din would go overwhelmingly against ratification, and the "no" vote might approach two-thirds in Ninewa. This prospect unsettled the Shia Arabs, since defeat of the referendum would mean redrafting the constitution under a new National Assembly.

At this point, Sunni Arab leader Mahmoud Mashaddani reached out to me. He said that several Sunni Arab leaders would be willing to support ratification if a few changes were made in the text. He explained that if six specific changes were made, which he had already discussed with the Kurds, a group of influential Sunni Arab leaders could sign on. I told him that I wanted a letter attesting to their conditional support.

Later that day, I met with Hakim, who agreed in principle to small changes. At the same time, he warned that Shia Arab patience was running out. He suggested that the Sunni Arabs were "toying" with me, that they would not compromise, and that I was wasting my time. He suggested waiving the requirement that gave three provinces a potential veto over ratification. I cautioned him about changing the rules at this late date.

In the ensuing days, I shuttled back and forth between the Sunni Arabs and other leaders. In Washington, senior leaders were skeptical that we could find common ground among the Iraqis. I may have contributed to that view myself. Hadley told me that he had seldom detected so much fatigue, frustration, and anger in my voice. In truth, I was at the point of exasperation.

On October 11, after a final series of frenetic exchanges, I was able to secure agreement among Iraqi leaders on the changes. The constitution would provide for a fast-track process to consider amendments under the next National Assembly, which would give Sunni Arabs another run at the issue of federalism. The De-Baathification Commission would be subordinated to the National Assembly, which Sunni Arabs believed would curb the abuses of the commission. Iraqis agreed to a compromise formulation on national identity. Sunni Arab leaders secured agreement that the federal government would control Iraq's antiquities and that the state would promote cultural activities and institutions. And finally, in a move I did not understand at the time, Sunni Arabs secured agreement that the constitution would recognize that "practicing sports is a right of every Iraqi." Years later, an Iraqi colleague explained to me that the Sunni Arabs were hedging against a Taliban-style Shia rule in which women would be banned from sports.

Iraqi leaders announced these final changes four days before the national referendum on ratification.

The following day, at a large meeting at the National Assembly, key Sunni Arab leaders announced their support of the draft constitution, citing these amendments.

President Bush, Hadley reported, now thought that I was some kind of a magician.

The political breakthrough was celebrated in the media of many Muslim-majority countries. In the United States, Iraq received positive coverage for the first time in a long while. I even received some positive coverage personally. While this was a political high point for Iraq in 2005—admittedly, not a high standard—I knew it was only the first step in the difficult process of stabilizing Iraq.

On October 25, the U.N. mission announced that the constitutional referendum had passed. Nationwide, 79 percent of Iraqi voters supported ratification. As expected, the referendum was voted down decisively in Al Anbar and Salah ad Din provinces, with "no" votes constituting 97 and 82 percent of total ballots, respectively. Ninewa was closer, with a 55 percent majority opposing ratification. Since this fell short of the two-thirds threshold, the constitution won ratification.

IRAQI LEADERS now faced a compressed timeline to organize their political coalitions and candidate lists for the December 15 election. I had previously hoped to facilitate the formation of cross-ethnic and cross-sectarian parties for this election. In light of the deep divisions over the constitution, however, I conceded that such an effort would be premature. Iraqis were not ready to organize based on issues rather than identity.

The party lists did not change a great deal. The Shia Islamist parties reconstituted their coalition to include SCIRI, Dawa, and Sadr's organization. The Kurdish parties formed a unified list. Iraqiyya expanded its coalition to embrace several smaller parties and independent candidates. Chalabi struck out on his own to create a party. A diverse set of Sunni Arab parties divided into two voting lists.

The fact that the Sunni Arab community committed to participating in the election, however, was a major achievement. My task force on Sunni Arab outreach set up meetings with dozens of Sunni political, tribal, religious, and social leaders. I impressed upon all of them the importance, for their communities, of participating in the election.

I even made my case to insurgent commanders. I went to meet some in jail, where they were being held by the coalition. I remember one conversation with the commander of an insurgent group. Taking the path of violence rather than political engagement, I argued, would destroy the Sunni Arab community. "Yours is the wealthiest community," I told him, "and the violence will make all the educated people run away. You will not get support for reconstruction, and employment will fall. All of this will produce a vicious dynamic that will destroy your people. Instead, you need to get involved in politics and build up your community."

He complained that the United States had created a government dominated by the Shia Arabs and Iran.

"I think *you* are working for Iran," I countered, pointing at him. "Do you think the United States wants Iran to take over Iraq? The United States has a limited number of troops in Iraq. We can't guard the border with Iran because you have us tied down in western Iraq. It is your fault that Iran is gaining influence in Iraq."

I could see he was at once processing and resisting my argument.

"We did not come to Iraq on a sectarian agenda," I stressed. "We want Iraq to succeed, but Iraqis will not succeed if they don't find a way to work together. That's what we want to see happen. However, if you attack us, we will defend ourselves. It's your choice on how you want to proceed."

My interlocutor ultimately told me that he wanted to work with us. He wanted help to move his family to Jordan, where they would be safe. Then, he explained, he wanted to be on our payroll and help align Sunni Arabs with the United States.

Over the course of many similar conversations, I became confident that the Sunni Arabs would participate in the December election and that the next National Assembly would fully represent the Iraqi people—a first step in forming a national unity government.

━ ⟨ ⟩ ━

ONE OF MY GREAT frustrations was that other countries—particularly Iran— were funneling millions of dollars into the election to support their allies and clients. The United States, meanwhile, did nothing to level the playing field for moderate and democratic forces. When our Iraqi allies approached me for financial support, I had to tell them that U.S. policy did not allow money to be provided to influence foreign elections. I doubt they believed me, assuming instead that we were supporting someone else.

As Iraqis campaigned for the December 15 election, I asked President Bush what could be done about this. I stressed that this election could be decisive to the success or failure of Iraq. We were spending tens of billions of dollars and losing American troops, yet we were refusing to make a small investment to counter Iran's machinations. Tehran's political intervention had the potential to derail everything we were doing. The United States had provided covert assistance for elections in Europe after World War II, when democratic parties faced stiff competition from Moscow-backed Communist parties. Surely there was something we could do here and now.

Though President Bush seemed sympathetic to my argument, he said that there was nothing he could do.

━ ⟨ ⟩ ━

THREE DAYS BEFORE the December 15 election, Casey and I met with three leaders of the Iraqi Accord Front—Tariq Hashimi, Adnan Dulaimi, and Khalaf Ulayyan. All were prominent members of the country's Sunni Arab leadership. Hashimi, a member of the Mashhadan tribe, had earned a master's degree in economics before leaving Iraq to lead a Sunni Islamist party in opposition to Saddam. Dulaimi was an Islamic studies professor at Baghdad University during Saddam's reign. The Iraqi government's recent decision to remove Dulaimi from his position as head of a prominent Sunni endowment had sparked outrage in the Sunni Arab community. Finally, Khalaf Ulayyan, a sheikh, had co-founded the Iraqi National Dialogue Council, one of the three parties in the Iraqi Accord Front. Unlike his colleagues, who wore Western pants and jackets, Ulayyan arrived in full Arab garb and a headdress.

The group mentioned that the Sunni Arab insurgency might stand down from violence during the election. Ulayyan offered to issue a public statement to this effect and work his contacts in the armed opposition; he knew that I knew his son was a commander in the insurgency.

I encouraged him to do so but was skeptical that anything would come of it. Although I had found the group to be reliable interlocutors during our talks over the elections, I highly doubted their claims on the insurgency. Casey and I had previously tried to reach local cease-fires with insurgents in pockets of western Iraq. We had had limited success and never thought that a broad cease-fire was feasible.

As promised, the Iraqi National Dialogue Council issued a public statement calling for the "honorable resistance" to cease operations for five days beginning on December 13.

On Election Day, Casey traveled all over the country to monitor the voting. That evening, he returned with good news, saying, "There was nothing going on out there all day."

Maybe our view that the insurgents lacked a central leadership was wrong. If one conversation with one political leader could lead to a nationwide standdown, the insurgency must have some kind of a leadership that could order concerted actions.

I took all of this in as Iraqis—both Sunni and Shia Arabs—celebrated the election.

Now it was time to consult Iraqi leaders on the formation of a national unity government. When Hakim asserted that a Shia Arab–Kurdish coalition would form the next government, I disagreed with him both privately and publicly. I was determined to bring Iraqi leaders of all communities together into a national unity government. Only then, I thought, would Iraqis reconcile differences that were fueling the violence. And as we succeeded in forming a unity government, perhaps we could pull insurgents out of the fight.

TWENTY-THREE

FORGING A NATIONAL UNITY GOVERNMENT

BAGHDAD, DECEMBER 2005–MAY 2006

THE RESULTS OF THE DECEMBER 2005 ELECTIONS WERE IN. THE MAIN COALITION OF Shia Islamist parties won 128 seats. Because the constitution required a two-thirds majority in the 275-member parliament to select the president and prime minister, the Shia Arab coalition could not form a government alone.

A national unity government was not going to come about on its own. Ruba'i, the national security advisor, brought a message from Sistani, urging me to help form a unity government. Mashaddani and Allawi both told me they supported a unity government. Talabani endorsed the idea as well, noting that the Kurds and Sunni Arabs could form a bloc to balance any undue influence by the Shia Arabs.

Yet many Shia Islamist leaders preferred to re-create a Shia-Kurd alliance to shut out the Sunni Arab and secular parties. Jaafari, who expected to continue on as prime minister, and Hakim made statements that bordered on triumphalism. I could see that going down this path would further alienate the Kurds and Sunni Arabs and exacerbate sectarian violence.

As I worked toward a unity government, I concluded it was time for bold political moves on Sunni Arab outreach. Casey and I reconvened the Sunni

Arab Advisory Council, the group that had used its contacts with the insurgents to prevent violence on Election Day. At the meeting, the Sunni Arab leaders were preoccupied with issues that I had now heard many times: the rising Iranian influence in Iraq; detainee abuse by the Ministry of Interior; coalition raids against people's homes; and Iraqi security forces that were being recruited almost exclusively from among the Shia Arab community.

Sadly, some of their complaints were valid. I, too, was worried about Iran's influence, particularly within Shia Arab militias. Reports had conclusively determined that the most deadly type of roadside improvised explosive device—the so-called "explosively formed projectile," or EFPs—was being produced in Iran. Shia Arab militias had used it to kill and maim coalition and Iraqi troops. And recently, coalition forces had raided an Iraqi government–operated detention center and discovered a torture chamber.

Also at this time, Allawi told me he could facilitate a meeting with commanders of the insurgency who were interested in a dialogue. Casey and I decided to pursue it, and President Bush authorized us to go forward with the initiative.

I met with Allawi's contacts at his home just outside the Green Zone, and then Casey and I asked David Litt, the head of political-military affairs, and Major General Rick Lynch, the co-chairs of our task force on Sunni Arab outreach, to follow up. Lynch, who looked the part of a senior army officer, put his feet up on the coffee table, held a cigar between his fingers, and proclaimed, "Now I am diplomat!"

Litt and Lynch reported that the insurgent commanders were requesting a general cease-fire with the coalition, with a catch: they still wanted to fight the Iraqi government. This was a nonstarter for us, but it did open a dialogue that helped us understand the nature of the insurgent leadership and the degree to which groups were reconcilable. I held several meetings in Jordan and Saudi Arabia with tribal leaders, former Baathists, and others with ties to the insurgency. The main obstacle to a deal was that our interlocutors wanted a comprehensive settlement with agreements on everything from ministerial appointments to security timetables. But until we knew them better and could assess their ability to deliver on a deal, we preferred starting with more local cease-fires, which could build confidence and produce a broader agreement down the line. We kept the Iraqi government informed about these discussions.

Meanwhile, the Iranians were taking notice of my activities. Tehran had its claws deep into the Shia Arab political elite and had developed strong ties with the Kurdish parties, creating the basis for a reliable anti-Sunni Arab coalition. Whenever I met with Shia Islamist leaders, I would survey the room and count how many I knew, from my sources, to be on Iran's payroll.

Iran had also encouraged—and funded—the formation of multiple Shia Islamist parties and militias. These armed groups included the Badr Organization, affiliated with SCIRI, and the Mahdi Army, linked with Sadr's political organization. Iranian operatives regularly came to Iraq and met with militia leaders to plan operations. Within the Mahdi Army, Iran maintained special units controlled directly by the Quds Force of the Iranian Revolutionary Guard Corps. They received lists of Sunni officers that Tehran wanted eliminated.

Iran had a stranglehold on the Shia Islamist parties. If any leader of these parties strayed from the Iranian line, Tehran would discipline him by cutting off money or even mobilizing militias against him. Iranian influence was amplified by its relationship with Sistani, who was an Iranian citizen. Sistani's son Rida served as a conduit between Najaf and Tehran.

Iran used the growing violence in Iraq to make the point to the Shia Arabs that their relationship with Iran was crucial to their survival.

I wanted to give the Shia Arabs an alternative to Iran, which I thought required reconciliation with Sunnis. This would need to include engaging the reconcilable Sunni insurgents; the building of balanced Iraqi security forces; and persuading Iraq's Arab neighbors to accept the Iraqi Shia as fellow Arabs.

The Iranians understood my game. Shortly after the December election, Talabani met with Qasem Soleimani, the head of the Quds Force, which was responsible for Iran's unconventional warfare and paramilitary operations. Soleimani was the man in charge of Iran's policies in Iraq. He told his Iraqi interlocutor that he understood what I was trying to do and would not allow it to succeed. He also warned Talabani that there would be grave consequences for Iraq, as well as for particular Iraqi groups, if they cooperated with my plan.

Subsequently, I learned that Soleimani had been ranting about me. "Khalilzad is singularly the worst person in the world," he said, noting that he "personally wanted to come to Iraq and kill this Khalilzad."

If our political efforts to create national unity had triggered this vitriol, I thought, we must be on the right track.

Political maneuvering among Iraqis escalated in January. Everyone quickly agreed to appoint a Kurd as president, a Shia Arab as prime minister, and a Sunni Arab as speaker, an arrangement that replicated the balance in the previous government. Talabani emerged as the consensus pick for president.

A few parameters struck me as obvious. The prime minister had to enjoy broad support. The main Iraqi parties needed to form a national unity government that included all the principal Shia Arab, Kurdish, and Sunni Arab parties. The ministerial portfolios needed to be divided equally, and the key security portfolios—interior and defense—needed to be held by nonsectarian figures with no links to armed militias.

To my surprise, Washington saw it differently. President Bush asked whether consensus decision-making might become too cumbersome to work effectively.

I strongly believed, though, that Iraq could not move forward unless its leaders started working together. This structure would not alter the distribution of power—the prime minister would be from the largest faction, and ministerial positions would be divided in proportion to the results of the elections—but the divisions and the distrust produced by sectarian violence had to be overcome. And if an agreement could be developed among key leaders in the cabinet, passing laws would be easier in the parliament.

With some encouragement, Iraqi leaders recognized the need for collaborating and building consensus. They soon began to contribute ideas proactively to the process.

◄ ►

SENATOR BARACK OBAMA made his first visit to Iraq at this time. I had first met Senator Obama during my confirmation hearing, where he had appeared more concerned about withdrawing from Iraq than he did in understanding the details of the conflict. In the hearing, Obama had repeatedly asked, before leaving hastily for another meeting, whether I intended to negotiate an agreement for "permanent" bases in Iraq.

During this field visit, Obama said very little; the other senators in his delegation asked the questions in the formal meetings. I explained to them my thoughts on a unity government. Talabani then hosted a dinner for the group. While it was clear that Obama was still becoming familiar with Iraqi politics, I found him to be thoughtful and analytical. I told Talabani and other Iraqi leaders that he was a rising star and encouraged them to engage the young senator.

The visit and my remarks on the unity government appear to have had an impact on Obama. After returning to Washington, he told President Bush that while he disagreed with the administration's approach on Iraq, he had confidence in me as ambassador. Later, in a revised edition of his book *The Audacity of Hope,* he mentions both our meeting and the dinner.

◄ ►

BECAUSE THE SHIA ISLAMIST bloc had received the most votes, it would have the right to nominate a prime minister and organize the government. In these negotiations, I was the only foreigner in the room, so Talabani declared me to be an "honorary Iraqi." Nuri al-Maliki, a senior official of the Dawa Party, attended the meetings. Jaafari did not attend, even though he wanted to be nominated again.

Perhaps as a result of Jaafari's conceit, another candidate, Vice President Mehdi of SCIRI, was soon angling to displace him.

I liked both Jaafari and Mehdi personally but was not sure that either was a suitable candidate. Jaafari was an academic by temperament. On his first visit to Washington as prime minister, he used most of his meeting with President Bush to lecture him about the achievements of Presidents Washington, Jefferson, and Lincoln. He had presumably wanted to demonstrate his wide-ranging knowledge, but at one point, President Bush shot me a look that seemed to say, "What's the point of this?"

During Jaafari's tenure, cabinet meetings were unfocused and meandering, sometimes dragging on for seven, eight, or nine hours. Whenever Casey and I were asked to attend meetings of the Ministerial Committee on National Security, we would look for opportunities to escape as soon as we had transacted our necessary business.

Mehdi was personally appealing. His political history was checkered, but he was not dogmatic. Over the decades, he had moved from secular parties to the Communist Party to SCIRI. He was well known in Washington from his days as the finance minister in the Allawi government. Some in the NSC pushed for his candidacy as prime minister, but his candidacy was problematic. SCIRI was receiving extensive financial and political backing from Tehran. The party's militia, the Badr Organization, had been attached to the Iranian Revolutionary Guard Corps during the Iran-Iraq war. Mehdi was subordinate to Abdul Aziz Hakim in the SCIRI hierarchy.

As the dominant military power, the United States could have played a shaping role in the Jaafari-Mehdi contest. I discussed the issue with the president, Rice, and Hadley. President Bush had a positive attitude toward Hakim and had come to the conclusion, for reasons that eluded me, that Hakim liked him. Whenever political negotiations bogged down among the Iraqis, the president would inevitably suggest that he "call Hakim." But I typically needed all Iraqis to move toward a compromise, Hakim included, so I had to counter this impulse. Hakim would interpret personal calls from the president as validation of his position and double down as a result.

We were using more advanced secure video technologies at this point, so I could meet electronically with Rice and Hadley while they sat at their respective desks at the State Department and the White House. "If you want Mehdi to be the nominee," I told them, "I can put my thumb on the scale." In the end, Rice and Hadley decided not to take sides in the Mehdi-Jaafari contest.

INSTEAD, I FOCUSED on facilitating the intra-Iraqi decision process. The Kurds held the decisive votes in parliament. With their backing, the candidate of the Shia Islamist bloc was likely to secure the needed two-thirds threshold for becoming prime minister. The Kurds generally did not have a high opinion of Jaafari but were more divided on Mehdi. Talabani and Salih of the PUK were supportive, but Barzani expressed concern that Mehdi was too close to Iran.

The Sunni Arabs, too, were divided. Hashimi was supportive of Mehdi, but the other two leaders of his bloc were opposed. They pointed to evidence of SCIRI's deep complicity in sectarian killings and abuse. Talking to members of the Shia Islamist bloc, including Dawa, I came away with the sense that not even they were happy with the options before them.

I decided to sit down with Mehdi and learn what he planned to do should he become prime minister. The discussion was inconclusive. I was dismayed that Mehdi, as a possible prime minister, seemed either to have little understanding of fundamental issues or, perhaps, was unwilling to show his hand. At the end of our meeting, I asked for his prediction on how the vote would go. He said that by his count, he would coast to victory over Jaafari. "I have it in hand," he said confidently.

But when the vote was taken in the caucus of the Shia Arab religious bloc a few days later, Jaafari defeated Mehdi by one vote.

EVEN AS WE WERE pushing for political unity and reconciliation, extremists on both sides, but especially al Qaeda in Iraq, were polarizing the country with an escalating campaign of violence. Sectarian groups had even infiltrated Iraqi security institutions. After the discovery of torture in Iraqi detention centers, I pressed Jaafari to launch an investigation. He did so only reluctantly, and the first report by his people amounted to a whitewash. He was well aware of the problems in the Ministry of Interior but did not intend to act.

For Iraq to continue receiving U.S. support, I forcefully told him, its government would need ministers of defense and interior who were nonsectarian and who had no affiliations with militias. Jaafari understood the point: I was accusing his current minister of interior, Bayan Jabr, of being complicit in the sectarian violence.

Shia Islamist parties were furious at me. They denied the more than obvious reality that Shia Arab groups even had militias at all. When I would raise the issue of sectarianism within the Ministry of Interior, Hakim would publicly attack me.

— ⟨ ⟩ —

MY EFFORTS to bring the fractious elements of the country together were dealt a severe blow on February 22 with a devastating terrorist bombing of the Golden Mosque in Samara, a sacred Shia shrine. In addition to being a spectacular historical monument, this wasn't just any mosque; it was the shrine where the Tenth and Eleventh Imams were entombed.

The attack was serious enough that I thought it might push Iraq into civil war. It was a masterstroke by the extremists.

Casey and I went to see Jaafari. I urged him to take strong action to prevent a meltdown. Already, we had reports that Shia Arab militias were mobilizing. Casey warned that a curfew was needed immediately.

Jaafari listened but was nonplussed, saying that Iraqis just had to "let off some steam."

Shocked, I asked, "Do you understand that scores of innocent Iraqis are being killed right now in the streets and in their homes?"

He brushed off the question.

As the conversation became more confrontational, I demanded to know whether he was simply going to let the Shia militias kill Sunnis with impunity.

Again, he gave no clear answer.

I became more direct: "If your people knew that the official responsible for all Iraqi security forces was taking this position, they would be shocked. They would not want you to be prime minister."

This startled him. "How long have you been here?" he replied angrily. "I know my people better than you do."

With Casey sitting beside me, I answered, "If you do not stop the killing, we will act unilaterally to do so."

I convened all the major Iraqi leaders for a meeting. "Iraq faces a moment of truth," I began. "This is your country, and you need to develop a plan to prevent Iraq from descending into civil war." For the first time, I saw fear in many of their eyes. They quickly decided to make a joint appearance on Iraqi media to condemn the bombing and urge Iraqis to remain calm.

I could see, as well, their sincere if belated recognition that a sustained effort at national reconciliation was critical. We convened a working group to think through how to proceed, even as Casey and I also mobilized an emergency response. Coalition forces took to the streets to prevent an escalation of violence. After a few days, we persuaded Jaafari to impose a curfew.

Soon thereafter the president convened a joint U.S.-U.K meeting. All of the American principals were present. Prime Minister Blair, who happened to be in Washington, also attended. In Baghdad, Casey and I were joined by the U.K. ambassador, William Patey. We reviewed the situation in the streets and our response. I described Jaafari's reluctance to come to terms with the crisis and his seeming indifference to the meltdown of his country.

"Can Jaafari be stopped from becoming prime minister?" President Bush asked.

"Yes," I replied, knowing the vote count in parliament from my canvassing of the Iraqi blocs.

My British colleague disagreed, arguing that the votes were still there for Jaafari.

By the end of the meeting, I had no doubt that the president wanted Jaafari out.

JAAFARI FOUGHT tenaciously to stay in office, testing Washington's patience.

I visited him at his home one day to try to get him to recognize realities. We sat in his garden, which had a small decorative moat running along the outer walls of the compound. At first I tried to get him to see that the other Iraqi groups did not think that he was the right leader. I got nowhere. He was acting as if he were already prime minister. I needed to be more direct, so I took him through the math of securing the two-thirds majority needed to become prime minister.

He dismissed this.

"With all due respect, we should read the constitution together," I said. "The rule is that the largest bloc can nominate a candidate for prime minister but that a supermajority of parliament is needed to approve him."

He was unmoved, and I left having made no headway.

Rice and U.K. Foreign Secretary Jack Straw met with Jaafari in Baghdad. They, too, pointed out, to no avail, that there was no way he could get enough support from the Kurds and Sunni Arabs for a two-thirds supermajority.

I asked President Bush to write a letter to Sistani asking him to intercede in the Jaafari impasse. Soon after the letter was delivered, Sistani called for solving the political deadlock by unifying the Iraqi nation. This was a clear message that he wanted a new candidate for prime minister.

I learned from Iraqis that Sistani and the Iranians had discussed the Jaafari situation, and had concluded that Jaafari's candidacy was not viable. Shortly thereafter, Soleimani came to Baghdad to deliver the same message.

The Dawa Party now indicated that they would come up with an agreeable nominee who could catalyze a unity government. Senior Dawa leader Ali Adeeb gained some currency. The leaders of the Shia Islamist alliance and the Kurdish bloc endorsed Adeeb, and Iran started to push for him over Jaafari.

I had some concerns about Adeeb, though. He maintained a residence in Iran, and his family lived there. I doubted that the leaders of the Arab world would reconcile with an Iraq led by Adeeb. If Adeeb became prime minister, the Sunni regimes of the Arab world would conclude that the United States was handing Iraq to the Iranians.

At the embassy, I tasked a small interagency group to go through the leadership profiles of dozens of Iraqi political figures and search for a better alternative. The group liked to joke that I wanted them to find "an Iraqi Karzai." There was some truth in this. Karzai was a Pashtun who could reach beyond his ethnic community and gain support from Afghanistan's smaller ethnic groups. We needed to find a Shia Arab who had the confidence of the Kurds and the Sunni Arabs, but no one seemed to fit the bill.

One morning, however, Jeff Beals, a talented young Foreign Service officer, walked into my office with another folder of profiles. "What about Nuri al-Maliki?" he asked.

I read through his bio. Maliki was an Iraqi nationalist. As an exile in Tehran, he had become disillusioned with the Iranian regime and had at one point refused to swear loyalty to Khomeini. He had taken up residence in Syria, but he did not seem to be working for Damascus. He had a good record during his term on the National Assembly's defense committee. The only worrisome point was that he seemed overly aggressive on de-Baathification.

I asked Beals to set up a meeting with Maliki.

WITH THEIR USUAL emphasis on speed, senior administration officials wanted to move forward with Adeeb. I warned Hadley that Adeeb might not be the right person to solve the sectarian problem. Besides, while I had some influence, in the end this was an Iraqi decision.

I would have preferred that the United States not be involved at all in the prime minister selection, but this was not possible under the prevailing circumstances. The Iraqi political class was too divided and constrained by parochial interests. Although Jaafari had been a failure, his Dawa Party still had the prerogative of proposing a replacement. Iran, moreover, effectively had a veto over the next selection. Given the enormous investment the United States was making in Iraq, the country's violence was not only an Iraqi responsibility but an American one as well. I thought we had a moral and strategic obligation to exercise the limited leverage we had in the matter, but we needed to do so with due modesty and with a recognition that intervening in another country's politics was a decision inherently fraught with grave consequences.

Beals called Maliki's office and asked for a meeting. Maliki called back and agreed to meet with me, but not in my residence. So we arranged to meet at the National Assembly building. I asked Patey and Beals to join me.

When I finally met with Maliki, I extended my hand to greet him and asked him how things were going. He replied gruffly, "You know everything. You are running everything. You got your way—Jaafari is out. I suppose you are here to tell me who is going to take his place." He was getting more and more worked up with every sentence. "You are in touch with Ayatollah Sistani. You are picking Ali Adeeb for prime minister. I hope that he meets with your approval." By this point, Maliki's every word projected resentment and anger.

"What about you as prime minister?" I asked.

Maliki was startled, rocking back slightly as my question was translated for him. He looked me directly in the eyes but was at a loss for words.

Next to me, the British ambassador was growing visibly agitated. He evidently believed that the selection of Adeeb, whom he perhaps preferred, was all settled.

After a moment, Maliki blurted out, "You vetoed me!"

This surprised me. I had never rendered an opinion on Maliki. I did not even know the Dawa leaders particularly well, since the party had not participated in opposition meetings before the war. Dawa leaders were invited to attend the meeting in Erbil but, even at that late stage, doubted that the United States was serious about toppling Saddam. They did not want to be used as a theatrical prop and therefore opted against attending.

"Who told you that?" I responded. "I took no view on your potential candidacy. I want to discuss this possibility with you right now."

Maliki's entire demeanor changed. The anger was gone. He leaned forward.

Patey now intervened, saying, "The decision has been made. Ali Adeeb will be the prime minister."

I asked the British ambassador to let me talk to Maliki privately.

Then I told Maliki that I had a few concerns, adding that if he could satisfy them, the United States would encourage Iraqis to rally behind him.

He asked me to name the issues.

I said that, first, the next government had to pursue political reconciliation seriously. Words were not enough.

Second, the prime minister had to take a balanced approach in combating both the insurgency and militias.

Third, I said, the prime minister would have to select defense and interior ministers who were not sectarian. To ensure that this was so, the United States would need to sign off on the appointees. Ministers with ties to militias would be unacceptable.

Fourth, the prime minister would need to reach out to the Arab world, particularly Saudi Arabia.

Finally, I said, the prime minister would need to move quickly to conclude agreements on distributing oil revenues, modifying de-Baathification, and other fundamental issues dividing the country.

Maliki instantly agreed to the first four points. He said that these conditions were perfectly aligned with his own views. De-Baathification, though, would require more extensive discussions. Over the next two days, however, we reached a satisfactory agreement on that matter as well.

Maliki had some advice for me, too. He thought the United States needed to change its military approach, and should hand over control of Iraqi security forces to the Iraqi government. He also talked extensively about the Dawa philosophy of government and how it compared with the Iranian system. Dawa believed in the will of the people. The Iranian regime, by contrast, was based on the belief that the clerics were the vice regents of God on earth. Maliki felt that the early Imams were indeed God's vice regents, but that with the disappearance of the Twelfth Imam in the ninth century, the "righteous rule belongs to the people until the hidden Imam reappears." Great and learned religious leaders could serve as sources of emulation but not as rulers.

"We have much to do to end the violence," I said as we parted.

He agreed. "We have to avert a war that could go on for thousands of years. Enough damage has been done by Iraqis fighting Iraqis." Then he added, "We need to change our strategy."

◄   ►

I MADE THE CASE for Maliki with Iraqi leaders. It was not a hard sell. Most praised him as "more Arab" and more independent of Iran. Sunni Arab leaders expressed some doubts about his willingness to modify de-Baathification. I told this to Maliki, and he again pledged to be forthcoming on the matter.

Since I knew the numbers were now there for Maliki, I considered the vote done. I called Hadley.

"There has been a slight change in plans," I explained. "A final deal on the prime minister is about to be closed, but it's not going to be Adeeb."

Hadley, in unusually colorful language, asked who it would be.

I answered, "We got Maliki."

I had mentioned Maliki in cables, but Hadley asked who he was. I directed him to the CIA biographic profile but also offered my view that he was better for our purposes than Adeeb. "Please tell the president that we're almost there," I concluded the call.

—< >—

WITH THE SELECTION of prime minister settled in late April, Iraqis proceeded to form the rest of the unity government and establish its agenda and decision-making structures.

On the whole, I was content with the balance and choices of the new government. Where difficult trade-offs had to be made, I thought the Iraqis made reasonable concessions. For example, I had to help fend off a push by the Shia Islamist bloc to retain Jabr as minister of interior. In the end, nonsectarian candidates took over the security ministries while Jabr became minister of finance.

On May 20, 2006, the National Assembly overwhelmingly voted the national unity government into office. Though Washington was frustrated that the process had taken five months, I reminded them that with the interregnum and delays in the Senate confirmation process, government formation could be just as protracted in the United States.

As I walked into the Iraqi parliament for the swearing-in ceremony, I was gratified but worried. We had made great progress in bringing Iraqis together politically. However, the extremists, in both the Sunni Arab and Shia Arab camps, had advanced their agendas as well.

I worried that extremist violence was outpacing our efforts to bridge divides between Iraq's communities. I saw the mounting bodies in Baghdad's morgues as tragic testimony to the fact that we were not moving fast enough to pull Iraq back from the brink.

TWENTY-FOUR

STRUGGLING TO BREAK THE CYCLE OF SECTARIAN VIOLENCE

BAGHDAD, 2006–2007

HOW DO YOU STABILIZE A COUNTRY? SOME ARGUE THAT SECURITY MUST COME first—a secure environment allows groups to reconcile and develop constructive politics. Others contend that a political settlement is the essential foundation for security. Still others hold that political and security efforts must be pursued in tandem, because progress on one enables progress on the other.

As ambassador to Iraq, I embraced this last school of thought. I believed that the relative urgency of and balance between the two would vary depending on the circumstances.

As the government was formed in May 2006, I thought we had the right formula for political success. Iraq's three major political communities had created a power-sharing arrangement under a national unity government with an agreed agenda and a process for near-consensus decision-making on issues of national importance.

The problem was that political progress had not brought down the level of violence. In fact, since the bombing of the Golden Mosque in February, Sunni

Arab and Shia Arab extremists had fomented a cycle of sectarian violence that was overwhelming our political efforts.

In 2006, Casey and I tackled the challenge in a variety of ways.

Politically, I developed a good working relationship with Maliki, urging him to see the Sunni Arab insurgency and the Shia Arab militias as twin problems to be attacked simultaneously. I worked with Iraqi leaders to identify and address the major issues still dividing Iraq's communities. Militarily, Casey and I collaborated in reaching out to Sunni Arab insurgents who were willing to reconcile with the Iraqi government. Diplomatically, I tried to elicit support for Iraq from neighboring states. Casey and I grappled with the challenge of countering Syrian and Iranian efforts to destabilize Iraq.

—◄   ►—

I CAME TO SEE Maliki as a leader with mixed motivations. He had authoritarian and sectarian tendencies, but I was convinced that he could be a positive political force. My goal was to incentivize him to align with moderate political factions and distance himself from hard-line sectarians like the Sadrists.

It took Maliki some time to get his bearings as prime minister. During the summer and early fall of 2006, Casey and I were frustrated when Maliki thwarted our efforts to confront Shia Arab militias. Over time, though, he came to recognize the problem of the militias. As he became more confident in his role, he showed that he wanted to address the security problem decisively. Maliki repeatedly asked the coalition to change the policy under which the Multi-National Force–Iraq (MNF-I) retained control of Iraqi forces after they were trained. He wanted to command these forces so that he could act decisively against the Sunni Arab insurgents and Shia Arab militias.

Maliki found our decision-making process too ponderous. "You think you see an opportunity to strike a terrorist, so you collect intelligence on it," he once complained to me. "You then send the information to Washington, where another process of deliberations takes place before you are authorized to do something. Then, here in Baghdad, you plan and plan. Finally, by the time you decide to act, the terrorist has left Iraq and gone even beyond Afghanistan." He also believed that we were using force with too much discrimination.

Maliki's critique stirred up problems with the U.S. military, who suspected that he wanted more control of Iraqi units for sectarian purposes. Maliki's initial objection to using force against the Sadrists, who formed part of his political base in parliament, fueled that suspicion. We eventually agreed that the coalition would transfer control of some Iraqi forces provided that Maliki coordinated with us and was willing to use force against all groups who violently opposed the state.

The most important thing to understand about Maliki, I realized, was his near-existential fear of a Baathist coup. More than once, I would meet with him, and he would tell me about elaborate conspiratorial plots on the part of Sunni Arab leaders and former Baathists, who, he alleged, were scheming to take power. He watched like a hawk as the United States built and reformed Iraqi security forces, fearing that we were empowering individuals who would execute a coup. He was particularly suspicious of the intelligence service that the CIA was helping to build, which was led by a Sunni Arab.

One day, after he related a particularly far-fetched conspiracy theory to me, I leaned toward him and said, "Look, Mr. Prime Minister, I understand that you worry about the stability of the Iraqi government. But you are wasting your time. We have so many other things to do besides worrying about a coup. There are more than 150,000 coalition troops in Iraq, and we are committed to the success of the Iraqi government. How in the world do you think a coup could succeed with the U.S. military here in those numbers?" He listened but never relinquished that fear.

Still, Maliki was willing to take risks in pursuing political reconciliation and distancing Iraq from Iran, provided that he was confident in his relationship with the United States. He was carefully attuned to the balance of power in Iraq and would not make a move if he believed it entailed excessive risk to him, his party, his sect, or his government. But when I briefed Maliki on my efforts to reach out to Sunni Arabs and pull insurgents out of the fight, he endorsed my plan, albeit with reluctance. Eventually, he gave the coalition the green light to act against Shia Arab militias and authorized us to strike the secret cells—the so-called "special units"—within the Mahdi Army that were directly controlled by Iran.

I was pleased with Maliki's evolution, but knew that he still harbored sectarian and authoritarian impulses. While I thought we could help create the conditions in which he would emerge as a genuine national leader, I knew there were limits. We could not change who he was fundamentally, but we could, and did, shape his conduct in important ways.

IN THE LATTER half of 2006, I focused on helping Maliki and other Iraqi leaders implement the agreed-upon agenda for their national unity government.

I selected the most significant issues and framed them as "benchmarks" or "milestones" for the unity government. Maliki, at times, loudly objected to the terms, which he felt demeaned Iraq's sovereignty. But he worked hard to advance the agenda.

Our efforts produced decidedly mixed results. We made the most progress on reforming the Ministry of Interior. Casey and I declared that 2006
would be the "Year of the Police." The coalition did a thorough analysis of the
Interior Ministry, pulled police units out of deployment for retraining, and
re-vetted police and ministry officials.

These reforms won me no favors in Shia Islamist circles. Leaders of Shia
Islamist parties began to call me "Abu Omar"—a typical Sunni Arab male
name, which suggested that I was "father of the Sunnis."

We improved the capabilities of other institutions as well. My deputy
chief of mission, Daniel Speckhard, mobilized the embassy to field Provincial
Reconstruction Teams modeled on those in Afghanistan. Given the federal
nature of the Iraqi government and the delegation of authority to regional and
provincial bodies, I thought it was critical to strengthen the capacity of local
governments.

In late 2006 and early 2007, I mediated negotiations on a series of important draft laws, but Iraqi leaders did not push any of these over the finish
line during my tenure. President Bush encouraged me to spend a great deal of
time on the hydrocarbon law. The draft created a Federal Council on Oil and
Gas that would include officials in the federal government, representatives of
oil-producing regions and provinces, and other figures to plan and oversee development of Iraqi hydrocarbon resources. Most importantly, it balanced the
equities of the federal government and the KRG in developing and managing
oil resources. The draft law was approved by the cabinet at the very end of my
tenure. It was transmitted to the National Assembly, but there was little momentum behind modernizing the hydrocarbon sector through partnerships
and profit-sharing with international companies. The document that I helped
Iraqi officials develop is still the only full draft law for Iraq's hydrocarbon
industry.

I also prioritized de-Baathification. On the very last day of my ambassadorship, Talabani signed off on a draft law to reform the de-Baathification
process and submitted it to the cabinet. The draft law called for reducing the
scope of de-Baathification and reversing the purge of lower-ranking members
of the Baath Party. It shifted the focus toward prosecuting actual crimes of the
Saddam era in the judicial process. The de-Baathification draft law, too, never
advanced through the National Assembly.

On the most import issue—reconciliation—Iraqi leaders made very little
progress at all. In this respect, we were up against hard realities. I made the
case for pluralism to a Shia Arab leader at my residence one evening in late
2006.

"I agree with everything you say about reconciliation and pluralism," he
replied to me. "However, I see it differently. Sunni Arabs have dominated us

for hundreds of years. We want to dominate them for a couple of hundred years. Then we will implement pluralism."

Fortunately, these sentiments, while not atypical, were not representative either. Advocates of reconciliation frequently mentioned to me how common intermarriage was across sectarian lines and how some tribes were comprised of both Sunnis and Shias.

And Maliki, to his credit, did not express sectarian views publicly. Despite our disagreements on reconciliation, he believed that sectarianism was a transitional problem. As Iraq security improved and the unity government delivered on its promises, he thought that issue-oriented politics would gain in prominence. He spoke frequently, and emotionally, about his belief that the rule of law would assist in this transition.

By the end of my tenure, I had concluded that improvement in the security situation was necessary for reconciliation to gain traction.

—◄　　►—

IN TERMS OF military strategy, I had arrived in Iraq believing that a population-security "oil spot" strategy was the optimal approach.

In September 2005, the "Red Cell," which Casey and I had tasked with reviewing our political-military strategy, had called for a population-security campaign that would secure Baghdad neighborhood by neighborhood. The Red Cell report advised that, after securing Baghdad, the military campaign should work outward from the capital to secure cities and towns, one by one, along the country's two rivers, the Tigris and the Euphrates. It assumed that no additional coalition forces were available and argued that forces from the provinces should be redeployed to initiate the campaign in Baghdad. The report also argued that the planned force structure for Iraqi security forces was too small.

Casey was not enthusiastic. While he did not reject the Red Cell report outright, he wanted to prioritize the transition of security responsibilities to Iraqi security forces. I gave a copy of the document to Hadley when I visited Washington in September, urging him to take it up in the interagency process. He demurred, arguing that the issue should be moved up through the military chain of command.

One of my greatest regrets was that I did not press harder for the adoption of a population-security strategy in 2005. From Baghdad, I saw that population-security strategies were successful under Colonel H. R. McMaster in Tal Afar in 2005 and under Colonel Sean MacFarlane in Ramadi in 2006.

In advocating a strategy to transition the war to the Iraqis, Casey was on the same page as General Abizaid at CENTCOM and Rumsfeld. Patey told me that Prime Minister Blair raised the Red Cell report with President Bush, but because President Bush had not seen the document, Blair did not get any traction.

It's possible that the "oil spot" strategy would have been difficult to implement as early as 2005. The program to build up Iraqi security forces was gaining momentum but had not yet achieved critical mass. The Iraqi Police, which were at that point infiltrated by sectarian forces, could not be used to secure Sunni Arab areas. Though Sunni Arab outreach had produced political progress, the elements of the insurgency that would later form the Sunni Arab Awakening had not yet turned. This shift—perhaps the most important factor leading to the success of the later surge—began only in late 2006 and did not transform the military situation in western Iraq until 2007. It took a more balanced and assertive Iraqi political leader—Maliki—to move against the Shia Arab militias and create an evenhanded offensive against extremists in both communities.

I saw the balance sheet for U.S. military operations in 2006 as generally negative. The levels of violence continued to be so high that hardly any "conditions-based transition" of security responsibility to the Iraqis could take place.

Counterterrorism raids put pressure on the enemy and killed the head of AQI, Abu Musab al-Zarqawi, but were not transforming the strategic picture. There was no change in the overall level of enemy activities. It seemed the enemy could simply regenerate its ranks, even at senior levels.

Most troubling, the major military operations in 2006 were largely unsuccessful. MNF-I and Iraq's security ministries attempted to curb the spiraling sectarian violence in Baghdad through Operation Forward Together. Security incidents actually increased over 40 percent, and up to 2,000 Iraqis were being killed in sectarian attacks every month.

<hr />

CASEY AND I continued to engage potentially reconcilable insurgents. Most of our meetings did not achieve breakthroughs, but I did see some glimmers of hope among tribes in Al Anbar in late 2006. In the aftermath of Zarqawi's death, I made a series of visits to Al Anbar, starting with Fallujah and Ramadi, and discovered that tribal leaders were increasingly disillusioned with the terrorists.

At one point, the Marines, who had responsibility for western Iraq, asked to bring a delegation of tribal leaders to see me in Baghdad. I greeted the group of about fifteen people in a comfortable meeting room in the Green Zone. One of them was Abdul Sattar Abu Risha, whom I had met in Al

Anbar and who would later emerge as one of the principal leaders of the Anbar Awakening. I also recognized others in the room from my meetings in Jordan. The Marines told me that the tribal leaders had been quite insistent on paying me a visit.

As we made small talk, I sensed that the attitudes of this group were quite different from those of other Sunni Arabs tribal leaders and commanders with whom I had met. When we turned to business, the Iraqis bluntly said that the United States and the tribes of western Iraq should come together to pursue our common interest in defeating al Qaeda in Iraq.

I was taken aback.

The Iraqis explained that AQI wanted to create a civil war within Islam, between Sunnis and Shias. They also complained about the brutal treatment of their communities by AQI, noting that life in the town of Qaim under the terrorists was like living in a totalitarian state.

I mentioned that the accounts of daily life and the brutality of the terrorists reminded me of the stories I had heard about life under the Taliban.

They said that AQI and the Taliban were cut from the same cloth. They stressed that their communities wanted to develop a partnership with the United States.

I endorsed the idea wholeheartedly, noting that this was exactly what was needed in western Iraq.

The Iraqis were delighted at my response. One of the leaders commented that I should be named "Abu Omar." At least the Sunnis and Shias could agree on one thing.

The tribal leaders asked whether they would be able to cooperate with the Baghdad government, given Iran's influence. I conceded that Iran had significant influence but noted that the United States also had clout. I told them that I had talked with Maliki about this meeting and that he was supportive. I promised that I personally would serve as an intermediary with the Iraqi government.

When the tribal leaders raised the issue of Sunni Arab detainees, I said that I would look into any individual cases that they raised.

For the remainder of my time in Iraq, I followed the efforts of the Marines to support Iraqi tribal leaders against AQI. I worked the issue at the national level, while they did so locally.

—◄   ►—

I ALSO TRIED to persuade U.S. friends in the region to embrace the Iraqi national unity government. I urged Saudi Arabia, Jordan, the United Arab Emirates, and Turkey in particular to support our Sunni Arab outreach efforts. It was unusual for an ambassador in one country to engage with the governments of its neighbors, but I took it upon myself when I saw that Washington was not being proactive enough. To their credit, our ambassadors in these countries did not protest when I met one on one with counterparts in these countries.

I advised Maliki to make his first visit abroad as prime minister to Saudi Arabia. He agreed. Before his visit, I went to Saudi Arabia and met with King Abdullah. The king had been a severe critic of developments in Iraq since our invasion. I bluntly described the challenges we faced, including Iran's conduct. King Abdullah replied that he appreciated my candor: "I look in your eyes and know you are telling the truth."

I told the king that Maliki was an Arab, not a Persian. I stressed that although he led a Shia Islamist party, he was an Iraqi nationalist. I argued that Maliki could reduce Iraq's dependence on Iran if the Arab world engaged Iraq and worked with its leaders. This was a tough sell. The king complained that Iranian influence was so pervasive that Iraqis were speaking Farsi in the Ministry of Defense. Ultimately, however, the king agreed to receive Maliki.

Maliki's visit went well, but the relationship between the leaders did not gel. King Abdullah honored Maliki by sending the crown prince to meet him at the airport and granting the Iraqi leader a one-on-one meeting. Maliki was almost elated when he reported back to me afterward. However, the king later accused Maliki of reneging on commitments that he allegedly had made in their one-on-one session.

I later learned that the Saudis believed that Maliki agreed to three requests from the king: reinstate certain Baathist army officers, meet with insurgent leader Harith al-Dhari, and prevent the hanging of Saddam. Iraqis dispute this view. In any case, Maliki did not follow through on the three items. When I later spoke with the king about Maliki, he snapped back, "Don't talk to me about that liar." I was unable to arrange a second meeting for Maliki in early 2007.

Worse, the Saudis came to believe that Maliki was an Iranian agent. When I met with the king in early 2007, he took me into a private meeting room, where his chief of intelligence showed me a paper that the Saudis believed came from inside the Iraqi prime minister's office. It was purported to be an order, signed by Maliki, to assassinate a number of Sunni Arabs, all listed in the document. I told the king that this had to be a fabrication. If Maliki wanted to carry out such actions, which I disputed, he would not be so stupid as to sign an order to that effect on the official letterhead of his office. Whoever created the fabrication achieved the desired effect—neither I nor my successors were ever able to get Saudi-Iraqi relations back on track.

I discussed the same issues with King Abdullah of Jordan. Many Sunni Arab Iraqis, particularly from Al Anbar Province, had taken refuge in Jordan.

The king's government facilitated contacts with tribal leaders. King Abdullah was more open than other Sunni regional leaders to engaging Iraq's Shia Arab leadership.

I seized every opportunity I had to advance Sunni Arab outreach through regional actors. When Washington ignored Turkish Foreign Minister Abdullah Gul's offer to convene Sunni Arab Iraqis and U.S. officials, I took matters into my own hands. I called Gul and said that if he would organize the Sunni Arabs, I would attend. Gul was startled that I did not wait for clearance from Washington. He embraced the chance to work with us, and our efforts eventually helped persuade Sunni Arabs of the Iraqi Islamic Party to join the political process.

I was less successful in challenging Syria and Iran.

Syria was not only providing safe haven to the Sunni Arab insurgency, it was allowing a flow of foreign fighters to come through its territory. In 2005 I raised the issue with Washington.

I suggested that we give Damascus an ultimatum: if they did not cut off the flow of foreign fighters, the United States would close the airport and destroy its runways. Washington deliberated briefly on my idea and then rejected it, arguing that the foreign fighters would simply find another route. I asked for alternative strategies to address Syrian conduct. None was forthcoming.

Iranian-supported militias, meanwhile, were attacking coalition forces. Rockets and mortars fired at the Green Zone invariably came from Shia Arab neighborhoods where the Badr Organization or the Mahdi Army were dominant. Together with General Casey, we gave detailed briefings to Talabani, Jaafari, and Maliki on Iran's activities. They raised the issue with Tehran, but nothing changed on the ground.

I sensed that Iran was trying to domesticate the Sunni Arabs so that the community would never again raise its head.

Based on conversations with Iraqis who interacted extensively with Iranian officials dealing with Iraq, I became very impressed with the analytical skills of the Iranians. Their analyses and calculations were much better than those of Western intelligence agencies or even neighboring Arab regimes. The Quds Force had an enormous number of Iraqis on its payroll, sometimes at low levels and other times at much higher levels. Iran also allowed the families of Iraqi political figures to live in Iran or send their children to school in the country.

I found the Iranians to be very cynical operators. They seemed to treat Iraq's Shia Arabs as cannon fodder. I sometimes told Shia Islamist leaders, who were close to Iran, that I believed Tehran wanted to turn Iraq into a smoldering ruin that the Iranians could then control with ease. Some of my interlocutors quietly concurred with my view. In fact, on one occasion, Maliki told us that he believed that Iran was behind the bombing of the Golden Mosque.

I struggled to get the Bush administration to develop a strategy for the Iran problem. Washington had a contradictory policy. It spoke loudly against Iran, and it refused to talk with the Iranians. But it was not willing to take on Iranian activities in Iraq. I did not see the logic of this approach. Talks would have offered the prospect of influencing Iran, though this would certainly have been difficult. However, if we were not going to engage the Iranians, I felt that we should have used other means, including force, to thwart their strategy.

I confronted senior administration officials with the contradictions in our policy. In 2006 I repeatedly asked for the authority to engage the Iranians in Iraq, just as I had done with Iranian officials while in Afghanistan. They ignored my requests.

Frustrated, I raised the issue with President Bush directly at an NSC meeting. He authorized me to engage the Iranians. Hakim then traveled to Iran and met with Ayatollah Khamenei. He convinced Khamenei that a dialogue between the U.S. and Iran was in the interest of Iraq, Iraqi Shias, and Iran itself.

Upon his return, Hakim told me that the Iranians wished to engage in a dialogue not only about Iraq, but about all the issues dividing the United States and Iran. Khamenei blessed the initiative. Tehran put together a team from across the Iranian foreign and security departments to attend the meeting in Baghdad. I planned to wave off discussions of issues other than Iraq, the only one over which I had authority.

For reasons that remain unclear to me, Washington did an about-face and canceled the meeting at the last minute. Khamenei, Hakim informed me, concluded from the incident that the Americans could not be trusted and were not serious about diplomatic engagement with Iran. Late in my tenure in Baghdad, the Bush administration reversed course again and allowed carefully circumscribed talks on Iraq. But Washington never authorized the kind of continuous engagement that might have shaped Iran's conduct.

In a SVTC meeting with President Bush, I described what Iran was doing and how harmful it was to the prospects for success. "We're being patsies!" I finally exclaimed in exasperation. After thinking for a few seconds, the president instructed me and Casey to "do something about it."

Casey and I decided to target Quds Force officers when they traveled to Iraq. An opportunity came on December 21. I had already gone to bed when my aide Ali Khedery called in the middle of the night. A senior Quds Force officer was going to be staying at Hakim's residence. The military wanted guidance on whether to raid the SCIRI leader's house. This presented a dilemma. While it would create a major diplomatic incident, it would also send a strong message. When Casey and I learned that the officer would be staying not in Hakim's house proper but in another building in the compound, we authorized the raid. The operation went forward without a hitch. Coalition forces arrested the Quds Force officer and took him in for interrogation.

Hakim was outraged, complaining that coalition forces had violated his home.

After I heard out his complaints, I decided to toy with him at first. "Technically," I noted, "this was not your home—it was a separate building on your compound."

This elicited an even angrier response. He demanded that the United States never again take actions that disrespected him in this way.

I then moved toward him and said, "You are a powerful political leader in Iraq. You are no longer an opposition leader in need of Iranian support for your existence and for your political survival in the face of Saddam's brutality."

The Iraqi government then formally raised the matter with us. Foreign Minister Zebari protested that the Iranians were in Iraq legally, on diplomatic business.

"Since the Iranians were here on diplomatic business," I replied, "you must have a diplomatic note. Could I see it? Could I see the visas?"

I then told Zebari in forceful terms that the Iraqi government had to stand up to Iran's violation of Iraqi sovereignty.

A similar action took place in the KRG when we learned that Quds Force officers were crossing the border. Casey and I authorized a raid, captured part of the group, and arrested and interrogated the Iranians.

I took up the issue with Talabani, who had recently met with Soleimani in a village near the border. "Iraqis are being too deferential to Iran," I told him. "It is inappropriate for you, the president of Iraq, to be meeting clandestinely with an Iranian intelligence officer."

Talabani explained that Soleimani did not want to come to Baghdad because he was afraid that he might be arrested.

For the remainder of my tenure, Quds Force operatives no longer blatantly traveled into the country to conduct consultations and joint planning. I am convinced that if we had combined diplomatic engagement with forcible actions we could have shaped Iran's meddling decisively.

—<   >—

THE CYCLE OF sectarian violence escalated in the fall of 2006, faster than we could respond. I felt physically sickened at times by reports of what Iraqis were doing to other Iraqis. I received regular briefings about Iraqis being tortured with drills, burnings, and beatings. Family members who went to collect the bodies of their loved ones would, in turn, be detained, tortured, and killed.

The level of brutality in Afghanistan had not even remotely prepared me for what was awaiting us in Iraq.

Even the way the execution of Saddam was carried out in December 2006 showed the depth of the sectarian problem. The timing and circumstances almost seemed designed to inflame sectarian tensions.

I was in Dubai at the time, and the last few days had been a whirlwind. The plan was for my family to meet me in Dubai for Christmas break. All of us had bad colds, me worst of all. I had gone to bed early, only to be awakened a few hours later by an agitated Alex. My phone had been ringing wildly, and he had finally picked it up and said, "Ambassador Khalilzad's phone." Our political counselor Margaret Scoby, assuming it was me, launched into her report: "Sir, I am here with the prime minister, and they want to move ahead with Saddam's execution. We're pushing back but they are insisting that they will move forward within the next hour. We need guidance from you, sir." Shocked, Alex and Max rushed to wake me up.

I asked for Maliki. After he confirmed the report, I said, "You are the leader of a Muslim country. Usually, a leader releases prisoners, as a show of mercy, on the occasion of Eid. Do you really want to hang a former head of state on that holiday?"

Maliki claimed he had reports that terrorists planned to seize a school, hold the children hostage, and demand Saddam's release. He also started to nitpick with me about when Eid actually began, based on the Shia calendar.

"Don't play those kinds of games with me," I responded. "You're the prime minister of Iraq and have the authority to make this decision." I counseled him to think things over while I consulted with Washington.

I spoke with Rice and Hadley. We went back and forth about what to do. In the end, I was told that the United States should respect Maliki's authority.

When I relayed to Maliki that we would defer to his judgment, he said the execution would take place as planned. The United States turned over Saddam, who was in our custody, to the Iraqis. The hanging took place amid macabre jeering by Iraqi security personnel, who appeared to be Sadrists. It was all captured on a handheld video recording. The graphic nature of the sectarian scene reverberated throughout the Muslim world.

Casey and I made sure to show requisite respect by transporting Saddam's body on a U.S. helicopter to Saddam's relatives in Tikrit.

Still, I received a number of irate phone calls about Maliki's recklessness. The Saudis were particularly furious. During my next trip to Riyadh, Interior Minister Nayef bin Abdulaziz reminded me that there were millions of pilgrims at the time in Mecca, both Sunnis and Shias. The execution could have triggered a massive conflict that the Saudis would not have been able to contain. Nayef suggested that this, in fact, had been Maliki's goal.

When Karzai called to convey his best wishes for the holiday, he remarked that the sectarian nature of the execution had surprised him. Only now, he acknowledged, did he fully understand the depth of the sectarian problem in Iraq.

—◄   ►—

I HAD BEEN away for four years. A few times, I tried to plan trips to Vienna, but they had to be canceled at the last minute. All of this was causing strain in the family.

The only solace was that Cheryl and Max were happier in Vienna than in Doha. Cheryl knew the city, had friends there, and felt at home. Max had entered the Vienna International School, where he became the captain of the basketball team. I called the principal of his school once a month or so to check on him. The report was always positive.

During this period, Jack Keane, a retired four-star general, visited me. He was part of a small group of experts at the American Enterprise Institute who had worked up a proposal for a "surge." Keane told me that the group favored a deployment of additional forces to adopt a population-security strategy. I liked the concept but did not get the impression that the group had made much headway with the Bush administration.

As far as I knew, three main alternative strategies were being debated within the administration. The first was what was described to me as the "80 percent solution": the United States should unify the Shia Arabs and the Kurds—who accounted for 80 percent of the population—and arm and equip them to defeat the Sunni Arab extremists. The vice president's office had proposed this plan.

In an NSC meeting, I reiterated points I had made in a cable beforehand. The 80 percent solution would exacerbate the problem. It would unite Sunni Arabs behind the extremists at a time when we needed to separate the two. I recounted the progress that we had made with Sunni Arab political and tribal leaders. I also pointed out that both Shia and Sunni extremists were the problem, and that we needed to empower moderates and isolate both sets of bad actors. My analysis seemed to resonate with President Bush.

Another strategy emerged from the Iraq Study Group, a commission created by Congress and led by Baker and former representative Lee Hamilton. The commission called on me to testify in November as the group neared the end of its fact-finding and deliberations. In preparing my statement, I told Maliki and other Iraqi leaders that I wanted to convey their ideas directly to the Iraq Study Group.

Casey and I arrived at Maliki's office shortly before my departure for Washington. The principals sat in large chairs at one end of his meeting room while staff members took seats along the wall. The prime minister, as always, came prepared for the meeting, with a sheet of paper listing the steps he wanted the United States to take.

Two points stood out to me.

The first was Maliki's request to give him full control over Iraqi security forces. He wanted to take charge, personally, as commander in chief. He believed that the United States was far too cautious in the use of force and intended to strike hard against the enemy, with far less concern for collateral damage.

The second significant point was easier to miss. Maliki asked the United States to provide "a guarantee of the Iraqi political system." I dwelled on this point for a minute as Maliki spoke. He was asking in effect for the United States to guarantee Iraq's democratic form of government. I saw this as the newest iteration of Maliki's paranoia about a coup. Maliki knew that as long as Iraq remained democratic, Shia Arabs would play a leading role. He made it clear that this guarantee would enable him to take more risks for reconciliation.

Soon after I arrived in Washington, I met with the Iraq Study Group. I presented an alternative approach that called for giving Maliki control over Iraqi forces and putting Iraqis in the lead. At the same time, I wanted authorities and resources to be able to shape the conduct of Iraqi leaders and groups. I needed the ability to use covert funding to create relationships of influence and incentivize actors through rewards and punishments. I recommended that U.S. forces shift to specialized missions: training and advising Iraqi forces, controlling the Iranian border, and conducting counterterrorism operations against high-value targets.

I also advised that U.S. forces should allay the principal fears of the two communities—that Sunni Arabs would conduct a coup against the Iraqi state, and that Shia Arab militias would conduct atrocities in Sunni Arab areas.

I took questions for a brief period. I was struck by the number of "Iraq 101" questions—basic questions about a very complex situation.

I was unimpressed with the conflicted nature of the Iraq Study Group's final report. It called for redeployments, a euphemism for withdrawals, and for leaving trainers in Iraq, who would be vulnerable if larger forces did not remain in the country. It also suggested, in seeming contradiction, that we should consider sending additional U.S. forces for a brief period of time.

The third alternative strategy, which originated in the State Department, called for U.S. military disengagement and the rapid transfer of security responsibilities to the Iraqis. Advocates of this position argued that Iraq could not be salvaged. Iraq had fallen into a civil war, and the United States should not be a party to such a conflict.

I opposed this option and took it up with Rice. I argued that Iraq was not in a full state of civil war. The institutions of the state—the government, military, and police—were holding.

Rice believed that sending more troops would not make a significant difference. She argued that the U.S. government had an obligation to minimize U.S. exposure and loss of American lives.

I agreed that more troops would not make a difference if they followed the same strategy. I added, however, that sending more forces as part of a better strategy would make sense.

Only after I arrived in Washington did I realize how far thinking about the surge had progressed in the White House. I had always taken at face value what every senior general had told me: additional U.S. combat forces were simply unavailable. However, when I was briefed on the elements of the surge option—which involved sending five additional combat brigades and shifting to a population-security counterinsurgency strategy—I was immediately sympathetic. I could not judge whether this escalation would be sufficient to quell the sectarian violence, but I thought the stakes in Iraq were weighty enough to give it a try.

In late 2006, Rice and Hadley invited me to dinner at the Watergate and asked for my thoughts on a surge. When I endorsed this option, Rice asked if I'd be interested in staying on as ambassador to implement the new policy.

My impression, though, was that the inquiry was largely a courtesy. I had already served, under exhausting circumstances, longer than any other U.S. ambassador to the country. By the time they found a replacement, my tenure might stretch to three years. Given how proactive President Bush had been in recruiting me for the ambassadorships to Afghanistan and Iraq, I assumed, since he had not done the same this time around, that he was not especially keen on my staying in Baghdad. Gates was taking over for Rumsfeld, and General David Petraeus was replacing Casey. So the president may have felt that a new ambassador should be deployed as well.

Rice asked me to submit my views on the surge through official channels.

I responded with a cable endorsing the surge. I thought additional U.S. forces, in combination with the increasingly capable Iraqi forces, could bolster security in Baghdad. We needed to keep pressing Maliki to move against Shia Arab militias. At the same time, we needed to persist in efforts to recruit Sunni Arabs to our side. At this point, I believed that we could capitalize on AQI's brutal treatment of the local population, which was alienating local Sunni Arabs in Al Anbar.

Casey was not happy about my cable. He walked into my office and argued that I was weighing in on an issue that was outside my lane. I informed Casey that, in the context of the ongoing review of our Iraq strategy, I had been asked to send my views. I didn't mind, I added, if he forwarded his views on political, economic, and diplomatic issues affecting Iraq.

I engaged Maliki on the surge. President Bush wanted Maliki to commit publicly to using force in a nonsectarian manner before the United States doubled down with additional forces and a new strategy. Maliki agreed, provided that MNF-I transferred more Iraqi forces to his control. I thought Maliki's request was reasonable, assuming that he would work through the chain of command, which would ensure that his actions were visible to MNF-I. We also agreed that the United States would expand Iraqi forces and provide better equipment and training.

Unlike some of our officers in the field, President Bush was impressed by the fact that Maliki sought more responsibility. Still, the president had doubts about Maliki's willingness to transcend sectarian loyalties.

Maliki made a statement that he believed would satisfy President Bush's conditions. Yet the president was not fully satisfied. He asked me to go back to Maliki and press the Iraqi leader to make a clearer and stronger statement. After Maliki did so, President Bush authorized the surge.

PETRAEUS TOOK overall command in January 2007, ably supported by General Ray Odierno, who ran the coalition's military operations day to day. I had known Petraeus from his earlier work in running the train-and-equip command in Iraq. We got along well and continued the same pattern of morning meetings that Casey and I had convened. Petraeus reported on his tours of various neighborhoods. He made it clear that his focus would be to improve security for the Iraqi people. The transfer of security responsibility to Iraqis would be on hold for now.

As the new team took over, they endorsed the political strategy we had pursued—unifying moderates in each community against the Sunni Arab and Shia Arab extremists. Petraeus expressed support for my effort to press Iraqi leaders on the hydrocarbon law and de-Baathification reform.

I was struck by the improvement in the security situation even before the five additional combat brigades arrived. I credit this principally to the population-security campaign, but also to the fact that few mixed neighborhoods had survived the sectarian killings.

Maliki proved to be a strong and evenhanded leader during the surge. While he had sectarian impulses and deep suspicions of the Sunni Arabs, he was willing to keep those tendencies in check when he had confidence in, and was working closely with, the United States. In my time working with Maliki, he came to see both Sunni Arab and Shia Arab extremists as threats and was committed to waging a serious war against both.

More recent events have overshadowed the generally positive nature of Maliki's leadership during this period. The leader I worked with, and who collaborated with Petraeus and my successor, Ambassador Ryan Crocker, was what I call "Maliki I." He distanced himself from the Dawa Party and created a new political movement—State of Law—that he hoped would be cross-sectarian. During the surge, he referred to military actions as "State of Law operations."

In 2007, Maliki's military move to target the Mahdi Army and criminal mafias in Basra—Operation Knight's Charge—was a high point in his evolution as a national leader. This had major reverberations in Iraq. Every group, including the Kurds and Sunni Arabs, said that if Maliki needed additional forces, they would provide them. Maliki also moved against the Mahdi Army in Sadr City.

In the 2010 election, Maliki fielded a State of Law list that included both Shia and Sunni Arabs. Both his group and Allawi's Iraqiyya were cross-sectarian movements, unlike the Shia Islamist bloc that put Maliki into power after the 2005 election. While sectarian identity was still a major factor in Iraqi politics in 2010, there was a decided move toward voting based on issues and leadership. Maliki was also a key part of this evolution. I had hoped that Maliki and Allawi, who finished neck and neck in the voting, would form a grand coalition together with the Kurds, thus grounding the Iraqi government in a centrist, cross-sectarian, and cross-ethnic political alignment.

This was not to be. The tragedy of Iraq, and Maliki as a leader, stemmed from President Obama's decision to withdraw from Iraq, rejecting military recommendations to leave a substantial residual force in the country. As Washington and Baghdad undertook negotiations on the future of U.S. forces in Iraq, Maliki sought a comprehensive strategic partnership with the United States. The Obama administration responded with an offer of a token U.S. force.

Once Maliki concluded that he could not count on the United States, he became what I call Maliki II. Letting his sectarian instincts guide him, he purged opponents. He also threw his lot in with Iran, knowing that Tehran was the only power that could help or hurt him. He replaced qualified military officers in the Iraqi army with political cronies—a gutting of the army's leadership for which Iraq paid when Islamic State fighters went on the offensive in 2014.

Today, there is a mistaken impression that Maliki was a negative political force throughout his tenure. I disagree with this view. It was a tragedy that the United States, by acts of omission and commission, enabled Maliki I to evolve into Maliki II.

I LEFT IRAQ profoundly disappointed over the events of my ambassadorship. I was committed to the mission in Iraq, for the sake of both U.S. interests and Iraq's long-suffering people. I was saddened that my efforts had not proven decisive.

As I look back at the full arc of American involvement in Iraq, a number of lessons stand out in my mind:

Do not assume that local politics will take care of themselves in the aftermath of regime change. A good outcome requires U.S. support in catalyzing and supporting a national compact over the long haul.

Geopolitical vacuums are dangerous things. When the United States intervened in Iraq, it created a vacuum that was filled by bad actors: al Qaeda, Syria, and Iran. These actors, skilled at using violence to polarize society, made everything in Iraq harder by several orders of magnitude.

Foster conditions that bring out the better instincts of local leaders. Good leaders can be found, and leaders with mixed motivations can be persuaded to behave better than they might on their own. This may require sustained U.S. engagement. As the United States disengaged after the surge, Maliki's relapse into sectarianism and authoritarianism was not only foreseeable, it was foreseen. It was also avoidable.

Exercise presidential command. I saw President Bush's evolution as a leader. While I would fault the president for the inadequacy of his deliberations before the invasion, the same cannot be said of his engagement with Iraq policy during my ambassadorship. He asked probing questions about the military situation and weighed more systematically the benefits and risks of alternative courses of action. Careful presidential command proved the decisive factor in the implementation of the surge strategy.

Finally, *pursue political and security efforts in tandem.* The success of the surge has fostered a narrative that security has to come first before political efforts can be effective. I disagree. In fact, I believe that the surge could not have succeeded without the political efforts that came before: the drafting of a constitution, Sunni Arab political participation, the formation of a national unity government, the election of a new prime minister, and outreach to Sunni Arab tribal leaders and reconcilable insurgents. Politics and security advanced together during the surge, allowing Iraqis to rescue themselves from a cauldron of sectarian violence.

TWENTY-FIVE

PERMANENT REPRESENTATIVE TO THE UNITED NATIONS

NEW YORK, 2007–2009

IN LATE 2006, WHEN RICE AND HADLEY INVITED ME TO DINNER AT THE WATERGATE, they asked me what I would like to do if the president decided to appoint a new ambassador to Iraq. I offered my resignation, but Rice said that the president wanted me to stay in the administration until the end.

I was tempted to relay my interest in becoming secretary of state or national security advisor, but I decided that Rice and Hadley would not be particularly receptive.

Instead, we discussed three possibilities.

One option was to serve as a presidential envoy for the entire Middle East. The second option was to become Rice's deputy at the State Department. The third was to take the post of permanent representative to the United Nations.

I drafted a proposal for Rice on the authorities I would need to be given in order to accept the Middle East envoy position. The only way to be effective in the role, I concluded, was for Rice to instruct the regional bureaus to report to me. I never received a clear response from Rice, but I got the sense that she was not amenable to this condition.

Instead, when John Bolton's recess appointment ended, in early January 2007, the president asked me to serve at the United Nations.

My preparations for the United Nations post were different from those I had undertaken for Iraq and Afghanistan. I had little interaction with the president or principals about the substantive agenda that I would pursue. The president reminded me that he had lived in the U.N. permanent representative's residence at the Waldorf Astoria in New York when his father held the position. The beds, he noted, were soft and comfortable, something I needed after roughing it in Afghanistan and Iraq.

While the president was obviously kidding, the residence was, in fact, unique. Most countries own a town house or at least an apartment in New York for their representatives. Oddly, the United States is the only country that does not. Rather, it rents, for the staggering sum of more than $60,000 a month, an apartment on the Waldorf's forty-second floor.

The wasteful spending aside, I had no quarrel with my new home, which represented a welcome upgrade from my last assignments. For my sons, the highlight of New York was the residence staff, especially the housekeeper, Dorothy Burgess, a woman from the Caribbean, and the chef, Stanton Thomas, who, in addition to his acerbic commentaries on world affairs, also taught them to prepare a few dishes guaranteed to impress their dates.

The residence's enormous dining room and equally large living room were reserved for official functions and therefore always had to be immaculate and bare of anything personal. I found that social gatherings could advance our diplomacy in subtle ways and began to host events, including a gigantic Fourth of July party attended by the permanent U.N. representatives.

We added a few events of our own as well.

When my family's favorite artist, Kehinde Wiley, held an exhibit in Harlem, I invited my colleagues to the event, followed by dinner in a local restaurant. Some of the representatives asked me privately if I was sure that the outing would be safe. Through the Art in the Embassy program, we were able to borrow a Kehinde Wiley piece for display in the dining room: a large portrait, in Renaissance style, of an African American athlete. A delegation from the African Union was particularly excited not only by the artist's work, but also by his African first name.

⟵   ⟶

RELATIONS BETWEEN the United States and the United Nations had sunk to new lows over the war in Iraq. Still, I viewed the U.N. as an important institution that could advance U.S. interests.

The key, I thought, was to maintain a realistic understanding of the purpose and structure of that body, how it functioned, and what it could and could not achieve.

My views on the U.N. had been influenced by my experiences as ambassador.

In Afghanistan, I had worked closely with the U.N.'s Brahimi and Arnault. The United Nations not only supported but actively enabled efforts to stabilize Afghanistan and set the country on a path to democracy, all at a time when Washington was still sorting out its longer-term strategy.

The United Nations' unique convening powers, credibility, and field experience in crisis areas were helpful. U.S. cooperation with the U.N. was a concrete example of burden-sharing at a time when the United States was otherwise taking on ever-greater responsibilities.

I was less impressed by the United Nations' work in Iraq. With Brahimi's departure in 2004 as U.N. envoy to Iraq, the United Nations' role, never particularly significant, had declined even further. I worked with Brahimi's successor, Ashraf Qazi, who provided a channel to Sistani, Sadrists, and Sunni leaders with whom the United States did not have direct contact. Qazi was helpful at times, but I had hoped that the United Nations would play a much larger role. The U.N. underperformed in assisting with Sunni-Shia reconciliation, resolution of the various conflicts between Kurdish authorities and the central government, and the integration of Iraq into the region.

— ⟨ ⟩ —

BEFORE MY confirmation hearings, I decided that I would use my time as permanent representative to focus on a few issues. I thought the situations in Afghanistan, Iraq, and Lebanon would benefit from a greater U.N. presence. On nuclear proliferation, I wanted to escalate U.N. pressure on Iran and North Korea. The massive humanitarian crisis in Darfur, I thought, called for U.N. intervention not only to save lives, but also to operationalize the international community's commitment to end genocide. Finally, I wanted to strengthen U.N. capabilities for peacekeeping operations.

In my confirmation hearings, I told the Senate how I intended to pursue these priorities. One of my ideas was to strengthen the U.N.'s caucus of democratic countries. The Non-Aligned Movement and the Group of 77—organizations composed of mostly developing countries—were driven by parochial views and an instinctive antagonism toward Israel and the West. It would take time for democracies from the global north and south to cooperate, and while I did not expect to turn the democracy caucus into a voting bloc that could undercut the NAM/G-77, I did hope to nurture it into an influential group down the road.

The presence of senior diplomats from around the world presented an opportunity to engage with my foreign conterparts on a broad scale. It was common to have two dinners on the same night, forcing me, as I used to joke, to sacrifice my waistline for my country. I saw them not as tedious duties to be tolerated but, rather, as opportunities to form friendships and establish rapport.

Still, I was under no illusions about the institution as a whole. It needed deep reform.

◄   ►

THE UNITED NATIONS IS structured like a small legislature but operates like a three-dimensional chessboard. At times, it feels like a bazaar. The degree to which countries' representatives to the U.N. have freedom of action varies. Some can make decisions; others are only mouthpieces for orders from back home. The intensity of national interests on particular questions varies. Group dynamics—manipulated by the more influential or ideologically committed states—are important. Bartering matters as well. States might vote a certain way on an issue on which they are ambivalent with the expectation of eliciting favors down the line.

I liked and respected Secretary General Ban Ki-moon, and we worked well together. A South Korean, Ban had witnessed his country's transformation from a war-torn, impoverished state to a vibrant, dynamic Asian democracy. He understood that without the U.S. security umbrella in Asia, this would never have happened.

Ban was well aware of the importance of the United States to the United Nations system. The tact and subtlety with which Ban managed the myriad stakeholders at the U.N. left some with the impression that he was too restrained; they were more accustomed to the flamboyant Kofi Annan. But I found Ban to be balanced, realistic, and quite effective. He cared deeply about climate change but knew that one could not advance a positive agenda by bulldozing or speechifying about it.

The power structure at the U.N. has its own internal logic. Nothing happens in the Security Council without the agreement of the five permanent Security Council members (the P5). Negotiations among the P5 have a certain predictability.

For Russia, the Security Council is an important part of its broader geopolitical strategy. Russia's assertive role in the Security Council reflects nostalgia for the days when it was a superpower. U.S. interest in an issue is a signal to Russia that Moscow, too, should be involved, constructively or not.

China views the United Nations as a vehicle for facilitating its rise as a global power. I would needle my Chinese colleagues, who tended to downplay their national ambitions, by joking that long into the future, the United States and China would become the "P2." For the most part, China exercises its power selectively, focusing on its interests in Asia and in resource-rich areas of Africa.

Britain and France have to navigate a tricky road. Their status as permanent members puts them in the same league as China, Russia, and the United States—flattering, perhaps, but increasingly an anachronism. They have tacitly redefined their role, seeking to represent European interests more generally. They also try to act as mediators and bridge-builders for the United States, Russia, and China. They usually vote in concord but have different concerns and diplomatic cultures. Nationalistic France demands to be seen as an independent actor, which makes it unpredictable. Sometimes France flaunts its disagreements with the United States. A moment later, France will champion some shared cause with dramatic flair. The United Kingdom emphasizes its "special relationship" with the United States. At times, I found this attitude to be patronizing, as though the British were the brains behind the operation and we Yankees were just the muscle acting on London's guidance. On occasion, they could be less than forthright. It helped that my British counterpart, John Sawers, and his wife, Shelley, were an engaging couple who became good friends.

MOST OF MY WORK centered on the Security Council, but the General Assembly had independent powers when it came to U.N. reform, the budget, and human rights. The General Assembly president is elected on an annual term from a regional rotation and has the authority to establish ad hoc working groups. I worked with two presidents of the General Assembly. I had a good relationship with former Macedonian foreign minister Serjan Kerim. His successor, former foreign minister of Nicaragua Migel d'Escoto Brockmann, was more difficult. A onetime foreign minister of the Sandinistas, d'Escoto's views had moderated over the years, but his fiery rhetoric against the United States had not. Within days of assuming the General Assembly presidency, d'Escoto lashed out against the United States. Having made headlines a few years earlier for calling President Reagan a "butcher," d'Escoto labeled President Bush as Reagan's "spiritual heir" and blamed him for making the world "far less safe and secure than it has ever been."

My dealings with d'Escoto were eased by an unusual coincidence. On her father's side, Cheryl can claim Nicaraguan ancestry. The Benard family has historically played a prominent role in the country's politics. They helped build the national railroad and championed the idea of a Nicaragua Canal, which lost out to the Panama Canal. Cheryl presented d'Escoto with a dove of peace she had made herself. He displayed this gift in his office.

Over time, he became more receptive to my argument that, as the General Assembly president, he should act as a bridge between members.

⎯⎯⎯   ⎯⎯⎯

TO PREVAIL in the General Assembly, it was necessary to work a complex system of voting blocs, regional groupings, pivot states, and personalities. Many of the groups were semi-anachronistic or were driven by material concerns cloaked in moralistic ideology. They advocated policies to transfer resources from Western, developed states to themselves. Anti-Zionism and anti-Americanism were rallying cries that served to drown out substantive, fact-based discussion.

The other influential blocs were organized by region. The NAM/G-77 was most important. The regional groups echoed the views of regional organizations outside the United Nations to varying degrees. The Arab Group could usually count on the NAM/G-77 on Middle East issues, and the Africa Group could do so on development and climate change. The positions of the African Union were virtually identical to those of the Africa Group. The Organization of the Islamic Conference, however, had mixed success in pressing its positions through the Arab or Asia-Pacific Groups, given that their memberships did not entirely overlap.

The voting blocs knew that their influence depended on cohesion and consensus, which created opportunities for intransigent or dominant countries to play outsized roles. Often, extreme positions advanced by more radical members emerged as the group's shared position. Cuba's role in the NAM/G-77 was the most striking case of this dynamic. Most countries went along with the group's leadership, effectively giving the leadership a proxy to decide issues on their behalf. When I would confront permanent representatives about why their countries had supported a particular position, they would often throw up their hands in resignation and say they had no choice but to go along with the group.

Each bloc had its dominant members, but the sources of their influence varied. In the cases of Brazil, Japan, Germany, Mexico, South Africa, and Egypt, it was their geopolitical power. However, geopolitical power was not enough to guarantee influence at the United Nations. Nigeria, for example, rarely played a leadership role. Countries such as Indonesia generated influence through their effectiveness in resolving problems. Other countries benefited from having unusually effective permanent representatives.

Munir Akram of Pakistan was among my most difficult interlocutors. He was openly anti-American, and I knew he could deliver on his threats to galvanize other countries behind him. When the Pakistan People's Party prevailed in the 2008 general elections, I used my long-standing friendships in the party to lobby for a friendlier permanent representative.

Fortunately there were also individuals whom I used to call good United Nations corporate citizens. Some of the smallest states could wield great influence in this respect. Lichtenstein was a leader on United Nations reform. San Marino's permanent representative, over his luncheon table or at the golf course, had tremendous success as a convening power. I worked particularly hard at building relationships with the more capable and constructive permanent representatives.

BEFORE I STARTED my posting, George H. W. Bush invited me to Kennebunkport to offer some advice. Reflecting on his own time as permanent representative, he urged me not to underestimate the importance of small gestures. It was important, he said, to show respect for all countries, regardless of their size and importance. One should go to their national days and visit their missions. This squared with my own intuition.

I made an effort to meet and engage respectfully with emissaries, whether or not they were from large or friendly states. I understood that on particularly divisive issues, the permanent representative was often on a tight leash from the government back home. Individually, though, their travel and constant interactions with people from all over the world tended to moderate their outlooks. Insofar as engagement could yield results, permanent representatives were among the most likely members of adversarial regimes to communicate our interests reliably and objectively within their systems.

GIVEN THE OUTSIZED role that the Security Council gave to Russia, I knew it would be critical to establish a productive relationship with my Russian counterpart, Vitaly Churkin. He had served as the permanent representative for eight years, far longer than any of the other P5 representatives. A former child actor who had played a role in a film about Lenin's youth, Churkin was a mentee of the hard-line Russian foreign minister Sergei Lavrov, who himself had served as United Nations permanent representative for a decade.

My tenure at the United Nations coincided with a series of aggressive steps by Russia. In fact, the first major conflict with which I dealt involved a

U.S.-Russia clash over Kosovo. The United States and Europe sympathized with Kosovo's drive for independence from Serbia. While we hoped that both Kosovo and Serbia, as separate countries, could modernize, democratize, and eventually join the European Union, Russia feared that an independent Kosovo would weaken Serbia and ally with the West.

Churkin pushed for a United Nations fact-finding mission to the region. He believed that once international observers saw realities on the ground, they would change their views on the independence question. The fact-finding mission backfired for the Russians. After touring the region and meeting with NATO officials, my colleagues and I concluded that local circumstances favored Kosovo's independence. I was amazed by the progress Kosovars had made in establishing institutions after the devastating war in the 1990s. I was struck by the fact that Kosovo had myriad ethnic groups—including a thriving Egyptian Albanian diaspora—and nearly all favored independence. Kosovo's president, Fatmir Sejdiu, was a promising leader. And the planning at NATO for how to facilitate independence in a stable way was impressive.

China, while concerned that Kosovo's independence could create a precedent for the national aspirations of Taiwan and Tibet, ultimately decided that this was a European matter and agreed to stay out of the fray.

There was no scenario in which Russia would acquiesce to Kosovo's independence, so the United States and its European allies on the Security Council faced two challenges. First, we needed to persuade Secretary General Ban Ki-moon not to stand in the way in the event that Kosovo declared independence. Second, we needed to ensure that the Security Council would not block Kosovo's move for independence.

On May 11, we introduced a resolution endorsing United Nations mediator Martti Ahtisaari's plan for Kosovo's supervised independence. I proposed various ideas to address Russian concerns related to the Serb minority in Kosovo. Churkin remained unmoved. We decided to postpone a vote on the Kosovo resolution until after the G-8 summit in June, where Rice and Lavrov were scheduled to meet. When Rice and Lavrov were unable to reach a deal, it was back to the drawing board.

By mid-July, it was clear that Churkin would not budge. This left me with two options. One was to push the issue to the brink and force a Russian veto. This would demonstrate to the world that Russia was responsible for obstructing progress on Kosovo.

Ban preferred the second possibility. So long as there was a deadlock, the United States, Britain, France, and he himself could use the United Nations Interim Administration Mission in Kosovo (UNMIK) to lay the groundwork for independence. Ban was willing to instruct UNMIK to devolve authorities away from the United Nations to the Kosovars with an eye toward self-rule for the region. This struck me as a sensible plan. When talks with the Russians eventually collapsed, Ban's approach facilitated Kosovo's independence in February 2008.

In the weeks that followed, I would find myself randomly having my hand pumped in ecstatic gratitude by elevator operators, taxi drivers, and people on the street—Kosovars living in New York.

WE ALSO ACHIEVED an early success in reforming the United Nations due to an issue involving North Korea. My deputy, Mark Wallace, presented evidence to me that the United Nations Development Program (UNDP) was skirting international restrictions on North Korea, even to the point of hiding evidence that Pyongyang was producing counterfeit currency. This was a genuine scandal—Cash for Kim, as it became known. UNDP officials denied U.S. allegations and threatened "retaliation" against the State Department. Reports by the *Wall Street Journal* and the *New York Times* drew further attention to the scandal. Representative Ileana Ros-Lehtinen introduced legislation to limit United Nations funding, and the House passed a resolution criticizing the Security Council.

That was all well and good, but the attacks soon focused on Ban, who, in fact, was making a sincere effort to investigate the matter and who was a determined proponent of United Nations reform. When the United Nations Ethics Office found that UNDP higher-ups had retaliated against the whistleblower who had disclosed the scandal, Ban swiftly took action.

I felt that the process was playing out appropriately and was concerned that inflammatory press leaks by American officials would backfire. When I asked Wallace to stop irking the UNDP through further leaks, I was surprised to see the conservative press turn on me. The *National Review* editorial board, in an article entitled "He's No Bolton," alleged, falsely, that I was trying to "rein Wallace in" and "help the UNDP make the scandal go away." Benny Avni at the *New York Sun* accused me of "unilateral disarmament."

Eventually, thanks in large part to Ban's cooperation, the entire UNDP program in North Korea was suspended pending the results of the United Nations investigation. UNDP ultimately tightened its oversight of UNDP-funded projects around the world.

MY EFFORTS TO implement deeper reforms in the United Nations were less successful. In any discussion on United Nations reform, debates would arise over the Security Council's composition. India, Japan, Brazil, South Africa, and Egypt, among others, were pushing for reform of the Security Council, arguing that the Council's existing membership did not reflect power realities in the world. Each believed that it should become a permanent member.

I reminded them that any plans for expanding the Security Council required the U.S. Senate to modify the United Nations treaty, which required a two-thirds majority vote. The way to sell Security Council reform to the United States, I advised, was to build it into a larger deal involving reform of the United Nations as a whole. As a starting point, I raised an issue that virtually everyone recognized: the United Nations' excessive, ballooning, and often senseless mandates. Mandates generally required the U.N. to assign and fund groups that research and report on various issues. Once launched, mandates lived on forever, often long past any reasonable shelf life. Some mandates merely created a pretext for experts to convene annually and, at the end of their meeting, crank out a carbon copy of the prior year's report.

When I proposed liquidating some mandates, the Middle East states immediately protested. Ever suspicious of U.S. motives, they assumed that this was a ruse to eliminate the Palestinian mandates—which, it is true, were perennial targets of Israel and its supporters in the United States. I suggested that we explicitly exclude the Palestine-related mandates from consideration.

That took care of one set of critics, but others alleged that the United States was only eliminating mandates so it could channel freed-up funds toward its own priorities. I promised that any savings derived from eliminating mandates would be transferred toward United Nations economic and development programs aimed at the poorest countries.

I agreed to allow the NAM/G-77 to identify which mandates we should review first. I expected no pushback if we started with the Economic Commission for Europe (ECE), which was not only spending United Nations funds on one of the wealthiest regions of the world but was duplicating tasks being performed by the European Union. Still, the NAM/G-77 saw the review process as a potential threat to their interests, even if they agreed with my view of the ECE. And my European colleagues, who were allies on the reform front, lost their enthusiasm when they saw that the ECE was at risk.

While the exercise over mandates did temporarily give the United States the moral high ground in the reform debate, it was an overall failure.

—◄   ►—

BY THE TIME I assumed the Security Council presidency, in May 2007, the ongoing crisis in Lebanon was flaring up again. A few months earlier, the Lebanese opposition, comprised mostly of Hezbollah and pro-Assad parties, had taken to the streets. The immediate catalyst for the protest was the United Nations special tribunal to investigate the assassination of former prime minister Rafiq Hariri. For the Hariri tribunal to proceed with its investigation, the Security Council needed to establish the court directly under its Chapter VII authority.

Some argued that a United Nations investigation would destabilize an already volatile situation in Lebanon, but I was persuaded of the need to proceed with the tribunal. The Christian and Sunni elements of the fractured Lebanese government were determined to respond to Hariri's murder but were powerless to do so. I did not see how, without outside help, they would overcome divisions in the country and the constellation of forces backed by Hezbollah and Syria. After some initial reluctance, Lebanese Prime Minister Fouad Siniora, as well as Saad Hariri, Rafiq's son, who had taken over the reformist March 14 Alliance led by his father, concluded that the only way to launch a serious investigation and bring the culprits (almost certainly Hezbollah and/or Syrian assailants) to justice was by internationalizing the matter.

My French counterparts were particularly supportive of the Hariri tribunal. Saudi Arabia, Egypt, and a number of other Arab countries were also sympathetic, given their relationships with Hariri and their support for Lebanon's Sunnis.

Russia was the biggest obstacle. Churkin argued that the tribunal would exacerbate divisions within Lebanon. This concern, while reasonable, was a pretext for Moscow's real concern: the fate of Syrian leader Bashar al-Assad, Russia's only ally in the region.

I suggested to Churkin that doubling down behind Syria would be costly for Russia. Moscow would effectively stand in front of the world as the only obstacle to justice in a crime that clearly violated international law.

To their credit, the Russians decided not to stand in the way of the tribunal.

⟨ ⟩

AS I SETTLED into New York, my colleagues in the Security Council, time and again, accused the Bush administration of disrespecting and disliking the United Nations. When my protestations to the contrary failed to persuade anyone, I made them an offer. I would take them to see President Bush so that they could judge for themselves. The president agreed to invite all of the permanent representatives on the Security Council. We scheduled the trip for June 2008.

"Prepare your toughest questions," I instructed. "Don't hold back!"

Once in the White House, the group found itself totally disarmed by the president's charm and willingness to engage. President Bush mentioned the substantive phone call he had had with Russian president Vladimir Putin earlier in the month. I got the impression that Churkin had not been aware of this phone call, which seemed to take the wind out of his sails.

"What happened?" I needled them afterward. "I was expecting a confrontation with the president!" Partly, I think, they were being courteous diplomats. But several of them conceded afterward that they had given too much credence to press stereotypes about the president.

PRESIDENT BUSH, all in all, was more pragmatic than ideological in his approach to the United Nations. One issue, however, particularly grated on him: the United Nations' failure to take action against the genocide in Darfur.

President Bush brought a singular determination to the issue, even when his senior advisors showed little interest. A week before I started work in New York, he asked me to join him at his speech at the Holocaust Museum in Washington, where he invoked the genocidal policies of the Nazi regime as part of his plea for action in Darfur. The president outlined a comprehensive strategy, promising Security Council sanctions and an expanded arms embargo if Sudanese president Omar al-Bashir continued to defy the international community.

The greatest roadblock to United Nations action on Darfur was China. My Chinese counterpart, Wang Guangya, was soft-spoken and genuinely congenial. Wang had studied in the U.K. and at the John Hopkins School for Advanced International Studies. He picked his battles carefully and engaged mainly where Chinese interests were directly in play. Unfortunately, Sudan was one of them. In addition to China's traditional reluctance to support Western humanitarian interventions—especially those that could legitimate the Responsibility to Protect doctrine—Beijing was loath to impose sanctions on an oil-exporting state with which it maintained friendly relations.

By late May, President Bush had decided that Bashir was not serious about cooperating with the United Nations. On the advice of the Pentagon, he decided not to take unilateral military action against Sudan or even to enforce a no-fly zone to prevent Khartoum from using its airpower. I would have advocated such measures, but I was not consulted. Instead, he announced that the United States would pursue a new Security Council resolution to apply further sanctions, impose an expanded arms embargo, and push for African Union peacekeepers.

In our private discussions, Wang revealed that his main concern was protecting China's preferential oil agreements with Khartoum. Since the oil fields were in South Sudan, Beijing favored an intervention that would prevent the Darfur conflict from spilling across the country without threatening the Bashir regime's hold on power.

The idea of a joint African Union–United Nations peacekeeping force had come up before. Bolton had pressed hard for a United Nations peacekeeping force but had opposed a "joint command" arrangement, which reminded him of the "mushy formulation" that led to the 1993 tragedy in Somalia. Rumsfeld agreed with him. At this point, however, it was clear to me that we had pushed the United Nations process as far as it would go. Since the president had ruled out military action, a hybrid force was the best deal we could expect. On July 31, the Security Council unanimously adopted Resolution 1769, authorizing a 26,000-strong hybrid force.

Unfortunately, this force did not have a big impact. By the time the United Nations–African Union Mission in Darfur (UNAMID) deployed, most of the killings and displacements had already occurred. Where the attacks by the Janjaweed fighters continued, UNAMID was incapable of protecting civilians, given its weak mandate and inability to disarm militias.

I strongly believe that the Responsibility to Protect doctrine deserves the support of the United States and the international community. The spotlight on Darfur is a testament to the efforts of the NGOs, faith-based organizations, and other human rights groups that brought the issue to the fore, but it also illustrates how difficult this principle of protection is to implement.

MEANWHILE, TROUBLE WAS brewing on the Iran nuclear front. By the summer of 2007, intelligence estimates had shown that Iran could have 3,000 centrifuges operating by the end of the year.

The nuclear issue took another turn in November 2007, when the intelligence community released its National Intelligence Estimate (NIE) on Iran's nuclear program. The report stated in part, "We judge with high confidence that in fall 2003, Tehran halted its nuclear weapons program." I remember remarking to my staff that we had scored a goal against ourselves. The fine print of the NIE indicated that the weaponization program had been halted, but that Iran was continuing its enrichment activities. As I knew from my days as a proliferation scholar, enrichment was the long pole in the tent—the hardest task in building a uranium-fueled bomb. Yet the NIE, which suggested that Iran had desisted from its pursuit of nuclear weapons, had made my job at the Security Council considerably more difficult.

In this context, I received an invitation to speak at the World Economic Forum. My comments on U.S. policy were entirely unremarkable. To my surprise, however, I was soon facing a firestorm of controversy. The reason was that the Iranian foreign minister, Manouchehr Mottaki, was part of the same forum.

Should I have stomped away when the organizers seated him on the same platform?

The United States and Iran participated in the same public forums all the time at the United Nations. And I met with Iranian counterparts informally from time to time, as when Kissinger invited me and Zarif to his apartment for lunch.

According to press reports, however, senior White House and State Department officials were furious at me for "freelancing."

Rice summoned me to discuss the issue. The press reported that she was going to scold me for the incident. Perhaps she wanted to create that impression. In fact, though, she was not upset at all, but merely asked that I keep her informed whenever I was scheduled to speak in the vicinity of Iranian diplomats. She added that some White House officials were simply disgruntled by her increasingly conciliatory Iran policy and were taking it out on me. "Don't worry," she advised, "about people who don't know how the world works."

I continued to press for tougher sanctions on Iran. Russia, China, and Europe predictably diluted what the United States sought. Wang agreed to go along with a broad array of restrictions so long as they did not touch Iranian oil. Long conversations with Churkin brought Russia's views to the surface: Moscow genuinely felt threatened by the prospect of a nuclear Iran but also did not want relations to be normalized between Iran and the West, which would lead Iran to turn away from Russia. So the ideal for Russia was a state of hostility between Iran and the West, short of war, along with a set of constraints against Iran's nuclear weapon. The Europeans were prepared to confront Iran so long as they could protect their own economic interests. They would gladly sanction economic transactions that disproportionately affected the United States.

Unlike other resolutions, drafts of Iran-related resolutions were shared with the remaining Security Council members only after the P5+1 had reached a general agreement. This frustrated the elected members, who knew from press reports that a resolution was being negotiated but were effectively sidelined until the very end. Typically, though, elected members understood the importance of the issue and agreed to adopt the P5+1 text with no more than minor adjustments. But on the latest Iran resolution, three states were holding out: Indonesia, Libya, and South Africa.

Indonesian representative Marty Natalegawa was reluctant to impose sanctions against fellow Muslims. Libya's Giadalla Azzuz Belgassem Ettalhi, a longtime minister in the Qaddafi regime, remembered his own battles with the Security Council over weapons of mass destruction and was uneasy about the escalatory nature of the council's approach to Iran. South Africa's

Dumisani Kumalo argued that all countries had a right to enrich uranium and develop a nuclear program for "peaceful uses."

France offered to take the lead in bringing South Africa and Libya on board. When French representative Jean-Maurice Ripert could not persuade his counterparts, he personally flew to the capitals of South Africa and Libya, parked himself there, and refused to leave until the heads of state agreed to vote in favor of the resolution.

I was to take the lead on persuading Indonesia. In private, Natalegawa offered no substantive disagreement with my points. The issue, he confided, was about domestic politics in Indonesia, where Iran was popular. Rice tried to call Indonesian prime minister Susilo Bambang Yudhoyono, the country's first head of government to come to power through direct elections. He refused to accept the phone call, and Indonesia ultimately abstained.

On March 3, the Security Council voted 14–0–1 in favor of Resolution 1803. It was, on the whole, a tactical victory for the international community but a strategic victory for Iran. Tehran bought time for its nuclear program and exposed how little appetite there was for even modest sanctions.

A CONSTANT DILEMMA I faced in the Security Council was whether the United States should veto problematic resolutions or try for compromises. I would typically receive conflicting advice. Hard-liners preferred to demonstrate U.S. resolve through generous use of its veto power. More conciliatory voices argued that this was a bad precedent because it undermined the spirit of cooperation that we needed in return. The debate was particularly salient on issues involving Israel, where the inordinate number of anti-Israel resolutions regularly forced American vetoes.

In January 2008, after an escalation in rocket attacks from Gaza, Israel moved to seal the border completely. The Security Council convened an emergency meeting. The Europeans tried to bridge the gap between the United States and the Arabs, but their efforts amounted to a statement of moral equivalency between Hamas's aggression and Israel's defensive response. I was prepared to use a veto if necessary, but a 14–1 vote against the United States at the Security Council was hardly desirable.

As the sole Arab state on the Security Council, Libya pursued a one-sided resolution calling for an immediate cessation of Israeli military operations. The Libyan resolution gained the support of all of the other Security Council members.

To make matters worse, the resolution became a campaign issue. Both Senators Obama and John McCain sent me letters requesting that any Gaza resolution not be biased against Israel.

Could the situation be deescalated without a veto?

I announced that we would support the Libyan resolution on one condition: that it included a reference to the cessation of "terrorist rocket attacks" from Gaza. This seemingly minor edit won the approval of every Security Council member except one: Libya.

Already reluctant to criticize Hamas, the Arabs instantly recognized the damage that would be done if they agreed to a Security Council resolution that characterized the rocket attacks as "terrorism." Libya withdrew the resolution without a vote.

Ultimately, throughout my tenure at the United Nations, I never had to use the U.S. veto to defend our interests.

◄ ►

ON MARCH 29, 2008, Zimbabwe held general elections. Violence erupted as it became clear that Robert Mugabe's challenger, Morgan Tsvangirai, may have prevailed. Assistant Secretary of State for African Affairs Jendayi Frazer called on Mugabe to step down.

On April 29, the Security Council convened a special session on Zimbabwe. Russia and China declared that sanctions were off the table. The pressure was now on South Africa, which enjoyed the greatest influence over the Mugabe regime. No amount of intransigence by the Mugabe regime persuaded South Africa to support Security Council action.

Inaction at the United Nations prompted the G-8 to convene in July 2008, where heads of state agreed to a text calling for sanctions against the Mugabe regime. I introduced a resolution to impose an arms embargo and targeted sanctions against the regime's senior members.

Russia and China again promised to veto the sanctions resolution. Given his anti-Western and anticolonial ideology, Mugabe was a more favorable partner for them than Tsvangirai, who was eager to integrate Zimbabwe into the international community.

I made a promise to Churkin and Wang: "Now that you have blocked Security Council action, Zimbabwe is on your head. You will have to explain how you're going to fix this situation. And I'm going to raise the matter every two weeks in front of the Council. I will remind the world what the veto of Russia and China has produced and what it hasn't produced for the people of Zimbabwe."

Most appalling to me was the conduct of South Africa's representative, Dumisani Kumalo, at the Security Council. In the 1970s, Kumalo had been forced to flee South Africa due to his activism against apartheid. He had received asylum in the United States and led a long campaign for United Nations sanctions against the South African regime.

I warned Kumalo that South African president Thabo Mbeki's mediation efforts were doomed and that the crisis would deteriorate without Security Council action. Kumalo responded that Zimbabweans should resolve the issue on their own.

"If it weren't for sanctions," I reminded him, "you wouldn't be sitting here and South Africa would not be the country it is." As for his clichés about respect for Zimbabwe's sovereignty, I reminded Kumalo that his country's policies were making the people of Zimbabwe dependent on international handouts. The European Union, United States, and U.K. at the time were providing upward of 50 percent of Zimbabwe's basic foodstuffs through the United Nations and NGOs.

None of my arguments made a difference.

Whenever I subsequently spoke out about the crisis, my African allies privately praised me. My tough words gave them greater leeway to criticize South Africa's cynical approach. Indeed, the one consistent request I received from dissidents and human rights activists was to keep making public statements, which let both Mugabe and reformers on the ground know that someone was paying attention.

Peter Godwin, in his book *The Fear*, argues that U.S. pressure on Mugabe during this period made Mugabe realize that his regime was not secure. Within a few months, Mugabe had broadened the base of his government and entered into a power-sharing agreement with Tsvangirai. It wasn't the outcome I would have liked. Genuine change, I knew, could not occur until Mugabe and his regime were out. But it was the best we could do under the circumstances.

◄   ►

IN THE SUMMER OF 2008, Russian tanks moved into Georgia.

I first sensed that there was trouble in August 2007, when Georgia's permanent representative, Irakli Alasania, came to see me. Alasania's father, a general in the Georgian army, had died in Abkhazia at the hands of rebel forces when his son was still a child. Since 2004 Alasania had engaged closely in the issue of Abkhazia, a part of Georgia controlled by Russian forces. Georgian President Mikheil Saakashvili had appointed him chairman of the Abkhazian government-in-exile and then assigned him to handle Georgian-Abkhaz peace talks.

Alasania briefed me on a Russian missile attack and asked for an emergency meeting of the Security Council. I supported that request, but others on the Security Council wanted to wait. Looking back, I wish we had taken greater steps at this stage to deter Russian aggression. I could have pressed for an expanded United Nations mission on the ground, perhaps, or taken steps to internationalize the conflict in Abkhazia and South Ossetia under the United Nations, as had been done in Kosovo in the 1990s.

On August 7, 2008, the Russian military moved tanks into Georgia. The Security Council convened an emergency session, but three days of intense negotiations produced no resolution. On August 11, a shocked Rice called me with a readout of her phone call with Lavrov. The Russian foreign minister had proposed a secret deal between Russia and the United States. Lavrov's key demand was simple: "Saakashvili must go." Rice refused and vowed to inform the world that the Russian foreign minister had secretly demanded the overthrow of a democratically elected president.

I revealed to the Security Council what Rice had told me, calling the Russian demand "totally unacceptable."

Churkin admitted that Lavrov and Rice had had a "confidential phone call" and proceeded, indirectly, to confirm my accusation: "Regime change is an American expression. But sometimes there are occasions, and we know from history, that there are different leaders who come to power, either democratically or semi-democratically, and they become an obstacle."

Churkin and I had dealt squarely with each other over the past year. This time, however, Churkin was unapproachable. He viewed Rice's decision to leak the phone call with Lavrov as an unforgivable breach of trust.

There was sympathy at the Security Council for Russia's position on Georgia, but Lavrov's attempt to secretly oust Saakashvili was a step too far. China sent a resounding signal through its decision to abstain rather than join Russia's veto of the Georgia resolution.

The pressure was clearly getting to Churkin. Our exchanges in the Security Council were becoming acrimonious to the point that Churkin accused me of engaging in "Trotskyite diplomacy."

Cheryl became alarmed that things were starting to get personal and suggested a "time-out." She called Churkin's wife, Irina, and invited her and her husband over for tea. The Churkins told us that they had spent their honeymoon in Georgia. They reminisced about the beautiful natural settings, the wonderful food, and the friendly people there. In each little village they hiked to, locals, upon learning that they had newlyweds as guests, produced bottles of champagne and toasted the young couple. It was a nice break, but I'm afraid it did not bridge our differences at the council.

At a United Nations General Assembly meeting a month later, Rice and Lavrov met for the first time since the Georgia crisis. They agreed to push for a new resolution on Iran to demonstrate that differences over Georgia would not affect U.S.-Russia cooperation on Iran's nuclear program. In selling the resolution at the Security Council, I had no better ally than Iranian president

Mahmoud Ahmedinejad. Thanks to his over-the-top speech at the General Assembly, even Indonesia supported Resolution 1835.

—◄ ►—

IN THE YEARS AHEAD, I expect little fundamental change in the United Nations or its role in the world. Despite its many problems, the Security Council is still the world's most prestigious and weighty international institution. But I do not anticipate that Security Council reform will become a priority.

It is possible that the United States will agree to enlarge the Security Council and even add new permanent members. But I would be surprised if the United States allowed new members to hold veto rights, which would diminish the Security Council's ability to function.

The Chinese want to appear supportive of the NAM/G-77 desire to add as many members from their ranks to the council as possible, but also worry about the prospect of historic regional rivals, namely Japan and India, becoming permanent members. Because China is confident of its place in the P5, it is showing some readiness to accept reform.

The Russians are firmly against diluting current veto authority. They oppose any diminished role for the Security Council and are concerned that rising powers will challenge their special position in the United Nations.

The United Kingdom and France are conflicted. They, too, understand the argument that their own place on the P5 is anachronistic. Within the European Union, Germany has growing reason to question why only France and the United Kingdom should be entitled to permanent seats. The consolidating of their seats into one European Union seat with rotating representation is a possibility—one I would favor as part of a deal to ensure greater representation for Asia.

On the whole, I remain pessimistic about the prospects for wider reform at the U.N.

The current financing structure illustrates the fundamental dilemma facing reformers. In 2013, seventeen countries (representing less than 9 percent of the total membership) paid over 80 percent of the U.N. budget. The remaining 176 contributed the rest of the budget yet could easily decide how and on what initiatives to spend those funds. Those with the highest financial stake in sound management and operational efficiency have limited leverage beyond cutting off funding—a problematic scenario.

Increasingly, principal donors are concluding that there are better alternatives to the excesses, mismanagement, and ineffectiveness of the United Nations. I believe that the trend will continue toward investing in voluntary contributions for specific programs or channeling development assistance through national, regional, or other channels rather than U.N. agencies like the UNDP.

──◄   ►──

TOWARD THE END of my time at the U.N., some of the fiercest debates I encountered were over the dinner table at home. Cheryl was rooting for Hillary Clinton in the Democratic presidential primaries. Max was a fierce proponent of Obama. Alex and I supported McCain. I joked that my wisest course was to remain neutral.

The election of Obama stunned my fellow diplomats at the U.N. How could an African American with the middle name of *Hussein* prevail in a general election?

"Maybe," I would respond, "America is an exceptional nation after all."

PART III

AMERICA IN THE WORLD

TWENTY-SIX

A MORE DANGEROUS WORLD

2016 AND BEYOND

THE WORLD WAS A DIFFERENT PLACE IN 1992, WHEN I WAS ASSESSING U.S. STRAT-egy as a Pentagon planner—one that seemed very favorable to the United States. The Gulf War victory infused our leaders with self-confidence after a long period of self-doubt following the Vietnam War. More importantly, the bipolar system of the Cold War ended with the disintegration of the Soviet Union and the utter discrediting of Communist ideology.

I was even relatively optimistic about the Middle East. I did not think that Iran, which had just emerged from the Iran-Iraq war with a devastated military and economy, was in any position to exploit the Iraqi defeat in the Gulf War. Al Qaeda had been formed, but Osama bin Laden had not yet de-clared jihad against the United States.

Nearly a quarter century later, global trends are exacerbating threats that the United States is not well positioned to address. Among the most signifi-cant are the collapse of order in many developing countries; the rise of terror-ism and extremism; Europe's triple crises of a loss of confidence in Brussels, threats from Putin's Russia, and the conflicts of the greater Middle East; and the Chinese push for regional hegemony.

WHY HAVE global politics shifted in such problematic ways?

It would be a mistake, in my view, to put undue emphasis on U.S. policy. The processes set in motion after the Cold War—such as the spread of democracy, market economies, and globalization—were probably bound to narrow the gap between the United States and others. Still, I believe that avoidable U.S. errors contributed to the unfavorable trend lines we now face.

One is the decline in U.S. military power relative to other powers—and therefore the decline in our capacity to deter dangerous actors. The 1992 Defense Policy Guidance implied that the United States should maintain such overwhelming military capability that others would be deterred from even attempting to achieve parity with it. Today, although the U.S. military still enjoys technological superiority and, in absolute terms, is far more integrated and capable than it was in 1992, it has declined in relative terms.

I do not believe that the United States presently is overextended as a world power; but it will become so if it maintains its current world role without the economy returning to trend-line growth. Even during the heights of the Afghanistan and Iraq wars, the United States was able to meet its global obligations. I am concerned, though, that either overextension or too dramatic a retrenchment from the world will become a real threat if we do not get our economic house in order.

We face a broader internal issue: the failure of the United States to achieve bipartisan consensus behind a grand strategy after containment. We are missing a clear sense of priorities and an understanding of which goals merit what level of investment. The result has been great exertions when crises erupt, followed by impatience and hasty disengagement.

While I am an optimist by nature, I fear that it would not take much to unleash a catastrophic series of events. As difficult as the world is today, it could get much worse if the United States retreats.

The United States protects access to the Persian Gulf, holding the line against a regional conflagration that would instigate an oil price shock. The ill-considered disengagement from Iraq, the resulting rise of ISIS, and the conflict in Syria offer a taste of what would happen amid a further U.S. withdrawal. Already regional powers were doubling down behind their proxies in the Iraqi and Syrian civil wars, but the assertion of Russian power has made these wars even more dangerous. Moscow has returned as a significant player in the geopolitics of the region—a factor that, until now, had been absent since the Cold War. Other great powers, particularly China and the Europeans, are also becoming more involved in the Middle East, which points to the beginning of a chaotic multipolar trend in the face of American retrenchment.

Confidence in the U.S. to manage regional security has declined. Some are hedging by building relations with rivals, including China and Russia. However, I do not see how the United States could avoid defending a narrow set of interests. For example, if sectarian war were to spread to the Shia areas of eastern Saudi Arabia, where ten million barrels of oil are produced every day, we could not remain uninvolved. Facing the prospect of a major recession at home from disruptions in global energy markets, I believe that any president would undertake a large-scale U.S. intervention in defense of Saudi Arabia, much like in Desert Shield.

Conflict between Saudi Arabia and Iran would disrupt global energy markets. Without a stabilizing American presence, oil shipments would shut down. A similar scenario played out during the 1987 "tanker war" of the Iran-Iraq war, which, incidentally, escalated into a direct military conflict between the United States and Iran.

Iran's nuclear program makes these scenarios even more dangerous. I do not have much confidence in a nuclear deal that restricts Iran's activities only for a few years. I doubt that other actors would show restraint in the event that Iran is allowed to restart large-scale enrichment or rushes to produce a nuclear bomb.

The Obama administration calculates that the nuclear deal will moderate Iranian behavior. Predictions of this sort, in my view, should not inform U.S. policy. While the people of Iran have long wished to rejoin the international community, the leadership's confrontational policies have continued unabated.

If Iran's nuclear capabilities continue to mature, the most probable scenario is that Saudi Arabia will acquire nuclear technology from Pakistan. Turkey and Egypt, I believe, would also pursue nuclear programs. The United States would need to think seriously about extending its nuclear umbrella to the Gulf States. In almost any scenario, the world would need to contend with a higher chance of nuclear weapons falling into the hands of terrorists.

Regional demand for Pakistan's nuclear technology would create risks of its own. Pakistan suffers from weak internal political cohesion, with three major ethnic groups pursuing historic claims to nationhood. The gap separating the wealthy and the poor is enormous, and the government has chronically failed to invest in education or create opportunity for its people. Rapid population growth is putting stresses on water resources and services. It is no exaggeration, in my judgment, to call Pakistan a fragile or even failing state—a particularly dangerous one beset by extremism.

Americans tend to believe that peace among great powers is the natural condition of the world. It is not. It is within the power of the United States to preserve the peace. However, this cannot be done on the cheap. Neither can it be accomplished without great talent and skill on the part of America's leaders.

◄   ►

LOOKING FORWARD, I believe the United States should, in the short term, focus on combating terrorism and ending the civil wars in Iraq and Syria. Longer term, we should focus on normalizing the geopolitics of three regions: the Middle East, Europe, and the Asia-Pacific. The U.S. should strengthen its transatlantic and transpacific alliances by adapting them to the new, dangerous circumstances on the horizon. At the same time, it should promote a balance of power in key regions while seeking opportunities to reconcile differences among major actors. As part of this effort, the United States must retain the military capability, forward presence, and surge capabilities to act as the ultimate balancer. The U.S. will also need to enhance its capabilities in advancing liberal, democratic ideals.

The problems of regional rivalry, sectarian conflict, and state collapse in the Middle East pose the most difficult and immediate challenges. The fundamental solutions, I believe, are to promote a regional balance of power, strengthen moderate and progressive states, and undertake with others the heavy lifting of fostering internal political settlements in Syria and Iraq.

The first step should be to strengthen our friends and partners in the Middle East, the Caucasus, and Central Asia. Some, such as Jordan and Morocco, actively oppose the extremism that has roiled the region. Others, such as the resource-rich countries of the Caucasus and Central Asia, have secular governments that can reform toward greater openness in an evolutionary manner. Still others, such as Afghanistan, are inclusive if struggling democracies. Improving governance and economic development in these states is perhaps our greatest lever in effecting a balance of power.

I do not think the United States should take sides in the overall sectarian conflict between Sunnis and Shias. This means that we should be open to relations with all states that are backing sectarian forces, including Iran. But for the foreseeable future, the U.S. will have to strengthen the military capabilities of Saudi Arabia and the Gulf States so there can be a balance of power in the region.

The United States will need to maintain efforts to combat terrorism. While drone strikes and other kinetic activities are needed, the U.S. should put much greater emphasis on mobilizing indigenous forces who themselves oppose extremism and terrorism. This requires the U.S. to foster a positive, alternative vision for the region's peoples.

The United States should establish a new diplomatic forum for dialogue on the region's problems. Realistically, it might be necessary to push back against Iran's gains in Yemen, Syria, and Iraq before forming such an institution. Currently, Saudi Arabia and the Gulf States, perceiving that Iran is in a position of strength, may not have the confidence to move toward negotiations.

The model for a new Middle Eastern regional organization might be the Association of Southeast Asian Nations (ASEAN). In conversations with friends, I have encountered a great deal of skepticism about this proposal. My former colleague at RAND, Angel Rabasa, notes that Middle Eastern economies are unlikely to transition from dependence on energy to interdependent, manufacturing-based export economies—a factor that drove regionalization in Southeast Asia. But I would remind critics that not long ago, Southeast Asia was regarded as the Balkans of Asia, a region involved in several major conflicts. ASEAN helped the region escape a long period of conflict.

Fear is often the motivation that leads states to take diplomatic steps that many thought impossible before. The horrific rubble of the Syrian civil war has made a powerful impression on every state in the region. Just as the religious wars of Europe eventually provided an impetus for a rules-based order through the Westphalian system, we should consider whether talks to end the Syrian stalemate might lay the groundwork for a broader forum for dialogue, which could focus, at first, on issues of common interest such as the environment, freedom of navigation, and reconciliation.

Even if ASEAN offers a useful precedent, however, regional states are unlikely, at this point, to take the lead in creating a new regional architecture. I would urge the United States to make regional multilateralism a priority sooner rather than later. The longer the conflict in Syria goes on, the more the region's states will fracture, which will make regional diplomacy even more difficult.

The charter of an ASEAN-like institution for the Middle East should have several elements. It should articulate a principle of mutual acceptance, resolving that the beliefs of all Muslims are equally valid; set forth a program to promote unity and end sectarian conflicts; and identify areas where countries of the Gulf can work on common practical challenges.

The United States should steer regional dialogue toward an internal political settlement in Syria. The key is for regional players to think through power-sharing arrangements that can create a durable peace. This will require buy-in from all of the major communities in each country. It is likely that decentralized, federal, or even confederal arrangements, in which the national government has limited functions and each community governs areas where its people predominate, would work best. The status of the Kurdish region in Iraq, which has its own constitution and security forces but participates fully in the national government, may be a model, even as Iraq itself is likely to fragment and birth an independent Kurdistan. Enabling the parties to reach such an agreement might require the equivalent of a Bonn conference, where competing local groups and their regional allies are all present.

Just as the United States invested resources, energy, and time in "normalizing" the geopolitics of Europe and East Asia during the Cold War, we must make a generational commitment to do so in the Middle East. If we do not undertake this work, the externalities of the problems of the region—extremism, terrorism, and regional conflict—will impose an enormous cost on the world over time.

A strategy of "balance and reconcile," however, can work only if it preserves great power peace even while attending to the unique challenges of the greater Middle East.

A newly assertive China is the principal challenge in the Asia-Pacific. China has ample incentives to test the seriousness of the U.S. commitment to East Asian security, perhaps by pressing claims in the South China and East China Seas, or in the event of a North Korean collapse. I would advise the next president to enhance the U.S. presence in the Asia-Pacific region. The U.S. and its allies need a joint approach regarding the contested maritime issues in the East China Sea and the South China Sea, one that draws red lines where necessary but employs diplomacy to avoid the risk of escalating crises.

A new Asia-Pacific forum for confidence-building, which includes all the countries of the region and reaffirms the U.S. role as an Asia-Pacific power, could catalyze regional cooperation. The model that comes to mind is the Organization for Security and Co-operation in Europe (OSCE), which has succeeded in establishing basic rules and processes to manage regional disputes. With U.S. prodding, the Helsinki Accords could serve as a model for the charter of an Organization for Security and Co-operation in the Asia-Pacific. It would complement the multiple regional organizations and groups already in place, and would complete the security architecture of the region. Perhaps the best candidate to evolve into this role is the East Asia Summit. It has the right membership, but to perform a role similar to OSCE, it must be institutionalized with a clear mandate and structures. As a rising power that seeks to preserve its freedom of action, China may oppose these proposals. But they are an important, cooperative piece of the architecture the region needs to preserve stability and prosperity.

Wider society-to-society contacts with the countries of the Asia-Pacific would yield enormous dividends for the United States over the long term. In this respect, the Trans-Pacific Partnership trade agreement is an excellent initiative, one that could be reinforced by expanding cultural exchanges, supporting binational foundations that promote links among civil society organizations, and encouraging young people to attend American universities. The challenge, in this respect, will be with China, which has recently imposed draconian restrictions on the operations of foreign NGOs. Diplomacy and economic engagement will not be enough to counter Chinese restrictions, as our policy elite has generally assumed since the 1990s; the United States will need to be proactive in reaching out to Chinese civil society.

A strategy of "balance and reconcile" would make Europe a higher priority. We need to support Europeans who are striving to restore confidence in the European project. After missing an opportunity in the early 1990s to support Yeltsin and his reformist government, the United States, together with NATO and other European partners, must meet the Russian threat at every level.

Russia is pursuing a hybrid approach through a mix of Spetsnaz forces and propaganda, along with new infantry equipment, electronic warfare, and rapid mobility capabilities. NATO must also develop the capacity to compete on the levels of political action, irregular warfare, and strategic communications.

Bolstering Europe's frontline states will raise the costs of Moscow's aggression. It is well within U.S. and allied capabilities to help Ukrainians bog down the Russians and force them to negotiate a reasonable settlement. The United States should partner with the Baltic states and Georgia to upgrade those states' defense capabilities. These efforts need not preclude transactional cooperation with Russia on issues such as the International Space Station and counterterrorism.

The OSCE could be used as a regional forum to defuse the crisis along Russia's periphery and ultimately draw Russia into Europe. With more developed peacekeeping capabilities, the OSCE might produce breakthroughs in the "frozen conflicts" in Eastern Europe and the Caucasus.

— ≻

TO CARRY OUT this "balance and reconcile" strategy, the United States will need to improve its capabilities in several areas.

I would urge the next president to take to heart lessons from recent history about presidential leadership. As Peter Rodman has written in his book *Presidential Command*, the most effective foreign policy presidents have personally engaged in deliberations on major decisions, particularly regarding the use of force. Rather than asking for consensus recommendations, they requested multiple options from their advisors, which highlighted differences with regard to the benefits, costs, and risks of action and inaction. The next president should also restore the system used by President Eisenhower for strategic planning, which enabled his administration to chart long-term strategies and connect budgets and spending to his priorities.

The conventional wisdom regarding an operational National Security Council needs to be reconsidered. My own experiences have persuaded me that the NSC staff, by virtue of its proximity to the president, is uniquely equipped to run transparent, active processes. The NSC staff understands what the president wants and is less encumbered by bureaucratic interests and procedures. Accelerating Success in Afghanistan is a concrete example of how this process can work.

I fear that we are not prepared for conflicts of the future. Despite sizable investments in Special Forces and, more recently, drones, conflicts in the Middle East have exposed the limits of the military instrument.

I am not necessarily calling for a less active U.S. role in small-scale conflicts. Indeed, the United States will need to seize opportunities to shape conflicts early and proactively to avoid more costly entanglements later. We could have removed Saddam in 1991 without destroying Iraqi institutions, and we could have managed the Syrian conflict far more effectively had we intervened with a no-fly zone and support for the moderate Syrian opposition when the demonstrations against Assad were largely peaceful.

I am suggesting, however, that the United States undertake direct military interventions, especially the deployment of large ground forces, with more caution. Frequent swings between great exertions and great retreats are a recipe for overextension and backlash.

I am particularly concerned by the imbalance between our diplomatic and military instruments. I have never understood the U.S. reluctance to negotiate with adversaries. Isolation, in my experience, rarely alters behavior in the right direction. In our regional strategies, I would seek out opportunities to bring adversaries and aggressive states into multilateral forums where the United States and its partners can together narrow differences, create rules of the road, and solve problems. Talks are not the same as capitulation.

Strengthening our diplomatic instrument requires a number of steps. The first is simply to increase funding for the State Department and other civilian agencies. To respond rapidly to changing circumstances, civilian agencies, like the military, need flexible operational funding. Also, the State Department needs to develop a stronger capability to develop and implement regional strategies. One option to consider is for the State Department to develop the equivalent of the regional combatant commanders in the military: individuals who are not tied to the interagency process and have the necessary authority and resources to shape policies over an entire region. They should work and travel jointly with the regional combatant commander.

Another needed change is to reform the "watch and report" culture of the State Department. It is not, today, a mission- and results-oriented institution with an operational and expeditionary ethos. On the bright side, I am convinced that a historic opportunity exists to catalyze such cultural change. An entire generation of diplomats—many of whom I got to know during my service in Afghanistan and Iraq—understands how to execute unconventional initiatives.

Exploiting this opportunity will take years of patient work. The State Department recruitment process will need to be overhauled to prize such values as entrepreneurship, public advocacy skills, and strategic thinking and invest in the career development of young Foreign Service officers to give them not just the skills of a generalist but also deep expertise in specific regions. One way might be to allow Foreign Service personnel to credential themselves in disciplines such as economics and military affairs, or specialized skills such as project management, that will lead to preferential access to certain positions. While reform is hard, it is in the long-term interest of the State Department to give young people meaningful work beginning with their very first assignments. The best talent will not gravitate to a system that consigns them to processing visas for years in the hopes that a decade later they will secure meaningful work.

The U.S. government would also benefit from the creation of think tanks that serve as centers of excellence for regional studies. I am amazed that whenever a crisis emerges in a particular country, the first reaction seems always to be: "We don't know who these people are." This problem can be redressed at modest costs. A set of think tanks could undertake studies to provide a baseline, granular knowledge of developing countries. They could serve as platforms for joint research and analysis of economic development strategies by local experts or officials. They could host fellows from the region, American universities, and departments and agencies in the U.S. government. Then, when the need arises to tap deep expertise on a country or region, the U.S. government would have that knowledge on standby.

Growing disorder in the world will compel the United States, whether we like it or not, to engage in state and nation building in difficult settings. We therefore need to develop stronger capabilities and mechanisms to succeed in these operations.

I strongly believe that when we deploy military force, we need to improve civil-military integration. In our current way of doing things, this depends on the luck of fielding like-minded ambassadors and commanders. Instead, it would be better for them to plan a joint strategy and deploy together. The next administration should also undertake a major review, like the Goldwater-Nichols Commission in the 1980s, to design an integrated civil-military command for expeditionary operations.

The vital task of training national military and police forces calls for the next president to direct a part of the army to providing standing capability for these tasks. Currently, this work is performed by ad hoc organizations, such as the Multi-National Security Transition Command–Iraq during the Iraq War. Dedicated units would develop the doctrine and skills to be able to reform security institutions and train and equip indigenous forces rapidly, which in turn would accelerate the process of stabilizing countries after conflicts. There is no capacity more essential than this one.

At the State Department, state and nation building merits the establishment of a new expeditionary "cone" staffed with senior officials able to surge deployments from standing capabilities. The cone should also be supported by a civilian reserve of specialists with the expertise needed to catalyze economic growth and establish governmental services. Without such standing and reserve capabilities in civilian agencies, the U.S. government will inevitably turn to the military.

To enable the strategic use of development programs, USAID should be split into two components. The capabilities for emergency humanitarian and disaster relief, a relative strength of the current USAID, could remain in an agency separate from the State Department. But the rest of USAID's development functions should be integrated into the political and economic cones of the State Department. It makes no sense to separate programs to strengthen governance and economic performance in developing countries from the department charged with shaping the overall bilateral relationship. This change would more readily integrate development activities into U.S. strategy, inject operational capabilities into the Foreign Service, and accelerate the needed change in the State Department's culture.

The current practice of relying on U.S. contracting firms to carry out development programs needs to change. In the 1950s and 1960s, USAID in fact had a great deal of specialized development expertise in such areas as infrastructure development and agriculture. Direct contracting with local firms in host countries would also wean the United States off the least effective of the U.S. contractors, with their exorbitant overhead.

No recent administration has addressed the mismatch between its rhetoric on democracy and the practical investments that are necessary to build democratic institutions over the long term.

Our biggest shortcoming, in my judgment, is the failure to translate civil society efforts into party-building activities that ultimately allow liberals to compete effectively in elections. I learned the hard way in Afghanistan and Iraq that illiberal actors are often best prepared to take advantage of elections. We are weakest in supporting the consolidation phase of a democratic transition, when new leaders must stand up to institutions to deliver security, rule of law, and services.

Even the darkest days of my ambassadorships in Afghanistan and Iraq did not fundamentally diminish my support for promoting democracy abroad. While I am concerned about the global backsliding in democracy and human rights, pessimism about democracy's future, I think, is ultimately belied by polls across the world that consistently register high support for democracy, human rights, and the rule of law.

My experiences in Afghanistan and Iraq in some ways made me more optimistic about the U.S. role in promoting democracy. The reason is that, as an implementer on the ground, I realized that a small number of capabilities and reforms could have made the difference between major successes and defeats on the democracy front. I attribute the recent resurgence of authoritarianism, in large part, to the sorry but hardly inevitable shortcomings of new democracies in addressing practical governance challenges.

I would prioritize two changes. We must be willing to provide support to liberal democratic parties in order to level the playing field in elections. Perhaps my greatest frustration as U.S. ambassador was my inability to assist liberal parties that were competing with adversaries financed by rival, authoritarian powers.

Compare my situation with that of James Clement Dunn, the U.S. ambassador to Italy from 1946 to 1952. In response to his alarming reports that Italy could fall to the Moscow-backed Communist Party in the 1948 elections, the Truman administration authorized "covert psychological operations" under Dunn's direction. Dunn coordinated between American businesses, trade unions, and CIA front organizations to channel assistance to the Christian Democratic Party and the Socialist Workers Party. The resulting landslide victory for anti-Communist forces not only helped secure Italy's alliance with the West, but also inspired, in historian Kaeten Mistry's words, "the development and organization of American political warfare" to "meet the broader Soviet challenge."*

The president and Congress should draw lessons from these and other case studies and allow ambassadors and intelligence officials to use discretion in backing liberal parties in sensitive elections.

More generally, the United States will need to cultivate democratic counter-elites in a more systematic way. One of the most astonishing lessons to

---

*Kaeten Mistry, *The United States, Italy and the Origins of Cold War: Waging Political Warfare, 1945–1950* (Cambridge University Press, 2014), p. 3.

me of the Afghanistan and Iraq campaigns was how a small number of democratically minded leaders, educated in the West, could play positive, outsized roles under the right circumstances. Ghani and the team of Afghan exiles who returned to Kabul in 2002 offer a good example. I would support the creation of an American version of the Soviet Union's Lumumba University, which trained a cadre of Soviet-backed parties and officials of client states in the developing world. Our version would train individuals from developing countries in the work of promoting democracy and making institutions deliver after a democratic transition—skills that are not and, in all likelihood, never will be taught in U.S. universities.

During the Cold War, the United States established the Congress of Cultural Freedom, which created the infrastructure for publications and intellectual discourse aimed at advancing democratic values against the ideological challenge of communism. I recommend establishing an analogous but global effort for today's world. I believe it should extend into the Muslim world, where many like-minded thinkers and political actors thirst for such engagement. I would emphasize lessons in how to establish the rule of law, foster inclusive economic growth, and reform educational institutions to encourage critical thinking, reason, and innovation. It is through such undertakings that the United States can contribute to the long game of promoting moderate political forces in China, Russia, and the Muslim world.

THE ABOVE RECOMMENDATIONS are far-reaching but well within the capacity of the United States.

America enjoys a unique appeal around the world. Despite declines in support for the U.S. in some places like the Middle East, a recent Pew poll among forty countries found that the median level of favorable opinion of the U.S. stood at 69 percent in 2015.

More so than any other nation, the United States celebrates the power of individuals and their desire for self-actualization. Tradition and history do not have a strong hold on the American psyche. Our national culture affirms that individuals should not be consigned to a certain destiny by chance of birth.

Our unmooring from family, tradition, and social bonds certainly has costs. I felt these costs acutely as an immigrant. Ultimately, however, I believe that this quality allows the country to continually reinvent itself—a benefit that, in my mind, is worth the trade-offs.

One consequence of our relative detachment from history is our pragmatism—our belief that there is a solution to every problem. I was always surprised as ambassador by the degree to which my Americanized mentality was at odds with the prevailing local cultures that shaped my early life. Even in the darkest moments of my ambassadorships, my American colleagues and I shared an instinct to experiment and innovate, an attitude quite at odds with our foreign counterparts' tendency to see problems as permanent and solutions as the inevitable start of new problems.

At the international level, we have a historically unique talent for coalition building. Many predicted that NATO and our East Asian "hub-and-spoke" alliances would wither in the absence of a Soviet threat. This proved to be incorrect.

We are able to mobilize others because we seek a rules-based international order that benefits even our adversaries. There has never been a power in world history that has enjoyed as much predominance as the United States yet has imposed as many self-limitations. We establish international organizations knowing they will constrain American power. We proactively seek international legitimacy. And we conduct debates in a political system that welcomes engagement from actors around the world.

The United States has an unparalleled capacity for what Brzezinski calls "reactive mobilization." The U.S. interventions in World Wars I and II entailed massive mobilizations of the U.S. economy, which tipped the balance of power in these conflicts. The response to the threat posed by the Soviet Union in the Cold War, which was sustained over forty-five years, showed similar capacity and ingenuity. After 9/11, the fact that the United States could, within months, use the global reach of its military and the agility of its diplomacy to lay down a new political order in Afghanistan showed that we had not lost this talent to respond in the moment.

I saw this capacity at a personal level. In Afghanistan I met Americans who had joined the military or the State Department after 9/11 because they had worked in downtown Manhattan and witnessed the horrors of the World Trade Center attacks. In Iraq, the number of individuals who joined the Coalition Provisional Authority from private life and stayed on for multiple tours in Iraq was inspiring. Think tanks helped to develop the ideas for the surge in Iraq. The proliferation of Arabic speakers and Middle East experts since 9/11 stands in my mind as a remarkable achievement.

The United States is unmatched in its ability to facilitate collaborations between people of different societies. I have seen the power of these contacts through my involvement with the AFS program and, more recently, the American Universities in Afghanistan and Iraq and the National Endowment of Democracy. While it is hard to quantify the impact of these people-to-people contacts, it is noteworthy that authoritarian regimes blame our civil society organizations and their activities abroad for the so-called "color revolutions" that have ushered in democratic transitions around the world.

America's evolution into the world's first "universal nation" is also a source of strength. The U.S. ability and willingness to absorb immigrants has allowed the country to avoid the perils of demographic aging that are afflicting almost every other developed nation in the world. The case for allowing more highly skilled immigrants into the country seems self-evident to me.

More so than any other civilization, the United States has embraced the private sector as the primary driver of technological growth. More than two-thirds of research and development funding in the United States comes from the private sector. Private universities, financial markets, and venture capital firms promote a culture in which risk-taking is valued, encouraged, and rewarded.

I was astonished by the pace of technological innovation even in government. While I was ambassador to Iraq, General Stanley McChrystal created a system that allowed U.S. Special Forces to process intelligence from laptops or phones that were seized in one raid and, within hours, launch a follow-up raid based on this information.

My experience as ambassador to Afghanistan and Iraq, where I tried, often in vain, to inculcate a culture of private enterprise, made me realize how unusual it is to live in a country where people are willing to fail repeatedly in pursuit of new ideas. I would joke as ambassador that Afghan mothers were the bane of the country's economic future, since they encouraged their children to become government bureaucrats instead of entrepreneurs.

To beat the United States in technological innovation over the long term—and to do so decisively enough to close the enormous gap between them and us—other countries will need to experience a fundamental cultural shift. Even if our economic competitors double down on innovation, they will need to cope with the daunting challenges that come with wrenching breaks from tradition. I am skeptical that China will be able to do so without a profound debate over the merits of political freedom. In technological innovation, I am still betting on the United States.

This set of inherent strengths has enabled the United States to "normalize" the politics of troubled regions. The transformations of Europe and East Asia stand as salient examples. The great achievement of American statecraft has been to produce the most prosperous period of great power peace in world history. It is vital that the United States continue to play this catalytic role in maintaining peace.

As I think back to when I first arrived in America in 1966 as an exchange student, I realize that while a great deal has changed in the United States and in the world, the basic values of the United States—the things that make America a successful society and world power—have remained solid. We remain a people who respect the dignity of all individuals, and we retain a pragmatic capacity to address our own and the world's problems.

As ambassador to Afghanistan, I used to tell audiences that the genes of Afghans contain great potential. I would then recall that Rumi, the great poet, was born in northern Afghanistan; that the city of Balkh was once the second-largest city in the world and the seat of a great civilization; and that Afghans hundreds of years ago accomplished engineering feats such as underground canals to enable production of great agricultural exports to South Asia. I would ask why Afghanistan had declined. My answer was that failures in Afghan politics—leaders pursuing personal rather than national interests—had weakened the nation. These political failures, in turn, led to geopolitical calamities that enabled the Mongols and the Soviet Union to destroy the nation. As I learned at the University of Chicago, this is a common story line in the fall of great powers.

We have serious problems that cannot be wished away with rhetoric about American exceptionalism. I cannot help but lament that many of America's assets that I admired and, indeed, have taken for granted since immigrating to the United States have been eroding. As a graduate student, I assumed that the threats to social cohesion that I saw on the South Side of Chicago—family breakdown, poor schools, minimal social mobility—would become ever more isolated to small pockets of the country. Instead, they have become the norm in many lower-middle-class communities. Our leaders, and American society writ large, need to get serious about increasing growth, establishing fiscal balance, and restoring social mobility for the less fortunate among us. If we do, we will have the resources and social cohesion needed to address looming global challenges.

The current peace among the great powers is a signal U.S. achievement. Extending this record well into the twenty-first century will require renewed commitment to building a durable order in the critical regions of the Asia-Pacific, Europe, and the Middle East. To succeed, the United States must retain its capacities as a reactive mobilizer but also develop a greater ability to serve as a proactive shaper of regional political order. If we work with partners to implement a "balance and reconcile" strategy, we can both deter adversarial powers and leave the path open to their evolution into more constructive players. We can pave the way for liberalism, tolerance, and democracy to take root around the world.

AFTERWORD

WHILE I HOPE THAT THIS BOOK WILL ENDURE AS A WINDOW INTO A CRITICAL PERIOD in American foreign policy, I also wrote it with the country's current bout of pessimism in mind. The United States fell far short of its aspirations in Afghanistan and Iraq—a reality that weighs deeply on me. While it will take some time before the true impact of the United States' efforts in Afghanistan and Iraq become clear, in the near term, it is perhaps inevitable that the region's conflicts and the threat they pose will dominate our relations with the Middle East.

But although it is hard to overstate the difficulties in the greater Middle East today, there are decent people in the region who are searching for a way out of the crisis. Many of them would have not had a platform or a voice but for our interventions.

As we formulate an approach for the region, I hope that we can pull back from our growing division at home. I am deeply concerned by how partisan our foreign policy debates have become. I was hoping that it was just a transitory phase, but, in fact, the proliferation of new media—in their infancies while I was ambassador—are exacerbating the trend. Last year alone, the Obama administration pushed through the Iran nuclear deal that did not win a single Republican vote in Congress, while even internationalist Republicans derided the Trans-Pacific Partnership as "ObamaTrade." We need to find our way back to "one nation . . . indivisible."

These challenges notwithstanding, I remain optimistic. America was a miracle to me when I visited as a teenager, and, in this respect, my outlook has not changed. The United States is still a universal nation where immigrants can become part of the fabric of the country and where people from everywhere can cooperate and work together under the rule of law.

Our country's history demonstrates time and again that it is a mistake to bet against America. We have an unparalleled ability to rally, stand firm in the face of adversity, and come up with bold solutions. I am hopeful also because of the courage, commitment, and sacrifices that I saw from our military and civilians in the wars in Iraq and Afghanistan.

I'll conclude the book with the most important lessons I have drawn from my career. First, we are crucial to world order; dangerous vacuums emerge when the United States retreats. Second, partnering with the best elements in other countries may be the surest path to achieving our goals without over-extending ourselves. Third, we need to balance our determination and can-do vitality with humility, cognizant of the limits of our power.

It is our never-ending destiny as Americans to be a catalyst for positive change. Our values, interests, and responsibilities call for us to play a proac-tive role in the world. During this period of great turmoil, I hope we can learn from our experiences without being disheartened and defeated by them.

ACKNOWLEDGMENTS

I THANK MY FAMILY FOR THEIR LOVE AND SUPPORT DURING THE PERIOD OF MY PUBLIC service and in helping me do this book. They mean the world to me, and I love them very much.

I am grateful to President Bush and to all the friends and colleagues who gave me the opportunity to serve in government. Also I want to thank the men and women who served in my security detail teams in Afghanistan and Iraq, and the U.N. for keeping me safe.

As my time in government came to a close, President Bush and other colleagues in the administration encouraged me to write a memoir. As emotions from the Bush administration settled down and crises in the Middle East flared, I decided to pursue the project.

Cheryl, Alex, and Max helped a great deal. Marin Strmecki, one of my closest advisors, and Pratik Chougule, a recent graduate of Yale Law School, assisted me in all aspects of the process. I am thankful for their competence, expertise, diligence, and support.

My literary agent, Keith Urbahn of JavelinDC, and Elisabeth Dyssegaard, executive editor at St. Martin's Press, saw promise in the book at a time when interest in Afghanistan and Iraq books was fading. They worked patiently and conscientiously through multiple drafts before bringing the manuscript to print. They were assisted ably by St. Martin's Press production editor Alan Bradshaw and Karen Houppert, a distinguished freelance editor and assistant professor at Morgan State University.

My colleagues at Gryphon Partners and Khalilzad Associates provided critical help with the book even while managing their day-to-day responsibilities. I benefited greatly from Ambassador Alex Wolff's encyclopedic knowledge of the United Nations and Omar al-Nidawi's extensive experience in Iraq. Madison Estes, Holly Rehm, and Adam Tiffen helped keep the book project on track.

In reconstructing and relaying the stories that appear in the book, I relied not only on my own recollections, but also on secondary sources and interviews. A number of family members, friends, and colleagues provided information and useful insights, including:

- Paul Bremer
- Katherine Brown
- Daniel Byman
- JD Crouch
- Charles Dunbar
- Douglas Feith
- Patrick Fine
- Thomas Goutierre
- Richard Haass
- Karen Hughes
- Robert Karem
- Jack Keane
- Tory Khalilzad
- Ali Khedery
- Robert Kimmitt
- Andrew Krepenevich
- Bernard Lewis
- Lewis Libby
- William Luti
- Roman Martinez
- Aziza Monawar
- Hamid Monawar
- Malika Monawar
- Laurie Mylroie
- Robert Oakley
- Torkel Patterson
- Angel Rabasa
- Condoleezza Rice
- Donald Rumsfeld
- Robert Satloff
- David Sedney
- Abram Shulsky
- Christopher Straub

I want to acknowledge in particular David Barno, Ehsan Bayat, James Dobbins, and Stephen Hadley for reading the entire manuscript and offering their candid and constructive feedback. Also Colin Powell, who suggested rather than a policy book, I write a life story.

Any errors that appear in the book are my own.

INDEX

Abdullah, Abdullah, 90, 101–3, 105, 118, 121, 123, 125–6, 145, 148, 196, 204, 214
Abdullah of Jordan, 273–4
Abdullah of Saudi Arabia, 273
Abdur Rahman Khan ("Iron Amir"), 22–3, 111
Abizaid, John, 169, 270
Abrams, Creighton, 187
Abu Bakr, 13
Adeeb, Ali, 262–5
Afghanistan
  15 Point Agreement, 193
  Accelerating Success in Afghanistan, 179–88, 192, 205–6, 221, 224, 314
  actors, 198–211
  Afghan National Army (ANA), 2, 179, 181–2, 193, 200, 202–5, 223
  Afghan National Police (ANP), 179, 203, 205, 223
  Bagram Air Base, 1, 129, 187, 189, 192, 220–1, 235
  civic responsibility, 200–201
  Constitution of 1964, 127, 194
  Constitutional *Loya Jirga,* 194–7, 200
  drug trafficking, 205–8
  election of October 9, 2004, 212–18
  Hazaras, 24, 41, 85, 109, 121, 186, 190, 213–14
  infrastructure, 199–200
  Interim Authority, 124, 127, 128, 135, 137
  and Islam, 15
  Kabul-to-Kandahar highway, 199–200
  Loya Jirga (2002), 141–50
  Mazar-i-Sharif, 2, 9–10, 12–14, 16–21, 25, 28, 134, 137, 201–2
  Northern Alliance, 85–7, 90, 100–103, 115–27, 129, 133, 135, 142–8, 181, 192, 195–6, 204, 213–14
  Pashtuns, 9, 12, 23–4, 64, 87, 89–90, 102–3, 116–23, 127, 137, 142, 145, 148, 183–4, 196, 204, 210–11, 214, 262
  presidential palace, 2–3
  Soviet invasion and occupation of, 1, 3, 15, 52–3, 61–6, 110–11, 113, 118–21, 125, 130, 186, 196, 200, 208
  Tajiks, 24, 101, 109, 118, 121, 149, 182–3, 202, 213–14
  Taliban, 65–6, 84–90, 99–105, 114–21, 130–7, 145–7, 177–8, 183–4, 194, 197, 200–211, 219–23, 250, 272
  Turkomen, 24
  United States–Afghanistan Strategic Partnership declaration, 221
  Uzbeks, 24, 85, 121, 123, 125, 141, 183, 214
  warlordism, 84–5, 136–8, 146–7, 150, 179, 184–6, 194–6, 198, 201–5, 215, 223–4
Ahmedinejad, Mahmoud, 302
air strikes, 43, 97, 116, 124, 158, 192
Akram, Munir, 290
al Qaeda, 3, 65, 87–9, 96, 99–100, 102–4, 107–10, 112, 114–21, 137, 176, 208–9, 222, 307
al Qaeda in Iraq (AQI), 165, 227–9, 231, 259, 271–2, 280
Alasania, Irakli, 300–301
Alexander the Great, 2, 13
Ali, 9, 13–15
Ali, Hazrat, 134
Allawi, Ayad, 153, 225–6, 232, 245, 254–5, 258, 282
Amanullah Khan, 23, 101, 132, 141, 204
Amin, Haroon, 115
Armacost, Michael, 63–5, 70
Armitage, Richard, 137–8, 166
Arnault, Jean, 213–14, 286

Assad, Bashar, 293–4, 314
Assad, Hafez, 262
Association of Southeast Asian Nations
    (ASEAN), 311
Ataturk, Mustafa Kemal, 38
Atmar, Hanif, 199
Atta Mohammed Noor, 134, 186, 202–3
Austin, Lloyd, 192
Austria, 43–4, 48–9, 59–60
Azim, Ejaz, 54
Aziz, Tariq, 68–9

Badr Organization, 256, 258, 274
Baker, James, 74, 278
"balance and reconcile" strategy, 312–13,
    321
Ban Ki-Moon, 21, 287, 291–2
Barno, David, 186–93, 202, 204–5, 213, 234
Barzani, Massoud, 74, 153–4, 161–4, 166, 170,
    240–1, 246–8, 259
Barzani, Nechervan, 164, 166
Bashir, Omar, 295–6
Batatu, Hanna, 39, 40, 157
Bayat, Ehsan, 199
Beals, Jeff, 262–3
Bearden, Milton, 65
Berlusconi, Silvio, 142
Bhutto, Benazir, 54, 63
Biden, Joe, 80, 134–5
bin Laden, Osama, 3, 87–8, 103, 115, 128–9,
    165, 307
Blackwill, Robert, 184
Blair, Tony, 170–1, 205, 261, 271
Bolten, Josh, 108
Bolton, John, 285, 296
Bonn Agreement, 119–27, 131, 148, 150, 159,
    179, 185, 196, 213, 217
Brahimi, Lakhdar, 117, 119, 123, 126, 149,
    196–7, 209, 213, 225–6, 286
Bremer, Paul, 4, 172, 174–5, 176, 229–30
Broadwater, Colby, 162–3
Brzezinski, Zbigniew, 50, 319
Bureau of Overseas Buildings Operations
    (OBO), 192
Bush, George H. W., 72, 74–5, 77, 290
    administration, 65, 71–2, 77, 80, 83
Bush, George W., 2–4, 101, 128, 184, 250,
    283, 288, 294–5
    and 9/11, 107, 109–13, 139
    and Afghanistan, 135–6, 138–9, 142–3,
        150, 183–4, 179–80, 206, 208–9, 217,
        219, 221
    Bush Doctrine, 107
    and Darfur, 295
    and Iraq, 153, 156–8, 170, 173–4, 225–6,
        229–30, 244, 252, 255, 257–8, 261, 269,
        271, 275, 280–1
    Virginia Military Institute address (April
        2002), 139
Bush, George W., administration
    and Afghanistan, 113–17, 119, 149–50, 153,
        176, 182, 199–200, 211, 223
    and Iran problem, 275
    and Iraq, 151, 156, 165–7, 234, 275, 278

Card, Andrew, 110, 112
Casey, George, 218, 252–5, 258, 260–1, 267,
    269–70, 274–81
CENTCOM, 71, 159, 169, 179, 271
chador, 85, 89
Chalabi, Ahmed, 73–4, 151–3, 156, 159, 163,
    167, 170, 230, 251
Cheney, Dick, 73, 77, 81, 94–8, 116, 138,
    158–9, 179, 217–18
China, 77, 82, 94, 288, 291, 295, 297,
    299–302, 307–9, 312–13, 318, 320
Churkin, Vitaly, 290–1, 294–5, 297, 299, 301
Clarke, Richard, 96, 99–100, 103, 105
Cleveland, Robin, 181
Clinton, Bill, 80–2
    administration, 65, 87–9, 99
Clinton, Hillary, 189–90, 303
Coalition Provisional Authority (CPA), 4, 166,
    168–9, 172–4, 176, 193, 222, 227–32,
    260, 267–70, 274, 276, 281, 319
Cold War, 19, 65–6, 113, 307–8, 312, 318–19
    U.S. post–Cold War strategy, 76–82
communism, 37, 41, 50, 53, 55, 59, 61–2,
    64–5, 76, 83, 90, 120, 252, 307, 317–18
Congress of Cultural Freedom, 318
counter narcotics, 205–7
counterinsurgency strategy, 187, 222, 234,
    280
crisis of Islamic civilization, 2, 38, 108
Crocker, Ryan, 164, 171–3, 282

Daoud Khan, Mohammed, 12, 20, 44, 50
Darfur, 295–6
Dawa Party, 74, 152, 251, 258–9, 262–4, 282
Defense Policy Guidance (DPG), 77–82
d'Escoto Brockmann, Migel, 288–9
Dhari, Harith, 273
Dobbins, James, 117, 119–23, 125–6
Dostum, Abdul Rashid, 85, 116, 125–6, 134,
    137, 201–3, 214–15, 217, 223–4
Dulaimi, Adnan, 252
Dunn, James Clement, 317
Durrani dynasty, 12, 101

Egypt, 39, 44, 112, 118, 289, 293–4, 309
Eikenberry, Karl, 181–2
Eisenhower, Dwight D., 230, 314
explosively formed projectile (EFP), 255

Fahim, Mohammed, 116, 118, 121, 125–6,
    134–8, 142–6, 149, 181–3, 185, 193, 196,
    204, 213–14
Fatemi, Amin, 199
Fayez, Sharif, 199
Fazel, Akram, 198
Feith, Douglas, 95, 138
France, 80, 288, 291, 294, 298, 302
Franks, Tommy, 138, 159, 179
Freeburg, Paul, 73

G-8, 291, 299
Garner, Jay, 171–3
Geneva Accords, 62
Germany, 49, 77, 80, 119, 124, 126, 134, 141,
    289, 302
Ghani, Ashraf, 28, 43, 49, 182, 196, 198, 202,
    204, 224, 318
Godwin, Peter, 300
Gorbachev, Mikhail, 61
Great Britain, 2, 20, 22–3, 39–40, 170, 205–6,
    216, 263, 288, 291. See also United
    Kingdom
Griffith, William, 50
Gul, Abdullah, 161, 274
Gulf Cooperation Council, 70
Gulf War, 70–5

Hadley, Stephen, 4, 80, 95–6, 99, 115, 119,
    122, 137, 152, 163, 175, 181, 226–7, 250,
    258, 262, 264–5
Hakim, Abdul Aziz, 153–6, 163, 165, 167, 240,
    243, 245–9, 253–4, 258, 260, 275–6
Hakimi, Ikleel, 198
Hamilton, Lee, 278
Hamoudi, Humam, 238
Haqqani network, 177, 208, 222
Hashimi, Tariq, 240, 252, 259
Hekmatyar, Gulbuddin, 54, 57–8, 64, 121,
    142–3
Helsinki Accords, 312
Hosseini, Khaled, 18
Hughes, Karen, 109–10
human rights, 54, 74, 99, 147, 195–6, 199, 221,
    240–1, 245, 247, 288, 296, 300, 317
Hussein, Saddam, 54, 82, 96–9, 163, 228–9,
    252, 273
    death of, 277
    defeat of, 4, 170–1, 232

and Gulf War, 70–5, 97
and Iran-Iraq war, 67–8
and Iraq war, 168–72
and Operation Desert Fox, 82, 97
oppression of, 169, 172, 233, 239, 245, 276
and planning for post-Saddam Iraq, 151–66

Ibish, Yosuf, 40
India, 19–21, 23, 25, 55, 74, 112, 120, 177,
    210, 293, 302
Interrim Iraqi Authority (IIA), 170–1
Inter-Services Intelligence (ISI), 54–5, 65,
    84–5, 102–3, 183, 210
Iran, 15, 23, 51, 64, 84, 107, 113, 153, 182,
    194
    and Afghanistan, 85, 119–20, 125–6, 186
    constitution, 239
    influence of, 39
    Iranian Revolution, 113, 154, 256, 258
    and Iraq, 153–4, 164–5, 171–2, 215, 227–9,
        231–2, 244, 251–2, 255–6, 258, 261–2,
        267–8, 272–6, 282
    nuclear program, 286, 296–8, 301–9, 322
    Quds Force, 229, 256, 274–6
    shah, 39, 51–2
Iran-Contra scandal, 70, 115
Iran-Iraq war, 67–70, 154, 171, 258, 307, 309
Iraq
    al-Askari Mosque (Golden Mosque)
        bombing, 260, 266–7, 274
    al Qaeda in Iraq (AQI), 165, 227–9, 231,
        259, 271–2, 280
    Baath Party, 155, 163–4, 230, 269
    Baathism, 39, 68, 72, 154, 228–31, 233,
        255, 268, 273
    Baghdad conference, 170, 172–3
    Coalition Provisional Authority, 4, 166,
        168–9, 172–4, 176, 193, 222, 227–32,
        260, 267–70, 274, 276, 281, 319
    constitutional negotiations and drafting,
        237–51, 254
    counterinsurgency strategy, 187, 222, 234,
        280
    de-Baathification, 4, 163–5, 169, 230, 233,
        249–50, 262, 264, 269, 281
    election of December 15, 2005, 252–4
    Green Zone, 171–2, 234, 238, 247, 255,
        271, 274
    hydrocarbon law, 269, 281
    and Kurds, 73–4, 99, 152–6, 159–70,
        227–8, 231–2, 239–49, 251, 254–6,
        259–62, 278, 282, 286
    Multi-National Force–Iraq (MNF-I), 267,
        271, 281

Nasiriyah conference, 171
and national compact, 232–3, 244, 283
national unity government, 254–65
and population-security strategy, 270, 278, 280–1
and Red Cell report, 270–1
sectarian violence, 266–78
Transitional Administrative Law (TAL), 228
Transitional National Assembly (TNA), 238, 242, 244
troop surge of 2007, 278–83
U.S. invasion and occupation, 168–75
U.S. preparation for invasion, 151–67
U.S. withdrawal from, 282
Iraq Study Group, 278–9
Iraqi National Accord (INA), 225
Iraqi National Congress, 74, 170
ISIS, 308
Islamism, 2–3, 37, 64–6, 108–9, 113, 146, 170, 172, 177, 194, 231, 247
Shia, 226–7, 239–45, 247–9, 251, 254–60, 262, 265, 269, 273–4, 282
Sunni, 39, 55, 118, 241, 252
Ismail Khan, 125, 203–4
Israeli-Arab conflict, 37–8, 40–1, 43, 293, 298–9

Jaafari, Ibrahim, 235, 254, 258–63, 274
Jalali, Ali, 196, 199, 202, 204
Jamaat Islami, 39
Japan, 4, 77, 205, 213, 289, 293, 302
Jordan, 37, 245, 252, 255, 272–3, 310
Joya, Malalai, 195

Kaplan, Morton, 46
Karzai, Hamid, 3, 84–90, 102–3, 120–3, 131–8, 219–24, 262, 278
and Accelerating Success plan, 178–80, 183–6
awards Khalilzad King Amanullah Ghazi Medal, 23, 221
chosen leader of Afghan Interim Authority, 124–9
Constitutional Loya Jirga (CLJ), 122, 131, 194–7, 200
and election of October 9, 2004, 213–18
Emergency Loya Jirga of 2002, 142–9
Keane, Jack, 278
Kennan, George, 76–7
Kennedy, Ted, 80
Kerim, Serjan, 288
Khalidi, Walid, 40
Khalili, Karim, 186, 213

Khalis, Younis, 58–9, 64, 87
Khalilzad, Zalmay
as American Field Service (AFS) exchange student, 24–5, 26–34
appointed ambassador to Afghanistan, 176–88
appointed ambassador to Iraq, 1–5, 218–19, 221–2
appointed special envoy to Afghanistan, 128–9
appointed special envoy to the Free Iraqis, 151
awarded King Amanullah Ghazi Medal, 23, 221
and Baghdad conference, 170, 172–3
birth and naming of, 9–11
birth of son Alexander, 55–6
birth of son Max, 72
and Bonn conference, 119–27
childhood, 11–12, 13–20
at Columbia University, 50, 52, 55, 59
and Constitutional Loya Jirga, 194–7
and Daoud Khan, 20–2
death of sister, 11
as director of policy planning at Defense Department, 71–85
early education, 16–18, 22
family's emigration from Afghanistan following Soviet invasion, 52
first trip to Iraq, 68–9
granted U.S. citizenship, 53
and Iraqi opposition conference in London, 152–6
and Iraqi opposition conference in Salahuddin, 160–7
and Iraq's constitutional negotiations, 237–51
joins Bush administration, 93–6
joins Reagan's State Department's policy planning staff, 57–9
and kite fighting, 18–19
meeting with Khomeini in Paris, 50–2
and Nasiriyah conference, 171
and October Governance Agreement, 186
parents of, 10–12, 14–19
at Pan Heuristics, 47–8, 53
as permanent representative to the U.N., 284–303
at RAND Corporation, 65, 71, 82–3, 94
student at American University of Beirut (AUB), 36–44
student at Kabul University, 35–6, 39
student at University of Chicago, 45–50
surgery, 235

wife (Cheryl), 5, 42–3, 48–53, 56, 59–60, 72, 101, 106–7, 134, 153, 177–8, 188, 201, 226, 235, 278, 288–9, 301, 303
Khamenei, Ayatollah Ali, 165, 275
Khedery, Ali, 275
Khomeini, Ayatollah Ruhollah, 51–2, 67–9, 84, 262
Kosovo, 119, 291–2, 301
Kreisky, Bruno, 43
Krepinevich, Andrew, 234
Kumalo, Dumisani, 298–300
Kurdish Democratic Party (KDP), 74, 153
Kurdish Regional Government (KRG), 239, 241, 243, 247–8, 269, 276
Kurdistan, 153, 159, 161, 166, 170, 312. *See also* Iraq: and Kurds
Kuwait, 71, 73, 78, 97, 152

Lang, Patrick, 71
Lavrov, Sergei, 290–1, 301
Lebanon, 36–44, 49, 70, 129, 153, 163, 286, 293–4
Lee Kuan Yew, 150
Leghari, Farooq, 54
Levin, Carl, 80
Lewis, Bernard, 53, 67, 73, 187
Libby, Scooter, 71, 81, 94–5, 227
Libya, 39, 297–9
Litt, David, 255
Loya Jirga (Grand Assembly), 84, 87, 89, 102, 122–3, 125, 127, 131, 200
    Constitutional *Loya Jirga* (CLJ), 122, 131, 194–7, 200
    defined, 64
    Emergency *Loya Jirga* of 2002, 140–50
Luti, William, 156
Lynch, Rick, 255

MacFarlane, Sean, 270
Mahdi Army, 256, 268, 274, 282
Makiya, Kanan, 157–8
Maliki, Nuri, 258, 262–5, 267–8, 270–4, 277–83
Marshall, Andrew, 48
Mashaddani, Mahmoud, 249, 254
Massoud, Ahmad Shah, 90, 101–3, 105, 115–16, 118, 121, 183, 213
Massoud, Ahmed Zia, 118, 213–14
McCain, John, 298, 303
McChrystal, Stanley, 223–4, 320
McLaughlin, John, 137–8
McMaster, H. R., 270
Mehdi, Adel Abdul, 243, 258–9
Miller, Frank, 114

Mir, Hamid, 128–9
Mistry, Kaeten, 317
Mohseni, Ayatollah, 147
Mojaddedi, Sibghatullah, 195, 219
Mojahedin-e-Khalq (MEK), 165
Mudd, Philip, 106
Mugabe, Robert, 299–300
mujahedeen, 57–66, 141, 146
Mukhlis, Hatem, 157–8
Murphy, Richard, 70
Musharraf, Pervez, 184, 209–11
Muslim Brotherhood, 39, 64, 118
Mustafa Zahir, 124, 142
Muttaqi, Amir Khan, 86

Naderi, Nadir, 198–9
Nadiri, Homayoun, 203
NAM/G–77 (Non-Aligned Movement and Group of 77), 287, 289, 293, 302
Nasser, Gamel Abdel, 39, 44
nation building, 111, 115, 117, 134, 139–40, 149–50, 176–80, 211, 315–16
National Security Council (NSC), 57, 81, 88, 94, 96, 99, 105–9, 114–15, 119, 135, 155, 162, 179–80, 258, 278, 314
Natsios, Andrew, 199
Neumann, Robert, 36
Neumann, Ronald, 36
new world order, 77
Nicaragua, 70, 288–9
no-fly zones, 73, 97–9, 163, 295, 314
North Korea, 78, 82, 286, 292, 312
Northern Alliance, 85–7, 90, 100–103, 115–27, 129, 133, 135, 142–8, 181, 192, 195–6, 204, 213–14
nuclear weapons
    and Iran, 286, 296–8, 301–9, 322
    and North Korea, 82, 286
    and Saddam Hussein, 97–8

Oakley, Robert, 64–5, 97
Obama, Barack, 82, 223, 257, 282, 298, 303
    administration, 200, 222–4, 309, 322
Odierno, Ray, 281
Office of Management and Budget (OMB), 181, 192, 207
Office of Reconstruction and Humanitarian Assistance (ORHA), 159, 171, 174
Omar, Mullah, 87, 114
Operation Desert Fox, 81–2, 97
Operation Desert Shield, 309
Operation Desert Storm, 71–2
Operation Forward Together, 271
Operation Iraqi Freedom, 227–8

Operation Knight's Charge, 282
Operation Provide Comfort, 73
Operation Staunch, 68
Organization for Security and Co-operation in Europe (OSCE), 312–13
O'Sullivan, Meghan, 227
Ottoman Empire, 38, 40, 112

Pace, Peter, 138
Pacha Khan, 137–8
Pakistan, 19–22, 52–5, 62–6, 87–9, 100, 102–3, 176–84, 190–1, 208–11, 222, 224, 290, 309
Patey, William, 261, 263, 271
patragar, 88
Patriotic Union of Kurdistan (PUK), 74, 153, 170, 259
Patterson, Torkel, 109
Perras family (Khalilzad's AFS family in California), 27, 29–32, 188
Petraeus, David, 223–4, 280–2
Powell, Colin, 71, 73, 79, 96–8, 116–19, 138, 152, 170–1, 174, 184, 188, 192, 215, 218
Powell, Nancy, 208–9
Prophet Mohammed, 9, 13, 38, 58, 154

Qaddafi, Muammar, 39, 297
Qanooni, Younus, 101, 118, 121–3, 126–7, 134–5, 142–3, 145, 148–9, 195, 199, 204, 213–17
Qayumi, Mo, 198
Qazi, Ashraf, 286
Qutb, Sayyid, 39, 118

Rabbani, Burhanuddin, 64, 85, 90, 118–20, 123–6, 146, 199, 214
Rahim, Rend, 158, 232
Ramadan, 14, 119, 123–4, 127
Raphel, Arnold, 63
Raymond, Walt, 57
Reagan, Ronald, 57–9, 61–2
administration, 61–2, 68, 70, 101, 115
Reed, Jack, 190
Rice, Condoleezza
as NSC advisor, 4, 95–7, 99–100, 103, 105, 107–8, 110, 114–15, 118–9, 159–61, 174, 179
as secretary of state, 220–1, 226, 232–4, 244, 258, 261, 277, 280, 291, 297–8, 301
Rice, Don, 65
Rodman, Peter, 184, 313
Rome Group, 85, 90, 102, 120–4, 144
Rowen, Henry, 71
Ruba'i, Mowaffak, 240–1, 254

Rumi, Maulana Jalaluddin, 2, 13, 321
Rumsfeld, Donald, 4, 61, 94–8, 116, 133, 138–40, 158–9, 175, 178–9, 184, 197, 205, 217–20, 235, 271, 280, 296
Russia, 20, 37, 78, 80, 82, 98, 126, 146, 287–302, 307–9, 313, 318

Saba, Daud, 198
Sadr, Muqtada, 249, 251, 256, 267
Sadrists, 267, 277, 286
Salih, Barham, 74, 170, 259
Samar, Sima, 199
Sattar, Abdul, 100
Saudi Arabia, 55, 64, 73, 97, 255, 264, 272–3, 277, 294, 309–11
Sayyaf, Abdul Rasoul, 63–4, 146, 196
Schlesinger, James, 48, 53, 61
Schwarzkopf, Norman, 71–2
Scowcroft, Brent, 80, 115
Sedney, David, 191
Sejdiu, Fatmir, 291
September 11, 2001, 1–3, 66, 84, 87, 90, 105–9, 113, 115, 118–20, 139, 180, 319
Serbia, 291
shah of Iran, 39, 51–2
Shahryar, Ishaq, 89
sharia law and principles, 127, 147, 241
Sherzai, Gul Agha, 117, 134, 136, 147, 184–5
Shia Islam, origins of, 13
Shinwari, Fazl Hadie, 147
Shultz, George, 61–3, 65, 69–70, 130
Sirat, Abdul Sattar, 121, 123–4
Sistani, Grand Ayatollah Ali, 240–1, 243, 247, 249, 254, 256, 261, 263, 286
Soleimani, Qasem, 256, 261, 276
Solomon, Dick, 70
Sorley, Lewis, 187
Soviet Union, 19–20, 26, 41, 44, 50, 54–5, 58, 71
collapse of, 76, 78–9
Soviet-Afghan War, 1, 3, 15, 52–3, 61–6, 110–11, 113, 118–21, 125, 130, 186, 196, 200, 208
Speckhard, Daniel, 269
Starr, Frederick, 13
Stephanopoulos, George, 80
Straw, Jack, 261
Strmecki, Marin, 179, 191, 234
Sunni Islam, origins of, 13
Supreme Council for the Islamic Revolution in Iraq (SCIRI), 74, 153–6, 238, 251, 256, 258–9, 275
Syria, 39, 54, 228–9, 262, 267, 274, 283, 294, 308, 310–11, 314